RSF: The Russell Sage Foundation Journal of the Social Sciences

New Immigrant Labor Market Niches

VOLUME 4 • NUMBER 1 • JANUARY 2018

RSF: The Russell Sage Foundation Journal of the Social Sciences

ISSN 2377-8261

The Russell Sage Foundation

The Russell Sage Foundation, one of the oldest of America's general purpose foundations, was established in 1907 by Mrs. Margaret Olivia Sage for "the improvement of social and living conditions in the United States." The foundation seeks to fulfill this mandate by fostering the development and dissemination of knowledge about the country's political, social, and economic problems. While the foundation endeavors to assure the accuracy and objectivity of each book it publishes, the conclusions and interpretations in Russell Sage Foundation publications are those of the authors and not of the foundation, its trustees, or its staff. Publication by Russell Sage, therefore, does not imply foundation endorsement.

Board of Trustees

Sara S. McLanahan, *Chair*
Larry M. Bartels
Karen S. Cook
W. Bowman Cutter III
Sheldon H. Danziger
Kathryn Edin
Michael Jones-Correa
Lawrence F. Katz
David Laibson
Nicholas Lemann
Martha Minow
Peter R. Orszag
Claude M. Steele
Shelley E. Taylor
Hirokazu Yoshikawa

Mission Statement

RSF: The Russell Sage Foundation Journal of the Social Sciences is a peer-reviewed, open-access journal of original empirical research articles by both established and emerging scholars. It is designed to promote cross-disciplinary collaborations on timely issues of interest to academics, policymakers, and the public at large. Each issue is thematic in nature and focuses on a specific research question or area of interest. The introduction to each issue will include an accessible, broad, and synthetic overview of the research question under consideration and the current thinking from the various social sciences.

RSF Journal Editorial Board

Elizabeth O. Ananat, Duke University
Karen S. Cook, Stanford University
Sheldon H. Danziger, Russell Sage Foundation
Mesmin Destin, Northwestern University
Janet C. Gornick, The CUNY Graduate Center
Jennifer Hochschild, Harvard University
Mary E. Pattillo, Northwestern University
Becky Pettit, University of Texas at Austin
James Sidanius, Harvard University
Miguel S. Urquiola, Columbia University
Mary C. Waters, Harvard University

Copyright © 2018 by Russell Sage Foundation. All rights reserved. Printed in the United States of America. No part of this publication may be reproduced, stored in a retrieval system, or transmitted in any form or by any means, electronic, mechanical, photocopying, recording, or otherwise, without the prior written permission of the publisher. Reproduction by the United States Government in whole or in part is permitted for any purpose.

Opinions expressed in this journal are not necessarily those of the editors, editorial board, trustees, or the Russell Sage Foundation.

We invite scholars to submit proposals for potential issues through the *RSF* application portal: https://rsfjournal.onlineapplicationportal.com/. Submissions should be addressed to Suzanne Nichols, Director of Publications.

To view the complete text and additional features online please go to **www.rsfjournal.org**.

Russell Sage Foundation
112 East 64th Street
New York, NY 10065

ISSN (print): 2377-8253
ISSN (electronic): 2377-8261
ISBN: 978-0-87154-738-5

New Immigrant Labor Market Niches

ISSUE EDITORS
Susan Eckstein, Boston University
Giovanni Peri, University of California–Davis

CONTENTS

Immigrant Niches and Immigrant Networks in the U.S. Labor Market **1**
Susan Eckstein and Giovanni Peri

Part I. Immigrants and Labor Markets in Time and Space

Old Immigrants, New Niches: Russian Jewish Agricultural Colonies and Native Workers in Southern New Jersey, 1880–1910 **20**
Siobhan O'Keefe and Sarah Quincy

Offshore Migrant Workers: Return Migrants in Mexico's English-Speaking Call Centers **39**
Michaël Da Cruz

Part II. Labor Market Dynamics, Networks, and Workplace Experiences

Black Immigration, Occupational Niches, and Earnings Disparities Between U.S.-Born and Foreign-Born Blacks in the United States **60**
Tod G. Hamilton, Janeria A. Easley, and Angela R. Dixon

The Rise of Market-Based Job Search Institutions and Job Niches for Low-Skilled Chinese Immigrants **78**
Zai Liang and Bo Zhou

Filling the Niche: The Role of the Parents of Immigrants in the United States **96**
Xiaochu Hu

Bridging the Service Divide: Dual Labor Niches and Embedded Opportunities in Restaurant Work **115**
Eli R. Wilson

Part III. New Immigrants in Growing Sectors: High- and Low-Skilled Labor Market Niches

Israeli Infotech Migrants in Silicon Valley **130**
Steven J. Gold

Caring and Carrying the Cost: Bicultural Latina Nurses' Challenges and Strategies for Working with Coethnic Patients **149**
Ming-Cheng M. Lo and Emerald T. Nguyen

Learning to Fill the Labor Niche: Filipino Nursing Graduates and the Risk of the Migration Trap **172**
Yasmin Y. Ortiga

Immigrant Niches and Immigrant Networks in the U.S. Labor Market

SUSAN ECKSTEIN AND GIOVANNI PERI

Immigrants come to the United States to work and to improve their earnings and material living conditions, and in doing so, they often drive economic growth and local revitalization. Their labor market involvement may either supplement or displace employment opportunities for native-born populations, and immigrant groups can vary significantly in the economic success they achieve in this country. The consensus among economists who assess the macro effects of economic activity and among sociologists who address the impact of noneconomic forces on economic activity is that, on balance, the U.S. national economy—as well as immigrants themselves—benefit from their labor market contributions.[1]

The essays in this issue deepen our understanding of different labor market experiences of immigrant groups by drawing on the expertise and insight not only of economists and sociologists but also of demographers, geographers, and anthropologists who value interdisciplinary scholarship. Drawing on somewhat different but overlapping frames and methods of analyses, these essays enhance our understanding of the labor market experiences of new immigrants and of the opportunities and constraints they face in the economic niches in which they obtain work. The qualitative scholars contribute insight into the distinctive features and dynamics of different occupational niches that quantitative analyses fail to capture. At the same time, quantitative scholars elucidate the broad trends and regularities in labor market activity that are missed by case studies. Few quantitative sociologists talk of "niches," and virtually no economist does. They instead focus on "labor markets"—considered as broad aggregates of workers and firms—and on wage effects and wage differentials across immigrant groups and between immigrants and U.S.-born workers. Yet quantitative social scientists have come to recognize the large heterogeneity of skills in the native and immigrant populations and to understand that specific labor market involvements are also shaped by institutions and informal social dynamics.

Our own research spans these two approaches. Likewise, our goal in this volume is

---

Susan Eckstein is professor of sociology and international relations at Boston University. **Giovanni Peri** is professor of economics at the University of California–Davis.

© 2018 Russell Sage Foundation. Eckstein, Susan, and Giovanni Peri. 2018. "Immigrant Niches and Immigrant Networks in the U.S. Labor Market." *RSF: The Russell Sage Foundation Journal of the Social Sciences* 4(1): 1–17. DOI: 10.7758/RSF.2018.4.1.01. We thank participants in the "New Immigrant U.S. Labor Market Niches in the Era of Globalization" conference for their comments and suggestions and the Russell Sage Foundation for its support of the project. Direct correspondence to: Susan Eckstein at seckstei@bu.edu, Department of Sociology, Boston University, 100 Cummington Mall, Boston, MA 02215; and Giovanni Peri at gperi@ucdavis.edu, Department of Economics, University of California, 1 Shields Avenue, Davis, CA 95616.

1. National Academies of Science, Engineering, and Medicine (2016) shows small aggregate positive effects of immigration on total income and wages in the United States.

to combine the insights that scholars of different disciplines, making use of different methodologies, contribute to our understanding of immigrant labor market involvements. Giovanni Peri, a quantitative economist, has devoted much of his research to enriching the quantitative analysis of the labor market effects of immigrants by incorporating the important building blocks of immigrants' skill specificity, their complementarity to native-born skills, and the heterogeneity of their experiences into the quantitative models used to analyze immigrants in labor markets and understand their effects.[2] Susan Eckstein, a qualitative historical sociologist, has enhanced our understanding of immigrant and native-born labor market experiences by demonstrating that immigrant labor market experiences may be transnationally embedded in both the supply of labor for distinctive "niches" and the evolution of U.S.-formed immigrant niches. Her work highlights how immigrants do not merely respond to preexisting demand for particular labor but sometimes create demand for their labor. In other words, across the skill spectrum, they may construct new markets.

In combining the expertise of the scholars of diverse social science disciplines represented in this volume with our own respective areas of expertise, we hope to "open the box" of immigrant labor market dynamics with new synergy and insight into new immigrant labor market experiences. Simple quantitative statistics, case studies, and more sophisticated regression analyses are used together in this volume to highlight the "value added" of examining new immigrant labor market experiences from different analytic perspectives associated with different social science disciplines and different methods of analysis.

As coeditors of this volume, we begin here by describing first the characteristics of niches and then the occupational niches in which today's foreign-born workers cluster and are overrepresented relative to their percentage of U.S. employment. We then address the specific labor market sectors in which the main immigrant groups work. We explain the dependence of niching on demand for their skills, their abilities, and, more generally, their individual characteristics. Once an immigrant group gets a footing in a particular line of economic activity, in-group social networks and informal dynamics contribute to that group's continued association with the niche. Immigration and labor policies and institutional practices may also contribute, intentionally or not, to the ongoing involvement of particular immigrant groups in certain labor market niches. These forces impede unfettered market forces from determining who does what work, but in ways that may enhance economic production and productivity by inducing worker loyalty, commitments, and investments.

THE FORMATION OF IMMIGRANT NICHES

Many immigrants are concentrated in an occupation, or a segment of an occupation, that we call a "labor market niche": a specific line of work found either within a single community or nationwide. A specific line of work represents an "immigrant niche" if an immigrant group is overrepresented in it relative to the group's portion of the country's employment. Some occupations are dominated by immigrants in general; in other cases, specific immigrant groups are associated with specific labor market niches.[3] Some heavily "niched" immigrant groups come from particular regions of a country or from specific ethnic groups in a country. Armenians from Syria and Persian Jews, for instance, dominate specific retail store sectors; Indians from the state of Punjab are highly concentrated as employees

---

2. Peri (2015) illustrates how economists have expanded their analysis to more complex models and more sophisticated empirical approaches in which heterogeneity and occupation specificity (niching) play a very important role in the labor market analysis of immigrants.

3. Roger Waldinger and Mehdi Bozorgmehr (1996) define a niche as a line of work that employs a minimum of 1,000 people among whom one group's share is at least 150 percent of its share of the total labor market. Unlike our focus on the foreign-born, their focus is on ethnic groups, which may involve second and subsequent generations of immigrants.

of gas stations, while Indians from the state of Gujarat mainly work in the hotel and motel business (Dhingra 2012).

Immigrant niching is not new. Historically, distinctive groups of immigrants engaged in distinctive work. Niching was already taking place in the nineteenth and early twentieth centuries, as documented by several historical accounts of the Chinese (for example, Kwong and Miščević 2005) and other groups. Siobhan O'Keefe and Sarah Quincey (this issue) illustrate one of these historical examples. The authors detail how a large wave of Russian Jews was encouraged to settle in rural New Jersey and to engage in farming during the last decades of the nineteenth century. This was a somewhat special case in that these colonies were partially supported by Jewish philanthropists to divert the large flow of Russian Jews away from the cities where Jews had settled earlier, but the dynamic they produced in rural New Jersey was rather typical. As O'Keefe and Quincy show, the immigrants' arrival revitalized local markets, reducing natives' out-migration because of new opportunities to sell to and work for the new settlers. However, their presence increased the unemployment of local workers in similar jobs. Zai Liang and Bo Zhou (this issue), in turn, trace the occupational niches involving Chinese immigrants in the late nineteenth century that became the basis for Chinese immigrant niches and niche diversification in the last thirty years.

The main focus of this volume is on the features and dynamics of labor market niches that employ contemporary immigrants, commonly referred to as "new immigrants." We address the formation, perpetuation, and, in some instances, transformation and transnationalization of today's niches by the interplay of social and economic dynamics that sociology and economics—and secondarily other social sciences—can help us understand.

Even as labor market niching provides opportunities for immigrants, a group's successful occupation of a niche often closes opportunities for nongroup members. Sometimes tensions arise—or at least difficult coexistence—from the displacement of local workers or previous immigrant groups.[4] Tod G. Hamilton, Janeria A. Easley, and Angela R. Dixon (this issue) analyze whether the lower degree of niching in the U.S.-born African American community, documented using census data, is a determinant of their wage disadvantage relative to foreign-born blacks. While African- and Caribbean-born blacks tend to be more concentrated in specific niches than native blacks, the authors do not find this to be a significant determinant of their wage advantage.

CONTEMPORARY IMMIGRANT NICHES

The national origins of U.S. immigrants changed markedly in the last half-century; at the same time, the foreign-born share of the U.S. population reached levels not experienced since the 1920s, with record levels in absolute numbers. In this introduction, we focus (with the exception of the O'Keefe and Quincy essay) on immigrants who came to the United States after the enactment of the Immigration and Nationality Act of 1965. This legislation eliminated national-origins quotas and opened U.S. borders to persons from countries previously excluded.

Until 1965, most immigrants to the United States came from Europe. Today's immigrants, in contrast, come mainly from Mexico, Central America, China, India, and, secondarily, other Asian countries. Many of these immigrants work in distinctive labor market niches where they account for a high percentage of those employed. In some instances, they replaced earlier immigrants within the niche. Others carved out new niches of their own, often providing products and services not previously available.

Using American Community Survey (ACS) data from 2014, the most recent year available at the time of writing, table 1 shows the thirty occupations in which today's immigrants account for the largest share of employment. For each occupation, column 2 shows the share of immigrants employed and column 3 the average weekly wages of workers.

---

4. See, for instance, Jennifer Lee's (2006) analysis of tensions between Jews and Koreans in the New York retail store market.

Table 1. Occupations with Highest Shares of Foreign-Born Workers and Weekly Wages, 2013

Occupation[a]	Immigrant Share	Weekly Wage (in 2013 Dollars)
Graders and sorters of agricultural products	0.64	447
Plasterers	0.62	671
Textile sewing machine operators	0.60	488
Drywall installers	0.56	672
Dressmakers and seamstresses	0.55	602
Farmworkers	0.53	506
Roofers and slaters	0.50	643
Painters, construction and maintenance	0.50	649
Housekeepers, maids, butlers, stewards, and lodging cleaners	0.49	417
Pressing machine operators (clothing)	0.47	465
Masons, tilers, and carpet installers	0.45	704
Medical scientists	0.45	1,747
Shoe repairers	0.44	522
Taxi cab drivers and chauffeurs	0.42	609
Upholsterers	0.42	621
Packers, fillers, and wrappers	0.42	540
Physical scientists	0.41	1,572
Packers and packagers by hand	0.41	470
Laundry workers	0.41	481
Gardeners and groundskeepers	0.38	519
Art/entertainment performers and related	0.38	962
Computer software developers	0.37	1,888
Construction laborers	0.36	721
Carpenters	0.36	745
Butchers and meat cutters	0.35	598
Production helpers	0.35	605
Hairdressers and cosmetologists	0.34	487
Bakers	0.34	500
Parking lot attendants	0.34	507
Hand molders and shapers, except jewelers	0.34	755

Source: Authors' calculations from American Community Survey (ACS) 2014 data.
Notes: The sample includes people ages eighteen to sixty-five not residing in group quarters, working for salary for at least one week in the previous year. "Foreign-born" is defined as born outside the United States. Weekly wages are for workers who worked at least thirty-five weeks in the previous year for at least thirty hours per week.
[a] We use the definition of "occupation" contained in the variable "Occ1990," which has been constructed by the Integrated Public Use Microdata Series (IPUMS) in such a way as to be consistently defined over time.

These thirty occupations are those in which niching by specific groups of immigrants is most prominent. Although the ACS covers more than 300 occupations, ensuring the most accurate picture of the U.S. labor force, its classifications can be too broad to capture some very specific niches. For instance, nail salon workers—a specific niche we discuss later—occupy only a subgroup of the ACS occupation category "hairdressers and cosmetologists." Still, the ACS data on occupations do show the range of occupations in which immigrants cluster. The variety and diversity of these occupations span the skills and earnings spectrums. At one extreme are a variety of manually intensive craft niches in agriculture (graders, farmworkers), construction (plasterers, drywall installers, roofers, painters, carpenters, masons, tilers), and personal services (housekeepers, dressmakers, laundry workers, gardeners, hairdressers). These jobs tend to require physical skills that low-educated workers may have acquired already in their homeland and that are easily transferable to the U.S. labor market, such as construction skills and skills in personal services. Their pay scales vary considerably, from a low average in 2014 of $408 per week for housekeepers to $745 per week for carpenters. Sometimes immigrants take low-skilled jobs that build on work they did in their homeland without remuneration, such as when immigrant women work in the United States as nannies and housecleaners. Other immigrants learn skills in the United States for the jobs they take—for example, Vietnamese who become manicurists. At the low-skilled end of the work spectrum, the lowest-paying jobs are in agriculture, housekeeping, and hotel and personal services (housekeepers, laundry workers, shoe repairers), with weekly salaries below $500 per week in 2014. Moreover, there is often a wage gap in these jobs of around 20 to 30 percent between immigrants and natives.

At the other extreme are high-skilled science- and technology-intensive occupations for which demand has grown in recent decades, such as medical scientists, physical scientists, and computer software developers. Typically requiring college and postgraduate education, this work pays well. Computer programmers, the best paid among the occupations listed in table 1, earned on average $1,888 per week in 2014. Moreover, the table shows that in science, technology, engineering, and math jobs, such as physical scientists and computer software developers (as shown in Hanson and Slaughter 2016), immigrants earn the same as comparable natives, and sometimes even more. The knowledge of specific skills and the high quality of their academic education may be the reasons for such a reverse gap.

Table 2 shows that immigrants in the states where they make up large shares of the population dominate manually intensive niches, particularly in construction. For instance, in California, Nevada, New Jersey, New York, Maryland, Arizona, and Massachusetts in 2014, more than 61 percent of housekeepers and maids were foreign-born, while in California and Texas more than 65 percent of workers in construction occupations (roofers, painters, drywall installers) were foreign-born. And in all states with an important agricultural sector—California, Florida, Washington, and Oregon—more than 60 percent of farmworkers were immigrants. At the same time, 63 percent and 65 percent of medical scientists in Maryland and Massachusetts, respectively, were foreign-born. These two states have high-quality research and medical institutions.

Table 3 focuses on the numerically largest immigrant groups: Mexicans, Chinese, Indians, and the combined small Central American countries. For each of these immigrant groups, we show the five occupations that employ the largest share of the group. The niches identified in this table display an especially high degree of overrepresentation of these immigrant groups in the five occupations relative to native workers. We see in the table that Indian immigrants have the greatest occupational concentration, with 15 percent working as computer software developers and another 8 percent as computer analysts. These occupations offer high earnings and good career opportunities. The characteristics and evolution of the information technology sector, and Indians' role in it, are detailed later in this essay.

Like Indians, Chinese immigrants are heavily involved in computer-related and other high-skilled occupations, with 6 percent working as computer developers and 5 percent as managers and college instructors. In these jobs, both high-skilled Chinese and Indians build not only on schooling acquired before migration but also on the graduate education they obtain in this country, made possible by the accessible U.S. study visa program.

Unlike Indian immigrants, however, there are many Chinese in less-skilled and lower-paying jobs, such as cooks. Liang and Zhou (this issue) describe the expansion of different types and varieties of Chinese restaurants that cater not merely to Chinese but also to the broader U.S. population and that employ less-

Table 2. Top Thirty-Five State-Occupation Groups with the Highest Shares of Foreign-Born Workers, 2013

Rank	State	Occupation	Share of Immigrants
1	California	Textile sewing machine operators	0.93
2	California	Farmworkers	0.81
3	Texas	Drywall installers	0.81
4	California	Graders and sorters of agricultural products	0.78
5	California	Housekeepers, maids, butlers, stewards, and lodging quarters cleaners	0.78
6	California	Drywall installers	0.78
7	Hawaii	Housekeepers, maids, butlers, stewards, and lodging quarters cleaners	0.75
8	California	Wood lathe, routing, and planing machine operators	0.75
9	Nevada	Housekeepers, maids, butlers, stewards, and lodging quarters cleaners	0.73
10	Texas	Roofers and slaters	0.73
11	Texas	Masons, tilers, and carpet installers	0.72
12	Washington	Farmworkers	0.72
13	California	Gardeners and groundskeepers	0.72
14	New York	Taxi cab drivers and chauffeurs	0.71
15	Texas	Painters, construction and maintenance	0.71
16	Florida	Farmworkers	0.70
17	California	Packers, fillers, and wrappers	0.68
18	California	Packers and packagers by hand	0.68
19	California	Painters, construction and maintenance	0.68
20	California	Roofers and slaters	0.68
21	California	Assemblers of electrical equipment	0.67
22	New Jersey	Housekeepers, maids, butlers, stewards, and lodging quarters cleaners	0.67
23	California	Laundry workers	0.67
24	Massachusetts	Medical scientists	0.66
25	New York	Housekeepers, maids, butlers, stewards, and lodging quarters cleaners	0.66
26	California	Bakers	0.66
27	Oregon	Farmworkers	0.66
28	New Jersey	Packers and packagers by hand	0.64
29	Maryland	Housekeepers, maids, butlers, stewards, and lodging quarters cleaners	0.64
30	Massachusetts	Housekeepers, maids, butlers, stewards, and lodging quarters cleaners	0.64
31	Colorado	Housekeepers, maids, butlers, stewards, and lodging quarters cleaners	0.63
32	Maryland	Medical scientists	0.63
33	Arizona	Housekeepers, maids, butlers, stewards, and lodging quarters cleaners	0.62
34	Nevada	Miscellaneous food prep workers	0.62
35	Texas	Gardeners and groundskeepers	0.61

Source: Authors' calculations from ACS 2014 data.
Note: The sample and variables are defined as in table 1.

Table 3. Top Five Occupations for the Four Largest Immigrant Groups, 2013

Country/Region of Origin	Occupation	Occupation Share Within Country-of-Origin Group
Mexico	Cooks, variously defined	0.068
	Farmworkers	0.053
	Construction laborers	0.051
	Truck, delivery, and tractor drivers	0.041
	Janitors	0.040
Central America	Nursing aides, orderlies, and attendants	0.048
	Janitors	0.043
	Cooks, variously defined	0.036
	Housekeepers, maids, butlers, stewards, and lodging quarters cleaners	0.035
	Truck, delivery, and tractor drivers	0.035
India	Computer software developers	0.146
	Managers and administrators	0.080
	Computer systems analysts and computer scientists	0.078
	Cashiers	0.037
	Supervisors and proprietors of sales jobs	0.033
China	Computer software developers	0.064
	Cooks, variously defined	0.057
	Managers and administrators	0.051
	Subject instructors (high school and college)	0.051
	Computer systems analysts and computer scientists	0.035

Source: Authors' calculations from ACS 2014 data.
Note: The sample and variables are defined as in table 1.

educated Chinese workers. Chinese immigrants have creatively diversified this niche to include labor recruiters in specific regions of China and a domestic transport system to bring workers to restaurants across the United States.

Chinese immigrant involvement in low-skilled work dates back to the nineteenth century, when Chinese laborers were hired to construct the American railroad system; they also worked in service industries, such as laundries, that catered to coethnics in the urban neighborhoods where they settled (which came to be known as Chinatowns) as well as to other city-dwellers. Following enactment of the Chinese Exclusion Act in 1882, immigration to the United States from China was prohibited. The act was the first U.S. legislation to prevent a specific national group from immigrating; it would be followed by legislation in the 1920s that restricted immigration from other countries, especially countries other than those in northern Europe. When the Chinese Exclusion Act was repealed in 1943 and immigration resumed, Chinese gravitated anew to low-skilled jobs as cooks and launderers. However, after the Chinese government in the post-Mao period began aggressively promoting high-skilled economic development and lifting Maoist-era restrictions on emigration, growing numbers of high-skilled Chinese took advantage of U.S. postgraduate training and U.S. labor market opportunities.

By contrast, Mexicans, the largest foreign-born group in the United States, have the lowest average education level of any immigrant group (see Peri 2015) and have clustered in low-skilled manual occupations in construction (laborers), agriculture (farmworkers), and personal and food services (cooks, janitors). These occupations pay poorly, offer very limited opportunities for upward mobility, and subject workers to the risk of living below the poverty level. In several industries, Mexican immigrants and second-generation Mexicans occupy the least-skilled and lowest-paying jobs. Eli R. Wilson's essay (this issue) describes the work that Mexicans do in the restaurant industry in the "back of the house," mainly cleaning, restocking supplies, and preparing food; these jobs offer little if any opportunity for advancement. Contrasting their work with that of the better-paid, English-speaking "front of the house" customer service employees, Wilson notes that some second-generation Hispanics, being proficient in English as well as Spanish, have acquired language skills that enable them to attain jobs that bridge these two distinctive restaurant labor markets. In connecting the "low-skill" niche with the more dynamic, skilled customer service–oriented niche, these new immigrants, with their combination of manual and language skills, exemplify an important complementarity that opens up this industry not only to provide services, both new and old, in new ways but to expand employment opportunities as well.

Central Americans have a specialization pattern similar to that of Mexicans. Besides working as janitors and cooks, many of them—especially women—work as housekeepers and health aides. Those engaged in health care may improve their earnings opportunities over time. The expansion of the health care sector, particularly government-funded health care, combined with the aging of the U.S. population, has contributed to specific labor shortages, such as of licensed nurses. Such market forces may exert an upward pressure on the earnings possibilities for immigrant workers in this field, especially those who upgrade their skill sets and learn English. Like bilingual restaurant workers in "bridge" jobs, bilingual health care workers are especially well positioned to take jobs that provide a bridge between U.S.-born doctors and the fast-growing group of Spanish-speaking patients. (Hispanics now constitute the largest immigrant group in the United States.) Ming-Cheng M. Lo and Emerald T. Nguyen (this issue) describe the experiences of bilingual Hispanic health care workers, including the dilemmas they face in attempting to conform with professional standards while addressing cultural practices of Hispanic patients that are premised on different norms. They emphasize that more support and institutional change are needed to allow for effective cross-cultural bridging between doctors and patients.

Immigrants from other countries also play a central role in specific occupations or segments of occupations. For example, Vietnamese immigrants, who account for less than 1 percent of the U.S. population, are heavily involved in the nail care sector—the least-skilled and poorest-paying sector of the beauty industry—across America (see Eckstein and Nguyen 2011). Vietnamese have transformed the nail care industry and in so doing created demand for their work. They established "McNails," walk-in shops offering manicures and pedicures at a fraction of the price of beauty salons. Vietnamese immigrants have been easily able to do this work, which requires minimal English fluency. Before Vietnamese created McNails, only the well-to-do could afford nail care in the high-end hair salons that offered expensive manicures and pedicures as a secondary service for their clientele. The new model of nail care provided by Vietnamese has expanded demand for their services by lowering their cost, so that nail care is now within reach for people who previously could not afford it.[5] Standards for nail beauty in due course have risen, further expanding demand for manicurists and pedicurists.

The creation of this new service and market has benefited Vietnamese women, both as shop owners and as employees. However, conditions in nail care salons are far from ideal. Earnings, being contingent on the number of customers a salon attracts—which varies seasonally—are low and variable, and workers are exposed to toxic supplies. In addition, oppor-

---

5. In New York, however, Koreans and, more recently, Chinese are heavily involved in nail care, as detailed in the essay by Liang and Zhou (this issue). See also Kang 2010.

tunities for advancement are minimal, typically only to those who open their own salon; the most ambitious open multiple salons in different locations.

Many female immigrants from the Philippines—another of the top ten sending countries today—secure mid-skill jobs in nursing, a niche created by the U.S. and Philippine governments. U.S. immigration authorities extended special work visas to Philippine-trained nurses to meet the rising demand for nurse care in the United States that arose from both the aging of the American population and cost-cutting on the part of hospitals and other medical institutions. Nurses cost less than doctors to employ, and Filipina nurses cost less than American nurses. The Philippine government promoted the labor export strategy on the presumption that nurses who go overseas send remittances to the families they leave behind, providing a valuable source of income not only for the recipients but also for the government, which needs hard currency to finance imports and foreign debt payments. Meanwhile, private schools in the Philippines took advantage of the demand for nurse training for the U.S. labor market—to the point that they trained an oversupply of nurses relative to the number of nurses the United States would admit from the Philippines. While the schools profited, students bore the costs of training for U.S. jobs they could not attain. Yasmin Y. Ortiga (this issue) describes the unfortunate and unintended consequences of the outsourcing of U.S. health care training.

Other immigrant groups are associated with local labor market niches in the cities where they mainly live. For example, many Ethiopian and Eritrean immigrants in Washington, D.C., work as taxi drivers, an occupational specialization they acquired in the United States in response to local demand. Their involvement in this niche is city-specific: most immigrants from these countries live in the U.S. capital.

Black immigrants from Africa and the Caribbean are also associated with occupational niches. Hamilton, Easley, and Dixon (this issue) document that while foreign-born blacks, especially those from the Dominican Republic, Ghana, Nigeria, and Ethiopia, are likely to be employed in niche occupations (70 percent), U.S.-born blacks are the least-niched black group. U.S.-born blacks earn less than the other black groups they studied, but immigrant niching does not seem to explain this earnings differential.

Another new immigrant niche that mainly involves immigrants from Central America, the Caribbean, and the Philippines has arisen in response to demand for housekeeping and child care among the U.S. middle class. In providing affordably priced care, these immigrants have also generated demand for their services (see Brown 2011; Kasinitz and Vickerman 2001), such that middle-class women continue to work after they have children, with positive effects on their long-term earnings and their careers (see Cortés and Tessada 2011).

Xiaochu Hu (this issue) shows that highly educated immigrant groups also benefit from female niche work, including unpaid niche work. She analyzes how highly educated Chinese women benefit from the unpaid, family-based child care provided by their China-based parents, mainly their mothers. Taking advantage of the high priority given to family members in the current U.S. immigration preference system, Chinese grandparents come to the United States on special short-term visas. Hu shows that the unpaid child care provided by temporary immigrant grandparents increases the probability that their immigrant daughters with children will work for pay. Other immigrant groups also turn to immigrant grandparents for unpaid child care.

THE FACTORS ACCOUNTING FOR IMMIGRATION NICHE SPECIALIZATION

To organize our thinking about immigrants in labor market niches, we focus on four sets of factors that contribute to the new immigrant labor market niching: the skills that immigrant groups have to offer; their ability to address existing demand or create demand for new and expanded goods and services; the institutional practices and regulations of occupations; and the nature and strength of immigrant group ties that are useful in the world of work. These factors together create, sustain, and, under certain conditions, transform immigrant niche specialization, with other factors also playing a role at times.

Immigrant Skill Sets and Demand for Labor

The work done by immigrants hinges on demand for their skill sets. Many immigrants offer abilities and skills that differ from those of the native-born. These skills may include not just craftsmanship and specific competencies but also broader attributes such as a willingness to work, ability to endure outdoor conditions, punctuality, work ethic, and stamina.

The so-called new immigrants arrived in the United States as the economy shifted from being predominantly manufacturing-based to predominantly service-based, and they contributed to making this transformation possible. The shift foreclosed certain labor market options, while opening others. The industrial jobs that had employed Southern and Eastern European immigrants from the early to the mid-twentieth century declined as businesses moved their production offshore to countries where labor was cheaper and technological changes and mechanization reduced overall demand for manual labor in manufacturing. The manufacturing jobs that remain in the United States and employ the new immigrants are low-skilled jobs in the food-processing and meatpacking industries.

Interestingly, immigrants have displayed a high degree of versatility, filling niches in the service sector that require face-to-face interactions and cultural sensitivity; some observers in the 1980s thought that these requirements were not conducive to immigrant labor market incorporation. The ability of immigrants to introduce new services—for instance, in the food and restaurant sector (think of the current ethnic variety and new fusion varieties of restaurants in many cities)—have increased differentiation, adding consumption options for natives and improving their own economic welfare. This is documented for the restaurant sector by Francesca Mazzolari and David Newmark (2012), who show that the presence of immigrants widely increases the supply of restaurant varieties.

In other sectors, immigrants may displace native-born workers when employers prefer to hire the foreign-born if they perceive them to be more skilled, more disciplined, or willing to work for longer, less convenient hours or at lower pay. Immigrant contributions strengthen the economy and benefit consumers when lower costs reduce prices for the goods produced or the services offered. (Such an effect on local service prices is shown in Cortés 2008.) However, the natives or previous immigrants competing with new immigrants for jobs can experience reduced opportunities and downward pressure on their wages.

For several cognitive- and analytical-intensive occupations, new immigrants sometimes offer skills that U.S. companies strongly demand and that U.S.-born workers do not adequately provide because of the fast-growing demand. In particular, foreigners have contributed to innovation and productivity growth in the science and technology sector (see Peri, Shih, and Sparber 2015; Kerr and Lincoln 2010). Highly skilled immigrants have been crucial to the growth during the last thirty years of the information technology (IT) sector—which has revolutionized production in many industries—by bringing their skills and abilities to IT-intensive jobs and science, technology, engineering, and mathematics (STEM) jobs (see, for instance, Hanson and Slaughter 2016).

Although, as previously noted, Indians have played an especially important role as workers, entrepreneurs, and professionals in the IT and computer sector, they are not the only immigrant group to contribute to the development, transformation, and transnationalization of this sector. So too have Chinese and Taiwanese (see, for example, Yu-Ling Luo and Wei-Jen Wang 2002) and Israelis, as analyzed by Steven J. Gold (this issue).

Foreign-born workers are attracted to U.S. high-tech companies at the cutting edge of the industry worldwide because they pay well by international standards, and also because demand for electrical engineers, computer programmers, and software developers has soared since 1980. Many of the immigrants hired for these jobs are well trained abroad—for example, at India's famous Indian Institutes of Technology or in China's top universities. They obtain these coveted jobs because, on the one hand, they are highly skilled, and on the other, because U.S. immigration policy makes their employment possible. The United States prioritizes their admission by allowing U.S. employers to hire skilled foreign labor on special H-1B visas, for a maximum of six years. Since the turn of this century, over 80 percent of H-1B visas have gone to highly educated foreign professionals in computer-related occupations, and most of those have gone to Indians. These workers have been fundamental to Silicon Valley's ability to establish and maintain a global competitive edge in information technology.

Building on U.S.-acquired skills, capital, and networks, Indian immigrants have also formed their own start-up companies, in India as well as in the United States. In India, they have developed businesses that complement the work of U.S. firms. U.S. multinational companies in the high-tech sector have also turned to high-skilled, well-trained Indian immigrants to manage the subsidiaries they have established in India to capitalize on the talent and lower wages in the Indian market. In so doing, Indian immigrants have transnationalized, as well as transformed, this initially exclusively U.S.-based niche.

New immigrants also meet the demand for labor that native-born workers shun. Immigrants, for example, increasingly dominate hard, physically demanding, outdoor jobs in the agriculture and construction sectors. Even in skilled sectors of the labor market, immigrants fill many of the jobs that native-born workers find unattractive because of where they are located or the conditions of work. For example, many doctors from India work in the inner cities, where their U.S.-born counterparts resist working. Their willingness to take these positions is good for minority and poor patients in the inner cities, the economy, and the health of Americans.

In the last half-century, the entry of large numbers of native-born women into the labor force has in turn increased demand for low-paid, low-skilled labor to do the housekeeping and child care work that women used to provide, unpaid, within the household. Central American and Mexican immigrant women are employed for much of this paid labor.

Overall, new immigrant niches have evolved mainly in response to the growth and differentiation of the service sector—from manual and personal services for which there still is high demand (housekeeping, food preparation, child care, personal assistance) to knowledge-intensive and cognitive services at the other extreme (high-tech, human resources, research). New technology, new tastes, and new demand have interacted with the variety of skills, abilities, and attitudes of immigrants to create new niches and expand existing ones.

Institutional Regulations and Practices

In general, the federal government sets immigration policies that determine which foreigners, with which skill sets, may immigrate with work rights, and government policies dictate work conditions and requirements at both the local and national levels. The federal government also prioritizes the admission of foreigners with certain skills, as discussed earlier in the case of Indian IT workers and Filipina nurses. In addition, businesses, business groups, and other nongovernmental groups establish practices that affect immigrant work experiences.

Labor regulations also affect the work that immigrants do legally and, by default, illegally. Some immigrant groups can establish a footing in regulated work, while others face barriers. Many states limit jobs that require licenses to U.S. citizens and legal permanent residents and offer qualifying tests only in English or selective foreign languages, such as Spanish. Non-English speakers can qualify for licensed jobs only when the exams are offered in languages they know. For example, many Cuban doctors who immigrated with little proficiency in English and with training that did not meet U.S. standards failed tests to qualify for practicing medicine in the United States (Eckstein 2009, 99). Cuban American state legislators in Florida, where most Cuban immigrants settled, tried to get the state to bend regulations for Cuba-trained doctors. Otherwise, the Cuba-trained doctors who failed the Florida qualifying tests needed to find other lines of work.

Even low-skilled manicure work requires licensing, although the requirements are not as stringent as for doctors. Vietnamese have accessed nail care jobs, not merely because they attained the requisite skills, but because many states where they have settled offer the licensing exams in Vietnamese. Initially accessing the jobs informally, Vietnamese established themselves in the sector and then successfully pressed for the licensing exams to be offered in their native language. Thus, Vietnamese salon owners have been able to recruit low-wage workers from their homeland who easily meet licensing requirements.

Liang and Zhou (this issue) highlight the dependence of immigrant labor market niche involvement on immigrant employment agencies. With Chinese employment agencies channeling immigrants from certain regions of China to jobs across America—for example, in the restaurant sector—Chinese immigrants have become less dependent on the local labor market where they initially settled for work and Chinese businesses have become less dependent on local labor markets for workers. Supply and demand for certain types of labor have therefore become less geographically constricted, allowing for greater efficiency in matching workers' wants to employers' needs. These immigrant employment agencies, in turn, contribute to a professionalization and formalization of immigrant job recruitment.

Other, less formalized, non-state-based institutional practices also influence immigrant labor market involvement. Banks, for instance, may discriminate against immigrants on the presumption that, with their limited credit history, if any, they are high-risk borrowers. In the absence of access to bank capital, entrepreneurial immigrants have gravitated to activities that do not require a large initial investment, such as small food and concession stands. Other immigrants have established their own banks to fill the lending gap. For example, wealthy Cubans who fled their homeland after Castro came to power mainly settled in Miami, where some of them established banks that lent to fellow Cuban immigrants on the basis of trust, including trust established in Cuba before moving to America (Portes and Stepick 1993). The Small Business Administration (SBA) also favored Cuban immigrants over others in Miami. Thus, an exceptionally large number of Cubans opened small businesses in the city. Although they initially catered to persons from their shared homeland, over the years the more entrepreneurial businesses have reached out to others in the city, especially to the other Spanish-speaking Latin Americans who have also settled in Miami in recent decades. Cuban entrepreneurs have benefited from their command of Spanish and their cultural capital in the "new Miami," which has been dubbed the "northernmost Latin American city."

Vietnamese manicurists exemplify yet another source of investment capital to which immigrants have turned in the absence of access to bank capital: pooled family funds. Business opportunities in nail care are limited, but with pooled funds, Vietnamese have been able to enjoy the economic mobility associated with transitioning from being a worker to owning and managing a business (Eckstein and Nguyen 2011).

The least-skilled immigrants and those who came to the United States undocumented are mostly confined to the occupations that workers with better options leave unfilled, mainly in the agricultural and construction sectors. These jobs have the lowest entry barriers and are minimally protected by labor regulations. The work is low-paid and seasonal, with very high turnover, and it subjects workers to harsh working conditions; workers in agriculture, for instance, are exposed to toxic herbicides and pesticides, as well as to extreme heat or cold. Although many of the foreign-born in these jobs are responding to a demand for their labor, they often have been unable to attain immigration visas and the legal protections provided by legal entry. As such, they are particularly vulnerable to employer abuse and fear of deportation. Table 2 shows that the vast majority of farmworkers in California, Florida, and Washington—states with large agricultural sectors—are from Mexico. The jobs usually pay minimum wage, at best, and offer workers little legal protection. Undocumented immigrants represent a large share of those workers.

Regulations have combined with practices and traditions to attract specific immigrant groups not only to private-sector niches but also to some public-sector niches. The Irish, for instance, have a long tradition of working as police officers and firefighters in the cities where they mainly live (notably New York and

Boston). In general, however, citizenship requirements result in public-sector niches being occupied by more second-generation immigrants than first-generation immigrants.

Among return immigrants, a reverse type of niching may even take hold. Michaël Da Cruz (this issue) details the establishment by U.S. companies of call centers in Mexico to take advantage of much cheaper labor costs than in the United States. They rely on Mexicans who grew up in the United States and thus are proficient in American-style English; many of these returnees were deported because they were not authorized immigrants with rights to work in the United States. Bilingual expertise is a form of cultural capital, in this case in Mexico, for persons without formal credentials for more-skilled jobs. U.S. companies have set up similar call centers in Central American countries that also draw on U.S.-attained immigrant cultural capital.

Immigrant Network Niche Formation, Maintenance, and Transnationalization

People rely on social contacts to attain jobs, and immigrants are no exception, even when they turn to immigrant employment agencies. Immigrant groups become entrenched in distinctive lines of work through informal ties among "their own." Historically, friends and family have told immigrants about job opportunities where they work or in the same line of work and provided them with job contacts (Lafortune and Tessada 2012), and that remains true today. The tendency of new immigrants to attain work in "immigrant enclaves" has been analyzed at length by sociologists and economists (see, for example, Altonji and Card 1991; Card and DiNardo 2000; Gold 2000; Waldinger 2001; Wilson and Portes 1980).

Immigrant women are known to rely especially heavily on personal ties for securing work. Their networks channel them into work with clusters of other women from their country of origin (see Sassen 1995). Some occupations in the service sector, such as housekeepers and maids, are dominated by immigrant women from Mexico and Central America, who often learn of and secure jobs through people they know not only in the United States but also from their communities of origin in their homeland. Immigrant groups—Brazilians in particular—are known to informally sell rights to cleaning jobs as they leave them, either to take other jobs or to return to Brazil (Braga Martes 2011). Once some members of an immigrant group establish a beachhead in a certain line of work, other group members, including new arrivals, gravitate to the same work. Immigrants like to work where they know others.

Informal social networks thereby serve as fundamental building blocks for (often gender-specific) immigrant group labor market niching. The inclusionary dynamic within immigrant groups excludes immigrants from other countries, as well as the native-born, from attaining job information and job contacts. Such exclusion is not by design, but rather an unintended consequence of in-group relations. Inclusionary-exclusionary practices transpire across the labor market in work commanding different levels and types of skills.

The network dynamics that result in distinctive immigrant group concentration in specific niches extends to the small business sector, even to self-employment. The same networks that allow workers to find jobs among their coethnics encourage investments and firm ownership by immigrants in those niches. William Kerr and Martin Mandorff (2015) discuss Koreans coming to own most of the dry-cleaning shops where they previously worked, and Eritreans and Ethiopians owning and operating the taxi companies that first employed them. Meanwhile, Chinese own not only restaurants but, in recent years, the bus companies that transport Chinese to work in restaurants across the United States. Thus do immigrant networks contribute to business clustering. Small business ownership often builds on the ties as well as the expertise that immigrants from specific countries first acquired as workers in particular lines of work. Alternatively, newly arrived entrepreneurs and investors may focus on a sector where they already have ties with coethnics. Thus, both entrepreneurial and labor-driven immigrant networks contribute to the concentration of specific immigrant groups in specific economic niches.

The in-group ties that contribute to labor market niching may even extend beyond U.S.

borders, and not only to immigrant homelands but also to other countries. The close ties that today's immigrants maintain with friends and family in their country of origin have contributed to the transnationalization of niche activity in a variety of ways. Immigrant groups may develop their niche "vertically" across borders by establishing supply chains that extend to their country of origin. Because owners of niche businesses may prefer to hire immigrants from their homeland when looking for new workers, the supply chains may center on labor recruitment. Their common language makes communication easy, and they also share feelings of trust and loyalty. Moreover, the new arrivals are likely to work for less pay than more-established immigrants and to tolerate less attractive work conditions. The very establishment of an immigrant group niche in the United States may, in turn, inspire people in the homeland to acquire the skills required to work in the niche, knowing that, upon immigrating, they are more likely to attain work easily on the basis of their transnational ties. For example, Vietnamese first became involved in the manicure business in the United States, but once they established the niche, others began to train for the work in Vietnam so that they could secure employment as manicurists upon their arrival in the United States.

The networks of immigrants consolidated within U.S. niches can also evolve into transnational connections. For example, some immigrant group restaurateurs draw on food supply chains in their homeland. Economists have measured for a long time the transnational impact of immigrant networks on business by showing that countries with larger communities of immigrants from a specific origin tend to trade more with that country and also invest more there (see Rauch and Trindade 2002). By representing a bridge between two cultures and countries, the network of migrants in a labor market niche produces economic ties with the country of origin, promoting foreign investment and business there.

Members of an immigrant group may also take their niche work to other countries, expanding the niche "horizontally." Vietnamese, for example, have established nail salons in Europe that build on the U.S. "McNails" model, inspired by the work of friends and family in the United States.

The experience of Indians who have drawn on the capital, expertise, and networks they developed in Silicon Valley to establish related businesses in India points to another form of niche transnationalization: in what has been dubbed "brain circulation" (Saxenian 1994), Indians transfer not only technology but their expertise to the country from which they originated. The success of Indians in this high-tech niche has come to be transnationally embedded through networks of immigrants, return immigrants, and immigrants with economic interests spanning the United States and India. Their high-tech activity is no longer based in the American labor market (see Commander et al. 2008).

The top research universities have also come to be dominated increasingly by scholars immigrating from select countries. As universities have globalized the pool from which they recruit their "best and brightest," competition has become steeper for the U.S.-born. More competition allows for higher-quality scholars in universities, although it concomitantly crowds out opportunities for native-born researchers.

Foreign-born professors in U.S. universities, in turn, recruit graduate students from top schools in Europe, Asia, Latin America, and Israel through their connections with and knowledge of the schools these students attended abroad. Recruiting foreign graduate students creates networking channels for research projects, coauthorships, and technological transfer between U.S. and foreign universities. Moreover, immigrant groups, sometimes from particular foreign universities, dominate niches in U.S. university departments—for example, Russians in mathematics, Israelis in engineering, and Indians in computer science.

NICHE SPECIALIZATION AND ECONOMIC OPPORTUNITIES

The niches in which immigrant groups get involved often affect their long-term economic prospects. Niches differ substantially in the opportunities they afford. Some are relatively "flat," offering very limited opportunities for vertical career improvement. Other more complex and differentiated niches provide opportunities for immigrant job advancement and earnings improvements and contribute more to the economy at large.

Immigrant groups that get involved in low-wage, low-skilled niches experience few opportunities for economic advancement or career advancement. Most Mexicans and Central Americans have been stuck in low-paying niches in agriculture and construction, where their career opportunities are limited. This is a consequence of both their lower levels of schooling and the location of these jobs, which are primarily found in rural and economically stagnant communities. Thus, the economic possibilities for these immigrants are limited, both within and outside these niches.

In contrast, immigrant groups involved in more-skilled niches that offer within-niche economic opportunities are well positioned to build on their human and social capital. They may not only respond to but also create opportunities for themselves, including through niche transnationalization. Typically, niches in the information technology, medical science and research, and applied life science sectors offer such opportunities. Indians, highly educated Chinese, Israelis, and other Asian groups have been major beneficiaries of such expansive niche-based opportunities.

A related and interesting issue we know little about concerns the intergenerational transformation and evolution of niches. Does the second generation of immigrants find success within a niche, possibly occupying its higher ranks (that is, moving from workers to employers and managers)? Or do they find success after leaving the niche? Roger Waldinger's (1999) descriptions of some niches typical in New York (for example, in the garment and fashion industry) imply that second-generation immigrants (such as Italians and Israelis) have succeeded by climbing the job ladder to become designers and traders within that niche. Other researchers emphasize that the second generation tends to leave the parents' niche to achieve economic success. Second-generation Vietnamese, for example, rarely work as manicurists, because the work offers no stable income, exposes them to toxic chemicals, and pays poorly (Eckstein and Nguyen 2011). In this issue, Eli R. Wilson describes how a bilingual, U.S.-born second generation generates its own upward growth opportunities in the restaurant industry by advancing from the lower-ranked jobs typically filled by the first generation to the upper tiers.

CONCLUSION

Immigrant specialization in labor market niches that build on immigrant social networks and sometimes also on immigrant social institutions helps immigrants attain jobs upon their arrival in America. This specialization contributes to an efficient allocation of skills to jobs as immigrants with different human and social capital assets attain jobs that fill labor market needs and broaden demand for labor by creating new products and services. New immigrants respond to but also create markets for their labor, *as sociological dynamics help us understand*. The opportunities open to immigrants depend on the match between their assets and the robustness or flatness of the niches in which they become engaged.

Immigrants respond to conditions where they settle as best they can, not necessarily cognizant of the macroeconomic efficiency of their labor market involvements. Niching can be a valuable channel for immigrant labor market integration while simultaneously generating economic growth and efficient specialization, provided it does not introduce distortionary barriers and exclusion through niche-based immigrant institutions but keeps those niches open to the forces of competition. The high-skilled immigrant niches contribute the most to the economy, even if they leave some highly qualified U.S.-born workers on the sidelines.

This introduction has pointed to ways in which concepts and insights from sociology and economics can be combined to advance our understanding of the conditions that contribute to the formation of distinctive new immigrant niches and their unintended as well as intended consequences. The essays that follow examine in rich detail both general and specific immigrant labor market engagement from diverse disciplinary and methodological perspectives. Together, they deepen our understanding of how and why different immigrant groups have become associated with different lines of work across the skill spectrum, with different consequences for immigrants, for the native-born, for the country at large, and for immigrant countries of origin. We hope that these essays will inspire other studies that deepen our understanding of immigrant labor market experiences in the globalized economy in which we live.

REFERENCES

Altonji, Joseph, and David Card. 1991. "The Effects of Immigration on the Labor Market Outcomes of Less-Skilled Natives." In *Immigration, Trade, and the Labor Market,* edited by John M. Abowd and Richard Freeman. Cambridge, Mass.: National Bureau of Economic Research.

Braga Martes, Ana Cristina. 2011. *New Immigrants, New Land: A Study of Brazilians in Massachusetts.* Gainesville: University Press of Florida.

Brown, Tamara Mose. 2011. *Raising Brooklyn: Nannies, Childcare, and Caribbeans Creating Community.* New York: New York University Press.

Card, David, and John DiNardo. 2000. "Do Immigrant Inflows Lead to Native Outflows?" *American Economic Review* 90(2): 360–67.

Commander Simon, Rupa Chanda, Mari Kangasniemi, and Alan Winters. 2008. "The Consequences of Globalization: India's Software Industry and Cross-Border Labour Mobility." *The World Economy* 31(2): 187–211.

Cortés, Patricia. 2008. "The Effect of Low-Skilled Immigration on U.S. Prices: Evidence from CPI Data." *Journal of Political Economy* 116(3): 381–422.

Cortés, Patricia, and José Tessada. 2011. "Low-Skilled Immigration and the Labor Supply of Highly Skilled Women." *American Economic Journal: Applied Economics* 3(3): 88–123.

Da Cruz, Michaël. 2018. "Offshore Migrant Workers: Return Migrants in Mexico's English-Speaking Call Centers." *RSF: The Russell Sage Foundation Journal of the Social Sciences* 4(1): 39–57. DOI: 10.7758/RSF.2018.4.1.03.

Dhingra, Pawan. 2012. *Life Behind the Lobby: Indian American Motel Owners and the American Dream.* Stanford, Calif.: Stanford University Press.

Eckstein, Susan. 2009. *The Immigrant Divide: How Cuban Americans Changed the U.S. and Their Homeland.* New York: Routledge.

Eckstein, Susan, and Thanhnghi Nguyen. 2011. "The Making and Transnationalization of an Ethnic Niche: Vietnamese Manicurists." *International Migration Review* 45(4): 639–74.

Gold, Steven J. 2000. *Ethnic Economies.* San Diego, Calif.: Academic Press.

———. 2018. "Israeli Infotech Migrants in Silicon Valley." *RSF: The Russell Sage Foundation Journal of the Social Sciences* 4(1): 130–48. DOI: 10.7758/RSF.2018.4.1.08.

Hamilton, Tod G., Janeria A. Easley, and Angela R. Dixon. 2018. "Black Immigration, Occupational Niches, and Earnings Disparities Between U.S.-Born and Foreign-Born Blacks in the United States." *RSF: The Russell Sage Foundation Journal of the Social Sciences* 4(1): 60–77. DOI: 10.7758/RSF.2018.4.1.04.

Hanson, Gordon H., and Matthew J. Slaughter. 2016. "High-Skilled Immigration and the Rise of STEM Occupations in U.S. Employment." Working Paper 22623. Cambridge, Mass.: National Bureau of Economic Research.

Hu, Xiaochu. 2018. "Filling the Niche: The Role of the Parents of Immigrants in the United States." *RSF: The Russell Sage Foundation Journal of the Social Sciences* 4(1): 96–114. DOI: 10.7758/RSF.2018.4.1.06.

Kang, Miliann. 2010. *The Managed Hand: Race, Gender, and the Body in Beauty Service Work.* Berkeley: University of California Press.

Kasinitz, Philip, and Milton Vickerman. 2001. "Jamaicans in the New York Regional Economy." In *Migration, Transnationalization, and Race in a Changing New York,* edited by Robert Smith, Héctor Cordero-Guzmán, and Ramón Grosfoguel. Philadelphia: Temple University Press.

Kerr, William R., and William F. Lincoln. 2010. "The Supply Side of Innovation: H-1B Visa Reforms and U.S. Ethnic Invention." *Journal of Labor Economics* 28(3): 473–508.

Kerr William R., and Martin Mandorff. 2015. "Social Networks, Ethnicity, and Entrepreneurship." Working Paper 21597. Cambridge, Mass.: National Bureau of Economic Research.

Kwong, Peter, and Dušanka Miščević. 2005. *Chinese America: The Untold Story of America's Oldest New Community.* New York: New Press.

Lafortune, Jeanne, and José Tessada. 2012. "Smooth(er) Landing? The Dynamic Role of Networks in the Location and Occupational Choice of Immigrants." Working Paper 14. Santiago: Pontificia Universidad Católica de Chile, Instituto de Economía, Clio Lab.

Lee, Jennifer. 2006. *Civility in the City: Blacks, Jews, and Koreans in Urban America.* Cambridge, Mass.: Harvard University Press.

Liang, Zai, and Bo Zhou. 2018. "The Rise of Market-Based Job Search Institutions and Job Niches for Low-Skilled Chinese Immigrants." *RSF: The Russell Sage Foundation Journal of the Social Sciences* 4(1): 78–95. DOI: 10.7758/RSF.2018.4.1.05.

Lo, Ming-Cheng M., and Emerald T. Nguyen. 2018. "Caring and Carrying the Cost: Bicultural Latina Nurses' Challenges and Strategies for Working with Coethnic Patients." *RSF: Russell Sage Foundation Journal of the Social Sciences* 4(1): 149–71. DOI: 10.7758/RSF.2018.4.1.09.

Luo, Yu-Ling, and Wei-Jen Wang. 2002. "High-Skilled Migration and Chinese Taipei's Industrial Development." In Organization for Economic Cooperation and Development (OECD), *International Mobility of the Highly Skilled* (Paris: OECD).

Mazzolari, Francesca, and David Neumark. 2012. "Immigration and Product Diversity." *Journal of Population Economics* 25(3): 1107–37.

National Academies of Sciences, Engineering, and Medicine. 2016. *The Economic and Fiscal Consequences of Immigration,* edited by Francine D. Blau and Christopher Mackie. Washington, D.C.: National Academies of Sciences, Engineering, and Medicine, Division of Behavioral and Social Sciences and Education, Committee on National Statistics.

O'Keefe, Siobhan, and Sarah Quincy. 2018. "Old Immigrants, New Niches: Russian Jewish Agricultural Colonies and Native Workers in Southern New Jersey, 1880–1910." *RSF: The Russell Sage Foundation Journal of the Social Sciences* 4(1): 20–38. DOI: 10.7758/RSF.2018.4.1.02.

Ortiga, Yasmin Y. 2018. "Learning to Fill the Labor Niche: Filipino Nursing Graduates and the Risk of the Migration Trap." *RSF: The Russell Sage Foundation Journal of the Social Sciences* 4(1): 172–87. DOI: 10.7758/RSF.2018.4.1.10.

Peri, Giovanni. 2015. "Economic Performance of Immigrants Following the Immigration and Nationality Act of 1965." In *The Immigration and Nationality Act of 1965: Legislating a New America,* edited by Gabriel J. Chin and Rose Cuison Villazor. Cambridge: Cambridge University Press.

Peri, Giovanni, Kevin Shih, and Chad Sparber. 2015. "STEM Workers, H-1B Visas, and Productivity in U.S. Cities." *Journal of Labor Economics* 33(S1): S225–55.

Portes, Alejandro, and Alex Stepick. 1993. *City on the Edge: The Transformation of Miami.* Berkeley: University of California Press.

Rauch, James, and Vitor Trindade. 2002. "Ethnic Chinese Networks in International Trade." *Review of Economics and Statistics* 84(1): 116–30.

Sassen, Saskia. 1995. "Immigration and Local Labor Markets." In *The Economic Sociology of Immigration: Essays on Networks, Ethnicity, and Entrepreneurship,* edited by Alejandro Portes. New York: Russell Sage Foundation.

Saxenian, AnnaLee. 1994. *Regional Advantage: Culture and Competition in Silicon Valley and Route 128.* Cambridge, Mass.: Harvard University Press.

Waldinger, Roger. 1999. *Still the Promised City? African-Americans and New Immigrants in Postindustrial New York.* Cambridge, Mass.: Harvard University Press.

———. 2001. "The Immigrant Niche in Global City-Regions: Concept, Pattern, Controversy." In *Global City-Regions: Trends, Theory, Policy,* edited by A. J. Scott. New York: Oxford University Press.

Waldinger, Roger, and Mehdi Bozorgmehr. 1996. "The Making of a Multicultural Metropolis." In *Ethnic Los Angeles,* edited by Roger Waldinger and Mehdi Bozorgmehr. New York: Russell Sage Foundation.

Wilson, Eli R. 2018. "Bridging the Service Divide: Dual Labor Niches and Embedded Opportunities in Restaurant Work." *RSF: The Russell Sage Foundation Journal of the Social Sciences* 4(1): 115–27. DOI: 10.7758/RSF.2018.4.1.07.

Wilson, Kenneth L., and Alejandro Portes. 1980. "Immigrant Enclaves: An Analysis of the Labor Market Experiences of Cubans in Miami American." *Journal of Sociology* 86 (2, September): 295–319.

PART I

Immigrants and Labor Markets in Time and Space

Old Immigrants, New Niches: Russian Jewish Agricultural Colonies and Native Workers in Southern New Jersey, 1880–1910

SIOBHAN O'KEEFE AND SARAH QUINCY

We look at the effect of immigration shocks on native workers in a labor niche by testing how workers in the farm and nonfarm sectors were affected by the establishment of Russian Jewish agricultural colonies in southern New Jersey in the late nineteenth century. By following the same individuals across the 1880 and 1910 U.S. censuses, we avoid making assumptions about the substitutability of immigrants and native workers. Many native workers improved their occupational standing by transitioning to occupations complementary to agricultural and semiskilled factory work, the immigrants' main niches. We see no impact on farmers, probably owing to the structure of agricultural markets. We also find a decreased probability of out-migration for natives living near an agricultural colony, with occupational upgrading concentrated among stayers.

Keywords: immigration, native response, farming, spillovers

American history is populated by immigrants who came to the United States to escape persecution, economic disaster, and violence. Like other groups before them, 1.5 million Jews from the Russian Empire found their way to the United States, starting in 1881 (Spitzer 2015). The similarity of their plight to that of earlier immigrant groups was not lost on contemporaries. As William Stainsby (1901, 3–4), the chief statistician for New Jersey, wrote in a 1901 report:

They had been cast out as paupers; their humble homes in Russia had been taken from them, and they fled as did the Pilgrim fathers from tyranny and relentless persecution to a land they knew not, but with the promise of such assistance as would enable them to make homes for themselves and children, and where they would be free to worship God in their own way, assured of liberty and the protection of the laws.

Siobhan O'Keefe is a graduate student in economics at the University of California–Davis. **Sarah Quincy** is a graduate student in economics at the University of California–Davis

© 2018 Russell Sage Foundation. O'Keefe, Siobhan, and Sarah Quincy. 2018. "Old Immigrants, New Niches: Russian Jewish Agricultural Colonies and Native Workers in Southern New Jersey, 1880–1910." *RSF: The Russell Sage Foundation Journal of the Social Sciences* 4(1): 20–38. DOI: 10.7758/RSF.2018.4.1.02. Thank you to Katherine Eriksson and Giovanni Peri for invaluable guidance and to the seminar participants at UC Davis and the Russell Sage Foundation for comments. Direct correspondence to: Siobhan O'Keefe at smokeefe @ucdavis.edu, Department of Economics, University of California, 1 Shields Avenue, Davis, CA 95616; and Sarah Quincy at squincy@ucdavis.edu, Department of Economics, University of California, 1 Shields Avenue, Davis, CA 95616.

As the population of ethnic enclaves in U.S. cities swelled, some of these newcomers were dispersed to the countryside, where, with the help of aid agencies, farming colonies were established across the United States (Shpall 1950). We focus on the effects of the flagship agricultural colonies in southern New Jersey on native workers in both the farm and nonfarm sectors by combining longitudinal, individual-level data and new quasi-experimental variation. In their introduction, the economist Giovanni Peri and the sociologist Susan Eckstein discuss the potential displacement of natives in occupations that become niches for new immigrants. We examine the impact of new immigrants entering labor market niches—pockets of concentrated employment in specific occupations within a community—on the outcomes of natives both inside and outside the niches in a uniquely rural context.

Jewish charities funneled refugees and funds into clusters of farms across southern New Jersey chosen for their affordability and relative proximity to New York City and Philadelphia. Because no Russians lived in the area before the establishment of the first agricultural colony at Alliance in 1882, we can isolate the effect of the immigrant inflow. We compare the 1910 labor market outcomes of native-born men living next to the colonies in 1880 to the outcomes of native-born men living elsewhere in southern New Jersey. The influx of Russian immigrants was equivalent to approximately 1 percent of the total population in areas next to the agricultural colonies. Although restrictions on landowning in Russia had prevented Russian Jews from farming, they eked out a living in New Jersey as farmers, with the help of charity-funded training. To keep the Russian Jewish immigrants employed when demand for crops was low, international aid societies also helped construct factories in the colonies.

We find that men living near a colony were not only less likely to move away by 1910 but also more likely to upgrade to higher-paying jobs that were complementary to refugee-occupied niches. Men who lived near agricultural colonies had a 4.7 percent higher income in 1910 than men who did not live near a colony. In contrast to the positive results for the nonfarm sector, we find no effect of living near a colony on farmers, despite the influx of new farmers.

We begin with a brief literature review, followed by a thorough investigation of the historical context of this immigration shock. Next, we detail our data and describe our specification. Finally, we present and discuss our quantitative results.

LITERATURE REVIEW

The literature on the impact of immigration on the labor market outcomes of native workers is vast. Our study fits neatly into the intersection of historical work on the "Age of Mass Migration," more modern work using longitudinal, individual-level studies, and examinations of refugee and immigrant shocks using natural experiments.

At the heart of the debate on the effect of immigration on native worker outcomes lie two different potential assumptions about the extent of labor market similarities between native and immigrant workers. Data constraints often compel researchers to use cross-sectional survey data. Identification of this effect then requires an assumption on the extent of substitutability between immigrants and natives; before determining how immigrants affect workers, the researcher must decide how susceptible each worker's job is to an influx of immigrants. On the one hand, the economist George Borjas (1999) assumes immigrants and natives are completely substitutable within an education and work experience group. On the other hand, the economists Giovanni Peri and Chad Sparber (2009) allow for differences between native and immigrant workers; doing so shifts the direction of the impact on native wages from negative to zero. We will track the same individuals over time, allowing us to refrain from making either assumption. The economists Mark Partridge, Dan Rickman, and Kamar Ali (2008) have results consistent with other nationwide studies when looking specifically at rural areas, but they note that, for high-poverty regions, higher immigration is associated with higher in-migration of natives, suggesting that immigrants add to the economic vitality of a local area. Other researchers have used unexpected events as quasi-experiments to estimate the impact of immigrants on native workers. The economist David Card's 1990 examination of the Mariel Boatlift is probably the best-known use of this empirical strategy in the immigration literature; in using this method to examine the effects of a large and unexpected influx of Cuban immigrants on the Miami labor market, he finds no impact on the wages or unemployment rates of low-skilled workers already in Miami.

Modern longitudinal work has focused on European countries for data accessibility reasons. Several papers have treated a Danish refugee settlement program as a natural experiment. From 1986 to 1998, this program randomly dispersed new refugees to municipalities across the county. Looking at wages within Danish firms from 1993 to 2004, the economists Nikolaj Malchow-Møller, Jakob Munch, and Jan Rose Skaksen (2012) find that when firms increase their employment of low-skilled immigrant workers, the wages of native workers at the same firm drop significantly. However, a study that looked specifically at Danish farms found that farms that employ immigrants are larger, create more jobs, and have higher revenue (Malchow-Møller et al. 2013). In the work that is the most similar in spirit to ours, the economists Mette Foged and Giovanni Peri (2016) leverage this program to examine the long-term outcomes of low-skill native workers in cities that received a substantial shock of immigrants. Overall, they find a small positive mean effect on income for native workers from 1991 to 2008. Consistent with earlier work, low-skilled native workers were more likely to transition into occupations with less manual intensity as low-skilled immigrants arrived. On the migration margin, Danish-born workers were less likely to migrate away from their original municipality when more refugee immigrants moved into their municipality. Spillovers—the ripple effects of the immigration shock across the economy—provide some explanation for why these results differ from those of Malchow-Møller and his colleagues (2012). Although we use a similar time window, we focus more on skill upgrading and migration responses in a much less industrialized society.

In the literature on the Age of Mass Migration—the large wave of unchecked immigration into the United States from 1880 to 1913—most work has focused on the experience of immigrants, not native workers.[1] Some of this work complements our work focused on Russian immigrants. The economist Yannay Spitzer (2015) finds that pogroms did not drive Russian Jewish emigration to the United States. The economist Leah Platt Boustan (2007) concludes that demographic growth was a key driver of Russian Jewish immigration. Using a 1909 Immigration Commission report on weekly wages across industries and immigrant groups, the economist Barry Chiswick (1992) finds that Russian-born Jews' lifetime earnings profiles were higher than those of other immigrant groups, though still lower than those of natives, indicating that their language differences made them imperfect substitutes for native workers, just as the modern literature would suggest.

The economic historian Claudia Goldin (1994) provides the closest analog to our work. She combines city-level annual wages, decennial demographic information, and decennial industry-city wage series to look at the change in wages after immigration shocks, measured as the change in the share of the foreign-born population. Goldin concludes that immigration pushed down wages in the clothing and unskilled labor sectors. We complement this work by moving away from using aggregate data (and the substitution assumptions embedded in that method) to using longitudinal data. Further, we address the potential endogeneity of immigrants' locational choices and natives' economic outcomes by using a cleanly identified natural experiment.

Additionally, there is a specific literature on the impacts of refugees, much of it in the context of developing countries. Refugees require separate analysis because their migration is forced and external aid charities often ease

---

1. Classic works on immigration to the United States includes work by economists like Barry Chiswick (1992) and the two books by Timothy Hatton and Jeffrey Williamson (1998, 2005). More recent scholarship includes work by Ran Abramitzky, Leah Platt Boustan, and Katherine Eriksson (2012, 2014).

their transition. The economists Isabel Ruiz and Carlos Vargas-Silva (2016) examine a large inflow of refugees into Tanzania in the early 1990s as a result of ethnic conflicts in Burundi and Rwanda. Looking at individuals before the shock and then seventeen to nineteen years after it, they find evidence that individuals in areas that received a larger flow of refugees were more likely to be engaged in household agricultural work or self-employment rather than casual day work, where they would have competed with the incoming refugees. Although the economist Javier Baez (2011) finds immediate adverse health impacts for children in the areas that experienced these refugee inflows, the economists Jean-François Maystadt and Philip Verwimp (2014) present evidence of net economic benefits, although with substantial heterogeneity across occupations. Self-employed farmers were most likely to benefit from the refugee inflow, consistent with the occupational transitions that Ruiz and Vargas-Silva find. None of these studies take into account the outcomes of those individuals who migrated after the inflow, an important potential mechanism for natives' adjustment.

By combining a previously unused natural experiment with longitudinal data, we provide a minimally structured environment in which to test how native workers respond to the entrance of immigrants into their labor market, both generally and into their specific niche. Instead of having to impose how and if immigrants competed with native-born Americans, we can measure the impact directly. Additionally, this article is the first to our knowledge to examine this question in the Age of Mass Migration. Finally, with most previous work focused on urban labor markets, our examination of a rural context is novel. We turn next to the historical record to examine how Russian Jews ended up farming in some parts of southern New Jersey.

THE HISTORICAL CONTEXT

About half of the world's Jewish population in 1880 lived in the Pale of Settlement, an area of the Russian Empire consisting of most of modern-day Lithuania, Poland, Belarus, Moldova, Latvia, and Ukraine (Popper 2006, 2). This concentration did not come about organically. Beginning with decrees passed by Catherine the Great in the 1790s, Russian law confined the Jewish population to the Pale, wherein many already resided (Eisenberg 1995, 4). Jewish craftsmen found themselves pushed out by new factories, which often refused to hire Jewish workers (Popper 2006, 3). Such targeted policies resulted in widespread poverty. In 1849, only 3 percent of the Jewish Pale population owned any capital, and they were considered a "separate, inferior category," below even peasants (Eisenberg 1995, 5; Lederhendler 2008, 514). Jewish military conscripts were substantially shorter than non-Jewish conscripts, suggesting lower standards of living (Kopczyński 2011, 206).

After the assassination of Alexander II in 1881, the Russian government enacted the explicitly anti-Semitic May Laws. Jewish people could no longer move to rural areas or enter beyond a certain quota into schools or professional work. Further, villages could expel anyone deemed "undesirable" (Brandes and Douglas 1971, 18; Eisenberg 1995, 13). When mob violence erupted, Jewish workers in the more manufacturing-driven North had an easier time emigrating. Jewish people in the South were at the center of anti-Jewish violence and needed international aid to escape (Eisenberg 1995, 6–17; Spitzer 2015, 26). Pogrom survivors from the southern Pale joined people from nearby towns in a mass exodus to the Austro-Hungarian border town of Brody, where the refugees quickly exhausted the resources of international aid foundations (Spitzer 2015, 8).

The international community was divided on the "Jewish problem." European Jews did not want to absorb the refugee inflows on their own. German Jews worried that visibly supporting other Jews might violate their German citizenship, and French Jews were just entering the period of anti-Semitism characterized by the Dreyfus Affair (Eisenberg 1995, 63–65). Many in the Jewish community in the United States worried that an influx of poor, uneducated, Yiddish-speaking migrants bearing "the ineffaceable marks of permanent pauperism" would set them back socially (Osofsky 1960, 183). The Hebrew Emigrant Aid Society (HEAS) emissary declared to European aid societies that "America [was] not a poorhouse . . . [or] an asylum for the paupers of Europe" (Szajkowski 1950, 225). In the 1880s, American aid societies even paid to deport the poorest immigrants on cattle steamers to avoid saturation (Brandes and Douglas 1971, 122).

If the flood of refugees could not be stopped from entering the United States, however, then perhaps it could be diverted to undersettled areas. To that end, the international Jewish community settled on the idea of lending skilled, able-bodied refugees money to establish farms in the United States and Argentina (Osofsky 1960, 174–75; Shpall 1950, 124).

Although the larger Jewish philanthropic community in the United States wished settlers well, they also were trying to divert as many immigrants as possible away from large urban centers. This "marked antagonism" resulted in sites being chosen "with almost no thought to the agronomic phase of the colonization" (Goldstein 1921, 13). In 1881, thirty-four families from pogrom-stricken Kiev and Elizabethgrad left Brody for New York with the help of French charities and settled on a tract of land in Sicily Island, Louisiana, purchased by the HEAS (Shpall 1950, 129; Eisenberg 1995, 37). Histories attribute the selection of low-lying, mosquito-ridden, isolated land in the north of Louisiana to corruption or ignorance (Price and Shpall 1958, 84; Shpall 1950, 130; Eisenberg 1995, 38). In any event, a spring Mississippi River flood destroyed the colony's crops at the same time as it was struck by a malaria outbreak (Shpall 1950, 130–31). Other farm colonies followed across the western United States, and all failed quickly.

By mid-1882, it was clear that these colonies were not set up to survive without constant aid inflows. Even if several of the colonies did not fail, immigration continued to surge, suggesting that a more efficient system was imperative if the Russian newcomers were to be diverted from urban centers. In response, philanthropists were determined to find a site that had a good climate and was close to preexisting Jewish communities, where they would better serve as safety valves for continued elevated levels of immigration and more easily receive financial and religious support. New Jersey had recently appointed a commissioner of immigration, Augustus Seeman, who was a partner in a realty firm near Vineland. He was eager to bring immigrants into New Jersey, particularly if they were willing to buy his land. There was land with good soil available near the New Jersey Central Railroad, which connected to both Philadelphia and New York City, and the HEAS was happy to oblige (Shpall 1950, 22). Seeman's enthusiasm notwithstanding, southern New Jersey was not abnormally pro-immigrant. When the Russians arrived in Vineland, natives scorned them because they could not tell tomatoes from weeds (Brandes and Douglas 1971, 86).

Alliance, New Jersey, was thus established. Settlers were assigned land through a lottery: each family got twelve to fifteen acres of land with generous mortgage terms and a weekly wage for clearing the land. Income was supplemented by picking berries, working in the nearby cigar factory (which charities wooed to the area), or doing needlework at home (Stainsby 1901, 5). Several other colonies were subsequently established, and those that received help, like Carmel, Rosenhayn, and Norma, survived. Contemporary observers attributed the quick failure and abandonment of seven other colonies to a lack of start-up capital, stemming from either rank exploitation or mismanagement, not to the quality of the land itself (Stainsby 1901, 27; Eisenberg 1995, 105; Brandes and Douglas 1971, 67).[2]

The biggest colony, Woodbine, was founded in 1891 by one of the most prominent Jewish philanthropists of the age, Baron Maurice de Hirsch, who believed that farming was a healthy and ennobling endeavor that would raise the profile of the Jew no matter what external prejudice he faced; "rainfall," de Hirsch claimed, was "insensitive to religion" (Popper 2006, 11). When suburban land around New York City, Philadelphia, and Trenton proved too expensive and a deal for land near Newark fell through, the Baron de Hirsch Fund turned to a 5,000-acre plot twenty miles southeast of Vineland (Brandes and Douglas 1971, 114). Un-

2. We conducted falsification tests on the placement of these failed colonies and found no relationship between failed colony placement and 1880 characteristics of our matched sample (results available upon request). Natives living near these failed colonies are not considered treated in our analysis.

like the earlier colonies, industry was planned in Woodbine. The town included an electrical plant, larger houses, a hotel, a Russian bath, and many houses intended for factory workers (ibid., 115).

The climate was similar across the New Jersey colonies on which we focus our examination of immigrant shock: Alliance, Rosenhayn, Carmel, Norma, and Woodbine. Because the soil was ill suited for growing wheat or other staple crops, farmers grew a variety of fruits and vegetables for sale at market (Stainsby 1901, 8). In particular, the colonies were renowned in Philadelphia and New York for their sweet potatoes, berries, and farm animals (ibid., 20, 60). This fame may have derived in part from the marketing cooperatives that the farmers organized on their own initiative, starting in 1889 (Brandes and Douglas 1971, 96). The colonies expanded from 1,109 people in 1889 to approximately 2,227 in 1901 and 2,739 in 1919 (Robinson 1912, 65–67; Stainsby 1901; Rosenthal 1906; Goldstein 1921, 29).[3] The Jewish Agricultural Society (1954, 9) attributed the colonies' survival to settlers' innovation, daring, and frugality. While their hard work cannot be denied, it is certain that external aid also played a large role in the colonies' continued existence. For instance, well before the passage of the Federal Farm Loan Act, the Jewish Agricultural and Industrial Aid Society (JAIAS) provided Jewish farmers with farm improvement loans (Stainsby 1901, 95; Robinson 1912, 52–53).

Jewish aid societies remained heavily involved in the day-to-day lives of the colonists in other ways as well. To help the new farmers, who were so ignorant about farming that they did not know if potatoes grew above or below ground, the JAIAS published a Yiddish-language newsletter and sent experts to discuss innovations with them (Robinson 1912, 72; Brandes and Douglas 1971, 86). The nation's first agricultural secondary school was established in Woodbine in 1893 (Stainsby 1901, 22; Goldstein 1921, 22). Other educational directives established community libraries and education supervising bureaus, which helped the immigrants' children outpace natives in school (Eisenberg 1995, 148; Robinson 1912, 67).

These aid society efforts were helpful, but colonists needed still more. Despite the colonies' agricultural ethos, the aid societies realized very early that nonfarm employment would be needed to sustain the immigrants. The soil was workable, but still required substantial investment to sustain a family. With industry, "it should not take forty years to lead their brethren out of the wilderness" (Brandes and Douglas 1971, 120–26). After the first year in Alliance, charities donated $3,000 to fund factory construction to provide off-season employment (ibid., 58). After 1900, the JAIAS provided mortgages, below-market rent, and annual subsidies for factories willing to relocate to the colonies in order to keep Jewish families fed during the winter (Dubrovsky 1992, 20; Brandes and Douglas 1971, 149). Norma, in particular, enjoyed high economic and population growth after the construction of the Allivine Canning Company in 1901. The JAIAS helped build the factory to provide a local market for farmers' produce (Robinson 1912, 66). By 1919, there were twenty-one factories in the Jewish colonies, with more in the surrounding areas (Goldstein 1921, 41).

Anti-Semitism was present in southern New Jersey before the arrival of the Russian immigrants, but increased with the expansion of the colonies. In 1885, for example, the *Vineland Evening Journal* printed that Eastern European Jews had murdered one of their own, just as they killed Jesus Christ, reiterating the blood libel that had provided a spark for several Russian pogroms (Brandes and Douglas 1971, 173). Jewish businesses were open on Sundays, which proved to be a temptation for some neighboring Christians who went shopping in Rosenhayn. The *Vineland Evening Journal* suggested that businesses closing on Sundays was an "American custom" and that anyone open for business on that day should leave the country (ibid., 187–88). Anti-Semitism also flared up in the workplace. In September 1891, workers at a glass factory refused to work alongside Jewish workers, chased the Jewish workers through the streets, and went on strike until the factory fired the Jews for being "unfit to work" (Eisenberg 1995, 124).

---

3. Population in 1901 uses 1889 values for Rosenhayn owing to missing data.

However, even though there was some cultural tension, for the most part native-born Americans welcomed the work ethic and patronage of Jewish workers. When some accused the Jews of not being good workers, one employer wrote the local newspaper to dismiss those charges as "slanderous," and the founder of Vineland suggested that some non-Jewish farmers could learn from the colonists' diligence (Brandes and Douglas, 175). Other benefits came as spillovers from Jewish charity. When philanthropists' labor-oriented guidelines proved to constrain profits, some factories relocated to nearby Vineland (ibid., 156–59). These differential responses suggest that there may have been substantial heterogeneity in the effects of the colonial immigration shock on native worker outcomes.

We turn next to a quantitative analysis to distinguish just how native-born workers changed their labor market behavior after exposure to immigrants.

DATA

From the historical record, we can clearly locate areas in southern New Jersey with agricultural colonies. Starting in 1880, the Census Bureau divided counties into smaller districts in order to administer the census. Each census-taker would have been assigned one or more districts across which they would administer the census questionnaire to each household (Haddad 2012). Using these enumeration districts allows us to take advantage of finer and more precise locational variation in exposure to the immigrant shock. To our knowledge, we are the first researchers to use enumeration district–level variation in historical work. This gives us 108 localities in New Jersey with which to work instead of eight counties.

In southern New Jersey, the enumeration district boundaries follow each county's established municipal boundaries, called townships, which are analogous to local labor markets (Morse 2016).[4] Using the 1872 *State Atlas of New Jersey* (Beers 1872), we can match the colony locations to their census enumeration districts. The darkest-shaded townships in figure 1 denote the locations of the agricultural colonies. Only townships in southern New Jersey, here defined as Atlantic, Burlington, Camden, Cape May, Cumberland, Gloucester, Ocean, and Salem Counties, are included in our sample. We exclude the city of Camden, as our analysis focuses on more rural labor markets. Townships colored white in figure 1 did not contain any observations in our matched sample.

Given this township-level shock, we take men observed in both the 1880 and 1910 U.S. censuses as our unit of study (Ruggles et al. 2015). This time frame allows us to look at long-term outcomes, but other events occurring in those thirty years could affect our results.[5] Using a procedure similar to that observed in Abramitzky, Boustan, and Eriksson (2014), we take an 1880 observation and a 1910 observation as matched if they share a first and last name, share a state of birth, and have birth years within five years of each other. Names are cleaned using the New York State Identification and Intelligence System (NYSIIS), a phonetic algorithm, to correct for enumerator spelling errors. We first match those with the same birth year and remove them from the pool of available matches, then those with birth years within one year of each other, and finally those with birth years within two years of each other, also removing the latter two groups from the pool. Then we keep only those observations that are unique by first name, last name, and birth place within a centered five-year birth year window to ensure that the matches are unique and to maximize the probability that we have indeed found the same person in both censuses. We undertook further cleaning to create uniform occupation variables across our

---

4. There are slight deviations in enumeration district borders from modern township boundaries in south-central New Jersey, as mapped in figure 1. We have chosen to color townships based on the proximity of the majority of the township to a colony.

5. The 1890 census schedules were destroyed by a combination of fire and congressional mandate, and 1900 census schedules are still being digitized. We thank Katherine Eriksson for her assistance with the 1910 full-count data.

Figure 1. Agricultural Colonies by Township in Southern New Jersey

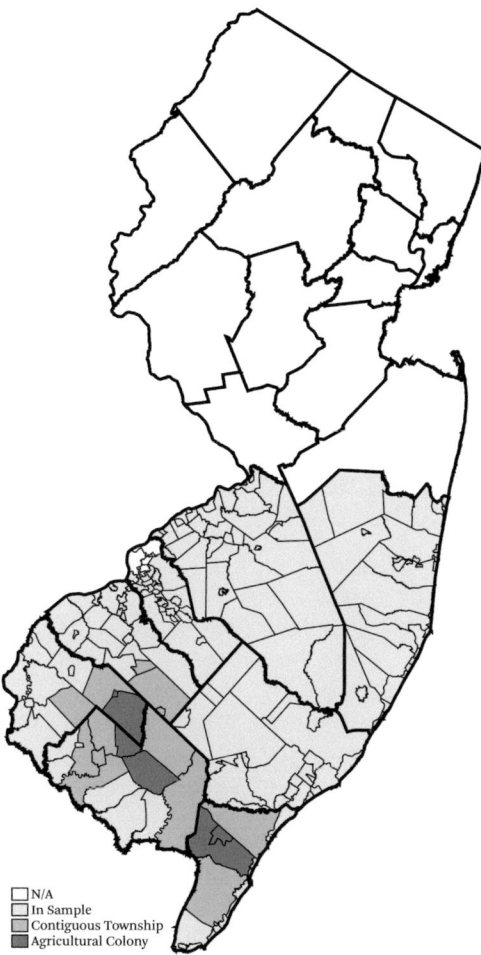

Source: Authors' calculations based on New Jersey Office of Information Technology 2010.

sample in 1910.[6] We restrict our sample to native-born men under age sixty-five in 1880 living in the counties described earlier. Although the matched sample is technically a panel data set, our specifications use it as a 1910 cross-section with preperiod information from 1880.

As we see in table 1, our sample began the period at age twenty-five. Most of them were living in rural areas, but fewer than 7 percent were farmers in 1880. One-fifth of the sample were exposed to a colony, and on average they were twenty miles away from a colony. The average occupational score is around that of a laundry operative or a fisherman. By the end of the period, their occupational score nearly doubled to the level of a teacher or a stonecutter. Well over half the sample migrated away from their initial county of residence. Appendix table A1 demonstrates the similarity between the entire 1880 southern New Jersey male population under sixty-five and our matched sample.

In 1880, when we first observe our matched sample, southern New Jersey was still very rural. Eighty percent of all people living in the area were classified as rural by the Census Bureau, and 28 percent were in a household with at least one person involved in agriculture. Given the rural nature of the area, it is not surprising that these townships were small. Their average population in 1880 was 1,944; the townships that received colonies were slightly smaller, with an average population of 1,872. An inflow of over 2,000 refugees would definitely have been noticed by the locals. The modal occupation category, representing 18 percent of men over age sixteen, was owning, managing, or renting a farm. Agriculture was also the most common industry in which to work, claimed by 43 percent of men who reported a sectoral specialization. This was an important economic niche for native workers as well. Ninety-nine percent of working-age men were literate, and 90 percent of them were born in the United States. There were no immigrants from the Russian Empire in the area in 1880 (Ruggles et al. 2015).

Midsize farms were the norm in southern New Jersey. In 1880, fewer than 8 percent were under ten acres and not even 1 percent were over five hundred acres. The average farm size was eighty-nine acres, and 13.8 percent were between ten and forty-nine acres; these farms were similar in size to those the colonists would later work (Haines and ICPSR 2010; Stainsby 1901). The average farm's output was $888, equivalent to approximately $21,800 in 2016. Although farming was still the dominant industry, manufacturing also had a presence in this area. Even Cape May County, the least

---

6. Additional information on the matching and cleaning processes described here is available upon request.

Table 1. Summary Statistics for Russian Jewish Immigrants in Agricultural Colonies in Southern New Jersey, 1880–1910

Variable	(1) Observations	(2) Mean	(3) Standard Deviation	(4) Minimum	(5) Maximum
A. 1880 starting point					
Age	3,693	25.010	13.817	0	65
Rural	3,693	0.704	0.454	0	1
Occupation score	3,693	15.589	13.504	0	80
Farmer	3,693	0.069	0.254	0	1
White-collar job	3,693	0.170	0.375	0	1
Craftsman	3,693	0.163	0.370	0	1
B. Colony distance					
Same or contiguous district of a colony	3,693	0.180	0.384	0	1
Distance to closest colony	3,693	23.884	12.353	0	64
C. 1910 outcomes					
Migrated	3,693	0.841	0.341	0	1
Occupation score	3,210	27.341	12.064	4	80
Farmer	3,693	0.135	0.341	0	1
White-collar job	3,693	0.290	0.454	0	1
Craftsman	3,693	0.180	0.384	0	1

Source: Authors' calculations based on 1880 and 1910 U.S. censuses.

developed, had thirty-six manufacturing establishments in 1880. On a per capita basis, the value of manufacturing output had already surpassed agricultural output, with manufacturing establishments producing about $104 of output per person in 1880 and farming producing about $50 per person (approximately $2,490 and $1,230, respectively, in 2016) (Haines and ICPSR 2010).

SPECIFICATION

To estimate the impact of newly arrived immigrants on native workers using this natural experiment and linked individual data, we use specifications of the following form:

$$Y_{id} = \alpha + \beta Colony_d + \gamma_i + \rho_{c(d)} + \varepsilon_{id}, \quad (1)$$

where i is the linked individual, d is the enumeration district, and c is the county of the individual's initial enumeration district. γ_i represents individual controls, which include controls for individuals' age and their initial occupational category. We considered clustering standard errors at the county level, but we would have run into the small number of clusters problem (Cameron and Miller 2015). Instead, we use robust standard errors and accept that our standard errors are likely to be reduced because there is some spatial correlation that remains unaccounted for in our estimates.

We control for variation in county economic composition stemming from proximity to either the Atlantic Ocean or Philadelphia with $\rho_{c(d)}$, which divides the townships in our sample into three categories: those in a county with an Atlantic border, those with a Philadelphia border, and those with neither. Thus, any initial conditions relating to port or major city activity are washed out.

$Colony_d$ is an indicator for whether an individual lived in a township with a colony or next to one with a colony. We chose this proximity measure to reflect the localized nature of rural labor markets at the time (Parman 2012). The *Vineland Evening Journal* expressed amazement that colonists walked about five miles from Alliance to Vineland to shop every day (Brandes and Douglas 1971, 172), but nonetheless immigrants walked from one township to another daily. We try a variety of distance-based measures and find similar results (available in appendix figures A1 to A3).

Y_{id} is either the native worker i's occupational standing in 1910 or an indicator variable that takes on a value of 1 for individuals who migrated out of their 1880 county of residence by 1910. Additionally, we examine the probability of entering three specific occupational niches: farming, white-collar work, or craftsman (skilled blue-collar work). Unfortunately, the Census Bureau did not collect earnings information at this time. We follow the lead of other economic historians by using occupational standing as a proxy for labor earnings (Abramitzky et al. 2014). Specifically, we use the occupational score calculated by the Integrated Public Use Microdata Series (IPUMS), which gives each occupation a score based on the median income of individuals in that occupation in 1950, measured in hundreds of 1950 dollars. For ease of interpretation, we convert these incomes to 2016 dollars using the consumer price index (CPI) deflator in the discussion of our results (Ruggles et al. 2015). For men who were younger than sixteen in 1880, we use the father's occupation score to measure economic status before the immigration shock (Abramitzky et al. 2014).

We are interested in the migration response of natives to the Jewish agricultural colonies. Migration away from the township-level shock is defined as moving away from the county of observation in 1880 by 1910. A main advantage of following the same individuals over time is the ability to examine this migration response. Migration, both westward and into cities, was a major force at this time. As seen in table 1, more than half of our sample migrated over this time period. Many of them moved to Philadelphia or other urban centers on the East Coast, and some of them moved west.

For this specification to give us a true estimate of the impact of these immigrants on native workers, we need to make a parallel trends assumption: in the absence of the colonies, the occupational and migratory patterns of native-born men in areas near a colony would have been the same as the patterns of those living farther away. As we are comparing the same individuals across time, we do not have to make assumptions about the comparability of people living in a given area in 1880 and in 1910. Owing to the quasi-random nature of the agricultural land selection process—the southern New Jersey tracts of land purchased by Jewish charities happened to be available for sale by newly appointed commissioner Seeman—we believe that any preexisting trends in our sample should be unrelated to the shock experienced by our treated group, that is, those who lived in or contiguous to a township with an agricultural colony.

Because the data necessary for an examination of pre-immigration shock trends in individual labor market outcomes do not exist, we look for possible pre-trend shocks at the county level.[7] Figure 2 shows average farm value, including crops and livestock, across the counties with and without colonies in our sample. While the no-colony group had more valuable farms, the trends in farm value appear to be similar, suggesting that no other economic trends were driving the selection of the colonies and that immigrants did not receive particularly unusable land.

Finally, to address any remaining concerns about international aid organizations' selection of local labor markets in which to invest within southern New Jersey, we use our matched sample to run the following regression:

$$C_{id} = \alpha + \delta X_i + \gamma_i + \rho_{c(d)} + \upsilon_{id}. \qquad (2)$$

C_d indicates if an enumeration district contains a colony or any treated individuals (adding enumeration districts that are contiguous to

---

7. Occupational information has been digitized only for a small subset of 1870 census returns. The sample from the counties relevant to our study is too small for meaningful analysis.

Figure 2. Average Farm Values in Southern New Jersey, 1860–1900

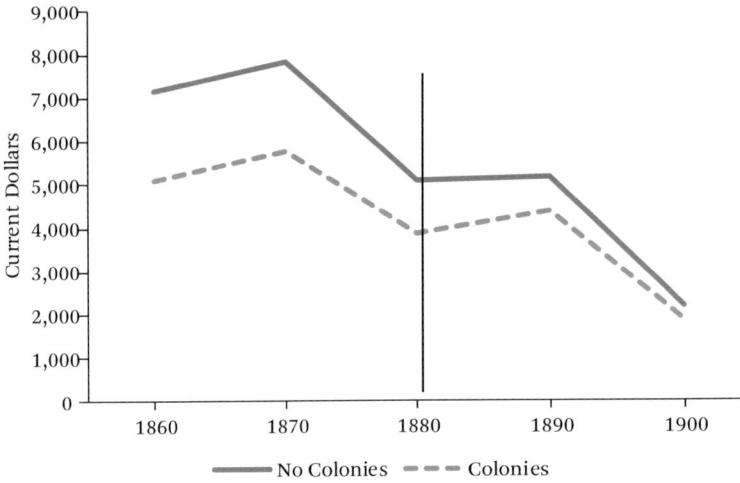

Source: Authors' calculations based on Haines and ICPSR 2010.

those with colonies). X_i is one of our three characteristics of interest: $occscore_i$, the 1880 occupation score of a matched individual; age_i, his 1880 age; or $farm_i$, the matched individual's household's farm status.[8] γ_i represents the individual's age and age squared in 1880 (included only when looking at occupation or farm status), $\rho_{c(d)}$ indicates if the enumeration district is in a county that borders either Philadelphia or the Atlantic Ocean, and v_{id} is a randomly distributed error term. We find no relation between the initial occupational score, age, or farm status of our matched sample and the location of the agricultural colonies. All the estimates, presented in appendix table A2, are very small in magnitude; none are statistically significant.

RESULTS

We present our quantitative results in tables 2 through 4. All subgroups are defined by initial period characteristics. We chose age and farm household as subgroups because age at the time of this event is likely to influence the spectrum of possible responses, and the introduction of the agricultural colonies may represent a different type of shock for farm households versus nonfarm households. We find that being next to a Jewish agricultural colony is associated with a 4.2-percentage-point decrease in the probability that a native-born worker would leave his 1880 county, which is similar to findings in Foged and Peri (2016). Given the general population's tendency to migrate at this time, the choice to stay implies positive impacts from immigrants. These migration results also rule out the story that natives left the treated areas, perhaps owing to competition with immigrants, and found better jobs in other labor markets. This result underscores the importance of using a matched sample; if we had compared areas contiguous to the colonies before and after the inflows, the two groups would have been systematically different because of this reduced probability of migration.[9]

Not only were workers in areas with inflows of refugees and international aid less likely to move, but they also experienced increases in occupational scores relative to workers in labor markets that were not next to colonies. As seen in panel B of table 2, native workers living next

---

8. A household is categorized by the Census Bureau as a farm household if it is located on a tract of land used for agricultural purposes or if any member of the household gives "farmer" as their occupation.

9. Note that, unless otherwise specified, all matched individuals are included in the following analyses, regardless of migration status.

Table 2. Russian Jewish Immigrants' Presence in Agricultural Colonies and Later Outcomes in 1910

	(1)	(2)	(3)	(4)	(5)
	All	Farm Household	Nonfarm Household	Under Age Sixteen	Age Sixteen and Older
A. Migration					
Colony	−0.0419*	−0.00598	−0.0587**	0.00493	−0.0587**
	(0.0218)	(0.0381)	(0.0265)	(0.0315)	(0.0274)
Observations	3,693	807	2,886	1,021	2,672
B. Occupational score					
Colony	1.277*	−0.261	1.893**	1.319	1.280
	(0.744)	(1.345)	(0.892)	(1.190)	(0.923)
Observations	3,210	723	2,487	938	2,272

Source: Authors' calculations based on 1880 and 1910 U.S. censuses.
Notes: The panel A dependent variable is an indicator that takes the value of 1 if an individual is observed in a different county in 1910 than in 1880. The panel B dependent variable is the individual's 1910 occupational score; to translate to approximate 2016 dollars, we multiply coefficients by 1,000. "Colony" indicates if the individual was in or contiguous to a township with a colony. Robust standard errors are in parentheses. All specifications include controls for age, initial occupation category, and proximity to Philadelphia and the Atlantic Ocean.
*$p < .10$; **$p < .05$; ***$p < .01$

to a Jewish agricultural colony earned $1,277 more (in 2016 dollars) in 1910. This represents a premium of approximately 4.7 percent at the mean 1910 occupational score. Although this is larger than the 2.4 percent wage premium found in Foged and Peri (2016), we also have an immigrant shock approximately double the size of the shock in that study. This response is primarily driven by men who started the period in nonfarm households. Their incomes increased $1,893 on average in 1910, a premium of 6.9 percent.

Next we look at natives' occupational sector choices in order to better understand the difference between farm and nonfarm households. The combined impact of the refugee labor shock and the philanthropic capital shock can be felt through natives' occupational choices. Part of this premium may be due to a shift away from farming, as shown in panel A of table 3. Younger men and men starting the period in nonfarm households were both relatively less likely to be in a farming occupation in 1910. For natives under the age of sixteen in 1880, there was a decline in the probability of being a farmer in 1910 of 3.5 percentage points when living near a successful agricultural colony. This is consistent with a complementarity story: as immigrants moved in and began to farm, more native-born workers could transition to better-paid, nonfarm occupations, particularly given the establishment of aid-supported industry nearby.

In fact, as demonstrated by panels B and C of table 3, workers near agricultural colonies in 1880, particularly those not living on farms at the time, were 3 to 4 percent more likely to be white-collar or crafts workers in 1910. This is an effect of approximately 10 percent relative to the mean for white-collar workers, and almost 25 percent for craftsmen. International aid organizations provided substantial funding in the colonies for Russian Jews to farm and work in factories, allowing native workers to reap the benefits of increased demand for positions that required more specialized training or intrapersonal skills, like mechanics or floor managers. We find additional support for this conclusion by examining the effect on occupation score separately for those who migrated and those who did not by interacting an individual's occupation score with his migration status. Because migration is also affected by the location of an agricultural colony, these

Table 3. Russian Jewish Immigrants' Presence in Agricultural Colonies and Occupation Choice in 1910

	(1) All	(2) Farm Household	(3) Nonfarm Household	(4) Under Age Sixteen	(5) Age Sixteen and Older
A. Farming occupation					
Colony	-0.0418**	-0.0375	-0.0400*	-0.0354	-0.0473**
	(0.0195)	(0.0395)	(0.0224)	(0.0334)	(0.0238)
Observations	3,693	807	2,886	1,021	2,672
B. White-collar job					
Colony	0.0429*	0.0123	0.0535*	0.0355	0.0433
	(0.0259)	(0.0497)	(0.0305)	(0.0537)	(0.0294)
Observations	3,693	807	2,886	1,021	2,672
C. Craftsman					
Colony	0.0344	0.00797	0.0471*	0.0153	0.0378
	(0.0223)	(0.0362)	(0.0278)	(0.0447)	(0.0259)
Observations	3,693	807	2,886	1,021	2,672

Source: Authors' calculations based on 1880 and 1910 U.S. censuses.
Notes: The dependent variables are indicators that equal 1 if the individual is employed in a farming occupation, a white-collar job, or a skilled craft. "Colony" indicates if the individual was in or contiguous to a township with a colony. Robust standard errors are in parentheses. All specifications include controls for age, initial occupation category, and proximity to Philadelphia and the Atlantic Ocean.
*$p < .10$; **$p < .05$; ***$p < .01$

conditional correlations are not necessarily causal but do provide additional information on the impacts of the colonies. Table 4 presents the results of the following regression:

$$occscore * \mathbf{I}(migration)_{id} = \alpha + \theta Colony_d + \gamma_i + \rho_{c(d)} + \varepsilon_{id}. \quad (3)$$

The exercise is repeated for both migrants and nonmigrants. We find the strongest positive effects on occupation status for individuals who did not migrate but stayed in southern New Jersey. Overall, the occupation score increases by 1.84, associated with an increase of $1,840 (in 2016 dollars), for native workers near an agricultural colony who did not move. Although this is a larger impact than we found in panel B of table 3, we cannot reject the hypothesis that the two coefficients are the same ($p = 0.58$). Although the coefficient of interest is negative for the regression focusing on those who moved, the results are also very imprecise and not statistically different from zero.

Given the nature of these refugee inflows, we cannot separately identify the impacts of the refugees and of the aid that accompanied them. We use the variation in funding within the colonies to test roughly whether increases in external aid provided an additional benefit to native workers. To do so, we add an interaction term to several of our main specifications to measure the specific effect of the Woodbine colony, which received the most investment and guidance from aid organizations. The extra funding associated with proximity to the Woodbine colony did not affect native outcomes more than proximity to other colonies did. Although the aid agencies' investment and programming are an important part of the effects we observe, we believe that this is evidence that our results are not solely driven by external aid flows, but also by immigration.

The concentration of this effect in nonfarm households across the initial occupational distribution indicates that native workers who were poised to compete with refugees in the labor market actually benefited from the im-

Table 4. Presence in Agricultural Colonies of Migrants and Nonmigrants and Occupation Score in 1910

	(1)	(2)	(3)	(4)	(5)
A. Nonmigrants	All	Farm Household	Nonfarm Household	Under Age Sixteen	Age Sixteen and Older
Colony	1.840***	0.834	2.279**	1.386	2.022**
	(0.696)	(1.024)	(0.894)	(1.029)	(0.881)
Observations	3,210	723	2,487	938	2,272
B. Migrants	All	Under Age Sixteen	Age Sixteen and Older	Semiskilled and Service	Laborer
Colony	−0.563	−1.096	−0.385	−0.0665	−0.743
	(0.929)	(1.647)	(1.132)	(1.433)	(1.166)
Observations	3,210	723	2,487	938	2,272

Source: Authors' calculations based on 1880 and 1910 U.S. censuses.
Notes: The panel A dependent variable is the individual's 1910 occupation score interacted with an indicator for if he had not migrated. The panel B dependent variable is the individual's 1910 occupation score interacted with an indicator for if he had migrated. "Colony" indicates if the individual was in or contiguous to a township with a colony. Robust standard errors are in parentheses. All specifications include controls for age, initial occupation category, and proximity to Philadelphia and the Atlantic Ocean.
*$p < .10$; **$p < .05$; ***$p < .01$

migrants' presence. Native-born workers near agricultural colonies moved into nonfarming niches that might not have existed otherwise at a higher rate, leading to higher occupational scores. Ultimately, the impact of these Jewish colonists on natives depended on both the natives and the market in which the two interacted. For farming households, we see no impacts across the board. Agricultural markets were already regionally integrated by 1880 (Kim and Margo 2004). The colonies' farms were just drops in the bucket compared to the larger markets in Philadelphia and New York, where both native and immigrant farmers sold their products. However, labor markets were more locally constrained by transportation. Individuals not engaged in farming were more likely to directly engage or compete with these newcomers. There appear to have been no knowledge spillovers from the colonies to native farmers from the large investments in refugee agricultural development, like the Woodbine school, and from refugees' agricultural innovations, like the marketing cooperatives. Within the agricultural niche, we do not find impacts either way from the immigrant shock.

CONCLUSION

Using the establishment and continued presence of Jewish agricultural colonies in southern New Jersey as a natural experiment, we have estimated the impact of an influx of refugees on native workers' long-term outcomes using rich historical data and fine-grained locational variation. Overall, our results are consistent with a complementarity story. Many workers, particularly young workers and workers with skills different from the immigrants', were able to make profitable adjustments to these labor market changes. Because rural labor markets in this period were relatively self-contained, spillovers from Jewish aid societies and immigrant innovations were concentrated in groups of natives who would have interacted with immigrants in the labor market. Although we see no impacts on farmers, men living in nonfarm households in 1880 were less likely to move away, and they upgraded their occupational standing. Philanthropic efforts to open factories benefited natives, who could shift toward crafts work or white-collar work in particular. The colonies' original intention was to divert part of the massive inflow of Russian Jewish immigrants away from cities and keep the ire of native-born Americans at bay. In retrospect, native-born Americans had no economic reason to be angry. Instead of crowding out the communities already established in southern New Jersey, immigrants and their funding created new opportunities for them.

The children of Russian immigrants and native-born Americans alike left the southern New Jersey colonies for bigger cities (Eisenberg 1995, 164). As observed in the 1920 census, these two groups' average occupational scores are incredibly close, suggesting that the colonies achieved the assimilation desired by Jewish philanthropists. Those who stayed provided the basis for a close-knit agricultural community that would attract Jewish refugees from Germany and Poland well into the 1950s (Eisenberg 1995, 168; Brandes and Douglas, 1971, 327). The JAIAS would not found more colonies on the scale of those in southern New Jersey, but it did continue to offer educational and financial support to new Jewish immigrants and to channel some of them toward southern New Jersey, suggesting that the JAIAS found the experiment to be a success.

Eventually, Jewish immigrants stopped electing to become farmers. Today the ease with which workers historically moved out of the agricultural niche has disappeared. Agricultural work is still a common niche for low-skilled modern-day immigrants (Eckstein and Peri, this issue), but the nature of their agricultural work and socioeconomic context are both very different from the work encountered by the Russian Jewish immigrants and the economic realities of their settlement in New Jersey. In modern agricultural work, immigrants are often seasonal workers in positions with little to no upward mobility. Many of them are undocumented, which leaves them particularly vulnerable to exploitation (Eckstein and Peri, this issue). A surge of immigrants into agriculture today would probably not be associated with occupation upgrades for those already adjacent to the niche, as happened in southern New Jersey in the late nineteenth and early twentieth centuries.

Another caveat limits the external validity of our results: unlike other immigrant settlements, the colonies received a large amount of institutional support. When demand within the agricultural niche slackened, charities helped attract capital to build factories and maintain employment for immigrants and native-born workers alike. Thus, an increase in the southern New Jersey labor supply did not make it more difficult for native-born workers to leave agriculture, in contrast to the Filipino nurses described by the sociologist Yasmin Y. Ortiga in this issue. Immigrants were not marooned within the niche either, unlike call center employees in Mexico City (Da Cruz, this issue). By becoming educated in farming, colonists could leave the niches they would have entered in urban areas. The differences in immigrant experiences between the agricultural colonies and other labor market niches discussed in this issue can be traced back to the continued involvement of Jewish charity, which provided another instance of the positive impact of coethnic proximity, as seen in work by the sociologists Ming-Cheng M. Lo and Emerald T. Nguyen (this issue). The colonies were good for the native-born Americans living nearby at least in part because of spillovers from Jewish charity.

If we take our results at face value, relocating immigrants to a new niche does not have a negative impact on native-born workers in the same labor market, particularly with continuing philanthropic involvement. Inserting immigrants into a labor market in which participants do not compete directly and providing them with training does not hurt native-born workers.

APPENDIX

Figure A1. Coefficients of Interest at Varying Degrees of Distance from a Colony, Occupation Score

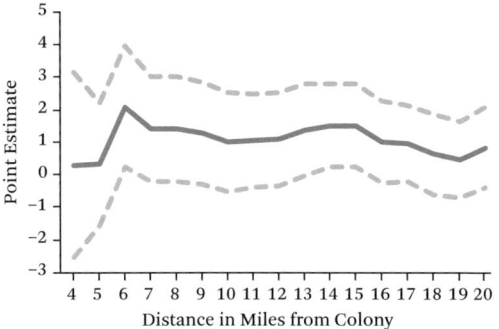

Source: Authors' calculations based on 1880 and 1910 U.S. censuses.
Notes: See notes to tables 1 through 4 for descriptions of dependent variables. Coefficient is an indicator for whether a colony is within X miles or less of an individual's enumeration district. Coefficient is in solid line, robust standard errors are in dashed lines.

Figure A3. Coefficients of Interest at Varying Degrees of Distance from a Colony, Probability of Farming Occupation

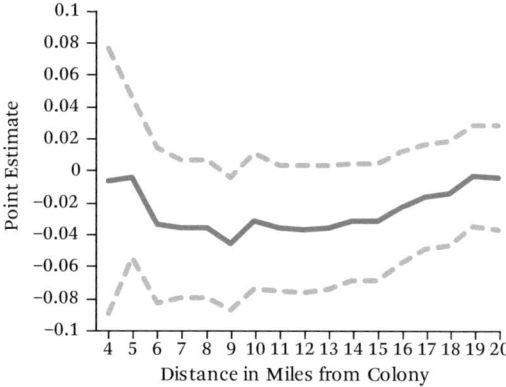

Source: Authors' calculations based on 1880 and 1910 U.S. censuses.
Notes: See notes to tables 1 through 4 for descriptions of dependent variables. Coefficient is an indicator for whether a colony is within X miles or less of an individual's enumeration district. Coefficient is in solid line, robust standard errors are in dashed lines.

Figure A2. Coefficients of Interest at Varying Degrees of Distance from a Colony, Probability of Migration

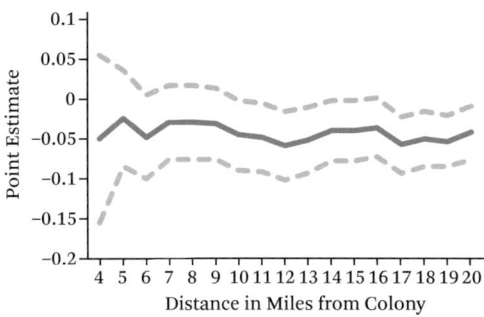

Source: Authors' calculations based on 1880 and 1910 U.S. censuses.
Notes: See notes to tables 1 through 4 for descriptions of dependent variables. Coefficient is an indicator for whether a colony is within X miles or less of an individual's enumeration district. Coefficient is in solid line, robust standard errors are in dashed lines.

Table A1. 1880 Balancing Table

	1880 Total	Matched
Age	32.22	25.01
	(17.58)	(13.82)
Percentage literate	99.1	98.9
	(9.55)	(10.5)
Percentage live on farm	32.6	22.5
	(46.9)	(41.8)
Occupational score	15.51	15.59
	(12.14)	(13.50)
Percentage white	93.7	85.9
	(24.4)	(34.8)
Observations	75,778	3,693
Match rate	4.87%	

Source: Authors' calculations based on 1880 U.S. census.
Notes: Standard deviations are in parentheses. Native-born males living in specified counties are included. Occupation score is for those with an occupation.

Table A2 tests the relationship between the 1880 characteristics of our sample and the location of the colonies. Column 1 is the most critical: it contains the results for our treatment variable as we define it in our main specification (1). These results support our decision to run our analyses as a cross-section with pre-period information.

Using our matched sample, we run the following regression, presented in appendix table A3:

$$Y_{id} = \alpha + \beta Colony_d + \theta Woodbine_d + \delta Colony_d * Woodbine_d + \gamma_i + \rho_{c(d)} + v_{id}, \quad (A1)$$

where i is the linked individual, d is the enumeration district, and c is the county of the individual's initial enumeration district. We run this regression for all Y_{id} described in the specification section. $Colony_d$ is an indicator for whether an individual was located in a township with a colony or next to one with a colony. $Woodbine_d$ is an indicator that equals 1 if the closest colony to enumeration district d is Woodbine, regardless of whether the township is contiguous to Woodbine. $Colony*Woodbine_d$ interacts these two and takes a value of 1 if the township is next to Woodbine. δ is the coefficient of interest in this table. γ_i represents individual controls, which include controls for

Table A2. Predicting Colony Placement with 1880 Characteristics

	(1) Contiguous or Colony	(2) Colony
1880 occupation score	0.000493	−0.000181
	(0.000535)	(0.000535)
Observations	3,693	3,693
1880 farm status	0.000893	0.000520
	(0.0162)	(0.00471)
Observations	3,693	3,693
1880 age	−0.000248	0.0000302
	(0.000358)	(0.0000829)
Observations	3,693	3,693

Source: Authors' calculations based on 1880 U.S. census.
Notes: The dependent variable is an indicator variable that takes the value of 1 if the individual's township satisfies the column category. Robust standard errors are in parentheses. All specifications include controls for age and proximity to Philadelphia and the Atlantic Ocean.
*$p < .10$; **$p < .05$; ***$p < .01$

Table A3. Woodbine Specific Effects on Main Outcomes of Interest

	(1) Occupation Score	(2) Migration	(3) Farming	(4) White-Collar Job	(5) Craftsman
Colony	1.368*	−0.0442*	−0.0401*	0.0542**	0.0294
	(0.786)	(0.0234)	(0.0214)	(0.0275)	(0.0231)
Woodbine	−0.977	0.101***	0.0324	−0.0102	−0.0861***
	(1.028)	(0.0300)	(0.0280)	(0.0355)	(0.0292)
Woodbine*colony	−0.230	−0.0277	−0.0264	−0.0778	0.0736
	(2.050)	(0.0608)	(0.0486)	(0.0694)	(0.0597)
Observations	3,210	3,693	3,693	3,693	3,693

Source: Authors' calculations based on 1880 and 1910 U.S. censuses.
Notes: Dependent variables are indicated by column titles. "Colony" indicates if the individual was in or contiguous to an enumeration district with a colony. "Woodbine" indicates if the closest colony to the individual was the Woodbine colony. Robust standard errors are in parentheses. All specifications include controls for age and proximity to Philadelphia and the Atlantic Ocean.
*$p < .10$; **$p < .05$; ***$p < .01$

individuals' age and their initial occupational category. As in our main specifications, we control for variation in county economic composition stemming from proximity to either the Atlantic Ocean or Philadelphia with $\rho c_{(d)}$, which divides the townships in our sample into three categories: those in a county with an Atlantic border, those with a Philadelphia border, and those with neither. μ_{id} is a random error term.

REFERENCES

Abramitzky, Ran, Leah Platt Boustan, and Katherine Eriksson. 2012. "Europe's Tired, Poor, Huddled Masses: Self-Selection and Economic Outcomes in the Age of Mass Migration." *American Economic Review* 102(5): 1832–56.

———. 2014. "A Nation of Immigrants: Assimilation and Economic Outcomes in the Age of Mass Migration." *Journal of Political Economy* 122(3): 467–506.

Baez, Javier E. 2011. "Civil Wars Beyond Their Borders: The Human Capital and Health Consequences of Hosting Refugees." *Journal of Development Economics* 96(2): 391–408.

Beers, Frederick W. 1872. *State Atlas of New Jersey.* New York: Beers, Comstock, and Cline.

Borjas, George J. 1999. "The Economic Analysis of Immigration." In *Handbook of Labor Economics,* edited by Orley C. Ashenfelter and David Card. Amsterdam: North-Holland Publishing.

Boustan, Leah Platt. 2007. "Were Jews Political Refugees or Economic Migrants? Assessing the Persecution Theory of Jewish Emigration, 1881–1914." In *The New Comparative Economic History: Essays in Honor of Jeffrey G. Williamson,* edited by Timothy J. Hatton, Kevin H. O'Rourke, and Alan M. Taylor. Cambridge, Mass.: MIT Press.

Brandes, Joseph, and Martin Douglas. 1971. *Immigrants to Freedom: Jewish Communities in Rural New Jersey Since 1882.* Philadelphia: University of Pennsylvania Press.

Cameron, A. Colin, and Douglas L. Miller. 2015. "A Practitioner's Guide to Cluster-Robust Inference." *Journal of Human Resources* 50(2): 317–72.

Card, David. 1990. "The Impact of the Mariel Boatlift on the Miami Labor Market." *Industrial and Labor Relations Review* 43(2): 245–57.

Chiswick, Barry R. 1992. "Jewish Immigrant Wages in America in 1909: An Analysis of the Dillingham Commission Data." *Explorations in Economic History* 29(3): 274–89.

Da Cruz, Michaël. 2018. "Offshore Migrant Workers: Return Migrants in Mexico's English-Speaking Call Centers." *RSF: The Russell Sage Foundation Journal of the Social Sciences* 4(1): 39–57. DOI: 10.7758/RSF.2018.4.1.03.

Dubrovsky, Gertrude W. 1992. *The Land Was Theirs: Jewish Farmers in the Garden State.* Tuscaloosa: University of Alabama Press.

Eckstein, Susan, and Giovanni Peri. 2018. "Immigrant Niches and Immigrant Networks in the U.S. Labor Market." *RSF: The Russell Sage Foundation Journal of the Social Sciences* 4(1): 1–17. DOI: 10.7758/RSF.2018.4.1.01.

Eisenberg, Ellen. 1995. *Jewish Agricultural Colonies in New Jersey, 1882–1920.* Syracuse, N.Y.: Syracuse University Press.

Foged, Mette, and Giovanni Peri. 2016. "Immigrants' Effect on Native Workers: New Analysis on Longitudinal Data." *American Economic Journal: Applied Economics* 8(2): 1–34.

Goldin, Claudia. 1994. "The Political Economy of Immigration Restriction in the United States, 1890–1921." In *The Regulated Economy: A Historical Approach to Political Economy,* edited by Claudia Goldin and Gary Libecap. Chicago: University of Chicago Press.

Goldstein, Phillip R. 1921. *Social Aspects of the Jewish Colonies of Southern New Jersey.* New York: League Printing Co.

Haddad, Diane. 2012. "Now What? All About Enumeration Districts." *Family Tree Magazine,* March 21. Available at: http://www.familytreemagazine.com/article/now-what-enumeration-districts (accessed May 5, 2016).

Haines, Michael R., and Inter-university Consortium for Political and Social Research (ICPSR). 2010. *Historical, Demographic, Economic, and Social Data: The United States, 1790–2002.* ICPSR02896-v3. Ann Arbor, Mich.: Inter-university Consortium for Political and Social Research, May 21.

Hatton, Timothy J., and Jeffrey G. Williamson. 1998. *The Age of Mass Migration: Causes and Economic Impact.* Oxford: Oxford University Press.

———. 2005. *Global Migration and the World Economy: Two Centuries of Policy and Performance.* Cambridge, Mass.: MIT Press.

Jewish Agricultural Society. 1954. *Jews in American Agriculture: The History of Farming by Jews in the United States.* New York: Jewish Agricultural Society.

Kim, Sukkoo, and Robert A. Margo. 2004. "Historical

Perspectives on U.S. Economic Geography." *Handbook of Regional and Urban Economics* 4(66): 2981–3019.

Kopczyński, Michael, 2011. "The Physical Stature of Jewish Men in Poland in the Second Half of the 19th Century." *Economics and Human Biology* 9(2): 203–10.

Lederhendler, Eli. 2008. "Classless: On the Social Status of Jews in Russia and Eastern Europe in the Late Nineteenth Century." *Comparative Studies in Society and History* 50(02): 509–34.

Lo, Ming-Cheng M., and Emerald T. Nguyen. 2018. "Caring and Carrying the Cost: Latina Nurses' Challenges and Strategies for Working with Coethnic Patients." *RSF: The Russell Sage Foundation Journal of the Social Sciences* 4(1): 149–71. DOI: 10.7758/RSF.2018.4.1.09.

Malchow Møller, Nikolaj, Jakob R. Munch, Claus Aastrup Seidelin, and Jan Rose Skaksen. 2013. "Immigrant Worker and Farm Performance: Evidence from Matched Empower-Employee Data." *American Journal of Agricultural Economics* 95(4): 819–41.

Malchow Møller, Nikolaj, Jakob R. Munch, and Jan Rose Skaksen. 2012. "Do Immigrants Affect Firm Specific Wages?" *Scandinavian Journal of Economics* 114(4): 1267–95.

Maystadt, Jean-François, and Philip Verwimp. 2014. "Winners and Losers Among a Refugee-Hosting Population." *Economic Development and Cultural Change* 62(4): 769–809.

Morse, Stephen P. 2016. "One Step ED Descriptions." Available at: http://stevemorse.org/ed/ed.php (accessed May 1, 2017).

New Jersey Office of Information Technology (NJOIT). Office of Geographic Information Systems (OGIS). 2010. *Municipalities of New Jersey, New Jersey State Plane. NAD83.* Trenton: NJOIT, OGIS.

Ortiga, Yasmin Y. 2018. "Learning to Fill the Labor Niche: Filipino Nursing Graduates and the Risk of the Migration Trap." *RSF: The Russell Sage Foundation Journal of the Social Sciences* 4(1): 172–87. DOI: 10.7758/RSF.2018.4.1.10.

Osofsky, Gilbert. 1960. "The Hebrew Emigrant Aid Society of the United States (1881–1883)." *Publications of the American Jewish Historical Society* 49(3): 173–87.

Parman, John. 2012. "Good Schools Make Good Neighbors: Human Capital Spillovers in Early 20th Century Agriculture." *Explorations in Economic History* 49(3): 316–34.

Partridge, Mark D., Dan S. Rickman, and Kamar Ali. 2008. "Recent Immigration and Economic Outcomes in Rural America." *American Journal of Agricultural Economics* 90(5): 1326–33.

Peri, Giovanni, and Chad Sparber. 2009. "Task Specialization, Immigration, and Wages." *American Economic Journal: Applied Economics* 1(3): 135–69.

Popper, Deborah E. 2006. "Great Opportunities for the Many of Small Means: New Jersey's Agricultural Colonies." *Geographical Review* 96(1): 24–49.

Price, George M., and Leo Shpall. 1958. "The Russian Jews in America: Second and Final Installment (Continued)." *Publications of the American Jewish Historical Society* 48(2): 78–133.

Robinson, Leonard G. 1912. "Agricultural Activities of the Jews in America." In *The American Jewish Year Book*, vol. 14, 21–115. Philadelphia: Jewish Publication Society of America for American Jewish Committee.

Rosenthal, Max. 1906. "Agricultural Colonies in the United States." In *Jewish Encyclopedia,* vol. 12. New York: Funk & Wagnalls.

Ruggles, Steven, Katie Genadek, Ronald Goeken, Josiah Grover, and Matthew Sobek. 2015. *Integrated Public Use Microdata Series: Version 6.0* (machine-readable database). Minneapolis: University of Minnesota. Available at: DOI: 10.18128/D010.V6.0.

Ruiz, Isabel, and Carlos Vargas-Silva. 2016. "The Labor Market Consequences of Hosting Refugees." *Journal of Economic Geography* 16(3): 667–94.

Shpall, Leo. 1950. "Jewish Agricultural Colonies in the United States." *Agricultural History* 24(3): 120–46.

Spitzer, Yannay. 2015. "Pogroms, Migration, and Networks: The Jewish Migration from the Russian Empire to the United States, 1881–1914." Unpublished paper. Brown University, Providence, R.I.

Stainsby, William. 1901. *The Jewish Colonies of South Jersey: Historical Sketch of Their Establishment and Growth.* Camden, N.J.: Chew & Sons.

Szajkowski, Zosa. 1950. "The Attitude of American Jews to East European Jewish Immigration (1881–1893)." *Publications of the American Jewish Historical Society* 40: 215–76.

Offshore Migrant Workers: Return Migrants in Mexico's English-Speaking Call Centers

MICHAËL DA CRUZ

This article examines the offshore bilingual (English/Spanish) call centers in Mexico City that serve as the entry into the labor market for young Mexican return migrants. Thanks to the English skills and cultural capital they gained from their experience in the United States, they are able to compete with more-skilled workers and are better suited to manage the cultural dimension of this transnational labor. Return migrants become stuck in this economic niche, however, owing to a lack of professional possibilities outside of the sector.

Keywords: return migration, Mexican 1.5 generation, offshore call centers, labor market incorporation, life stories

In joining the "new immigrant labor market niches" debate in the United States, this article analyzes an economic niche on the other side of the southern border: offshore call centers in Mexico City. It is well known that American firms make use of offshore call centers' services to fulfill a wide range of purposes: customer assistance, contact centers, banking, marketing and sales activities, technical support, and even health care services. With information and communication technologies (ICT) putting customers and workers separated by thousands of miles in direct contact, we are forced to rethink national and international divisions of labor (Freeman and Soete 1994; Richardson and Belt 2001).

In the late 1990s, ICT permitted India to become "the call center to the world," a role now filled by the Philippines (Lee 2015). Meanwhile, a strong call center industry developed in Latin American countries to offer bilingual services to an English-speaking market that increasingly includes a demand for Spanish-speaking services. To compete with India and the Philippines, Latin American call centers promote their higher cultural proximity to the United States. In Mexico, the majority of employees in call centers are students and graduates of the local universities (Da Cruz and Fouquet 2010; Micheli Thirión 2007, 2011).

How are offshore call centers in Mexico relevant to the debate in the United States about new immigrant labor market niches? Recently, one group of employees has been growing in size and even becoming, in some call centers, the main workforce: Mexican return migrants

Michaël Da Cruz is a postdoctoral fellow at El Colegio de la Frontera Norte in Tijuana, Mexico.

© 2018 Russell Sage Foundation. Da Cruz, Michaël. 2018. "Offshore Migrant Workers: Return Migrants in Mexico's English-Speaking Call Centers." *RSF: The Russell Sage Foundation Journal of the Social Sciences* 4(1): 39–57. DOI: 10.7758/RSF.2018.4.1.03. Direct correspondence to: Michaël Da Cruz at dacruz.michael@gmail.com, Departamento de Estudios Culturales, El Colegio de la Frontera Norte, Carretera escénica Tijuana, Ensenada, Km 18.5, San Antonio del Mar, 22560 Tijuana, Baja California, México.

from the United States. These are people who have been expelled from the United States and who, after returning to Mexico, enter this labor market niche and work directly with American customers located in the United States. Indeed, offshore call centers in Mexico can be considered extensions of the U.S. labor market beyond its political borders.

In this article, I examine how Mexican return migrants from the United States become workers at offshore call centers that cater to the U.S. market. I show that certain attributes of this migrant group account for their expertise in the skills necessary to participate in this labor market niche: their life experience in the United States, their mastery of the English language, and their knowledge of the cultural aspects of everyday life in the United States. This knowledge of U.S. culture compensates to some degree for their lack of educational qualifications for jobs that, despite being considered nonqualified, require high-skilled workers (Frenkel et al. 1998).

The article draws from research I conducted in Mexico City from 2010 to 2013, during which time I interviewed forty-three young return migrants employed in English-speaking call centers. I used a mixed method—a combination of biographical interviews, group interviews, and participant observation of everyday life with a select group from the sample. Observation took place during interviewees' free time. The biographical interview—an established method in migration studies (Rivera Sánchez 2015)—is the "method par excellence" when it comes to grasping such "lived experiences" (Demazière 2008, 16). It allowed me to understand the three phases of our interviewees' migration process: their life in the United States, their return to Mexico, and, above all, the pivotal process of deciding to return (for those who were not being deported). Life stories allow us to locate and understand such an important moment in the life trajectory, which can be identified as a "turning point" or bifurcation: the key moment when individuals question perhaps their entire life trajectory (Hughes 1997; Bidart 2009). This method also allowed me to collect in-depth descriptions of the labor insertion process in Mexico and call center work activity.

My sample is divided into two groups: those who migrated to the United States as adults and those who migrated as minors with their parents. The latter group is defined as the 1.5 generation of migrants (Rumbaut 2004). The young people in my sample had lived all their lives in the United States as undocumented immigrants, and they experienced their arrival back in Mexico as more akin to emigration than to a "return." The life trajectories of both those who were forced to return and those who decided to leave instead of accepting the conditions of life as an undocumented adult in the United States were highly subject to U.S. immigration laws (Gonzales 2011).

I set the stage by discussing the literature on return migration and labor market integration and the specific case of the Mexican 1.5 generation. I then explore features of offshore call centers in Mexico and Central America, focusing on the cultural component of this transnational labor. After describing my research method and the characteristics of my sample, I review empirical data on return migrant labor incorporation into Mexico City call centers. The article concludes with some final observations.

THE LABOR MARKET INCORPORATION OF RETURN MIGRANTS

Return migration is not a new topic in migration studies in Mexico, but it has never been more than a minor field of study, one that up until recently was limited to analysis of the return phenomenon in rural areas. However, the increase in unemployment in the United States due to the Great Recession, which led an unprecedented number of returns to Mexico, has prompted a need for further study.

From 2005 to 2010, 824,000 migrants returned to Mexico, three times more than the period between 1995 and 2000 (Giorguli Saucedo and Gutiérrez 2012) This sudden growth in the number of returns has renewed interest in the topic (Gandini, Lozano-Ascencio, and Gaspar Olvera 2015), especially with regard to the high number of people who have returned since 2008 and their reinsertion into the professional Mexican labor market (Mendoza Cota 2013; Padilla and Jardón Hernández 2014). These studies aim to understand the extent to which return migrants invest savings in their original community and invest skills acquired from their migrant experience in the United States. This approach is limited, as it has examined data on return migration from a geographic perspective only; in other words, it mainly focuses on migrant communities of origin. Such a focus may not account for return migration to someplace other than the point of origin of the migration process.

Return mobilities can be much more complex than the original migration (Cassarino 2004; Rallu 2007). People do not always go back to the place they came from, and their movements can also be influenced by the state of the labor market in their country of origin. Additionally, research on small cities and rural areas often depicts return migrants as entrepreneurs. This bias becomes evident in the high percentage of business owners emerging from these studies. Consequently, I decided to focus in my study of return migration, not on the community of origin, but rather on a labor sector characterized by a significant number of returnees: bilingual call centers offering English/Spanish service.

Before describing the population I studied, it is important to review the theories that draw an analytical link between return migration and professional reinsertion. Despite the fact that return migration is viewed less and less frequently as the final step of the migratory process, it is still analyzed under the prism of failure or success (De Haas, Fokkema, and Fihri 2015). This view generally conceives of two outcomes: lasting settlement in the community of origin or remigration (Rivera Sánchez 2015). What determines an individual's outcome? According to the structural approach, it is the context of the society of origin, more than competencies acquired and earnings accumulated during the migratory experience, that shapes the possibility—or the impossibility—of making use of them (Cassarino 2004). From Cerase (1974) on, it is understood that if the social or economic context is not receptive to innovation (whether economic or social), a return tends to lead to failure.

Therefore, transnational ties show their importance in that the longer migrants are absent from their community of origin, the more remote their expectations will be from the current context, owing to the changes that have occurred during their absence (Gmelch 1980). This is why successful return migrants tend to be those who regularly visit their homeland to keep in touch and remain socially visible in their community of origin (Conway, Potter, and St. Bernard 2009; Massey et al. 1987). These two aspects—the context in the home country and the duration of the migration or absence—determine whether the migrant will be able to transfer the human capital acquired during the migration experience back to the homeland (Battistella 2004). Together with the situation in the home country (security, politics, the economic situation, and so on), the local context of migrants' point of origin and the duration of their absence are the three main factors to consider when determining a good "return preparedness" (Cassarino 2014). It is also important to consider migrants' capacity to mobilize other resources such as tangible resources (such as financial capital), intangible resources (such as contacts, relationships, skills, and networks), and social capital (ibid).

THE MEXICAN 1.5 GENERATION IN THE UNITED STATES AND THEIR RETURN TO MEXICO

Most of the studies about return migration analyze "traditional migrants": those who emigrated as adults to work abroad and who later come back to their home country. The issues associated with return become increasingly complex when the migrants returning are those same migrants' children. Whether they are second- or third-generation, and whether or not they emigrated as children with their parents, the issues are not the same.

Since the beginning of the 2000s, the return of later-generation migrants has been at the center of a vast scholarly production. Their returns have been defined as next-generation returns (Conway, Potter, and St. Bernard 2009), transgenerational returns (Durand 2004), ethnic returns (Tsuda 2003), and counter-diaspora returns (King and Christou 2011). These studies show that even after two generations, people still migrate to the country of their parents or even their grandparents, not to a random other country. The reasons they cite for this decision range from sentimental affection and idealization of their country of origin and culture (Tsuda 2003; King and Christou 2011) to more pragmatic economic and social concerns.

The main economic and social concerns motivating their decisions to return are factors related to the difficulties they face in the United States: unemployment, racism, lack of family support, and so on (Conway, Potter, and St. Bernard 2009; Phillips and Potter 2009; Potter, Conway, and St. Bernard 2009; Reynolds 2011). In other words, they decide to return to their own or their parents' homeland in search of a better "quality of life" (Phillips and Potter 2009). These young people are ill prepared for return migration, mainly because of their weak ties with their origin country. But for some of them, the decision to return is a response to a more structured mobility strategy, especially among the university graduates, who take into account the lower competition in their country of origin (Conway, Potter, and St. Bernard 2009). The returns of these migrants tend to be more successful because they are better prepared and they have visited their origin country more frequently before they return.

This article analyzes a previously unstudied category of return migrants in Mexico: the 1.5 generation (Rumbaut 2004). This concept encapsulates the singular socialization experience of those who neither were born in their host country nor immigrated as adults. This distinction from the second-generation group is particularly relevant among Mexican migrants to the United States because the migratory status of Mexico's 1.5 generation is very often marked by its irregularity. As a consequence, these migrants' socialization is different from that of the children of Mexican immigrants born in the United States, who have American citizenship. Thus, it is relevant to distinguish 1.5-generation migrants from those who arrived as adults (first-generation) and whose socialization has been mainly linked to work. For the 1.5 generation, by contrast, school has been a central part of their socialization.

The Mexican second generation in the United States experiences numerous social and economic disadvantages: high college dropout rates; low rates of mastery of the English language compared to other immigrant communities; racism; a high incidence of incarceration; and one of the lowest rates of economic mobility. These disadvantages can be explained in part by the disappearance of the blue-collar jobs that once helped immigrants transition to more-qualified jobs (Waldinger and Feliciano 2004; Waldinger, Lim, and Cort 2007). The 1.5 generation suffers from these same difficulties, but these immigrants must also cope with the critical problem of irregular migratory status.

Their schooling experience also does not differ from that of their documented peers. Protected during their K–12 education by the Supreme Court's 1982 ruling in *Plyler v. Doe,* they adopt the same meritocratic American values transmitted by the school system as their schoolmates (Abrego 2006; Rojas García 2013). The sixteenth birthday marks the rupture of this protective sphere: as 1.5-generation migrants seek their driver's licenses and their first jobs, they have their first experiences as adults outside of the schooling system. These are the first moments when the young undocumented 1.5-generation Mexicans experience through praxis the implications of their migratory status.

In his study of the undocumented Mexican 1.5 generation's transition to adulthood, Roberto Gonzales (2011) calls this moment the phase of "discovering." He identifies the next phase as "learning to be illegal," a stage marked by drastically reduced social and economic expectations—especially for those who were academically successful and were planning to attend college (Gonzales 2011; Gonzales and Chavez 2012). The last phase, identified as "coping," is the moment when individuals once and for all abandon their expectations of upward social mobility and cope with all the implications and limitations of their illegal status. In my research, I identified return to Mexico as an alternative to the dashed hopes of the phase of coping; many 1.5-generation migrants saw return as an opportunity to break the glass ceiling they faced in the United States (Da Cruz 2014).

Before exploring the experiences of the 1.5-generation return migrants in the Mexican labor market and comparing them to the experiences of first-generation return migrants, let us first consider the role of offshore call centers in Mexico and Central America.

OFFSHORE CALL CENTERS IN MEXICO AND CENTRAL AMERICA: NEITHER ETHNIC ENTREPRENEURSHIP NOR PLANNED MIGRANT ECONOMIC NICHES

The call center industry in Mexico and Central America experienced constant growth from the mid-1990s until the present, becoming one of the principal sources of job creation in the region (Da Cruz 2014). There is strong competition between these countries to attract call center companies because call centers not only create many new jobs but offer a solution for those countries facing crisis in the job market for educated youth. However, with the exception of El Salvador (Da Cruz 2013), the sector has never shown a direct interest in employing return migrants.[1]

This explains in part why the workforce of Latin American call centers is made up mainly of local university and high school students (Da Cruz 2013; Da Cruz and Fouquet 2010; Del Bono and Bulloni 2008; Micheli Thirión 2007, 2011). This type of local workforce is a common feature in other developing countries, such as India and the Philippines (Holman, Batt and Holtgrewe 2007; Messenger and Ghosheh 2010). It is also interesting to note that in these countries the education level of call center workforces is generally above the national average. Mexico is no different from other Latin American countries: the vast majority of call center employees are high school students, university students, or recent university graduates (Da Cruz and Fouquet 2010; Micheli Thirión 2007, 2011).

Call centers maneuver to attract young employees and combat the high turnover common in the industry (Da Cruz and Fouquet 2010; Hualde, Tolentino, and Jurado 2014). As a growing sector in constant need of workforce renewal, the largest call centers use various strategies to target this population, including installing their facilities close to universities, awarding scholarships to their best employees, offering flexible schedules based on school timetables, and fostering a youthful atmosphere in their workplaces. Salaries for employees providing these outsourced bilingual services can also be considered high compared to many local qualified jobs. This is the context in which young return migrants find an entry into the Mexican labor market.

One question arises: considering the characteristics of the call center sector, particularly the level of workforce qualification, how have much less qualified young return migrants managed to enter this sector and compete with the existing workforce? My hypothesis is that, despite their lower level of qualifications, young returnees from the United States and Canada have other skills that give them a competitive edge over their coworkers.

While the cultural capital (Bourdieu 1979) derived from a migratory life can compensate for a lack of formal qualifications, there is some question as to the level of prior education that in fact is necessary for employment at a call center. Studies of call centers have reached the singular conclusion that there is a significant contradiction in this industry between its employment of a qualified workforce and the unqualified nature of the work, which is robotic and repetitive and offers no space for autonomy or creativity (Cousin 2002; Stanworth 2000). Call centers seek employees with high-level communication skills, which they attribute to university graduates (Belt, Richardson, and Webster 2002). At the same time, call center work is considered emotional labor: employees must be able to empathize with the client, convey a sense of good mood, and

---

1. The program "Meet Your Roots," led by the Export and Investment Promotion Agency of El Salvador (PROESA), which tried to attract young Salvadorans from the United States using the cultural argument and offering "well-paid jobs" in English-speaking call centers, was a great failure. Meanwhile, the call center Teleperformance promoted its Salvadoran services by arguing that the Salvadorans it employed had "English-neutral" accents owing to their time in the United States and ongoing links to it. Also, I interviewed some call center employees who had been deported to El Salvador and who told me that, in the professional orientation flyers they were given by American migratory authorities on the plane back to Salvador, call centers were listed first (Da Cruz 2014).

"smile on the phone." This aspect of the work probably explains the prominence in call center of women workers, to whom such skills are commonly attributed (ibid).[2]

Offshore outsourced services have these same requirements for employees, but with an additional dimension: an ability to close the cultural gap between the call center agent and the client. The quality of offshore call center service lies in the ability of the agent to make the client feel that the interaction is taking place "here and now" (Mirchandani 2012; Poster 2007; Puel 2003), with the "here" being the most crucial aspect. To mimic local flavor, call centers in India make use of a large panel of intercultural management skills, such as accent neutralization, cultural lessons, and an ability to express an interest in American baseball and football scores. To exhibit these skills, the employee needs to be immersed in clients' culture and everyday life. Winifred Poster (2007) defines the practices that firms implement to bridge a cultural gap as "national identity management." In North African call centers serving the French market, another common practice is to "Frenchify" the names of local employees (Nyobe 2015).

The quality of call center service partially depends on these assumed cultural similarities. Within the global outsourcing market, in fact, reducing cultural distance between operator and client is crucial and in the long run has a measurable economic impact. For example, in the Philippines and El Salvador, the need for workers with these skills among employers offering outsourced services has led to the creation of national educational programs that explicitly train the local population to be competitive in this arena (Da Cruz 2013; Friginal 2007). That these countries have undertaken such national measures can be easily understood when we consider that business processing outsourcing (BPO) activities may account for up to 10 percent of their GDP, as is the case in the Philippines (Lee 2015). With so much at stake, employers are glad to avoid the use of these cultural management tools by hiring young Mexican returnees from the United States—and to an even greater extent, the 1.5 generation who grew up there—because they can meet these job requirements with no such training.

RESEARCH SAMPLE

My study is based on forty-three in-depth biographical interviews with Mexican return migrants from the United States and, to a lesser extent, from Canada. At the time of the interview, they were between nineteen and thirty-five years old and employed by call centers in Mexico City. The ages of the migrants from the 1.5 generation corresponded more closely to the average age of call center workforces.[3] The returnees who had migrated to the United States as adults were older on average. (Almost all were older than thirty.) They had returned to Mexico between one and five years prior to the interview; most had come back two to three years earlier.

This sample is a snowball selection. Since I did not work in a call center, I gained access to the respondents through two gatekeepers—one male and one female—who were working in two different call centers.[4] From there, I asked each interviewee to provide a list of contacts, ideally individuals who did not work in the same call center.

Most interviewees (thirty-one) were male. Return migration to Mexico is predominantly a masculine phenomenon. The census data

---

2. The same gendered assumptions are made in services that predominantly employ male workers, such as help desks, which see men as more likely to be techies (Belt, Richardson, and Webster 2002).

3. All 1.5-generation interviewees were between eighteen and twenty-seven years old. Sixty-six percent of the Mexican call center workforce are younger than twenty-seven. Only 12 percent are older than thirty-five (IMT 2012).

4. I decided not to conduct the field research directly from a call center for two reasons. First, and most prominently, was that my oral English skills, and particularly my strong French accent, disqualified me for the job. Second, if I had taken opportunities to conduct observation from inside the call center, I would have risked misrepresenting myself; my respondents insisted that they would have reconsidered giving the interviews if they had believed that I was linked with company management.

show that 72 percent of returnees from the United States are male, and the percentage of males among those returning because they were deported is even more dramatic: 90 percent or more of these involuntary returnees are male (Gandini, Lozano-Ascencio, and Gaspar Olvera 2015). As such, the fact that all of my interviewees who were deported were male is not a surprise. At the same time, most of them worked in predominantly masculine services, such as sales and help desk activities.

Eleven U.S. states are represented in my sample, two of them most prominently: thirteen interviewees had lived in California, and eight in Texas.[5] Compared to the return migrant population I interviewed in Monterrey—almost all of whom had returned from neighboring Texas (Da Cruz 2013; Da Cruz and Fouquet 2010)—my Mexico City sample shows an uncommon variety of origin states. Likewise, their original provenance in Mexico is scattered. Almost one-third of the interviewees were from a Mexican state other than Mexico City and the neighboring Estado de Mexico. These data reinforce my initial position that studying return migration only from origin communities is limited at best. With only three exceptions, these migrants' period spent abroad had always exceeded five years.

To better understand how returnees had entered the Mexican labor market, I gave priority to interviewees with longer experience working in call centers. When I interviewed them, all but two interviewees had spent more than one year working in the industry in Mexico, and I was thus able to analyze the processes of professional insertion in greater depth. With this goal, I also chose respondents for the sample who represented different call center activities because they worked in different positions, from customer service to technical support and sales.

My sample is divided into two main categories. Young return migrants who had emigrated to the United States or Canada as adults (eleven males and four females) and 1.5-generation return migrants (twenty males and eight females). In the latter group, the great majority (twenty-six) had arrived in the United States before they were ten years old, and seven of them before they were six. I chose to study these two categories of migrants—who were socialized in distinctly contrasting ways—in order to understand the differences in how they found work and mobilized their specific skills when they arrived in Mexico.

The 1.5-generation interviewees were fluent in English; indeed, most of them considered English their first language. When they lived in the United States, they tended to speak Spanish with their parents and English with their brothers and sisters, cousins of similar age, and friends. There were many different reasons for their return to Mexico, depending on whether they had been deported or had made the decision themselves. The portrait painted of the global Mexican 1.5 generation in the United States (Chavez 2015) is very different from the circumstances of those in my sample: they were good students (two of them had graduated from college), with a high level of English fluency. They had experienced the glass ceiling, either in school or in their professional careers. Their choice to return to Mexico was generally the result of a variety of factors, but among the most important were the impossibility of upward social mobility and family separation. The desire to reunite with a loved one (a sibling or a partner) who had already returned to Mexico or been deported was a decisive factor for all but one interviewee. It is important to note that, even if this group was much more qualified than the average return population, six of the twenty-eight 1.5-generation respondents did not finish high school, five of them because they had been deported.[6]

The respondents who had emigrated to the

---

5. The other states were New York (four respondents), Georgia (four), Arizona (four), North Carolina (three), Illinois (three), Michigan (two), Utah (one), Missouri (one), and Tennessee (one). Four respondents had lived in Canada, and three had lived in more than one state.

6. In 2010, of all return migrants in the Mexican population, only 26.5 percent of the women and 17.7 percent of the men had finished high school (Gandini, Lozano-Ascencio and Gaspar Olvera 2015). In my sample, only eight of the forty-three interviewees had not finished high school.

United States or Canada as an adult corresponded much more closely to the traditional Mexican migration pattern. Their migratory experiences in these two countries were related to work—in sectors such as construction, the restaurant industry, and agriculture. It is important to note that, with the exception of two respondents, all had concluded their preparatoria (high school) before leaving Mexico. Again, family reunification after relatives had been deported or "voluntarily" returned for economic reasons (unemployment, health issues) were catalysts for their own return.

"THIS IS MY COUNTRY AND I DON'T EVEN KNOW IT!": ADJUSTING EXPECTATIONS AND PREPARING TO LOOK FOR WORK IN MEXICO

The first question that begs to be asked about the presence of young return migrants in Mexico City call centers is: how did they manage to penetrate this sector? With the exception of one interviewee who had been employed in a call center in Vancouver, Canada, no interview subject had previous call center experience before arriving back in Mexico. Moreover, only one was even aware of the existence of call centers before arriving in Mexico. So how did they make that jump? My research revealed that the majority of the interviewees were ill prepared for their return. Their accounts—especially those of the 1.5 generation—showed very little knowledge (if any at all) of the Mexican labor market reality. Most of them had imagined that their mastery of English would give them an edge in the labor market and afford them certain job opportunities, such as teaching English. The first problem they faced, however, was their lack of educational credentials, which are highly valued in the Mexican labor market. Then, like twenty-five-year-old Gloria, they realized that fluency in English would generally not be sufficient:

> This is the picture we have of Mexico in the United States: that it is Tierra de Nadie [No Man's Land] . . . that you can come here, do whatever you want, and nobody will say anything to you. This is the erroneous image they have of Mexico in the United States. Even for me, a Mexican, but well, because I lived there so many years, I came here myself with this idea, "I come from the United States, I speak better English than everyone else!" And suddenly you arrive here and, "What is this accent?" and a thousand things like that. "Where is the proof? Where is the certificate that shows you worked there?" And suddenly you realize you are inexperienced. . . . I didn't know what was a good or a bad salary here in Mexico. Well, I came from the United States, and of course I knew that I would not earn the same. So I was thinking that if they paid me more than a thousand pesos [about U.S.$60], it would be fine, no? [*laughter*] And in my first job, I was earning five thousand, they were giving me five thousand, so I thought, *Well, that is not so bad... It's great!* . . . And then Teletech called me: "Gloria, I offer you nine thousand pesos." And I was like, *Wow! I'm earning five thousand and now I will earn nine!* [*laughter*] (interview by the author, Mexico City, 2013)

Gloria's testimony is particularly illustrative: having lived in Dallas, Texas, from ages eight to twenty-two, Gloria had overvalued the importance of English-language skills in the Mexican labor market and was unable to gauge the cost of living and salary values in Mexico. The distance between her professional expectations and the reality in Mexico can be attributed to her weak transnational links with Mexico. A widening breach forms between members of the 1.5 generation and their families left behind when they were young because their illegal status carries too many risks; they and their families become increasingly unwilling to run those risks by making return visits. In fact, except for three of my 1.5-generation interviewees, none had previously returned to Mexico since immigrating to the United States. Another reason for their lack of preparation for the labor market may have been that, even with plenty of family support available—uncles, aunts, and grandmothers being cited most often—they did not have information about the labor market. This is easily explained by the low educational backgrounds of most of them and the lack of knowledge among their family members about the qualified job sector.

Migrants who left Mexico after the age of

eighteen encountered different problems upon their return. Most of them had labored in manual industries in Mexico before leaving for the United States, such as construction, food service, and agriculture. Upon their return, they tried to find jobs in which they believed they could reinvest the professional skills they had acquired in the North. Yet they quickly gave up when confronted with the much lower pay offered in these sectors in Mexico. This account from thirty-three-year-old José, who lived in Ann Arbor, Michigan, from ages nineteen to thirty-one, is representative:

> When I arrived here, my mom had taxis. But I came here with the idea of staying only two or three months before going back to the United States. So my mom said, "Hey, why don't you work with one of the taxis?" I told her yes. I got my driver's license and went to discover Mexico City, because I was very young when I left. And a lot of people were afraid, like, "This guy doesn't know what he's doing, he must be drunk!" I worked like one month, one month and a half. But the truth is that it wasn't enough money. My mom told me, "Don't worry. Take care of the car, gas it up, and be careful." . . . But then she began to say, "Hey, don't worry too much, but I do need you to bring me money!" She began to ask me to help with the bills, and it didn't seem fair to me. So she put me in touch with Sanborns, and I worked there for a month, but it was the same![7] The job didn't seem good to me. There was no possible comparison with the dollar. (interview by the author, Mexico City, 2012)

In light of such frustration, one can imagine how someone like José ends up at a call center. The call centers are visually omnipresent in urban hubs like Mexico City and Monterrey. This is an economic sector in constant search of workers, and advertisements, written in English, can be found in many public spaces, like buses, subway stations and trains, and on the streets. Another path to the call centers is the Internet. Putting great stock in their language competence, many began their job search with keywords like "English-speaking," "job," and "Mexico." The resulting list of job offers is dominated by call centers. Others published their curriculum vitae online. We learned from these interviewees that after publishing their curriculum vitae, they would almost immediately receive a call from a call center expressing interest. Very few interviewees found their first job in a call center through personal networks. The only ones who did so had a sibling who had returned before them. For instance, Miguel, who was twenty-seven years old and had lived in San Jose, California, from ages eight to twenty-five, had a brother working in the industry:

> And then I arrived here. . . . And fucking cultural shock, man! And then I saw my brother and it was like, "What the fuck, Jay? What's going on?" And then he told me what happened. And I saw that my brother was working. He had two jobs. . . . But when I arrived here I was like, "No kidding, you're working two jobs!" I thought it was going bad for him, you know? And him: "Yes, I've got two jobs. But here, as long as you speak English, you get a job at a call center like that!" [*snaps his fingers*] And I was like, "Not bad, you know?" And I asked, "And how much can you make?" And he told me, "I only make. . . ." How much did he tell me? 3,600, 3,800 . . . he was probably making $300 a fortnight. I was like: "Fuck . . . are you serious, man? No kidding . . . can you survive with that?" And he told me, "Yeah, everything is way cheaper here, the economy is way down in Mexico." He told me that, yeah, there are some places as expensive as in the United States, nice spots. But, well, you've got plenty of really cheap places! (interview by the author, Mexico City, 2013)

Applying for a job in a call center is simple: it consists of a phone interview and the furnishing of a requisite *preparatoria* diploma. Returnees who had not finished high school did not find this to be a stumbling block:

---

7. Sanborns is a well-known Mexican restaurant and pharmacy chain owned by the Mexican billionaire Carlos Slim.

when they mentioned that they had grown up in the United States and presented themselves as native English speakers, human resources departments waived this formal requisite. Interviewees said that just mentioning these details to recruiters would get them very interested.

As nineteen-year-old Juanito, who lived in Provo, Utah, from ages nine to eighteen (interview by the author, Mexico City, 2012), explained to us, "No curriculum [vitae], no cover letter, just your phone number and your email address." Having prerequisites waived eased an otherwise complicated professional transition for many returnees who did not have cover letters or proof of past employment. With other jobs, however, prerequisites were not waived for returnees; in fact, "they ask you [for] an arm and a leg," said Israel, a twenty-seven-year-old who lived in Atlanta, Georgia, from ages seventeen to twenty-six. "They ask you for so much stuff" (interview by the author, Mexico City, 2013). In call centers, by contrast, all of the subsequent recruitment filters were presented as formalities, particularly for the 1.5-generation returnees. If the interview in English was very easy, the basic computer knowledge test was also very simple for young people who had attended American schools and passed "half of their lives in front of a computer," as Gloria put it.

THE INVISIBLE DIMENSION OF CALL CENTER WORK

The "invisible dimension" of the work also explains the presence of young returnees in call centers. For some of our interviewees, their appearance was a strong handicap to finding a job once they had come back to Mexico. Call centers appeared to be their only employment opportunity. Many young return migrants who were part of Latino gangs in the United States carried on their bodies the marks of this previous association; upon returning to Mexico, these tattoos became stigmata (Goffman 1975), which foreclosed many job opportunities for them. The bad reputation that tattoos have in Mexico and Central America is directly related to their association with criminal organizations such as the Maras in El Salvador, where tattoos have even become sufficient reason for arrest within the framework of the Mano Dura law.[8] But not all of our tattooed interviewees were members of gangs. As they informed us, tattooing is a very common practice in the United States. They all mentioned how hard it was for them to find a job when, as Jorge said, "people don't trust you." Twenty-nine-year-old Jorge, who had lived in various U.S. states from ages nineteen to twenty-eight, added, "As soon as they see your tattoos, they think you're a criminal" (interview by the author, Mexico City, 2012). Gloria, whose arms are completely tattooed, described the problems her tattoos caused her even when she was employed in low-qualifying jobs:

GLORIA: And I came back, but in San Luis [Potosi], people are even more ... narrow-minded. So when I got off the bus, I had a T-shirt on, and everyone saw my arms. And they were looking at me like this. ... So I got here, and I'm someone who works, you know? So I looked for a job as soon as I arrived. And I found that the only available jobs in San Luis were in factories. And if you have tattoos, they don't give you the job.

AUTHOR: Did your tattoos bother you a lot?

GLORIA: I never told my boss [in her job previous to the call center], but you have to imagine: in this job I had to wear heels, with nice trousers and a shirt with the sleeves down to here [*she shows her wrist*]. So it was really hot, and I was there with my shirt. ... Everyone rolled up their sleeves, but I couldn't because it would have meant losing my job. ... In the U.S., you can wear whatever you want and people won't say: "Uh, this one's a gangster!" First, they see who you are, how you behave, and based on that, they judge you. In Mexico, on the other hand, if you don't dress correctly. ... The "how you look" is very important: "What will they say if I employ someone with tattoos? What will they say if I employ someone with purple hair?" Things like

---

8. Mano Dura (literally "firm hand") is a law of exception (2003) to fight against the criminal activities of gangs; it allows police to arrest individuals based on their physical appearance alone.

that. . . . And that didn't happen here at Teletech.

Interviewees who lived in more problematic neighborhoods encountered more than work-related difficulties because of their tattoos: their security was threatened as local gangs, assuming their appearance was the result of a gang experience in the United States, tried to recruit them. Tattooed young people were not the only ones who mentioned discrimination. The testimonies of gay returnees were very similar. The presence of these two minorities in Mexico City call centers has even given rise to jokes about alternative names for one of the main call centers: "Telegay" or "Homietech."[9] As a result, Mexican call centers have become places where "people that in the past didn't look at each other, or could even hate each other," now work together and sometimes become friends.

THE EMERGENCE OF A LITTLE UNITED STATES IN ENGLISH-SPEAKING MEXICAN CALL CENTERS

During their orientation, one particular practice left a mark on the returnees who were hired by call centers: the "circle reunions." This ritual seems to be very common in Mexican call centers. All the new members of a new recruitment wave are brought together to introduce themselves to each other and start getting acquainted. Nineteen-year-old Juanito found it be a positive experience:

> I remember that I felt at home very quickly. They organized these meetings in which everybody gets in a circle and each one tells the others who he is, what kind of music he likes [*imitating one of these conversations*]: "I'm Fulano, I like this kind of music, I like to go for walks, etc. etc."[10] I felt like I was home, because in the United States we always did this kind of thing the first day of school. . . . I think they do this kind of thing because they know well the backgrounds of the people they employ. (interview by the author, Mexico City, 2012)

Like Juanito, who lived in Provo, Utah, from ages nine to eighteen and was deported just before finishing high school, many 1.5-generation interviewees mentioned this practice in the call centers where they worked. It is a practice directly inspired by the American school system. Like Gloria, most of them found the circle reunion "kitsch," but it gave them a "homey feeling" that they had not felt until then since returning from the United States. In fact, with the exception of those who joined brothers or sisters who had already returned to Mexico, most of the interviewees had arrived in Mexico feeling that their migratory experience was an isolated case.

Even if most returnees had the support of their extended family when they arrived in Mexico, they quickly discovered a strong cultural gap between them and their Mexican relatives, and cohabitation rarely lasted long. This was especially true for the 1.5-generation interviewees. As a result, many felt isolated, misunderstood, and even discriminated against because of their appearance or the way they spoke Spanish, and some felt judged because of their behavior. In this context, call centers were more than just an employment niche: they played the important role of providing a place where for the first time young returnees could meet people who shared their background. Call centers became the place where they could rebuild what Marcelo Suárez-Orosco (1998, 52) calls a "safety background"—a place of shared meanings. It is easy to see this re-creation of a "Little United States" when walking past call centers like Teletech in central Mexico City; one can hear young Mexicans speaking fluent English together at lunchtime and after work in nearby bars.

As discussed earlier, the general requirement that applicants have at least completed high school was often waived for the returnees who were employed in these enterprises because call centers valued other skills they had acquired through their migrant experience—most obviously their mastery of the English language. Like other returnees, Gloria distin-

---

9. *Homie* originally meant "buddy." Here it refers to youngsters identified as being "from the hood" because they wear baggy pants, oversized shirts, and so on.

10. "Fulano" is the Mexican equivalent of "John Smith."

guished between the classroom English her local colleagues had mastered and her own more "natural" spoken English:

> Well, with English, it's not that I want to say that "I am wow!" but concretely, the English that they [local employees] speak and mine are very different. A big difference. And the difference is not only "my English is better," no? The problem is also that, let's make an example, I can tell you that I write better in English than in Spanish, and I often express myself better in English than in Spanish. But if you ask someone who studied English here what is past perfect and why you say it that way and not this way, they can explain it to you because they studied English like this at school. But I can't, because my English is native. So I can tell you when you said it wrong, but I can't explain why.... For me, it's something very natural! ... So it's complicated.... I have a disadvantage in this way, but in the end I have an advantage because they can't pronounce correctly, sometimes they don't understand, there are lots of sentences they don't get.

With their facility in English, 1.5-generation employees are the best at posing as American employees. Miguel was amused by some of his interactions with American clients:

> No, people speaking with us [*mentions his own case and that of two of his friends*] sometimes think that we're in the United States. Sometimes: "Oh, are you in New Jersey? Where in New Jersey?" [*laughter*] And I [say]: "I'm not in New Jersey, dude.... I'm in Mexico." And they're like: "Wow! Really? But you don't even have an accent!" "Yeah ... I lived like twenty years over there ... so I guess that's why." [*laughter*]

Since English was generally their first language, returnees, unlike their local colleagues, spoke the same English as their clients—or at least a form of English familiar to these clients. This ability to hide from clients that they are speaking with an employee located in another country plays an essential role in the quality of call center services. Interviewees noted that this aspect of the work was one of the most important when it came to understanding client dissatisfaction. Thirty-year-old Paloma, a local worker, described how her young returnee colleagues, particularly the ones who had grown up in the United States, could convey this sense of security to clients:

> The thing is that a lot of these people coming back from the United States are very pochitos.[11] They have this slang from the United States, and they even have this tone when they speak, and this can create a lot of insecurity for the American [client]. Because of the bad reputation, because of cultural references, they won't trust the person they are speaking with on the phone. But go figure: if a person calls and I, who have difficulties speaking English ... he won't call back. He won't call back because I will not be able to transmit to him the same security, that I really understood his problem.... But them (the pochos), even if they have this slang, they understand everything: "Okay, I understood you." (interview by the author, Mexico City, 2012)

MORE THAN A LANGUAGE: MASTERING THE GRAMMAR OF CULTURAL CODES

English fluency is not returnees' only advantage in call center jobs. As twenty-eight-year-old Ricardo, who had lived in Dallas from ages twenty to twenty-six, told us: "Speaking English helps you to do your job. But if you want to do your job correctly, or with quality, you need to know your clients, you need to have had some contact with them before so you can understand their forms of thinking. This helps you. A lot!" (interview by the author, Mexico City, 2011).

In this exercise of "presentation of self" (Goffman 1973), the activity is more than a basic linguistic exchange: it is a total cultural in-

---

11. Diminutive of pocho. The term referred originally to Mexican Americans, Chicanos, Mexicans who lost their culture. Today Mexicans use it more commonly in reference to young Mexicans who grew up in the United States and are assimilated to gang culture or urban cultures like rap or hip-hop.

teraction, one that is all the more significant for taking place on an international scale (Mirchandani 2012; Poster 2007). After mentioning the linguistic dimension of their work, all of the interviewees agreed that their life experience in the United States had given them an advantage over local workers: they had mastered the cultural codes of their clients and could manage the diversity of these clients. Their familiarity with these cultural codes gave them a considerable advantage in their interactions, for example, with some Puerto Rican and African American clients.[12] Local employees were often simply unable to comprehend these clients' accents.

On this subject, one of our interviewees told us that when African American clients ("from the hood") called, local employees commonly transferred the call to him. For some of the returnees, this was one of the dimensions they most valued in their job: their work briefly taking on a social dimension that they were the ones most capable of attending to successfully. Indeed, their ability to manage what might have been problematic situations for other workers conferred on them a particular status, which became a driver of self-esteem for some of them. This dimension of the job helped them experience a solidarity link with these client communities, in contrast to the negative attitude of their local colleagues, who did not understand, as Ricardo said, "what it is to live in the United States":

> Another thing is that [the local workers], they study [English], but they don't have relations with these people, the daily problems people have there. When these people talk to you, they ask you . . . or they tell you their problems: "I couldn't pay my bill because. . . ." You understand because you've been there. At best, the ones who are undocumented and who do have services like AT&T, they can't get welfare and so they have to pay all at once and medical care in the U.S. is so expensive! And you can understand them, no? It's not only a matter of getting rid of these people for work, no? You understand their problems better because you experienced the same situations. The truth is that it is very different. They [the local workers] take their job as very mechanized, and you, it is like you are a little bit more involved. . . . Let's say you understand them. When you have the experience of how it is there, you understand everything.

OUTSIDERS AMONG THE OUTSIDERS: RETURNEES WHO EMIGRATED AS ADULTS

For return migrants who had moved to the United States after reaching adulthood, the situation was somewhat different from the experience of the 1.5-generation returnees. They did not have the same skills as the 1.5 generation, especially the latter's mastery of English and computing skills. As such, they can be considered outsiders even more so than the 1.5 generation returnees in that they related even less to the standard qualified workers who normally made up the call center workforce. Many of them had never envisaged themselves working at an office job: "I never imagined that one day I would work at a desk job," said José.

The main difference in the discourse of these returnee migrants can be seen in their argument that, more than the cultural capital gained in the United States and mentioned by the 1.5 generation as their main advantage, they acquired the competencies that gave them access to this kind of job through their migration experience and what they learned about American work values. To them, their migratory experience was an educational experience that allowed them to acquire new skills and become "better workers," and they were now applying these new skills in their current job. Like their 1.5-generation colleagues, they insisted that their life experience in the United States, living among the American people, gave them a serious advantage in their job by enabling them to understand aspects of American culture. One of those making this argument was Mario, a thirty-two-year-old who had lived in New York City from ages twenty to twenty-nine:

---

12. Puerto Rican and African American clients were the examples most often cited by the interviewees and even by the local employees.

They ask you what the weather's like. I don't know why Gringos love to know about the weather so much. If there were no Weather Channel, they'd all die! And in conversation, it's something they bring up without even thinking about. They ask you: "Hey, how's the weather?" It's a way to start the conversation. So you tell them, "Around seventy, eighty," something they like, you know? Whatever . . . these little things help you a lot. These little guys who learned English at school but who never lived with the raza, they don't understand.[13] There are some things, like, that a Gringo doesn't like you lying to him. If you lie to him and he realizes it, he doesn't insult you, but he doesn't let you escape until you tell him why you lied to him. A Gringo doesn't like you to apologize. A Gringo, after hearing "I'm sorry" three times, is like "Wow, this guy is crazy." Once is enough. One "I'm sorry" is the max. So when you know all that, it's way easier, of course! (interview by the author, Mexico City, 2012)

Although they had not moved to the United States until adulthood, these returnees did not consider themselves local workers, and they emphasized the strong differences between themselves and the local workers, especially with respect to work values. They tended to make dichotomous comparisons between "here and there," opposing Mexican values (which characterized the local employees) to American values (which characterized themselves). Males who had emigrated as adults were particularly prone to refer frequently to American values, citing American punctuality versus Mexican lack of punctuality, the merit system versus the old-boy network, pride in work done well versus a blasé attitude, and believing that the "customer is king" versus mocking American values. They believed that their adherence to American work values was the reason why, even though they were not as proficient in English as their 1.5-generation colleagues, their work was particularly valued by their employers.

FINDING AN ECONOMIC NICHE IN OFFSHORE CALL CENTERS

One of the reasons for the preponderance of returnees in the call center industry is that it offers what can be considered good salaries. For the university-educated employees entering the labor market in markedly increasing numbers in the last ten years, call center jobs are attractive because they offer higher salaries than the salaries offered in some other qualified jobs (Micheli Thirión 2007). Although taking a call center job represents a move into another professional sector, these returnees, with their lack of educational qualifications, have few well-paying alternatives. Some interviewees had held jobs outside the call center sector, but the incomes were lower, a fact that was even more relevant to those who lacked educational qualifications: "For someone who only finished high school, it's good money," said Mario. "In other jobs, you can get six or seven [thousand pesos]. Eight is a lot. . . . I looked for what paid best. And I only finished high school, and if you have only that here, the truth is that those jobs are badly paid. That's why, since I came back, I've only worked in call centers. You speak English and that's it!"

We received many testimonies from interviewees who had tried to work in other sectors but ended up coming back to the call centers, mainly because of the income. There certainly are jobs that offer equivalent or superior incomes, but they may require higher qualifications or have inferior working conditions (in particular the number of working hours required): "I think all these people who come back from the United States, well, they find themselves in a place where they don't get their hands dirty and where they're well paid," said Roberto, a thirty-two-year-old who had lived in California and Missouri from ages twenty-two to thirty. "Look, for me, who was working as a builder, they're paying me the same amount of money and I am not killing myself" (interview by the author, Mexico City, 2012).

Roberto, who had worked double shifts in

---

13. *Raza* is a Mexican term for the common people, or the folk. It differs from the meaning attributed to it by Mexican Americans, who use it specifically to refer to Mexican people.

the construction sector and the restaurant industry when he was in the United States, stressed an important point: a lot of the interviewees had worked in "3D" (Dirty, Dangerous, Demanding) jobs while living in the United States. Therefore, many of them considered their current position a step up the social and professional ladder, from 3D jobs to a desk job. They also maintained that their current call center jobs offered them good working conditions in comparison with other jobs that they could find in the Mexican labor market. Mario and twenty-eight-year-old Adrian, who had lived in Chicago from ages eight to twenty-five (interview by the author, Mexico City, 2012), had this lively exchange:

MARIO: This is the advantage compared to other jobs. Here, you work from seven to four, with one and a half hours for lunch, and it's from Monday to Friday. You get out at four and "see you!" This is one of the advantages: you have a good salary, and it doesn't kill you. No, really, it doesn't kill you. How can you kill yourself sitting in a chair?

ADRIAN: In the worst-case scenario, you get fat! [*laughter*] . . . Look, my girlfriend earns like 12,000 [pesos] a month, with vouchers.[14] But no kidding, she works twelve hours a day, she's always tired. She does nothing after work because she's tired. And she's also bilingual. She also worked in Teletech, but only for two months. But now, in the hotel, she earns 12,000 pesos, sometimes even more with tips. But no kidding, she works twelve hours a day, six days a week.

At the same time, these young returnees found themselves in a paradoxical situation. On the one hand, they were able to earn a salary that was hard to match in other jobs with equivalent qualifications. On the other hand, they were stuck in the call center sector because they would have run the risk of lowering their income or encountering inferior working conditions if they moved to another sector.

As a consequence, they tended to develop careers in the call center sector, which is not a uniform sector. Some call centers pay more but offer less security, featuring short campaigns and short contracts; others give employees the opportunity to augment their salary with many bonuses; other call center jobs are lower-paid but come with a wide array of social security benefits (permanent contract, medical care, vouchers, housing credits, and so on). Each return migrant seemed to prefer one or another type of call center, according to their own individual needs. Thus, young single men tended toward the less secure jobs, which enabled them to earn more money more quickly, while older men with children tended to take more secure positions whose benefits were better aligned with their family's security and long-term plans.

The female return migrants were different; indeed, they showed the highest inclination to choose ascendant careers in the call center industry. There seemed to be two main reasons for this tendency. Female respondents stressed the importance of the age factor, which made career changes more difficult for them. They were more aware than men of the impact of getting older faster in the Mexican labor market. The women were also much more likely than their male counterparts to speak about their desire for independence.[15] In addition to age and desire for independence, the stigma of tattoos in Mexico made call centers appear to be the only option for those who had them. Gloria was glad that remaining with the call center was a career option for her:

I learned a lot. Really. I never thought I would get it so easy. I learned a lot, and I like it. . . . It's not what you plan to do when you're a kid (*laughter*): "Ah, I want to work in a call center!" I don't know, perhaps it sounds bad, like

14. If they earned the bonuses (a fixed salary of 10,000 pesos plus 2,000 pesos in bonuses), Mario and Adrian would also earn about 12,000 pesos in the call center.

15. Among eight 1.5-generation female interviewees, five said that they had suffered conjugal violence within their first relationship after returning to Mexico. This experience—as described in off-the-record testimonies—was heavily related to their desire of independence.

other employees say to me: "You sound really whiny! How can you want to stay here?" Well, I want to stay here, and the reason is that I am very aware that I have tattoos, that I'm not so young . . . that to pursue a career now, it would be complicated.

CONCLUSION

Call centers appear to be the principal entry into the labor market for young returnees when they arrive back in Mexico. Some of the deported migrants I interviewed even reported that U.S. migration authorities pointed them toward this labor market sector. Although their language skills make them suitable for employment in English-speaking call centers, most returnees cannot aspire to jobs that require higher education as well as English skills because they lack formal qualifications. This explains why the majority of interviewees, after imagining that call center employment would be a transitional situation for them, were stuck years later in the same sector: it offered a higher salary than other nonqualified jobs. Last but not least, the invisibility of their work receiving calls allowed tattooed individuals—some of them former gang members in the United States—to enter the formal labor market after their previous attempts at employment had been met with rejection because of their stigmata.

The cultural capital that these return migrants accumulated during their lives in the United States had put them on a par with a local workforce of university students and graduates, who were more qualified but lacked the returnees' unique capital. Mexican call center employees are generally expected to have at least completed high school, but even returnees who lack this prerequisite are employed in these enterprises. As anticipated, call centers value more highly the other skills possessed by returnees, which are closely tied to their migrant experience. Besides a mastery of English, their knowledge of American culture is a crucial skill that they bring to the call center workplace. Confronted with American customers, they can understand a wide range of situations that are unfamiliar to their local colleagues, such as American regional accents and slang and day-to-day situations that they themselves experienced in the United States. Additionally, values learned in the American labor market are highly prized by call center employers: punctuality, the idea that the client is always right, and pride in "work well done." The interviewees felt that these attributes run counter to the Mexican way of working. Returnees reinvest the human capital they acquired during their U.S. migration experience as a set of skills in this economic sector, despite their weak preparation for call center work. This confirms that the structural context in the origin country is the main factor in human capital transferability.

Return migrants consider their jobs in call centers financially and socially rewarding: they have a formal job rather than the informal jobs they held in the United States; in progressing from "3-D" jobs in the United States to a desk job in Mexico, their status has been elevated; and they earn a good salary compared to what nonqualified jobs, and even some skilled jobs, would offer in Mexico. Finally, job security is not a concern in a sector that is continuously looking to renew its workforce; some even move from one call center to another, according to the benefits that they can obtain.

Nevertheless, returnees experience the paradox of occupying an advantageous position, considering their level of qualifications, while also being trapped in one labor market niche. Their lack of skills would make it difficult to find a better job in another sector, and any such job they found would most likely offer a much lower salary.

The young returnees working in English-speaking call centers in Mexico reflect the complexity of the international division of labor in a time of economic globalization and intense human mobility. New communication technologies, beyond their capacity to compress space and time, have allowed the creation of unprecedented forms of "migrations" of work without the bodies (Aneesh 2006) and created an unexpected scenario: an expelled migrant can find himself working, from within his country of origin, for the very country from which he was expelled.

REFERENCES

Abrego, Leisy J. 2006. "I Can't Go to College Because I Don't Have Papers: Incorporation Patterns of Undocumented Latino Youth." *Latino Studies* 4(3): 212–31.

Aneesh, A. 2006. *Virtual Migration: The Programming of Globalization.* Durham, N.C.: Duke University Press.

Battistella, Graziano. 2004. "Return Migration in the Philippines: Issues and Policies." In *International Migration: Prospects and Policies in a Global Market,* edited by Douglas S. Massey and J. Edward Taylor. Oxford: Oxford University Press.

Belt, Vicki, Ranald Richardson, and Juliet Webster. 2002. "Women, Social Skill, and Interactive Service Work in Telephone Call Centres." *New Technology Work and Employment* 17(1): 20–34.

Bidart, Claire. 2009. "Bifurcations biographiques et éléments de l'action." In *Bifurcations,* edited by Marc Bessin, Claire Bidart, and Michel Grossetti. Paris: La Découverte.

Bourdieu, Pierre. 1979. *La distinction: Critique sociale du jugement.* Paris: Les Éditions de Minuit.

Cassarino, Jean-Pierre. 2004. "Theorising Return Migration: The Conceptual Approach to Return Migrants Revisited." *International Journal on Multicultural Societies* 6(2): 253–79.

———. 2014. "A Case for Return Preparedness." In *Global and Asian Perspectives on International Migration,* edited by Graziano Battistella. Basel, Switzerland: Springer International.

Cerase, Francesco P. 1974. "Expectations and Reality: A Study of Return Migration from the United States to Italy." *International Migration Review* 8(26): 245–62.

Chavez, Leo R. 2015. "Uncertain Futures: Educational Attainment and the Children of the Undocumented Mexican Immigrants in the Greater Los Angeles Area." In *Cracks in the Schoolyard: Confronting Latino Educational Inequality,* edited by Gilberto Q. Conchas and Briana M. Hinga. New York: Teachers College Press.

Conway, Dennis, Robert B. Potter, and Godfrey St. Bernard. 2009. "Repetitive Visiting as a Pre-return Transnational Strategy Among Youthful Trinidadian Returnees." *Mobilities* 4(2): 249–73.

Cousin, Olivier. 2002. "Les ambivalences du travail: Les salariés peu qualifiés dans les centres d'appel." *Sociologie du travail* 44(4): 499–520.

Da Cruz, Michaël. 2013. "Usos de la cultura transnacional en la economía globalizada: Los estudiantes y los migrantes teleoperadores en los centros de llamadas bilingües de Monterrey (México) y San Salvador (El Salvador)." In *Ser migrante latinoamericano, ser vulnerable, trabajar precariamente,* edited by Roberto Benencia, Fernando Herrera Lima, and Elaine Levine. Barcelona: Antrophos.

———. 2014. "Back to Tenochtitlan: Migration de retour et nouvelles maquiladoras de la communication: Le cas des jeunes migrants employés dans les centres d'appel bilingues de la ville de Mexico." PhD diss., Aix-Marseille University.

Da Cruz, Michaël, and Anne Fouquet. 2010. "La figura del operador mundializado: Jóvenes trabajadores en los call centers de Monterrey." In *Cuando México enfrenta la globalización: Permanencias y cambios en el área metropolitana de Monterrey,* edited by Lilia Palacios. Monterrey: Autonomous University of Nuevo León.

De Haas, Hein, Tineke Fokkema, and Mohamed Fassi Fihri. 2015. "Return Migration as Failure or Success? The Determinants of Return Migration Intentions Among Moroccan Migrants in Europe." *Journal of International Migration and Integration* 16(2): 415–29.

Del Bono, Andrea, and María Noel Bulloni. 2008. "Experiencias laborales juveniles: Los agentes telefónicos de los call centers offshore en Argentina." *Trabajo y sociedad* 9(10): 1–21.

Demazière, Didier. 2008. "L'entretien biographique comme interaction négociations, contre-interprétations, ajustement de sens." *Langage et société* 1(123): 15–35.

Durand, Jorge. 2004. "Ensayo teórico sobre la migración de retorno: El principio del rendimiento decreciente." *Cuadernos geográficos* 35(2): 103–16.

Freeman, Christopher, and Luc Soete. 1994. *Work for All or Mass Unemployment? Computerised Technical Change into the 21st Century.* London: Pinter.

Frenkel, Stephen J., May Tam, Marek Korczinski, and Karen A. Shire. 1998. "Beyond Bureaucracy? Work Organization in Call Centres." *International Journal of Human Resource Management* 9(6): 957–79.

Friginal, Eric. 2007. "Outsourced Call Centers and

English in the Philippines." *World Englishes* 26(3): 331–45.

Gandini, Luciana, Fernando Lozano-Ascencio and Selene Gaspar Olvera. 2015. "El retorno en el nuevo escenario de la migración entre México y Estados Unidos." Mexico City: Consejo Nacional de Población (CONAPO).

Giorguli Saucedo, Silvia E., and Edith Y. Gutiérrez. 2012. "Migration et développement: De l'ambivalence à la désillusion?" *Hommes et migrations* 1296(2) : 22–33.

Gmelch, George. 1980. "Return Migration." *Annual Review of Anthropology* 9: 135–39.

Goffman, Erving. 1973. *La mise en scène de la vie quotidienne: La présentation de soi*. Paris: Éditions de Minuit.

———. 1975. *Stigmate: Les usages sociaux des handicaps*. Paris: Éditions de Minuit.

Gonzales, Roberto G. 2011. "Learning to Be Illegal: Undocumented Youth and Shifting Legal Contexts in the Transition to Adulthood." *American Sociological Review* 76(4): 602–19.

Gonzales, Roberto G., and Leo R. Chavez. 2012. "'Awakening to a Nightmare': Abjectivity and Illegality in the Lives of Undocumented 1.5-Generation Latino Immigrants in the United States." *Current Anthropology* 53(3): 255–81.

Holman, David, Rosemary Batt, and Ursula Holtgrewe. 2007. *The Global Call Centre Report: International Perspectives on Management and Employment*. Ithaca, N.Y.: Cornell University.

Hualde, Alfredo, Hedalid Tolentino, and Mario Jurado. 2014. "Trayectorias laborales en los call centers: Empleos sin futuro?" In *La precariedad laboral: Dimensiones, dinámicas, y significados*, edited by Rocío Guadarrama, Alfredo Hualde, and Silvia López. Tijuana: El Colegio de la Frontera Norte.

Hughes, Everett. 1997. *Le regard sociologique: Essais choisis*. Paris: Éditions de l'EHESS.

Instituto Mexicano de Teleservicios (IMT). 2012. "IMT Research." *Contact Forum* 15(45): 6–41.

King, Russell, and Anastasia Christou. 2011. "Of Counter-Diaspora and Reverse Transnationalism: Return Mobilities to and from the Ancestral Homeland." *Mobilities* (6)4: 451–66.

Lee, Don. 2015. "The Philippines Has Become the Call-Center Capital of the World." *Los Angeles Times*, February 1, 2015.

Massey, Douglas S., Rafael Alarcon, Jorge Durand, and Humberto González. 1987. *Return to Aztlan: The Social Process of International Migration from Western Mexico*. Berkeley: University of California Press.

Mendoza Cota, Jorge E. 2013. "Migración de retorno, niveles educativos, y desarrollo socioeconómico regional de México." *Estudios sociales* 21(42): 55–85.

Messenger, Jon C., and Naj Ghosheh. 2010. *Offshoring and Working Conditions in Remote Work*. Basingstoke, U.K.: Palgrave Macmillan.

Micheli Thirión, Jordy. 2007. "Los call centers y los nuevos trabajos del siglo XXI." *CONfines de relaciones internacionales y ciencia política* 3(5): 49–58.

———. 2011. "El sector de call centers: Estructura y tendencias: Apuntes sobre la situación de México." *Frontera norte* 24(47): 145–69.

Mirchandani, Kiran. 2012. *Phone Clones: Authenticity Work in the Transnational Service Economy*. Ithaca, N.Y.: Cornell University Press.

Nyobe, Sara. 2015. "Quelle GRH pour des salariés en situation de domination culturelle?" *Management et avenir* 4(78): 99–117.

Padilla, Juan M., and Ana E. Jardón Hernández. 2014. "Migración y empleo: Reinserción de los migrantes de retorno al mercado laboral nacional." Mexico City: La Fundación Internacional y para Iberoamérica de Administración y Políticas Públicas (FIIAPP) and Instituto de Estudios y Divulgación sobre Migración (INEDIM).

Phillips, Joan, and Robert B. Potter. 2009. "Quality of Life Issues and Second-Generation Migration: The Case of 'Bajan-Brit Returnees.'" *Population Space and Place* 15(3): 239–51.

Poster, Winifred R. 2007. "Who's on the Line? Indian Call Center Agents Pose as American for U.S.-Outsourced Firms." *Industrial Relations: A Journal of Economy and Society* 46(2): 271–304.

Potter, Robert B., Dennis Conway, and Godfrey St. Bernard. 2009. "Transnationalism Personified: Young Returning Trinidadians 'in Their Own Words.'" *Tijdschrift Voor Economische En Sociale Geografie* 100(1): 101–13.

Puel, Gilles. 2003. "Géographie des centres d'appel." *Réseaux* 21(119): 203–36.

Rallu, Jean-Louis. 2007. "L'étude des migrations de retour: Données de recensement, d'enquête et de fichiers." In *Migrations internationales et retour au pays d'origine*, edited by Véronique Petit.

Paris: Centre Population et Développement (CEPED).

Reynolds, Tracey. 2011. "Caribbean Second-Generation Return Migration: Transnational Family Relationships with 'Left-Behind' Kin in Britain." *Mobilities* 6(4): 535–51.

Richardson, Ranald, and Vicki Belt. 2001. "Saved by the Bell? Call Centres and Economic Development in Less Favoured Regions." *Economic and Industrial Democracy* 22(1): 67–98.

Rivera Sánchez, Liliana. 2015. "Narrativas de retorno y movilidad: Entre prácticas de involucramiento y espacialidades múltiples en la ciudad." *Estudios políticos* 47: 243–64.

Rojas García, Georgina. 2013. "Transitioning from School to Work as a Mexican 1.5er: Upward Mobility and Glass Ceiling Assimilation Among College Students in California." *Annals of the American Academy of Political and Social Science* 648(1): 87–101.

Rumbaut, Rubén G. 2004. "Ages, Life Stages, and Generational Cohorts: Decomposing the Immigrant First and Second Generations in the United States." *International Migration Review* 38(3): 1160–1205.

Stanworth, Celia. 2000. "Women and Work in the Information Age." *Gender, Work, and Organization* 7(1): 20–32.

Suárez-Orozco, Marcelo M. 1998. "Introduction: Crossings: Mexican Immigration in Interdisciplinary Perspectives." In *Crossings: Mexican Immigration in Interdisciplinary Perspectives*, edited by Marcelo M. Suárez-Orozco. Cambridge, Mass.: Harvard University Press.

Tsuda, Takeyuki. 2003. *Strangers in the Ethnic Homeland: Japanese Brazilian Return Migration in Transnational Perspective*. New York: Columbia University Press.

Waldinger, Roger, and Cynthia Feliciano. 2004. "Will the Second Generation Experience 'Downward Assimilation'? Segmented Assimilation Reassessed." *Ethnic and Racial Studies* 27(3): 376–402.

Waldinger, Roger, Nelson Lim, and David Cort. 2007. "Bad Jobs, Good Jobs, No Jobs? The Employment Experience of the Mexican American Second Generation." *Journal of Ethnic and Migration Studies* 33(1): 1–36.

PART II

Labor Market Dynamics, Networks, and Workplace Experiences

Black Immigration, Occupational Niches, and Earnings Disparities Between U.S.-Born and Foreign-Born Blacks in the United States

TOD G. HAMILTON, JANERIA A. EASLEY, AND ANGELA R. DIXON

Using data from the 2000 U.S. census and the 2010 to 2014 waves of the American Community Survey, we examine the importance of occupational niches in explaining earnings disparities between U.S.-born blacks and black immigrants in the United States. Our results show that, relative to U.S.-born blacks, most black immigrant subgroups have similar or greater representation in occupational niches. Employment in a niche occupation has a small but positive association with earnings, and the returns to niche employment are greater for black immigrants, particularly black immigrant women. Niche employment does not, however, explain earnings disparities between U.S.-born and immigrant blacks.

Keywords: niches, occupation, earnings, blacks, immigrants

Every census of the U.S. population since 1970 has shown that, even after adjusting for a standard set of labor market characteristics, black immigrants from the English-speaking Caribbean (West Indies) have higher labor force participation rates, higher employment rates, and higher earnings than U.S.-born blacks. A number of studies have also shown that West Indian immigrants have become the primary source of labor in sectors of the economy once dominated by U.S.-born blacks (Waldinger 1996; Waters 1999). Although researchers have examined whether selective migration, differential patterns of discrimination, or differences in cultural practices explain disparities between the two groups (Hamilton 2014; Ifatunji 2016; Model 2008; Sowell 1975, 1978, 1981, 1983; Vickerman 1998; Waters 1999), few have

---

Tod G. Hamilton is assistant professor of sociology and faculty associate of the Office of Population Research at Princeton University. **Janeria A. Easley** is a postdoctoral fellow in the Department of Sociology at the University of Pennsylvania. **Angela R. Dixon** is a graduate student in the Department of Sociology and the Office of Population Research at Princeton University.

© 2018 Russell Sage Foundation. Hamilton, Tod G., Janeria A. Easley, and Angela R. Dixon. 2018. "Black Immigration, Occupational Niches, and Earnings Disparities Between U.S.-Born and Foreign-Born Blacks in the United States." *RSF: The Russell Sage Foundation Journal of the Social Sciences* 4(1): 60–77. DOI: 10.7758/RSF.2018.4.1.04. We thank participants in the "New Immigrant U.S. Labor Market Niches in the Era of Globalization" conference for their comments and suggestions and the Russell Sage Foundation for its support of the project. Support for our research was provided by grants from the Eunice Kennedy Shriver National Institute of Child Health and Human Development of the National Institutes of Health (P2CHD047879, T32HD007163). Direct correspondence to: Tod G. Hamilton at todh@princeton.edu, Department of Sociology, Princeton University, 128 Wallace Hall, Princeton, NJ 08544; Janeria A. Easley at jeasley@sas.upenn.edu, Department of Sociology, University of Pennsylvania, 3718 Locust Walk, McNeil Building, Suite 113, Philadelphia, PA 19104; and Angela R. Dixon at angelad@princeton.edu, Office of Population Research, Princeton University, Wallace Hall, Princeton, NJ 08544.

comparatively examined variation in the types of employment typically held by black immigrants and U.S.-born blacks or analyzed whether employment in ethnic niche occupations helps explain labor market disparities between the two groups.

A common feature of immigrant economic incorporation is the proclivity of new immigrants to gravitate toward a narrow set of economic activities (Eckstein and Peri, this issue; Waldinger 1996). The organization of economic activity can take different forms, such as ethnic economies or ethnic enclaves (Adelman, Huishien, and Tolnay 2006; Fong and Shen 2011; Light and Gold 2000; Portes and Jensen 1989; Portes and Manning 2005; Portes and Shafer 2007). One of the most common and basic forms of economic clustering, however, is ethnic niches—the overrepresentation of members of a particular ethnic group in a given set of occupations or industries.

Roger Waldinger (1996) shows that public-sector employment has been a niche for U.S.-born blacks since the 1990s. Conversely, Suzanne Model and Gene Fisher (2001) show that West Indian immigrants are overrepresented in a number of private-sector industries. Prior research has suggested that immigrant occupational niches provide employment opportunities for black immigrants, particularly less-skilled immigrants upon arrival in the United States, but considerable debate remains regarding whether niche-sector employment leads to greater earnings.

Most of the studies on ethnic niches among black immigrants have focused almost exclusively on the experiences of pre-2000 black immigrants from the English-speaking Caribbean residing in New York City (Model 1997a; Waldinger 1994). Between 2000 and 2013, the number of black immigrants in the United States increased by 56 percent: Caribbean immigration increased by 33 percent during this period, while African immigration increased by a remarkable 137 percent (Anderson 2015). Therefore, understanding whether niche employment provides pathways to economic integration for both African and Caribbean immigrants could provide valuable insights into the types of economic incorporation experienced by newer waves of black immigrants, as well as shed light on how niche employment shapes disparities among blacks by nativity in the United States.

This study has three goals. First, given the absence of research documenting the degree to which different black immigrant subgroups are employed in ethnic niches, we examine variation in niche employment for the major black immigrant subgroups: immigrants from the Dominican Republic, Haiti, Jamaica, Trinidad and Tobago, Guyana, Ghana, Nigeria, and Ethiopia. Second, we evaluate the degree to which niche employment explains variation in labor market outcomes between U.S.-born blacks and immigrant blacks. Finally, we look at whether the earnings return to employment in ethnic niches varies between U.S.-born and immigrant blacks as well as among black immigrants by birth country.

Our descriptive results show that, relative to U.S.-born blacks, a similar or greater proportion of individuals from every black immigrant subgroup is employed in an ethnic niche. Immigrant groups with the largest share of individuals employed in niche occupations hail from Ghana and Ethiopia, and the subgroups with the smallest share hail from Guyana and Jamaica. Our regression results show that employment in niche occupations has a small but statistically significant positive association with weekly earnings. However, ethnic niches do not account for earnings disparities between U.S.-born and immigrant black men and women. Results also show that, relative to U.S.-born blacks, the returns to niche employment are greater for black immigrants, particularly immigrant women.

THEORETICAL BACKGROUND

Researchers have proposed three primary explanations for labor market differences between native and immigrant blacks: cultural differences in attitudes toward work, disparate patterns of discrimination, and selective migration (Foner 1985; Hamilton 2014; Ifatunji 2016; Kasinitz 1992; Model 2008; Sowell 1975, 1978, 1981, 1983; Vickerman 1998; Waters 1999).

The Creation of an Ethic Niche

Mary Waters (1999) suggests that a combination of selective migration, network hiring, and discrimination by white employers produces a labor market advantage for black West Indian immigrants in New York. She argues that because black immigrants are immigrants, they are positively selected on a number of unobserved factors that lead to more favorable outcomes in the United States. Moreover, she contends, immigrants' point of reference regarding the value of a particular type of employment is their country of origin and the opportunities available in their home countries. As a result, at the food services firm that she studied, black immigrants placed greater value on the menial jobs available to them. According to Waters, the result was that West Indian immigrants stayed longer and worked harder at jobs that many Americans, black or white, would have considered dead-end employment. In addition, the firm relied on the social networks of existing immigrant employees to fill vacancies. These factors, combined with discrimination, make it virtually impossible for U.S.-born blacks to find employment in the firm.

The process that Waters (1999) describes is the creation of an ethnic niche. Waldinger (1996) outlines this general phenomenon for other ethnic groups in New York. Because of unusual demand for labor in particular occupations, the resources specific to particular ethnic groups, and differential discriminatory practices across industries and occupations, different ethnic groups gravitate toward different occupations or industries that offer avenues for upward mobility. Waldinger also shows that niches are dynamic and follow a process of ethnic succession whereby members of one ethnic group replace another ethnic group as the dominant workforce in the industry. Two primary factors drive the evolution of niches: better employment opportunities for a particular ethnic group outside of niche sectors, and, perhaps more importantly, immigration.

One of the most visible patterns of ethnic succession is the formation of different immigrant niches in segments of the economy that were once U.S.-born black niches (Waldinger 1996; Rosenfeld and Tienda 1999). Michael Rosenfeld and Marta Tienda (1999) show that Mexican immigrants are now dominant in segments of the economy once held by U.S.-born blacks. Waldinger (1996) also shows that West Indians and Dominicans have replaced U.S.-born blacks as the dominant workforce in many segments of the economy.

Both Waldinger (1996) and Rosenfeld and Tienda (1999) also highlight that while many U.S.-born black niches have been transformed into immigrant niches, U.S.-born blacks, particularly those who are moderately and highly skilled, have become the dominant workforce in many public-sector occupations. Waldinger notes that one of the key factors in the creation of modern U.S.-born black niches is stringent hiring practices that make it more difficult to discriminate. Consequently, U.S.-born black niches tend to form in large private-sector industries and in the public sector. Firms in large industries, being highly visible, are forced to engage in more transparent hiring practices, and the public sector's bureaucratic hiring protocols, which tend to reduce discrimination, help U.S.-born blacks gain employment.

Earnings and Immigrant Occupational Niches

Prior studies show that occupational niches lead to employment opportunities for both new immigrants and U.S.-born blacks, particularly less-skilled new immigrants (Waldinger 2001). However, the evidence regarding the earnings benefits of employment in niche occupations is mixed.

Research has shown that the benefits of niche employment vary by industry and sector of the labor market (Model 1997a; Wilson 2003). For example, Jennifer Lee (2013) finds that, for Asian immigrants, the relationship between occupational niches and earnings depends on whether the niche is in a low-tech or high-tech industry. Steven J. Gold (this issue) shows that Israeli immigrants also tend to gravitate toward high-paying jobs in the technology sector. There is robust evidence that African Americans, because of lower levels of discrimination in public-sector niches, fare particularly well in these niches (Logan and Alba 1999; Rosenfeld and Tienda 1999; Waldinger 1994). Using data from 1990, Waldinger (1996) also finds that African Americans have higher wages in public-sector niches than in the dominant economy. In contrast, he shows West Indian and Dominican immigrants have lower wages when employed in niche occupations than when employed in non-niche sectors.

The economic benefits of employment in niche sectors also vary by gender. When comparing how nonwhite groups fare in the dominant labor markets of New York and London, Model (1997b) finds that ethnic niches are more beneficial for West Indian female immigrants in New York than for West Indian male immigrants.

The Current Study
Most of the extant literature on black immigrant ethnic niches focuses on the employment experiences of immigrants from the Caribbean. Less is known about the impact of niche-sector employment on earnings disparities between black immigrants from the Caribbean and those from Africa.

There are several reasons to expect black immigrants from sub-Saharan Africa to have different patterns of employment than black Caribbean immigrants. The first relates to education. Among individuals ages twenty-five and older, 30 percent of the entire U.S. population has a college degree or an advanced degree, and 20 percent of U.S.-born blacks have a college degree. This figure is 20 percent for immigrants from the Caribbean and a remarkable 35 percent for immigrants from Africa (Anderson 2015). Although niches can form in high-skilled occupations, much of the existing research suggests that niche employment benefits less-skilled immigrants in occupations where it is easy to bypass bureaucratic hiring procedures and little formal training is needed to start employment (Waldinger 1996). Consequently, it remains an open question whether the patterns of labor market concentration for newer and more-educated waves of black immigrants from Africa will be similar to those for black immigrants from the Caribbean, and whether the benefits to niche occupations will vary across the groups.

Second, the gender composition of immigration varies considerably for immigrants from the Caribbean and those from sub-Saharan Africa. Women represent more than 50 percent of the stock of immigrants from the West Indies. Moreover, relative to West Indian men, West Indian women have a longer tenure of U.S. residence and are also often the family member who initiated the migration decision (Foner 2009; Model 2008), a factor that affects both the likelihood and type of niche employment (Kasinitz and Vickerman 2001). By contrast, men account for a greater proportion of flows from sub-Saharan Africa and also tend to be the primary migrant. These factors, in combination with the gendered nature of occupations in the United States, make it likely that men and women from the two regions would cluster in different types of occupations.

Finally, many of the seminal papers documenting patterns of ethnic niching among blacks were written using data from the 1990s. Given the changes in the U.S. economy since that period, during which many occupations requiring lower levels of skill have been eliminated, it is unclear whether the economic returns to niche employment have remained stable since the 1990s or how the returns to ethnic niching vary across a more diverse black population. Such variation could help explain differences in labor market outcomes between U.S.-born blacks and black immigrants.

We address these gaps in the literature by examining three questions: (1) Is there variation in the degree to which U.S.-born blacks and foreign-born men and women are employed in occupational niches? (2) Does niche-sector employment explain wage disparities between black immigrants and U.S.-born blacks? (3) Do the earnings returns to niche-sector employment vary among blacks?

DATA, MEASURES, AND METHODS

Data
This study uses data on black men and women between the ages of twenty-five and sixty-four taken from the 5 percent Integrated Public Use

Microdata Series (IPUMS) of the 2000 U.S. census and the 2010 to 2014 waves of the American Community Survey (ACS) to evaluate labor market differences between native and immigrant blacks (Ruggles et al. 2015). In this study, blacks are defined as individuals who self-identify as black and who do not reside in institutions or group quarters. To avoid including individuals in the immigrant sample who are more similar to natives than to immigrants, we exclude people who were born abroad to American parents and those born in Puerto Rico. Because one of the primary goals of this study is to examine the impact of occupational niches on earnings, we exclude individuals for whom we do not have occupation data and individuals who are in school, out of the labor force, or in the military.

Blacks are separated into two categories: U.S.-born blacks and immigrant blacks. Immigrants are defined as individuals who were born outside of the United States. We divide the black immigrant population into nine primary source countries: the Dominican Republic, Haiti, Jamaica, Trinidad and Tobago, Guyana, Ghana, Nigeria, and Ethiopia.

Ethnic niches are created and maintained based on the strength of coethnic social networks (Waldinger 1996). Consequently, the influence of ethnic niches on labor market opportunities must be studied in areas with relatively large numbers of coethnics. In this study, we examine occupational niches in the fifteen metropolitan statistical areas (MSAs) that had the largest black populations in 2014 (Anderson 2015): New York–Newark–Jersey City, NY-NJ-PA; Miami–Fort Lauderdale–West Palm Beach, FL; Washington-Arlington-Alexandria, DC-VA-MD-WV; Boston-Cambridge-Newton, MA-NH; Atlanta–Sandy Springs–Roswell, GA; Philadelphia-Camden-Wilmington, PA-NJ-DE-MD; Orlando-Kissimmee-Sanford, FL; Los Angeles–Long Beach–Anaheim, CA; Houston–The Woodlands–Sugar Land, TX; Minneapolis–St. Paul–Bloomington, MN-WI; Chicago-Naperville-Elgin, IL-IN-WI; Dallas–Fort Worth–Arlington, TX; Baltimore-Columbia-Towson, MD; Seattle-Tacoma-Bellevue, WA; and Columbus, OH.

Measures and Methods

Dependent Variable

Weekly earnings is the outcome of interest. This variable is generated by summing a respondent's wage or salary income with any positive business or farm income, divided by the reported number of weeks worked in the previous year.

Independent Variables

Education and work experience are standard predictors of earnings (Borjas 1986, 1987; Model 2008). To account for these factors, each equation includes years of education and predicted work experience (age-education-6). To capture the nonlinear effect of work experience on earnings, work experience squared is also included in each model. Research suggests that labor market outcomes vary by marital status (Correll, Benard, and Paik 2007; Korenman and Neumark 1991). To account for this factor, each model includes a variable indicating whether an individual is married with the spouse present. In addition, because some immigrants do not speak English or speak English poorly, each equation includes an indicator variable that equals 1 if an individual reports not speaking English or not speaking English well, and 0 otherwise (Chiswick 1991; Chiswick and Miller 1995). To account for the geographic clustering of different immigrant groups, the regression models also include an indicator for the exact metropolitan area in which a respondent resides. Finally, to capture differences in labor market conditions over time, the survey year of each observation is included in each regression.

Immigrants have less favorable labor market outcomes and are more likely to be employed in niche occupations when they first arrive in the United States because they are unfamiliar with the U.S. labor market. As they adapt to the host labor market, however, immigrants improve their labor market outcomes and are more likely to work outside of niche sectors of the economy (Borjas 1985; Waldinger, Bean and Bell-Rose 1999). We account for this factor in our regression models by including a set of variables that control for tenure of U.S.

residence. Labor market outcomes vary considerably by gender in the United States (Model 2008). Moreover, while some occupational niches are gender-neutral, others are extremely segmented by gender. Consequently, we analyze labor market outcomes separately for male and female immigrants.

To evaluate the importance of occupational niching for blacks, we create an odds ratio where the numerator represents the odds of working in a particular occupation for a particular group, and the denominator represents the odds of working in the same occupation for all other persons in the labor force (Rosenfeld and Tienda 1999, 100).

Using this measure, an odds ratio of 1 indicates that an immigrant group is proportionally represented in a particular occupation relative to other ethnic groups (Rosenfeld and Tienda 1999). An odds ratio greater than 1 means that a group is overrepresented, and an odds ratio of less than 1 means that a group is underrepresented in a particular occupation. While the analytical threshold for defining an occupational niche is arbitrary, consistent with prior studies, we define a group as having a niche in an occupation if the odds ratio is greater than 1.5 (Lee 2013; Wilson 2003).[1] The odds ratio is calculated separately for each group, in each of the fifteen metropolitan areas, and in each survey year.

We construct the occupational niche variable using the "OCC1990" variable contained in the IPUMS samples of the 2000 census and the 2010–2014 five-year file of the American Community Survey. The OCC1990 variable is a modified version of the 1990 Census Bureau occupational classification scheme. The original 1990 occupation scheme contained 514 categories. OCC1990 combines a number of occupational categories to maximize the variable's consistency over time. The resulting OCC1990 classification scheme contains 389 categories. To avoid small cell sizes, we further collapse these 389 categories down to 79 categories. Given that occupational niches vary across time and place, we allow niches to vary across both metropolitan areas and survey years. For example, the construction of the niche variable allows black Jamaican immigrants to have a different set of niches in Washington, D.C., and in New York. It is also possible for the exact set of niches to vary in 2000 and 2010 for black Jamaican immigrants. Moreover, an occupation is not considered a niche unless at least 200 individuals are employed in it in a given metropolitan area and year (Wilson 2003). We treat the 2010 to 2014 time period as a single cross-section of data to allow for sufficient sample sizes across time periods.

The Empirical Model

The following equations show the fully specified empirical models used in the study. Models are estimated using ordinary least squares (OLS) regression.

$$Log(Y_i) = X_i\beta + C_i\gamma + A_i\theta + T_i\pi + \varepsilon_i, \quad (1)$$

$$Log(Y_i) = X_i\beta + O_i\delta + C_i\gamma + A_i\theta + T_i\pi + \varepsilon_i, \quad (2)$$

$$Log(Y_i) = \alpha_1 niching + X_i\beta + C_i\gamma + A_i\theta + T_i\pi + \varepsilon_i, \quad (3)$$

$$Log(Y_i) = \alpha_1 niching + O_i\delta + X_i\beta + C_i\gamma + A_i\theta + T_i\pi + \varepsilon_i. \quad (4)$$

In equation 1, Y is weekly earnings. X is a vector of standard social and demographic characteristics that include predicted experience, predicted experience squared, education, marital status, an indicator for each of the fifteen metropolitan areas, English proficiency, and citizenship status. C is a vector of dummy variables identifying immigrants' country of birth. The reference group for these variables is U.S.-born blacks. A is a vector of dummy variables indicating how long an immigrant has lived in the United States; these variables are set to 0 for U.S. native-born individuals, and the reference group is immigrants who have resided in the United States for more than fifteen years. T is a vector of dummy variables indicating the survey year of each observation. Equa-

---

1. We also estimate models in which occupational niches are defined by an odds ratio of 2. This change does not affect any of the substantive findings reported in this article.

tion 1 serves as the base model for the study and establishes the magnitude of the wage gap between black immigrants and native blacks.

Equations 2 to 4 attempt to isolate the impact on earnings of employment in a particular occupation from the impact of employment in an occupation that is an occupational niche. Immigrants' social networks might help new immigrants find employment in an occupation where their group clusters. After employment is secured, niche employment might not offer any additional benefits. Under this scenario, after controlling for occupation, the niche variable might not have a significant association with earnings. Alternatively, if employment in an occupation with a relatively large number of coethnics leads to greater earnings than employment in the same occupation with a limited number of coethnics, then, after controlling for occupation, niching would have a statistically significant positive association with earnings.

To examine these possibilities, equation 2 augments equation 1 by including O, a vector of dummy variables that identify the occupation of each respondent. Consequently, wage differences among blacks in equation 2 are based on wage variation between immigrants and native blacks employed in the same occupation. Equation 3 augments equation 1 by including an indicator for whether an individual is employed in a niche occupation. Finally, equation 4, the full model, includes both O and an indicator for whether an individual is employed in a niche.[2] Equation 4 examines whether ethnic niche employment is statistically associated with earnings after adjusting for differences in occupation. This niche variable is estimated using variation among individuals with the same occupation.

Given that the impact of niching on earnings varies across origin countries, we also estimate regression models based on equation 4 that include a set of interactions between country of birth and the niche indicator.

Descriptive Results

Table 1 shows descriptive statistics for native and immigrant black men and women, with the immigrant sample stratified by birth country. Tables 2 and 3 show descriptive statistics for individuals employed in niche occupations and for those employed outside of niche occupations, respectively.

Across the subgroups identified, table 1 shows considerable variation in niche employment. U.S.-born blacks and black immigrants from Guyana had the smallest proportion of individuals employed in occupational niches (36 percent). Among Caribbean immigrants, those from the Dominican Republic (55 percent) and Haiti (55 percent) had the largest percentages of individuals employed in niche occupations, and those from Guyana (36 percent) had the smallest share. Among the three countries from sub-Saharan Africa, Nigeria (52 percent) had the smallest share of individuals employed in niche sectors, ten percentage points less than Ghana and thirteen percentage points less than Ethiopia.

In addition, table 1 shows considerable differences in weekly earnings across the subgroups. For example, black immigrants from Nigeria ($1,062) had higher weekly earnings than U.S.-born blacks ($859) as well as all the other black immigrant subgroups. In contrast, immigrants from the Dominican Republic ($652) and Haiti ($685) earned the least.

The demographic and socioeconomic characteristics of blacks in the sample also vary substantially. Looking at educational attainment, one of the strongest predictors of earnings, table 1 shows that, on average, U.S.-born blacks had 13.27 years of education. Among all blacks, black immigrants from the Dominican Republic had the lowest (11.97) mean years of education, and immigrants from Nigeria had the highest (15.11) mean years of education.

Table 1 also indicates that immigration patterns differ significantly between immigrants from the Caribbean and those born in Africa.

---

2. In supplemental analysis, tables 4 and 5 were reestimated using data for each survey year. The substantive results from these analyses are the same as those presented here. For simplicity, we use the same arguments to represent the coefficients in equations 1 to 4. However, we are not assuming that the coefficient values or error terms are constant across the empirical models.

Table 1. Descriptive Statistics of Analytic Sample by Country of Birth

	(1)	(2)	(3)	Caribbean (4)	(5)	(6)	(7)	African (8)	(9)
	U.S.-Born Blacks	Dominican Republic	Haiti	Jamaica	Trinidad and Tobago	Guyana	Ghana	Nigeria	Ethiopia
Occupational niche: index value 1.5	0.36	0.55	0.55	0.37	0.43	0.36	0.62	0.52	0.65
Social and economic characteristics									
Positive earning	859.31	652.40	684.57	840.26	855.91	884.77	879.07	1061.77	770.33
Education	13.27	11.97	12.30	12.98	13.04	13.15	13.45	15.11	13.38
Experience	22.66	25.16	25.98	25.51	25.84	25.48	23.60	22.52	20.91
Speaks poor English	0.00	0.38	0.18	0.00	0.00	0.00	0.03	0.01	0.07
Female	0.55	0.50	0.51	0.56	0.55	0.55	0.42	0.41	0.46
Married	0.37	0.42	0.50	0.46	0.46	0.51	0.48	0.62	0.49
Citizen		0.54	0.58	0.64	0.60	0.71	0.50	0.59	0.57
Years of U.S. residence									
Zero to five years		0.11	0.09	0.08	0.05	0.07	0.19	0.17	0.21
Six to ten years		0.15	0.13	0.12	0.12	0.13	0.23	0.15	0.24
Eleven to fifteen years		0.15	0.18	0.16	0.18	0.16	0.20	0.20	0.21
Sixteen to twenty years		0.17	0.18	0.17	0.14	0.18	0.14	0.18	0.13
More than twenty years		0.41	0.42	0.48	0.51	0.45	0.24	0.30	0.20
Observations	313,262	2,306	14,340	18,972	5,499	3,864	2,961	5,062	2,915

Sources: 2000 U.S. census of population and 2010–2014 American Community Survey (ACS).

A larger share of immigrants from African countries were more recent arrivals. For example, column 4 shows that 8 percent of Jamaican immigrants came to the United States within the last five years. In contrast, column 8 shows that 17 percent of Nigerian immigrants arrived during this period. Similarly, 48 percent of immigrants from Jamaica had resided in the United States for more than twenty years, compared to only 30 percent of Nigerian immigrants.

Tables 2 and 3 show descriptive statistics for individuals who were and were not employed in niche occupations, respectively. Together, these tables highlight two interesting data patterns. First, with the exception of Nigerians, across the subgroups, individuals employed in occupational niches earned considerably less than those employed outside of occupational niches. Second, individuals employed in niche occupations had lower mean years of education than those employed outside of niches, suggesting that niching is more common among less-educated blacks.

Multivariate Results

This section presents OLS regression models of log weekly earnings. Column 1 of table 4 shows estimates from our base model (equation 1) for the entire male sample. It establishes our baseline estimates before adjusting for occupational niching or occupational composition. The results from this model show that, with the exception of black immigrants from Jamaica, Trinidad and Tobago, and Guyana, the adjusted earnings of all other black immigrant subgroups were lower than or similar to those of U.S.-born blacks, the reference group. Relative to U.S.-born black men, men from Ethiopia had the largest earnings deficits. Column 1 of table 4 also shows how male immigrants' earnings changed the longer they live in the United States. Immigrants who have resided in the United States for more than fifteen years are the reference group for the years of U.S. residence variables. The coefficients on years of U.S. residence variables are universally negative, and less negative for the categories showing longer tenures of U.S. residence. These results suggest that immigrants' earnings increase the longer they live in the United States, a finding consistent with prior studies (Hamilton 2014).

Column 2 of table 4 presents estimates from equation 2, which includes a set of dummy variables for a person's current occupation. Among male immigrants from the Caribbean, controlling for current occupation has no impact on earnings disparities between U.S.-born blacks and black immigrant men from Haiti. Relative to the results in column 1, however, accounting for occupation differences reduces the estimate on the Jamaica coefficient by 42 percent, from 0.07 to 0.04. Moreover, while the Trinidad and Tobago and Guyana coefficients are both statistically and substantially significant in column 1, they lose their significance after accounting for respondents' occupations. This change suggests that differences in earnings between U.S.-born blacks and black immigrants from Trinidad and Tobago and Guyana are driven largely by differences in the distribution of occupations held by members of each group.

Among immigrants from Africa, columns 1 and 2 show that controlling for occupation has no substantive impact on the Ghana or Ethiopia coefficient. By contrast, adjusting for occupation changes the significance and increases the adjusted earnings deficit for immigrants from Nigeria, changing the coefficient from –0.04 to –0.08. This result suggests that, relative to similarly skilled U.S.-born black men, black men from Nigeria tend to hold jobs in better paying occupations.

Column 3 of table 4 presents estimates based on equation 3 for men, which includes a variable that captures whether the respondent is employed in an occupational niche. Importantly, this model does not include controls for occupation. Consequently, comparing the results from columns 1 and 2 to those in column 3 allows us to examine the degree to which adjusting for occupational niches differs from adjusting for occupation. In other words, we can see whether controlling for niche employment, characterized by the overrepresentation of own-group members in a particular occupation, and simply accounting for occupation has a different impact on earnings disparities among blacks.

Consistent with the descriptive results, column 3 shows that men employed in niche oc-

Table 2. Descriptive Statistics of Analytic Sample by Country of Birth Among Individuals Who Work in an Occupational Niche

	(1)	(2)	(3)	Caribbean (4)	(5)	(6)	(7)	African (8)	(9)
	U.S.-Born Blacks	Dominican Republic	Haiti	Jamaica	Trinidad and Tobago	Guyana	Ghana	Nigeria	Ethiopia
Social and economic characteristics									
Positive earning	715.85	532.65	584.16	756.88	795.85	749.48	809.24	1097.34	681.38
Education	12.76	11.15	11.61	12.60	12.78	12.50	13.15	15.02	13.04
Experience	23.14	27.51	27.54	27.14	27.11	27.04	23.99	22.72	20.81
Speaks poor English	0.00	0.49	0.23	0.00	0.00	0.01	0.03	0.01	0.08
Female	0.54	0.53	0.57	0.74	0.67	0.61	0.47	0.48	0.46
Married	0.34	0.41	0.49	0.43	0.42	0.51	0.47	0.62	0.47
Citizen		0.47	0.55	0.63	0.58	0.68	0.51	0.60	0.55
Years of U.S. residence									
Zero to five years		0.14	0.10	0.08	0.06	0.09	0.20	0.17	0.23
Six to ten years		0.16	0.15	0.13	0.12	0.17	0.25	0.17	0.25
Eleven to fifteen years		0.17	0.19	0.18	0.19	0.16	0.20	0.22	0.22
Sixteen to twenty years		0.17	0.19	0.17	0.14	0.18	0.14	0.18	0.13
More than twenty years		0.37	0.38	0.44	0.49	0.40	0.21	0.27	0.17
Observations	105,911	1,236	7,831	6,838	2,217	1,346	1,764	2,542	1,786

Sources: 2000 U.S. census of population and 2010–2014 ACS.

Table 3. Descriptive Statistics of Analytic Sample by Country of Birth Among Individuals Who Do Not Work in an Occupational Niche

	(1)	(2)	(3)	(4)	(5)	(6)	(7)	(8)	(9)
				Caribbean				African	
	U.S.-Born Blacks	Dominican Republic	Haiti	Jamaica	Trinidad and Tobago	Guyana	Ghana	Nigeria	Ethiopia
Social and economic characteristics									
Positive earning	939.50	799.24	809.17	889.50	900.78	962.06	995.36	1023.29	936.21
Education	13.64	12.98	13.17	13.20	13.24	13.52	13.96	15.20	14.02
Experience	22.42	22.27	24.04	24.55	24.89	24.58	22.94	22.31	21.11
Speaks poor English	0.00	0.25	0.12	0.00	0.00	0.00	0.03	0.01	0.05
Female	0.55	0.45	0.43	0.45	0.47	0.51	0.33	0.33	0.46
Married	0.39	0.42	0.51	0.48	0.49	0.51	0.50	0.61	0.52
Citizen		0.63	0.62	0.65	0.62	0.73	0.49	0.58	0.61
Years of U.S. residence									
Zero to five years		0.09	0.07	0.07	0.05	0.07	0.18	0.18	0.18
Six to ten years		0.13	0.12	0.11	0.11	0.10	0.18	0.14	0.21
Eleven to fifteen years		0.14	0.17	0.15	0.17	0.16	0.21	0.18	0.19
Sixteen to twenty years		0.18	0.17	0.16	0.14	0.19	0.14	0.18	0.15
More than twenty years		0.46	0.47	0.50	0.53	0.48	0.28	0.33	0.26
Observations	190,524	1,070	6,509	12,134	3,282	2,518	1,197	2,520	1,129

Sources: 2000 U.S. census of population and 2010–2014 ACS.

Table 4. Regression of Log Weekly Earnings for U.S.-Born and Immigrant Black Men

	Men				
	(1)	(2)	(3)	(4)	(5)
	Base Model	Occupation Fixed Effects	Niching	Full	Interaction
Country of birth (reference: U.S.-born blacks)					
Caribbean countries					
Dominican Republic	−0.04	−0.05*	−0.03	−0.06*	−0.07*
	(0.02)	(0.02)	(0.02)	(0.02)	(0.03)
Haiti	−0.05***	−0.05***	−0.04***	−0.05***	−0.06***
	(0.01)	(0.01)	(0.01)	(0.01)	(0.01)
Jamaica	0.07***	0.04***	0.06***	0.04***	0.04***
	(0.01)	(0.01)	(0.01)	(0.01)	(0.01)
Trinidad and Tobago	0.03*	0.00	0.03*	0.00	0.00
	(0.02)	(0.02)	(0.02)	(0.02)	(0.02)
Guyana	0.05**	0.02	0.05**	0.02	0.03
	(0.02)	(0.02)	(0.02)	(0.02)	(0.02)
African countries					
Ghana	−0.02	−0.02	0.01	−0.02	−0.03
	(0.02)	(0.02)	(0.02)	(0.02)	(0.03)
Nigeria	−0.04**	−0.08***	−0.02	−0.09***	−0.09***
	(0.01)	(0.01)	(0.01)	(0.01)	(0.02)
Ethiopia	−0.17***	−0.16***	−0.14***	−0.16***	−0.06*
	(0.02)	(0.02)	(0.02)	(0.02)	(0.03)
Years of U.S. residence (reference:					
more than fifteen years)					
Zero to five years	−0.20***	−0.15***	−0.20***	−0.15***	−0.15***
	(0.02)	(0.02)	(0.02)	(0.02)	(0.02)
Six to ten years	−0.07***	−0.05***	−0.06***	−0.04***	−0.04***
	(0.01)	(0.01)	(0.01)	(0.01)	(0.01)
Eleven to fifteen years	−0.04**	−0.03*	−0.04**	−0.03*	−0.03*
	(0.01)	(0.01)	(0.01)	(0.01)	(0.01)
Occupational niche: index value 1.5			−0.12***	0.02***	0.02***
			(0.00)	(0.01)	(0.01)
Dominican Republic x niche					0.03
					(0.04)
Haiti x niche					0.03
					(0.02)
Jamaica x niche					−0.02
					(0.02)
Trinidad and Tobago x niche					0.00
					(0.03)
Guyana x niche					−0.01
					(0.04)
Ghana x niche					0.02
					(0.03)
Nigeria x niche					0.02
					(0.03)
Ethiopia x niche					−0.16***
					(0.04)
Observations	157,071	157,071	157,071	157,071	157,071
R-squared	0.17	0.25	0.17	0.25	0.25

Sources: 2000 U.S. census of population and 2010–2014 ACS.
Note: All models also control for education, experience, experience squared, English proficiency, marital status, citizenship, survey year, and a set of dummy variables for metropolitan area.
*p < .05; **p < .01; ***p < .001

cupations earned less than men who are not employed in non-niche occupations (−0.12). Relative to the results in column 1, our baseline model, the inclusion of the occupational niche variable into the regression model has either no effect or a very modest impact on most of the birth country coefficients. Two notable exceptions are the results for men from Nigeria and Ethiopia. Relative to the results from column 1, the coefficients on Nigeria and Ethiopia increase in magnitude (become less negative). This finding suggests that men from these two countries tend to find employment in low-earnings niche occupations.

Because column 3 does not include occupation, the niche variable is based on variation across occupations. Consequently, the niche variable captures both the impact of employment in a particular occupation and the impact of employment in an occupation in which own-group members are overrepresented (a niche). To determine whether the results in column 3 are driven by variation in the distribution of occupations held by respondents, column 4 of table 4 uses a regression model that takes into account both occupation and niching. After controlling for respondent occupation, the occupational niche variable remains statistically significant, but the sign on the coefficient changes from negative to positive. This result suggests that among individuals with the same occupation, those for whom that occupation is a niche earn more.

Comparing the results in column 2 to those in column 4 provides insights into whether niche-sector employment is a primary driver of earnings disparities among blacks. Note that the coefficients on the birth country variables in columns 2 and 4 of table 4 are nearly identical. Thus, after accounting for occupation, niche employment does not explain earnings disparities between U.S.-born blacks and most subgroups of black immigrants. Together, these results suggest that niching is more likely to occur in low-wage occupations. When U.S.-born blacks and black immigrants with the same occupation are compared, however, niche employment, on average, is modestly associated with greater earnings.

To determine whether the association between niche employment and earnings varies across subgroups, in column 5 we interact the niche indicator with each birth country indicator. In these models, the main effect for occupational niching represents the relationship between niching and wages for U.S.-born blacks, while the coefficients on the interaction terms represent the additional impact of niching on wages for a particular foreign-born group. The coefficient on the occupational niche variable in column 5 is positive and statistically significant, suggesting that U.S.-born black men employed in niche sectors earn approximately 2 percent more than comparably skilled U.S.-born black men employed outside of niche sectors. With the exception of the interaction term for Ethiopian immigrants, all the interaction terms are statistically insignificant, suggesting that there are no additional returns to niche employment for most black immigrant men relative to U.S.-born men. Ethiopian men employed in niche occupations earn approximately 16 percent less than U.S.-born black men employed in niche occupations.

Table 5 shows the results of these models for the sample of women. Column 1 of table 5 shows that women from Jamaica, Trinidad and Tobago, Guyana, and Ghana had significantly greater earnings than U.S.-born black women. In contrast, relative to U.S.-born black women, black immigrant women from the Dominican Republic and Ethiopia had lower adjusted earnings and women from Haiti and Nigeria had similar adjusted earnings. Column 2 shows how earnings disparities among black women change after adjusting for variation in current occupation. The inclusion of occupational controls has no substantive impact on the Jamaica, Trinidad and Tobago, and Guyana coefficients, suggesting that the differences in the distribution of occupations do not explain disparities between these groups and U.S.-born black women. In contrast, the coefficient on the Dominican Republic, Ethiopia, Haiti, and Ghana variables increases in magnitude after accounting for occupation. This result suggests that relative to U.S.-born black women, these immigrant women tend to gravitate toward lower-paying occupations.

Similar to the results for men, column 3 shows that black women employed in niche

Table 5. Regression of Log Weekly Earnings for U.S.-Born and Immigrant Black Women

	Women				
	(1)	(2)	(3)	(4)	(5)
	Base Model	Occupation Fixed Effects	Niching	Full	Interaction
Country of birth: (reference: U.S.-born blacks)					
Caribbean countries					
Dominican Republic	-0.16***	-0.10***	-0.15***	-0.10***	-0.10**
	(0.02)	(0.02)	(0.02)	(0.02)	(0.03)
Haiti	0.00	0.05***	0.02	0.04***	-0.04**
	(0.01)	(0.01)	(0.01)	(0.01)	(0.01)
Jamaica	0.08***	0.09***	0.10***	0.08***	0.06***
	(0.01)	(0.01)	(0.01)	(0.01)	(0.01)
Trinidad and Tobago	0.05***	0.05***	0.06***	0.05***	0.03
	(0.01)	(0.01)	(0.01)	(0.01)	(0.02)
Guyana	0.05**	0.04*	0.05**	0.04*	0.05*
	(0.02)	(0.02)	(0.02)	(0.02)	(0.02)
African countries					
Ghana	0.08***	0.11***	0.11***	0.11***	0.05
	(0.02)	(0.02)	(0.02)	(0.02)	(0.03)
Nigeria	0.03	-0.02	0.05**	-0.02	-0.07**
	(0.02)	(0.02)	(0.02)	(0.02)	(0.02)
Ethiopia	-0.08***	-0.03	-0.06**	-0.04	-0.04
	(0.02)	(0.02)	(0.02)	(0.02)	(0.03)
Years of U.S. residence (reference: more than fifteen years)					
Zero to five years	-0.21***	-0.14***	-0.21***	-0.14***	-0.14***
	(0.02)	(0.02)	(0.02)	(0.02)	(0.02)
Six to ten years	-0.14***	-0.08***	-0.13***	-0.08***	-0.09***
	(0.01)	(0.01)	(0.01)	(0.01)	(0.01)
Eleven to fifteen years	-0.07***	-0.04**	-0.06***	-0.04***	-0.04***
	(0.01)	(0.01)	(0.01)	(0.01)	(0.01)
Occupational niche: index value 1.5			-0.10***	0.03***	0.01
			(0.00)	(0.01)	(0.01)
Dominican Republic x niche					0.01
					(0.04)
Haiti x niche					0.16***
					(0.02)
Jamaica x niche					0.08***
					(0.01)
Trinidad and Tobago x niche					0.06*
					(0.02)
Guyana x niche					-0.01
					(0.03)
Ghana x niche					0.11**
					(0.04)
Nigeria x niche					0.10**
					(0.03)
Ethiopia x niche					0.03
					(0.04)
Observations	195,300	195,300	195,300	195,300	195,300
R-squared	0.19	0.29	0.20	0.29	0.29

Sources: 2000 U.S. census of population and 2010–2014 ACS.
Note: All models also control for education, experience, experience squared, English proficiency, marital status, citizenship, survey year, and a set of dummy variables for metropolitan area.
*$p < .05$; **$p < .01$; ***$p < .001$

occupations earned less (−0.10) than women employed outside of niche occupations. Column 3 also indicates that accounting for niche employment either has no impact or modestly increases the magnitude of the immigrant birth country variables relative to column 1.

The model used in column 4 controls for both occupation and niche employment for women. Similar to the results for men, after including occupation controls, the occupational niche variable remains statistically significant, but the sign on the coefficient changes from negative to positive, suggesting that women employed in niche occupations earn slightly more (0.02) than similarly skilled women employed outside of niche occupations. Again similar to the results for men, the fact that results in column 4 of table 5 are virtually identical to those found in column 2 implies that differences in occupations between immigrant and U.S.-born black women account for more of the variation in weekly earnings between the groups than differences in niching patterns.

Finally, column 5 looks for differences in the relationship between niching and wages across groups. In contrast to the results for U.S.-born men, niching is not significantly correlated with wages for U.S.-born black women. Also in contrast to the results for men, niching is significantly and positively correlated with greater wages for five of the eight immigrant women subgroups. This finding suggests that the niche result in column 4 is primarily driven by immigrant women.

DISCUSSION

Four key findings emerge from this study. First, consistent with prior research, after adjusting for a standard set of labor market characteristics, only black immigrant men from the English-speaking Caribbean (Jamaica, Trinidad and Tobago, and Guyana) had greater earnings than U.S.-born black men. Black immigrants from the other countries studied had similar or lower adjusted earnings. In contrast, every subgroup of black immigrant women except Dominicans and Ethiopians had earnings similar to or greater than those of U.S.-born black women. Second, after controlling for occupational choice, employment in an occupational niche has a small, positive association with earnings (approximately 2 percent for men and 3 percent for women). Models interacting niche employment with country of birth show that the returns to niche employment are similar for U.S.-born black men and most country subgroups of black immigrant men. In contrast, relative to U.S.-born black women, most subgroups of black immigrant women have greater earnings returns to niche employment. Finally, although we document variation in both niche employment and returns to niche employment for earnings, the results suggest that niching does not account for earnings disparities among blacks in the United States.

These findings raise two important questions about the role of niche-sector employment in understanding earnings disparities among blacks in the United States.

1. Why does niche-sector employment seem to play such a limited role in labor market disparities among blacks in the United States? Waldinger (1996) shows that the clustering of coethnics in particular occupations or industries is largely a network-based phenomenon. The social networks found within particular ethnic communities facilitate the flow of information about job opportunities to other coethnics seeking employment. Although our results suggest that this phenomenon may lead to the clustering of different immigrant groups in particular occupations, they also suggest, after accounting for choice of occupation, that the overrepresentation of coethnics within an occupation does not account for earnings disparities between blacks in the United States.

These results are largely consistent with prior research. Model (1997a) compares the economic attainment of ethnic group members within their ethnic economy industries with that of "outsiders" in the same industries. She finds few differences in economic attainment. Together, these findings suggest that occupation choice itself is more consequential than employment in an occupation with a large number of coethnics for understanding earnings disparities among blacks by nativity.

2. What explains variation in the returns to niche employment among blacks? Among men, returns to niche employment for earnings are statistically similar for both U.S.-born and most black immigrant subgroups. This finding suggests that black men in general tend to form niches in sectors where the presence of coethnics does not facilitate upward mobility. Similar to U.S.-born black men, black immigrant men tend to niche in occupations such as motor vehicle operators, cleaning services workers, and security guards. The presence of niches in these occupations may provide access to jobs, but because they tend to be low-paying jobs that offer few opportunities for advancement, the role that coethnics can play in aiding upward mobility is limited.

In contrast to the results for men, subgroups of black immigrant women from both the Caribbean and sub-Saharan Africa had greater returns to niche employment than U.S.-born black women. This suggests that immigrant women tend to form niches in occupations where the presence of coethnics is beneficial. Like immigrant men, black immigrant women tend to form niches in low-paying occupations with few opportunities for advancement (such as private household work), but a number of niche occupations for immigrant women offer considerable pathways for upward mobility. For example, health care occupations, such as nurses and nurse's aides, are two of the largest niches for women from both sub-Saharan Africa and the Caribbean (authors' tabulations). Both of these occupations offer coethnics pathways to aid each other to upward mobility. Additionally, many of the primary niches that employ U.S.-born black women are in the public sector (Kasinitz and Vickerman 2001; Waldinger 1996). Although these occupations offer opportunities for upward mobility, they often require advanced education, and their more bureaucratic workplaces, with stringent hiring and promotion protocols, may mitigate the influence of coethnic ties (Kasinitz and Vickerman 2001).

Our results also show that the returns to niche employment vary among black immigrant women, among whom Haitian women have the largest returns to niche employment followed by women from Ghana and Nigeria, then by women from Jamaica and Trinidad and Tobago. This variation is likely to be driven by differences in education and U.S. tenure across the groups, which could lead to the formation of different types of niches as well as region-specific demand for female labor.

CONCLUSION

During the 1990s and 2000s, waves of black immigrants drastically changed the composition of the black population in the United States. Although flows of black immigrants from the Caribbean to the United States date back to the early 1900s (Model 2008), fewer than 60,000 black individuals migrated to the United States from Africa prior to 1990. In contrast, 323,000 black Africans migrated during the 1990s, and another 353,000 between 2000 and 2005 (Kent 2007).

Immigrant occupational niches, an important aspect of the assimilation process for many immigrants, are often associated with favorable labor market outcomes (Lee 2013; Waldinger 2001). Despite the growing demographic diversity of the black immigrant population, few studies have examined the degree to which occupational niche employment explains variation in earnings between U.S.-born blacks and black immigrants or among black immigrants. Our findings show that while occupational niche employment does not explain variation in earnings between the two groups, niche employment remains an important aspect of the economic incorporation of black immigrants, particularly immigrant women.

REFERENCES

Adelman, Robert M., Hui-shien Tsao, and Stewart E. Tolnay. 2006. "Occupational Disparity in a Migrant Metropolis: A Case Study of Atlanta." *Sociological Spectrum* 26(3): 269–87.

Anderson, Monica. 2015. "A Rising Share of the U.S. Black Population Is Foreign Born." Washington, D.C.: Pew Research Center.

Borjas, George J. 1985. "Assimilation, Changes in Cohort Quality, and the Earnings of Immigrants." *Journal of Labor Economics* 3(4): 463–89.

———. 1986. "The Self-Employment Experience of Immigrants." *Journal of Human Resources* 21(4): 485–506.

———. 1987. "Self-Selection and the Earnings of Immigrants." *American Economic Review* 77(4): 531–53.

Chiswick, Barry R. 1991. "Speaking, Reading, and

Earnings among Low-Skilled Immigrants." *Journal of Labor Economics* 9(2): 149-70.

Chiswick, Barry R., and Paul W. Miller. 1995. "The Endogeneity Between Language and Earnings: International Analyses." *Journal of Labor Economics* 13(2): 246-88.

Correll, Shelley J., Stephen Benard, and In Paik. 2007. "Getting a Job: Is There a Motherhood Penalty?" *American Journal of Sociology* 112(5): 1297-1339.

Eckstein, Susan, and Giovanni Peri. 2018. "Immigrant Niches and Immigrant Networks in the U.S. Labor Market." *RSF: The Russell Sage Foundation Journal of the Social Sciences* 4(1): 1-17. DOI: 10.7758/RSF.2018.4.1.01.

Foner, Nancy. 1985. "Race and Color: Jamaican Migrants in London and New York City." *International Migration Review* 19(4): 708-27.

———. 2009. "Gender and Migration: West Indians in Comparative Perspective." *International Migration* 47(1): 3-29.

Fong, Eric, and Jing Shen. 2011. "Explaining Ethnic Enclave, Ethnic Entrepreneurial and Employment Niches: A Case Study of Chinese in Canadian Immigrant Gateway Cities." *Urban Studies* 48(8): 1605-33.

Gold, Steven J. 2018. "Israeli Infotech Migrants in Silicon Valley." *RSF: The Russell Sage Foundation Journal of the Social Sciences* 4(1): 130-48. DOI: 10.7758/RSF.2018.4.1.08.

Hamilton, Tod G. 2014. "Selection, Language Heritage, and the Earnings Trajectories of Black Immigrants in the United States." *Demography* 51(3): 975-1002.

Ifatunji, Mosi Adesina. 2016. "A Test of the Afro Caribbean Model Minority Hypothesis." *Du Bois Review: Social Science Research on Race* 13(1): 109-38.

Kasinitz, Philip. 1992. *Caribbean New York: Black Immigrants and the Politics of Race*. Ithaca, N.Y.: Cornell University Press.

Kasinitz, Philip, and Milton Vickerman. 2001. "Ethnic Niches and Racial Traps: Jamaicans in the New York Regional Economy." In *Migration, Transnationalization, and Race in a Changing New York*, edited by Héctor R. Cordero-Guzmán, Robert C. Smith, and Ramón Grosfoguel (Philadelphia: Temple University Press).

Kent, Mary Mederios. 2007. "Immigration and America's Black Population." *Population Bulletin* 62(4): 1-16.

Korenman, Sanders, and David Neumark. 1991. "Does Marriage Really Make Men More Productive?" *Journal of Human Resources* 26(2): 282-307.

Lee, Jennifer C. 2013. "Employment and Earnings in High-Tech Ethnic Niches." *Social Forces* 91(3): 747-84.

Light, Ivan, and Steven J. Gold. 2000. *Ethnic Economies*. Bingley, U.K.: Emerald Group.

Logan, John R., and Richard D. Alba. 1999. "Minority Niches and Immigrant Enclaves in New York and Los Angeles: Trends and Impacts." In *Immigration and Opportunity: Race, Ethnicity, and Employment in the United States*, edited by Frank Bean and Stephanie Bell-Rose. New York: Russell Sage Foundation.

Model, Suzanne. 1997a. "Ethnic Economy and Industry in Mid-Twentieth-Century Gotham." *Social Problems* 44(4): 445-63.

———. 1997b. "An Occupational Tale of Two Cities: Minorities in London and New York." *Demography* 34(4): 539-50.

———. 2008. *West Indian Immigrants: A Black Success Story?* New York: Russell Sage Foundation.

Model, Suzanne, and Gene Fisher 2001. "Black-White Unions: West Indians and African Americans Compared." *Demography* 38(2): 177-85.

Portes, Alejandro, and Leif Jensen. 1989. "The Enclave and the Entrants: Patterns of Ethnic Enterprise in Miami Before and After Mariel." *American Sociological Review* 54(6): 929-49.

Portes, Alejandro, and Robert D. Manning. 2005. "The Immigrant Enclave: Theory and Empirical Examples." *The Urban Sociology Reader* 38: 583-94.

Portes, Alejandro, and Steven Shafer. 2007. "Revisiting the Enclave Hypothesis: Miami Twenty-Five Years Later." *Research in the Sociology of Organizations* 25: 157-90.

Rosenfeld, Michael J., and Marta Tienda. 1999. "Mexican Immigration, Occupational Niches, and Labor-Market Competition: Evidence from Los Angeles, Chicago, and Atlanta, 1970 to 1990." In *Immigration and Opportunity: Race, Ethnicity, and Employment in the United States*, edited by Frank Bean and Stephanie Bell-Rose. New York: Russell Sage Foundation.

Ruggles, Steven, Katie Genadek, Ronald Goeken, Josiah Grover, and Matthew Sobek. 2015. *Integrated Public Use Microdata Series: Version 6.0* [dataset]. Minneapolis: University of Minnesota. DOI: 10.18128/D010.V6.0.

Sowell, Thomas. 1975. *Race and Economics.* New York: David McKay.

———. 1978. "Three Black Histories." In *Essays and Data on American Ethnic Groups,* edited by Thomas Sowell and Lynn D. Collins. Washington, D.C.: Urban Institute.

———. 1981. *Ethnic America: A History.* New York: Basic Books.

———. 1983. *The Economics and Politics of Race: An International Perspective.* New York: William Morrow.

Vickerman, Milton. 1998. *Crosscurrents: West Indian Immigrants and Race.* New York: Oxford University Press.

Waldinger, Roger. 1994. "The Making of an Immigrant Niche." *International Migration Review* 28(1): 3–30.

———. 1996. *Still the Promised City? African-Americans and New Immigrants in Postindustrial New York.* Cambridge, Mass.: Harvard University Press.

———. 2001. *Strangers at the Gates: New Immigrants in Urban America.* Berkeley: University of California Press.

Waldinger, Roger, Frank Bean, and Stephanie Bell-Rose. 1999. *Immigration and Opportunity: Race, Ethnicity, and Employment.* New York: Russell Sage Foundation.

Waters, Mary C. 1999. *Black Identities: West Indian Immigrant Dreams and American Realities.* New York and Cambridge, Mass.: Russell Sage Foundation and Harvard University Press.

Wilson, Franklin D. 2003. "Ethnic Niching and Metropolitan Labor Markets." *Social Science Research* 32(3): 429–66.

The Rise of Market-Based Job Search Institutions and Job Niches for Low-Skilled Chinese Immigrants

ZAI LIANG AND BO ZHOU

Increasingly, market-based job search institutions, such as employment agencies and ethnic media, are playing a more important role than migrant networks for low-skilled Chinese immigrants searching for jobs. We argue that two major factors are driving this trend: the diversification of Chinese immigrants' provinces of origin, and the spatial diffusion of businesses in the United States owned by Chinese immigrants. We also identify some new niche jobs for Chinese immigrants and assess the extent to which this development is driven by China's growing prosperity. We use data from multiple sources, including a survey of employment agencies in Manhattan's Chinatown, job advertisements in Chinese-language newspapers, and information on Chinese immigrant hometown associations in the United States.

Keywords: employment agencies, networks, Chinese immigrants, ethnic media, job niches

Immigration scholars have long noted that immigrant groups tend to concentrate in certain occupations as they adapt to the U.S. labor market (Eckstein and Peri, this issue). Historically, Irish immigrant women were known to work as housemaids, Jewish immigrants specialized in the garment industry, and Italian immigrants were heavily represented in the construction business (Lieberson 1980; Portes and Rumbaut 2001; Rischin 1962; Waldinger 1986, 1994). Chinese immigrants, one of the oldest immigrant groups in the history of the United States, are no exception. In their early settlement in the United States, Chinese immigrants were known to concentrate in two major occupations: restaurant work and laundry work (Chen 2015; Siu and Tchen 1988; Sung 1967). Restaurant-related work was cited as one of the occupations pursued by Chinese immigrants in the United

Zai Liang is professor of sociology at the State University of New York at Albany. **Bo Zhou** is a doctoral candidate at the State University of New York at Albany.

© 2018 Russell Sage Foundation. Liang, Zai, and Bo Zhou. 2018. "The Rise of Market-Based Job Search Institutions and Job Niches for Low-Skilled Chinese Immigrants." *RSF: The Russell Sage Foundation Journal of the Social Sciences* 4(1): 78–95. DOI: 10.7758/RSF.2018.4.1.05. The portion of the study using data from a survey of employment agencies in New York City's Chinatown was supported by the Russell Sage Foundation (88-10-06), whose support is gratefully acknowledged. The 2004 Survey of Chinese Immigrants was supported by the National Institutes of Health (NIH) (R01 HD39720-0) and the Ford Foundation (1025-1056). We thank Jian Cao for assistance with historical data from Chinese newspapers and Feinuo Sun for gathering critical data on Chinese immigrant hometown associations in the United States. The authors also thank three anonymous reviewers and editors for very constructive comments and suggestions. Direct correspondence to: Zai Liang at zliang@albany.edu, Department of Sociology, State University of New York at Albany, Albany, NY 12222; and Bo Zhou at bzhou3@albany.edu.

States as early as the 1860 census (Kwong and Miščević 2005).

Some have argued that discrimination by mainstream society limited Chinese immigrants' occupational choices. After all, the first discriminatory immigration law in the United States, passed in 1882, targeted Chinese immigrants. Today, however, the occupational patterns of Chinese immigrants have fundamentally changed. Chinese immigrants can be found in diverse occupations, from engineers in Silicon Valley to professors in academic institutions, from workers in state or federal government to soldiers who fought in Iraq. Compared to Mexican immigrants in the United States, Chinese immigrants occupy two labor market niches: high-skilled jobs, on the one hand, and low-skilled jobs, on the other. Data from the 2013 American Community Survey (ACS) reveal that 42 percent of Chinese immigrants worked in high-skilled occupations and 46 percent in low-skilled occupations.[1] Only about 10 percent of Chinese immigrants worked in restaurant-related jobs.

Our article focuses on low-skilled Chinese immigrants because upward mobility is often a challenge for them, owing to low levels of education and sometimes lack of legal status (Eckstein and Peri, this issue). One major occupation we study is the Chinese restaurant business, which employs a great many immigrant workers. By some accounts, there are more than 40,000 Chinese restaurants in the United States—more than McDonald's, Burger King, and Wendy's combined (Lee 2008). Besides the large number of Chinese restaurants, several large Chinese restaurant chains—such as Panda Express (now operating 1,500 restaurants in the United States) and P. F. Chang's—have changed the landscape of the Chinese food service industry in the United States.

The purpose of this article is threefold. First, in documenting the continuing significance of restaurant work among a large number of low-skilled Chinese immigrants, we argue that the recruitment mechanisms for employing these immigrants in restaurant work have changed from traditional migrant networks to market-based institutions, such as employment agencies, the media, and the Internet. Second, using data from a variety of sources, we show that this change in the recruitment process has been driven by two major forces—the diversification of the provinces of Chinese migrant origin and the spatial diffusion of businesses owned by Chinese immigrants. Our third goal is to explore some emerging new Chinese immigrant job niches and evaluate the extent to which these niches are driven by the growing prosperity of China, as manifested in the growing number of Chinese tourists and China's investment in the United States. We also discuss the potential implications of the market-based institutions now used to recruit Chinese immigrants. Will they lead to Chinese-owned businesses becoming more akin to modern organizations than to traditional mom-and pop-operations? Most of the other articles in this issue use either a qualitative or a quantitative approach (Eckstein and Peri, this issue); we combine the two approaches, and we also rely in some cases on nontraditional data sources.

THE EMERGENCE OF MARKET-BASED JOB SEARCH INSTITUTIONS

One key difference between immigrants who work in niche jobs today and immigrants who worked in niche jobs forty years ago is the change in the methods they used to find their jobs. In particular, today's low-skilled Chinese immigrants rely on market-based institutions more than earlier immigrant cohorts did. In carefully observing the Chinese community in New York, we have noticed some major, sociologically interesting changes. Strolling through Chinatown in Manhattan, Flushing in Queens, or Sunset Park in Brooklyn, we frequently see, among the dazzling signs of restaurants, driving schools, legal services, and hometown associations (HAs), the signs of employment agencies (EAs). We have also become aware of the growing presence of EAs in the Chinese immigrant labor market through Chinese-language newspapers and Chinese yellow pages. In New York City alone, our online search came up with 132 EAs (excluding some duplicated entries). The lion's share of EAs are

---

1. Authors' calculations from 2013 ACS data.

Figure 1. Distribution of Employment Agencies by New York City Borough, 2016

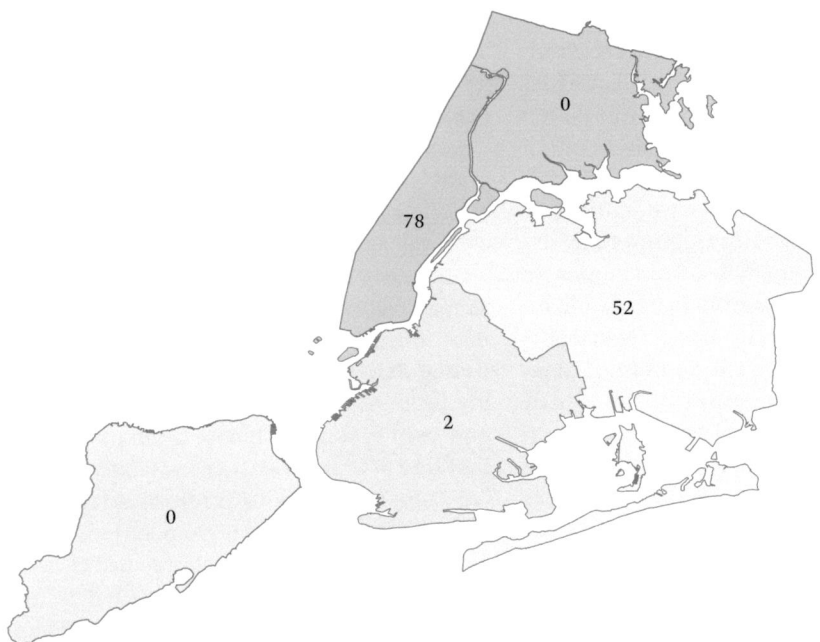

Source: Authors' compilation from "List of Employment Agencies by New York City Borough," 2017, available at: http://newyork.jinti.net/yellowpages/309_l0/ (accessed May 15, 2017).

located in Queens and Manhattan (see figure 1), and in Manhattan the vast majority are located in Chinatown, a main settlement area for low-skilled Chinese immigrants. The mushrooming of EAs is not only an East Coast phenomenon; a similar development has been reported in Los Angeles (Dolnick 2011). As students of immigration, we believe that this new pattern of job recruitment deserves our attention and further exploration.

NETWORK-BASED VERSUS MARKET-BASED JOB SEARCH PROCESSES

Much of the earlier sociological research on immigration focused on the so-called enclave economy, such as is found in Chinatown in Manhattan or among Cuban immigrants in Miami (Portes 2010; Wilson and Portes 1980; Zhou 1992). This literature continues and expands earlier work by Ivan Light (1984) and others who have explored the issues of immigrants and ethnic enterprises in the United States. Light's earlier work sought to explain variations in entrepreneurship by immigrant group, and he stressed the role of ethnic and class resources in the formation of immigrant enterprises. Subsequent sociological studies by Alejandro Portes (2010) and others (for example, Sanders and Nee 1987; Waldinger 1986) aimed to examine whether ethnic enclaves represent not simply a means of survival but an alternative vehicle for economic mobility. There is a consensus between the two strands of literature that immigrant workers become spatially concentrated in neighborhoods with an immigrant labor market based on a strong sense of immigrant identity and connection. For example, earlier immigrants who settled in Manhattan's Chinatown came mainly from Guangdong Province and spoke the same dialect. In this scenario—an immigrant group originating from the same place and being spatially concentrated in a particular neighborhood—migration networks work effectively to allocate immigrant labor for jobs in restaurants and laundry shops (the traditional Chinese immigrant job niches) (Massey, Goldring, and Durand 1994). Today the increase in the

Figure 2. Theoretical Framework

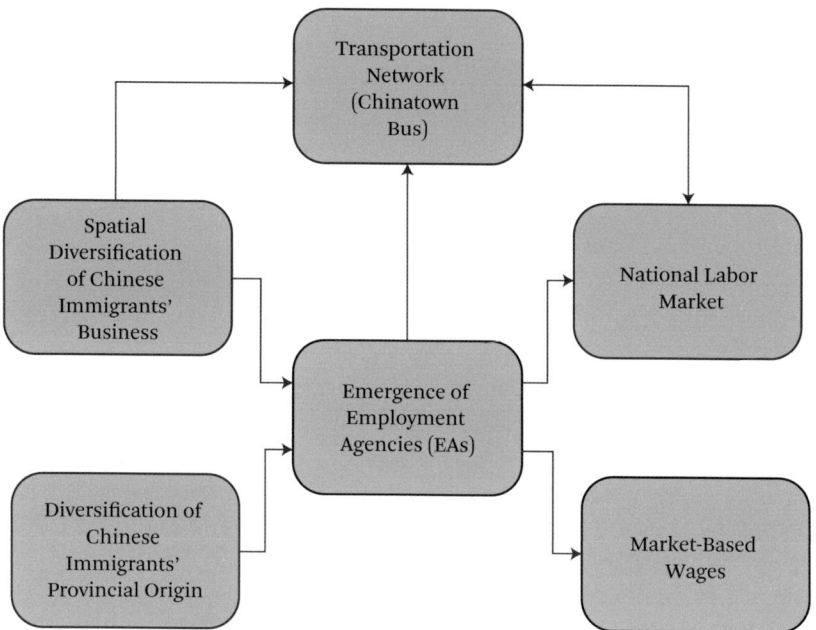

Source: Authors' compilation.

number of EAs reflects not only dramatic changes in the job search process for immigrants in the last two decades in the United States, but also changes in the size of immigrant groups, their origins, and the spatial diffusion of immigrant-owned businesses.

Figure 2 summarizes the logic and key components of our theoretical framework. Our core argument is that the emergence of EAs is a market-based response to two major forces: the diversification of Chinese immigrants' provinces of origins and the spatial diffusion of businesses owned by Chinese immigrants. This response has strong implications for both individual immigrants and the formation of a national labor market for low-skilled Chinese immigrants. For average low-skilled Chinese immigrants, we expect that market-based job searches will be more successful than searches conducted through a traditional migrant network. At the same time, the formation of a broad immigrant labor market has given rise to the establishment of national supply chain networks and immigrant-based transportation systems (such as Chinatown Bus). In turn, the national supply chain networks and transportation systems further strengthen and expand the broad labor market for Chinese immigrant workers. In the following sections, we elaborate our key arguments and present systematic empirical evidence.

DATA COLLECTION FOR THE STUDY

We have relied on multiple data sources for this study. The first is our own previous study of employment agencies in New York's Chinatown (Liang et al. 2015). We surveyed a total of thirty-two EAs in Chinatown, obtaining information on type of job, location, and salary for each sampled EA. Most of these EAs were located between Canal Street and East Broadway in Lower Manhattan rather than along Mott and Canal Streets, the traditional area of settlement for Cantonese immigrants. The majority of today's low-skilled Chinese immigrants no longer come from Guangdong Province but from Fujian Province, and they tend to settle along East Broadway. Another source of data for the present study is a 2004 survey of Chinese immigrants containing detailed information on respondents' job history, such as job changes, workplace location, and wages (for a detailed discussion of this survey, see Liang et al. 2008). We use these survey data to examine how immigrants' wages and wage growth are related to the job search methods they use.

The third data source is the Chinese-language newspaper *World Journal*. We use information on all job listings published on a day in February 2004, a day in February 2016, and another day in April 2016. Some employers posted one ad for several jobs. So, for example, we generated four positions in our data from an ad for a travel agency that needed four workers. For our analysis, we use two pieces of information from these job ads: types of jobs and locations of jobs.

To understand the growing diversification of the provincial origins of Chinese immigrants in the United States, we needed information on these provinces of origin, but this information was difficult to obtain. Typical data sources such as the U.S. census and the American Community Survey do not contain information on the province or state of immigrant origin. Thus, in collecting data on Chinese immigrant organizations, we assumed that the establishment of immigrant organizations from a specific Chinese province reflected a major increase in immigration from that province to the United States.[2] Given that most immigrant associations are headquartered in large cities or states with large populations of immigrants, we focused on Chinese immigrant organizations in New York City, Washington, D.C., California, and Texas.

We began the process by searching for 同乡会, the Chinese term for "hometown association," in selected locations (such as New York City). We looked through ten pages of search results looking for specific names of associations in that location. Sometimes we would find a useful link to an association's website and be able to obtain information on the year the association was established. Sometimes we found one website listing Chinese immigrant associations in a selected location (such as Washington, D.C.). Then we would search for reports on the anniversary events associated with each Chinese immigrant association in that location because they would help us identify the year the association was established. For example, an immigrant association having a twentieth-anniversary celebration in 2016 would have been established in 1996. When we could not find such information, we phoned or emailed the manager or another staff member of the Chinese immigrant association to inquire about the year of the association's founding.

Overall, the four data sources complement each other and provide a comprehensive portrait of the linkages among the diversification of Chinese immigrant origins, the spatial diffusion of Chinese immigrants, and the rise of market-based job search institutions. We should also mention some caveats: these data do have limitations. For example, our survey of employment agencies does not include jobs advertised in the *World Journal*. This limitation is overcome somewhat by our inclusion of the jobs posted in the Chinese-language newspaper. Likewise, our use of job information contained in the *World Journal* during the two months (February and April) may overlook potential seasonal variations. Finally, the information on Chinese immigrant associations obtained from the Internet is likely to be incomplete and to underestimate the number of Chinese immigrant associations in the United States.

THE INCREASING DIVERSIFICATION OF CHINESE IMMIGRANTS

In 2015, the U.S. Census Bureau reported that China had replaced Mexico as the number-one immigrant-sending country to the United States, as measured by migrant flow (Shah 2015).[3] The more than 150,000 Chinese immi-

---

2. The history of Chinese immigrant associations in the United States is consistent with this assumption. The Chinese Consolidated Benevolent Association was established in 1883 as the number of Chinese immigrants from Guangdong Province was increasing significantly (see the association's website at http://www.ccbanyc.org/eindex.html, accessed August 31, 2017). Likewise, the Fukien Benevolent Association of America (http://www.usfujian.com/viewthread.php?tid=21, accessed August 31, 2017) was established in New York City in 1942 because more and more immigrants from Fujian Province were arriving in the United States.

3. The Census Bureau defines an "immigrant" as a foreign-born person who was in a foreign country one year earlier and was living in the United States at the time of the American Community Survey.

grants who came to the United States in 2012 were recorded in the American Community Survey of 2013 (U.S. Census Bureau 2013). In 1990, there were 681,000 Chinese immigrants in the United States, and by 2000 that number had nearly doubled, reaching 1.2 million. By 2013, according to ACS data, there were 2 million Chinese immigrants, which is clearly an underestimate: a significant number of undocumented Chinese immigrants are often not counted in the official data.

To most casual observers, all Chinese immigrants are the same, or at least not that different. In reality, however, there are significant variations between the Chinese immigrants we observe today and Chinese immigrants thirty or forty years ago. Most Chinese immigrants in the United States before 1965 came from Guangdong Province in southern China and spoke Cantonese (Nee and Nee 1974; Sung 1967). They were often seen in Chinatowns in different cities and either worked in restaurants and laundry businesses or ran grocery stores and gift shops.

Today immigrants from China are fundamentally different and represent much broader origins in China—an immigration trend that has been recently reported on by National Public Radio (Wang 2016). In April 2016, the humorist Calvin Trillin (2016), a longtime *New Yorker* contributor, wrote a poem complaining that Americans could not keep up with the different Chinese regional cuisines. "Have they run out of provinces yet? / If they haven't, we've reason to fret." The poem may be innocent and humorous, but it actually created something of a global controversy: commentators from both the United States and China joined the debate (Li 2016; Ramzy 2016). The English edition of the influential *Global Times,* a newspaper published in China, ran its own poem, which began: "Have they run out of xenophobia?" (Li 2016).

That controversy aside, the mainstream media clearly take notice of the unmistakable immigration story: immigrants from different provinces and regions of China to the United States are becoming increasingly diverse. For scholars, the challenge is to document this diversification systematically. In the federal data collection system, we can obtain information on Chinese immigrants from the U.S. census and the American Community Survey and administrative data from the U.S. Department of Homeland Security. But none of these data sources identifies Chinese immigrants' province of origin in China. To overcome this challenge we decided to use data on Chinese immigrant hometown associations in the United States, on the assumption that a higher number of HAs for immigrants from certain provinces in China represents a larger volume of immigrants from these provinces. Of course, this approximation may not be entirely accurate.

Table 1 shows recent changes in Chinese immigrant hometown associations in the United States. The top panel reveals increasing provincial diversification over time in four major immigrant locations in the United States: New York City, Washington, D.C., California, and Texas. In 1965 in New York City, for example, three Chinese provinces were represented among Chinese immigrant hometown associations. By 2015, New York City HAs represented twenty-three provinces in China (out of thirty-one). Similar findings are revealed for Chinese immigrant HAs in Washington, D.C., California, and Texas. The lower panel of table 1 shows the total number of Chinese immigrant HAs in each location. We identified twelve HAs in 1965 in New York City that represented immigrants from three provinces of China. In addition to comparing HAs across time in New York City, it is informative to make comparisons between cities. Compared to New York City HAs, for example, HAs in Washington, D.C., represent more provinces in China (twenty-eight versus twenty-three). But this is only part of the story: New York City in 2015 had 130 HAs, nearly four times the number in D.C., suggesting that Chinese immigrants in the D.C. region may be more diverse, but there are many more Chinese immigrants in New York City than in D.C., as is consistent with the official account (Hooper and Batalova 2015).

Table 2 gives us more detailed information on how the change in HAs differs by province of origin. First, let us compare Guangdong and Fujian Provinces, using New York City as an example. In 1965, clearly the most important immigrant-sending province was Guangdong,

Table 1. Distribution of Chinese Hometown Associations in the United States, by Year

	Number of Chinese Provinces with Hometown Associations			
Year	New York City	Washington, D.C.	California	Texas
1965	3	0	1	0
2000	12	11	14	6
2010	15	21	22	10
2015	23	28	26	16
	Number of Chinese Hometown Associations			
Year	New York City	Washington, D.C.	California	Texas
1965	12	0	2	0
2000	33	9	18	4
2010	47	22	36	9
2015	130	36	57	19

Source: Authors' compilation.

Table 2. Distribution of Hometown Associations of Selected Chinese Provinces in the United States, by Year

	Number of Chinese Hometown Associations			
Province/Year	New York City	Washington, D.C.	California	Texas
From Fujian				
1965	1	0	0	0
2000	4	2	2	1
2010	6	3	2	1
2015	75	3	2	2
From Guangdong				
1965	9	0	2	0
2000	11	0	3	1
2010	12	1	4	1
2015	13	2	4	1
From Zhejiang				
1965	0	0	0	0
2000	4	0	3	0
2010	6	1	7	0
2015	8	1	8	1

Source: Authors' compilation.

which was represented by nine HAs in New York City, compared to only one Fujian HA. By 2015, the picture had changed dramatically: now there were seventy-five Fujian-based HAs, compared to only thirteen Guangdong HAs. At the same time, the number of HAs representing immigrants from Zhejiang Province (located in coastal China) had increased in both New York City and California.

Chinese immigrants from different provinces speak different dialects and are often embedded in their own networks. Even among immigrants from Fujian Province, a person from one Fujian town who runs a restaurant and needs to hire a worker might not know that someone from another town in Fujian is looking for a job. Thus, this Chinese restaurateur from Fujian Province, unable to staff his restaurant from his own small network of friends and relatives, has to look beyond it. In this case, the traditional network-based job search process has reached its limit. A different version of the strength of "weak ties" may apply here: job information and choice are limited for those immigrants who know only the job availability of those within their own province-of-origin network (Granovetter 1985).

THE SPATIAL DIFFUSION OF CHINESE IMMIGRANT ENTREPRENEURS

In addition to the diversification of Chinese immigrants' provinces of origin, we also observe spatial diffusion of Chinese immigrant entrepreneurs. Here we report results from a survey of eleven employment agencies that we carried out in Manhattan's Chinatown in 2011. Before discussing our findings from this survey, we give a brief overview of the history of EAs in New York City. In our interviews with owners of selected EAs, all mentioned that the first person to start an EA was Jackson Lee, an immigrant from Guangdong Province, although no one could say exactly when. In *New York Times* reporter Jane Lii's 1994 report on a case against Jackson Lee, however, a quote from Lee implies that his EA business started in 1969. This time frame is broadly consistent with the information from our interviews with other EA owners. For example, another EA owner, Mr. Yang, told us that when he first came to New York in 1973, he saw Jackson Lee's EA in Chinatown.[4] Mr. Yang also remembered that the fee for EA services was $30 at that time. (That today's fee of $30 to $35 is virtually unchanged after more than twenty years points to the fierce competition among modern EAs.) Although earlier EAs primarily provided services for immigrants from Guangdong and other Chinese immigrants, over time the number of EAs has expanded dramatically; now they cater mainly to immigrants from other provinces, such Fujian, and from northeast China. One key difference is that owners of EAs today are primarily immigrants from Fujian Province, because most restaurant owners in New York City are Fujianese immigrants.

We obtained all of the job listings of the EAs we surveyed—over 2,000 jobs in total. All of these jobs were in businesses owned by Chinese entrepreneurs. Most of them were jobs in restaurants (serving both Chinese food and Japanese food). For the most part, job applicants were Chinese immigrants, but some Latino workers also used the services of Chinese immigrant EAs. Just as in high-end restaurants in Los Angeles, there is a hierarchy among restaurant workers in Chinese restaurants (Wilson, this issue), where Latino workers tend to work mainly as busboys.

For our survey, the most important job information posted at an EA was the phone area code for each job, which could be perceived to imply an immigrant business in operation within the geographical boundaries of that area code. Thus, this job information could be used to examine the spatial locations of immigrant-owned businesses. Figure 3 shows the spatial distribution across the United States of these immigrant-owned businesses in 2011. From a survey of employment agencies in Chinatown in Manhattan, we can study the spatial diffusion of Chinese immigrant–owned businesses (mainly restaurants) across the United States. In figure 3, we see that Chinese immigrant businesses can be found in nearly all U.S. states, excepting only Montana, Wyoming, South Dakota, North Dakota, Idaho, and Nevada.

One implication of the expansion of Chinese immigrant–owned businesses across the country is that the labor demand is high and constant and there are no sizable local populations of Chinese low-skilled workers to depend on to meet that demand. Given how widespread these job locations are, even if business owners could find people in their migrant networks who are looking for jobs, there is no guarantee they would be willing to move. Thus, the recruitment of restaurant workers for the

---

4. Our interview with Mr. Yang was conducted on June 4, 2016.

Figure 3. Distribution of Jobs in Chinese Immigrant–Owned Businesses in the United States, 2011

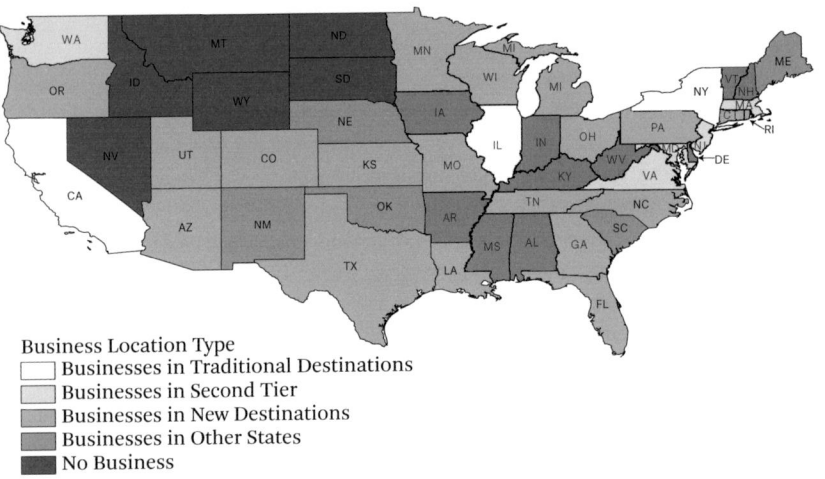

Business Location Type
- ☐ Businesses in Traditional Destinations
- ☐ Businesses in Second Tier
- ☐ Businesses in New Destinations
- ☐ Businesses in Other States
- ☐ No Business

Source: Authors' Chinatown employment agency survey, 2011.

whole country is better served by reliance on market-based institutions such as EAs, which can cast a much bigger net to identify workers willing to take these jobs, rather than traditional migrant networks.

A CHINESE-LANGUAGE NEWSPAPER AND THE NEW IMMIGRANT JOB NICHES

The second market-based job search institution on which we focus is the Chinese-language newspaper *World Journal* (世界日報). Established in 1976, the *World Journal* celebrated its fortieth anniversary in 2016 and is the most influential Chinese-language newspaper in the United States, with a circulation of about 300,000 (Zhou and Cai 2002). The *World Journal*'s coverage is broad, from news in the United States and New York City's Chinese community to news from mainland China, Taiwan, and Hong Kong, along with news on the economy and stock market. The *World Journal* also posts job openings. We use information from the *World Journal*'s job listings for three periods: April 2004, February 2016, and April 2016. Our decision to use data from these time periods was driven by the availability of job information for earlier time periods; we needed that earlier job data because we planned to examine any changes in job categories over time. Job information in the *World Journal* for 2016 was easier to obtain. We obtained data for two different months in 2016 to detect any seasonal variations.

Nancy Foner (2013), one of the immigration scholars who have studied ethnic media, reports that in New York City there are 198 magazines and newspapers published in thirty-seven languages; this high number of publications suggests the importance of ethnic media in many immigrant communities in New York City. In analyzing their systematic collection of information on ethnic media (including Chinese-language newspapers), Min Zhou and Guoxuan Cai (2002) ask whether ethnic media hinder or facilitate immigrants' assimilation into American society—for example, by providing information on purchasing a home or investing in education, or helping readers learn about American culture. Using information from two Chinese newspapers and interviews with nine Chinese immigrant women, Yu Shi (2009) examines the interaction between newspapers' discourse and the discourse of the working immigrant women among their readers.

None of these studies focus on the job search dimension of ethnic newspapers. As an information channel for job openings, newspapers differ from employment agencies. First, newspapers cover a much broader range of jobs, including not only restaurant jobs but all

Table 3. Job Advertisements in a Chinese-Language Newspaper, by Job Category, 2004 and 2016

	April 16, 2004		February 25, 2016		April 8, 2016	
	Number of Jobs	%	Number of Jobs	%	Number of Jobs	%
Nail salon jobs	238	19.80	453	31.20	171	16.16
Massage or tuina jobs	92	7.65	195	13.43	134	12.67
Restaurant jobs	408	33.94	348	23.97	340	32.14
Other jobs	464	38.60	456	31.40	413	39.04
Total	1,202	100	1,452	100	1,058	100

Source: World Journal, job advertisements in the New York City edition, April 16, 2004, February 25, 2016, and April 8, 2016.

other jobs that employers, large or small, are trying to fill. This broader coverage gives researchers a more comprehensive view of the immigrant labor market. Second, job ads in newspapers come and go quickly because employers have to pay for them and no one wants to pay more than necessary to advertise a job. The moment a job is taken, the ad is taken out of the newspaper. And finally, because newspapers cover diverse job categories on a timely basis, they are better positioned to capture new developments in the labor market—such as new labor market niches for immigrants.

In table 3, we present job distribution data that we collected from the *World Journal* for April 2004, February 2016, and April 2016. Interestingly, a higher proportion (31 percent) of nail salon jobs were advertised in February than in April (16 percent); salon owners were preparing for increased demand for nail services as the weather got warmer. Several additional observations can be made from table 3. First, for both years we see that restaurant jobs were among the most important job categories; this time-tested finding confirms that today's low-skilled immigrants continue to rely on restaurant jobs. Equally important, however, is another service job category: nail/massage/tuina. We combine these three types of jobs because all three are new jobs, not traditional niche-type jobs. Second, Chinese immigrants are latecomers in the nail salon industry, which was initiated by other Asian immigrants (Eckstein and Nguyen 2011). Recent reports suggest that Chinese immigrants are taking an increasingly larger share of this business in the market once dominated by Korean immigrants in New York City.[5] The declining share of Korean-owned nail salons is due to low immigration from Korea and low fertility in Korea combined with the unwillingness of second-generation Koreans to follow in their parents' footsteps. Third, a careful study of this job market shows that many nail salon jobs advertised in the *World Journal* are actually for nail salon businesses owned by Korean immigrants. This suggests that Chinese and Korean immigrants work together in the nail salon market.

The presence of Chinese immigrants in this market generated a great controversy in 2015 after a *New York Times* article reported violations of employees' labor rights by some nail salon owners, such as paying below minimum wage or requiring unpaid overtime (Nir 2015). That report prompted Governor Andrew Cuomo's immediate action to shut down some of these businesses and begin to implement new business standards and regulations, leading to many protests by Chinese and Korean business owners. In pursuing their case and publicizing

---

5. In the aftermath of Governor Andrew Cuomo's announcement of new regulations concerning the nail salon industry in New York State, nearly 500 Chinese nail salon owners showed up at meetings with state government officials (Zhu 2015). At present, most nail salon businesses in New York and along the East Coast are owned by Korean and Chinese immigrants (see Kang 2010; Yin 2016; Zhu 2015), while Vietnamese dominate this business on the West Coast (Eckstein and Nguyen 2011).

their side of the story, Chinese and Korean business owners have worked together to put pressure on the state to implement more practical and realistic policies so that their businesses can survive and workers can keep their jobs (Yin 2016; Zhu 2015).

From table 3 and detailed job distributions (not shown in the table), we also detect the influence of China's increasing economic prosperity on labor market niches in the United States. For example, the job categories of massage and tuina are clearly new job niches in the United States for low-skilled Chinese immigrants. Massage services have become very popular in China for the last three decades and accessible to middle-class customers. Anyone who travels to urban China can easily find massage services—both body massage and foot massage—everywhere, not only in fancy hotels but on street corners as well. The arrival of tuina in the United States from China is more recent. Tuina is a hands-on body treatment that uses Chinese Taoism to bring the eight principles of traditional Chinese medicine (TCM) into balance.[6] In China, the services of tuina professionals are often offered in some hospitals and clinics as a way to treat body pain and discomfort. Sometimes tuina is combined with massage to give massage service more legitimacy. Chinese immigrant entrepreneurs brought these newly popular massage and tuina services from China to the United States, first offering these services in cities with large immigrant concentrations, such as New York. The initial business strategy was to target Chinese tourists and middle-class Chinese immigrants, but businesses offering massage and tuina have now expanded to other clients besides Chinese, in other locations.

Another consequence of the growing influence of China's prosperity is the global reach of Chinese tourists. From 2011 to 2014, China was ranked number one in international travelers, and Chinese tourist spending rose from $40 billion in 2008 to $140 billion by 2014—a nearly fourfold increase (Feng and Zhang 2015). Of course, the United States is one of the most popular destinations for Chinese tourists. The number of tourists visiting the United States from China rose to 2.2 million in 2014, from 270,000 in 2005 (U.S. Department of Commerce 2015). This increase in Chinese tourists has generated labor demand for tourist-related jobs in the United States. Our data from Chinese newspapers reveal that tourism- and travel-related jobs account for about 2.1 percent of all job listings (not shown in table 3). For example, one travel agency alone was hiring four new workers. Of course, our data reflect only the demand for new workers in this industry and do not account for the immigrants who already work in these jobs. Besides tour guides, tour bus drivers are in particularly high demand.

Chinese shoppers are also having an impact on immigrant labor market niches in the United States. Compared to travelers from other countries, Chinese travelers are said to be "aggressive shoppers" with an enthusiastic desire for designer products. Major department stores such as Macy's try hard to entice Chinese tourist shoppers, and Woodbury outlet stores have many signs written in Chinese for Chinese buyers. In almost every major designer store, at least one salesperson can speak Mandarin Chinese. (Some of these retail workers are included in the category "other" in table 3.)

China's growing economic power is also reflected in U.S. companies' increasing interest in doing business with China and their search for bilingual workers who can speak both English and Chinese. For example, many sales jobs posted include jobs in long-distance telecommunications, global trading, and international express shipping. The demand for international express shipping services especially is mushrooming because of strong Chinese demand for U.S.-made products. These kinds of companies are quite visible in places like Flushing and Chinatown in New York. The *World Journal* also advertises jobs in English, such as the many import-export business jobs that require applicants to be bilingual—another sign of the economic interdependence between the United States and China, the two largest economies in the world.

In tables 4 and 5, we focus on the two most important job categories for low-skilled Chi-

---

6. For more information on tuina, see the Wikipedia entry at: https://en.wikipedia.org/wiki/Tui_na (accessed August 31, 2017).

Table 4. Massage and Tuina Job Advertisements in a Chinese-Language Newspaper, by Job Location, 2004 and 2016

	April 16, 2004		February 25, 2016		April 8, 2016	
	Number of Jobs	%	Number of Jobs	%	Number of Jobs	%
New York City	53	57.61	72	36.92	53	39.55
New York State (excluding New York City)	3	3.26	18	9.23	22	16.42
Other	36	39.13	105	53.85	59	44.03
Total	92	100	195	100	134	100

Source: World Journal, job advertisements in the New York City edition, April 16, 2004, February 25, 2016, and April 8, 2016.

Table 5. Restaurant Job Advertisements in a Chinese-Language Newspaper, 2004 and 2016

	April 16, 2004		February 25, 2016		April 8, 2016	
	Number of Jobs	%	Number of Jobs	%	Number of Jobs	%
New York City	187	45.83	159	45.69	172	50.59
New York State (excluding New York City)	62	15.20	62	17.82	76	22.35
Other	159	38.97	127	36.49	92	27.06
Total	408	100	348	100	340	100

Source: World Journal, job advertisements in the New York City edition, April 16, 2004, February 25, 2016, and April 8, 2016.

Table 6. Nail Salon Job Advertisements in a Chinese-Language Newspaper, 2004 and 2016

	April 16, 2004		February 25, 2016		April 8, 2016	
	Number of Jobs	%	Number of Jobs	%	Number of Jobs	%
New York City	165	69.33	138	30.46	60	35.09
New York State (excluding New York City)	65	27.31	196	43.27	81	47.37
Other	8	3.36	119	26.27	30	17.54
Total	238	100	453	100	171	100

Source: World Journal, job advertisements in the New York City edition, April 16, 2004, February 25, 2016, and April 8, 2016.

nese immigrants and examine their spatial distribution: jobs in nail salons, spas, and massage and jobs in restaurants. Confirming the findings from our employment agency survey, only about half of the job postings were located in New York City; the rest were located in other parts of New York State and other parts of the country. We should note that we are using the New York City edition of the *World Journal*, which also has Chicago and California editions.

Table 6 displays the spatial distribution of nail salon jobs. The nail salon business seems to have been diffused to other parts of New York State to a significant degree. In 2004, nearly 70 percent of the job ads for New York City were nail salon jobs; by 2016, that proportion had declined to 30 to 35 percent. One possible explanation is that the diffusion of these jobs was accelerated by Governor Cuomo's tightening of industry regulations after the 2015 *New York Times* report. What table 6 also reveals is that, as with Chinese restaurant workers, the nail salon business is becoming a broad national labor market.

IMPLICATIONS OF A MARKET-BASED JOB SEARCH PROCESS

The rise of market-based job search institutions has several implications for immigrant job outcomes as well as our conceptualization of the immigrant labor market (Sassen 1995). First, we argue that traditional network-based job searches have advantages and disadvantages. On the one hand, newly arrived immigrants are happy to get jobs through migration networks—that is, through friends, relatives, or shared hometown origins—but on the other hand, it is hard to negotiate wages for jobs obtained through networks if those wages are not consistent with market-based wages. Thus, immigrants obtaining jobs through networks may receive only the wages that employers can afford and are willing to pay, but not necessarily market wages. By contrast, jobs obtained through market-based institutions such as employment agencies and newspaper listings must pay market wages, for several reasons. First, with other employers also posting ads in employment agencies and newspapers, any employer that does not offer market wages is unlikely to receive job applicants (unless the job market is bad). Second, employers try to avoid high turnover rates, which are likely to occur if they do not offer market wages and their employees have an incentive to find better-paying jobs elsewhere. And third, because there is no prior connection between employers and job applicants—such as is the case in network-based employment—many applicants do not hesitate to negotiate for market-level wages or higher. For these reasons, we hypothesize that immigrants who obtain jobs through market-based job search institutions receive higher pay than they would in jobs obtained through migrant networks.

We test this idea using the 2004 survey of Chinese immigrants carried out by Zai Liang. We use logged wages for current job as the dependent variable. Job search methods include friends, relatives, neighbors, smugglers, employment agencies, newspapers, and direct applications to the employer. We group employment agencies and newspapers as market-based job search methods and classify the rest as network-based. We use ordinary least squares (OLS) regression to estimate the wage models and report the results in table 7.

As shown in table 7, immigrant men are paid more than immigrant women, and the duration of U.S. residence has a positive impact on wages; these findings are consistent with previous studies. We also find that age is negatively related to wages, probably, we suspect, because restaurant jobs are very labor-intensive, demand long hours, and are essentially a young person's game. Thus, older immigrants who stay in the restaurant business are not being rewarded as they would be in other businesses.

Surprisingly, there is no significant difference in wages between immigrants who obtained their current job through market-based institutions and those who relied on migrant networks. To further explore the linkage between job search method and wages, we use wage growth between the first job and the current job using job search method as one of the key independent variables. Here we find that wage growth for immigrants who found their current job through a market-based search method is significantly higher than wage growth for immigrants who found their current job through migration networks. It seems that the immigrants who found their jobs through market-based institutions were better informed about market wages and better able to negotiate with employers than immigrants who got their jobs through migrant networks.

Beyond wages, we also argue that immigrants' use of market-based job searches is part of a larger movement in the immigrant labor market of employers relying increasingly on market institutions rather than migrant networks for their business operations. In the restaurant business in New York's Chinatown, we observe a set of businesses that support res-

Table 7. OLS Regression Predicting Logged Hourly Wage and Growth of Monthly Wage for Chinese Immigrants, 2004

Variable	Logged Hourly Wage		Wage Growth	
	Coefficient	Standard Error	Coefficient	Standard Error
Age	0.03*	0.01	47.42*	21.46
Age*age	-0.0004**	0.00	-0.59*	0.25
Male	0.26***	0.04	354.20***	69.60
Married	-0.04	0.06	-73.89	92.99
With high school or higher education	0.05	0.05	53.31	74.63
Years in the United States	0.01*	0.00	19.87*	7.93
With legal status	0.04	0.04	27.72	63.36
Found job through market methods[a]	-0.07	0.04	139.26*	59.48
Poor English proficiency[b]	-0.15***	0.04	-193.89**	69.86
Working in restaurants	0.04	0.04	210.31**	67.47
Constant	1.20***	0.24	-855.12*	395.65
Adjusted R^2	0.265		0.263	
N	320		320	

Source: 2004 survey of Chinese immigrants by Zai Liang.
[a]The reference group for "found job through market methods" is "found job through social network."
[b]The reference group for "poor English proficiency" is "speaks English well or fluently."
*$p < .05$; **$p < .01$; ***$p < .001$

taurant operations for the whole country: buses that send immigrants to work in different states, printing companies that create menus for Chinese restaurants nationwide, kitchen equipment stores that supply restaurants, companies that produce cashier systems and surveillance cameras, and so on. In other words, the operation of Chinese restaurants, traditionally a mom-and-pop operation, has begun to resemble the operation of a modern industrial organization. Moreover, the rise of market-based institutions has prompted us to reconceptualize our notion of the immigrant labor market. No longer confined to singular enclaves in one location, the immigrant labor market is now often national in scope (Liang et al. 2015; Sassen 1995)—as is clearly the case for both the restaurant and nail salon businesses, based on the evidence we present here.

SUMMARY AND CONCLUSION

This article began with the observation that there has been a rise in market-based job search institutions, such as employment agencies and newspapers, in the Chinese immigrant labor market. We argue that this increase is driven by two major forces. One is the changing pattern of Chinese immigration, as reflected in both the large size and, especially, the diversification of immigrant provinces of origin. To the extent that network-based job searches rely on kinship and friendship ties and shared community of origin, any employer relying only on the limited number of people from his or her own community of origin looking for a job may soon reach the limit of the labor supply. This is likely to happen as employees themselves become entrepreneurs, start their own businesses, and need workers. In fact, this is exactly what happens in the restaurant business. Most of the restaurant workers we interviewed dreamed of having their own business down the road. The diffusion of Chinese immigrant businesses across the country further complicates the recruitment process as businesses open in places with no local low-skilled Chinese immigrant population and find it difficult to persuade those living in locations with large immigrant populations, such as New York City, to move to faraway places. These employers must rely on a larger potential pool of labor to recruit willing employees.

It is natural to wonder what the rise of market-based job search institutions means for average workers. Using Liang's 2004 survey of Chinese immigrants, we find that immigrants who obtained jobs using market-based institutions experienced higher wage growth than immigrants who obtained their jobs through migrant networks. This finding points to the limits of migrant networks and ethnic solidarity and the advantages of market mechanisms. One policy implication is that policymakers should design policies to help the employment agencies in the Chinese community and Chinese-language newspapers that are created by immigrants and immigrant entrepreneurs—for example, by providing guidelines for employment agencies to use in educating their employees. In the last few years, employment agency owners have reported that city government officials often visit their offices to see whether government policies and regulations are being followed and penalize agencies found not to be in compliance. In 2012, for example, officials from New York City's Consumer Affairs Bureau penalized employment agencies for failing to provide job assignment forms written in both English and Chinese and for not putting all labor contracts in writing (Wang 2012). Business owners complained that they did not know what policies should be followed in the first place. One agency owner complained that he had run his business for twenty years without knowing how contracts between workers and his agency should be written. Clearly, the city government could help these business owners by educating them about New York City policies that relate to employment agencies. In fact, under the strong encouragement of Governor Cuomo, New York State officials are already doing this for nail salon owners.

We also analyzed job listings in a Chinese-language newspaper, the *World Journal*. Not surprisingly, our findings confirm those from a survey of employment agencies that restaurant jobs continue to be the backbone of the low-skilled Chinese immigrant labor market. However, new niche jobs are emerging, such as nail salon jobs. In addition, we find evidence that the rising prosperity of China has implications for Chinese immigrant jobs in the United States. In particular, we show that the market for jobs that meet the growing needs of Chinese travelers to the United States is strong and likely to expand even further. Twenty years ago, Chinese visiting the United States were likely to be high-ranking officials, scholars, or upper-class citizens. Today China's international tourism industry has taken advantage of the growing economic wealth of the Chinese middle class, for whom travel to the United States and other countries has become more accessible. Jobs related to China's investment in the United States are also expected to grow. Chinese immigrants with English-language skills and cultural knowledge of both China and the United States are well positioned to take these jobs. Recently, the Asia Society released a report about China's investment in U.S. real estate (Rosen et al. 2016): between 2010 and 2015, both China and Chinese customers invested significantly in residential and commercial property in the United States. This is clearly good news for Chinese immigrants, both low-skilled and high-skilled, as job opportunities are likely to expand in sectors related to China's investment in the United States.

The spatial diffusion of Chinese immigrant businesses and increasing use of employment agencies to recruit workers have raised important theoretical questions about the study of ethnic enclaves such as Manhattan's Chinatown. Compared to Chinatown's traditional enclave economy, the new type of Chinese enclave we report on here continues to rely on Chinese immigrant labor but is no longer located in Chinatown in Manhattan. There are other striking differences as well. First, the new Chinese enclave economy serves mostly non-Chinese customers, raising interesting questions about intergroup contacts and assimilation. Moreover, some of these Chinese immigrant–owned businesses are located in minority neighborhoods, making the middle man minority thesis relevant as well (Min 1996). Second, we cannot use traditional measures to define an enclave economy, whether by residential location or job location in Chinatown, because most of the Chinese immigrant workers employed by today's Chinese immigrant–owned businesses do not work or live in Chinatown. However, Chinatown in Manhattan continues to play an important role as a transportation hub for immigrant workers, a center of supply chains, the home of Chinese-language media, a source of political mobilization, and the setting for social events and ceremonies such as weddings and the celebrations of hometown associations. This change in Chinatown's role is an important new development that deserves more attention from immigration scholars.[7]

We conclude with a methodological note for the study of immigration. As immigration scholars who specialize in quantitative research, we are used to relying on data from the U.S. census, national surveys—for example, the American Community Survey (ACS) and the Panel Study of Income Dynamics (PSID)—and administrative data. Such research is extremely valuable for understanding key issues for immigrants, such as broad patterns of spatial location, occupations, and family, but it is also limited in some ways. For example, we can learn almost nothing about immigrants' origins in their home countries, whether at the state and provincial or regional level. At a time when immigration scholars are recognizing the importance of links between origins and destinations and of transnationalism (Liang and Chen 2004; Singley and Landale 1998; Waldinger 2015), it is important to bring migrant origins back into the discussion.

Addressing these concerns, we have attempted to try some new approaches. Using data on immigrant hometown associations to gauge the diversification of Chinese immigrants met with some success. For immigration scholars, gaining knowledge of migrant origins is extremely important because different provinces represent differences in levels of socioeconomic development (rich versus poor, working-class versus middle-class), differences in immigration history, differences in cultures of entrepreneurship, differences in dialects, and, of course, differences in food tastes (as Calvin Trillin noticed). Likewise, ethnic media can also make valuable contributions to our understanding of the immigrant labor market. Although ACS data can tell us the proportion of immigrants who work in service jobs, Chinese-language newspapers describe these jobs more specifically: restaurant workers, nail salon workers, tour company bus drivers, workers in Chinese banks in New York City, and clerks in international shipping companies. Job ads in the ethnic media also provide an up-to-the-minute picture of labor market demand, which is useful for detecting changes in the labor market.

Recognizing the limitations of our approach of using job information from only a few moments in time, we nevertheless hope that we have demonstrated the utility of this approach well enough to encourage future researchers to explore it further. We are optimistic, particularly in these days of "big data," that the rich data available in ethnic media can be fully utilized to advance immigration research.

REFERENCES

Chen, Yong. 2015. *Chop Suey, USA: The Story of Chinese Food in America.* New York: Columbia University Press.

Dolnick, Sam. 2011. "Many Immigrants' Job Search Starts in Chinatown." *New York Times,* February 22, 2011.

Eckstein, Susan, and Thanh-Nghi Nguyen. 2011. "The Making and Transnationalization of an Ethnic Niche: Vietnamese Manicurists." *International Migration Review* 45(3): 639–74.

Eckstein, Susan, and Giovanni Peri. 2018. "Immigrant Niches and Immigrant Networks in the U.S. Labor Market." *RSF: The Russell Sage Foundation Journal of the Social Sciences* 4(1): 1–17. DOI: 10.7758/RSF.2018.4.1.01.

Feng, Ye, and Yue Zhang. 2015. "International Tourism of 100 Million Chinese." *Nanfang Weekend,* October 22, C13.

Foner, Nancy. 2013. *One Out of Three: Immigrant New York in the Twenty-First Century.* New York: Columbia University Press.

Granovetter, Mark. 1985. "Economic Action and Social Structure: The Problem of Embeddedness." *American Journal of Sociology* 91(3): 481–510.

---

7. We thank one anonymous reviewer for suggesting that we compare the traditional Chinese enclave economy with the new Chinese enclave economy.

Hooper, Kate, and Jeanne Batalova. 2015. "Chinese Immigrants in the United States." Washington, D.C.: Migration Policy Institute (January 28). Available at: http://www.migrationpolicy.org/article/chinese-immigrants-united-states (accessed May 16, 2016).

Kang, Millan. 2010. *The Managed Hand: Race, Gender, and Body in Beauty Service Work.* Berkeley: University of California Press.

Kwong, Peter, and Dušanka Miščević. 2005. *Chinese American: The Untold Story of America's Oldest New Community.* New York: New Press.

Lee, Jennifer 8. 2008. *Fortune Cookie Chronicles: Adventures in the World of Chinese Food.* New York: Twelve.

Li, Jingling. 2016."New Yorker Writer's Chinese Food Poem Sparks Racism Ruckus." *Global Times,* April 13.

Liang, Zai, and Yiu Por Chen. 2004. "Gender and Migration in China: An Origin-Destination Linked Approach." *Economic Development and Cultural Change* 52(2): 423–43.

Liang, Zai, Miao David Chunyu, Guotu Zhuang, and Wenzhen Ye. 2008. "Cumulative Causation, Market Transition, and Emigration from China." *American Journal of Sociology* 114(3): 706–37.

Liang, Zai, Jiejin Li, and Glenn Deane. 2015. "From Chinatown to Everytown." Revision of the paper presented to the 2012 annual meeting of the Population Association of America. San Francisco (May 3–5).

Lieberson, Stanley. 1980. *A Piece of the Pie: Blacks and White Immigrants Since 1880.* Berkeley: University of California Press.

Light, Ivan. 1984. "Immigrant and Ethnic Enterprise in North America." *Ethnic and Racial Studies* 7(2): 195–216.

Lii, Jane H. 1994. "Chinatown Agencies Fined over Job-Seekers' Fees." *New York Times,* August 14.

Massey, Douglas S., Luin Goldring, and Jorge Durand. 1994 "Continuities in Transnational Migration: An Analysis of 19 Mexican Communities." *American Journal of Sociology* 99(6): 1492–1533.

Min, Pyong Gap. 1996. *Caught in the Middle: Korean Communities in New York and Los Angeles.* Berkeley: University of California Press.

Nee, Victor, and Brett de Barry Nee. 1974. *Long Time Californ': A Documentary Study of an American Chinatown.* Boston: Houghton Mifflin.

Nir, Sara Maslin. 2015. "The Price of Nice Nails." *New York Times,* May 7.

Portes, Alejandro. 2010. *Economic Sociology: A Systematic Inquiry.* Princeton, N.J.: Princeton University Press.

Portes, Alejandro, and Rubén G. Rumbaut. 2001. *Legacies: The Story of the Immigrant Second Generation.* Berkeley: University of California Press.

Ramzy, Austin. 2016. "Calvin Trillin's Poem on Chinese Food Proves Unpalatable for Some." *New York Times,* April 7.

Rischin, Moses. 1962. *The Promised City: New York's Jews, 1870–1914.* Cambridge, Mass.: Harvard University Press.

Rosen, Kenneth, Arthur Margon, Randall Sakamoto, and John Taylor. 2016. "Breaking Ground: Chinese Investment in U.S. Real Estate." San Francisco: Special Asia Society and Rosen Consulting Group (May). Available at: http://asiasociety.org/new-york/events/breaking-ground-chinese-investment-us-real-estate (accessed May 19, 2016).

Sanders, Jimmy, and Victor Nee. 1987. "The Limits of Ethnic Solidarity in the Enclave Economy." *American Sociological Review* 52(6): 745–73.

Sassen, Saskia. 1995. "Immigration and Local Labor Markets." In *The Economic Sociology of Immigration,* edited by Alejandro Portes. New York: Russell Sage Foundation.

Shah, Neil. 2015. "Immigrants to U.S. from China Top Those from Mexico." *Wall Street Journal,* May 3.

Shi, Yu. 2009. "Re-evaluating the 'Alterative' Role of Ethnic Media in the U.S.: The Case of Chinese Language Press and Working-Class Women Readers." *Media, Culture, and Society* 31(4): 597–616.

Singley, Susan G., and Nancy S. Landale. 1998. "Incorporating Origin and Process in Migration-Fertility Frameworks: The Case of Puerto Rican Women." *Social Forces* 76(4): 1437–64.

Siu, Paul C. P., and John Kuo Wei Tchen. 1988. *The Chinese Laundryman: A Study of Social Isolation.* New York: New York University Press.

Sung, Betty Lee. 1967. *Mountain of Gold: The Story of the Chinese in America.* New York: Macmillan.

Trillin, Calvin. 2016. "Have They Run Out of Provinces Yet?" *The New Yorker,* April 4, 2016.

U.S. Census Bureau. Population Division. 2013. *2000–2013 Single Year American Community Survey.* Washington: U.S. Department of Commerce.

U.S. Department of Commerce. International Trade

Administration. National Travel and Tourism Office. 2015. "2014 Market Profile: China." Available at: http://travel.trade.gov/outreachpages/download_data_table/2014_China_Market_Profile.pdf (accessed May 18, 2015).

Waldinger, Roger. 1986. *Through the Eye of the Needle: Immigrants and Enterprise in New York's Garment Trades.* New York: New York University Press.

——. 1994. "The Making of an Immigrant Niche." *International Migration Review* 28(1): 3–30.

——. 2015. *The Cross-Border Connection: Immigrants, Emigrants, and Their Homelands.* Cambridge, Mass.: Harvard University Press.

Wang, Hansi Lo. 2016. "Leaving China's North, Immigrants Redefine Chinese in New York." *All Things Considered,* National Public Radio, January 16. http://www.npr.org/2016/01/26/463857599/leaving-chinas-north-immigrants-redefine-chinese-in-new-york (accessed April 24, 2016).

Wang, Lianxiang. 2012. "Employment Agencies Complained About NYC Consumer Affairs Bureau Writing Tickets." *World Journal,* May 6, C1.

Wilson, Eli R. 2018. "Bridging the Service Divide: Dual Labor Niches and Embedded Opportunities in Restaurant Work." *RSF: Russell Sage Foundation Journal of the Social Sciences* 4(1): 115–27. DOI: 10.7758/RSF.2018.4.1.07.

Wilson, Kenneth, and Alejandro Portes. 1980. "Immigrant Enclave: An Analysis of the Labor Market Experiences of Cubans in Miami." *American Journal of Sociology* 86(2): 295–319.

Yin, Yingzi. 2016. "Chinese and Korean Nail Salon Owners Protest in Albany." *World Journal,* March 1, C1.

Zhou, Min. 1992. *Chinatown: The Socioeconomic Potential of an Urban Enclave.* Philadelphia: Temple University Press.

Zhou, Min, and Guoxuan Cai. 2002. "Chinese Language Media in the U.S.: Immigration and Assimilation in the American Life." *Qualitative Sociology* 25(3): 419–41.

Zhu, Lei. 2015. "Chinese and Korean Nail Salon Business Owners Are United to Be Against New Regulations and Plan to Protect." *World Journal,* August 19, C3.

Filling the Niche: The Role of the Parents of Immigrants in the United States

XIAOCHU HU

Care-providing parents of immigrants fill a labor market niche in the receiving economy. My research examines the intergenerational support for working women in immigrant families in the United States. Using panel data derived from the Current Population Survey (CPS), I find that having a coresiding parent increases the labor force participation probability of foreign-born women with children by about 7.4 percent, and that the effects differ by birth region and educational level. I use a difference-in-differences approach to reinforce the finding that coresiding parents significantly alleviate the short-term labor force participation decline of foreign-born females after their transition to motherhood.

Keywords: niches, parents of immigrants, caregiving grandparent, intergenerational support, female labor force participation

The prevalence of intergenerational support for working women has been documented in many countries and cultures. When immigrants arrive and work in the United States, this support is likely to follow. In my research, I have investigated this transnationalized phenomenon and quantified the important yet neglected role of immigrants' parents in supporting their children in the U.S. labor market.

The main mechanism through which caregiving parents of immigrants increase female labor force participation is by increasing the availability of child care and reducing the cost of child care. As James Heckman (1974) found in his study of the labor force participation choices of mothers, living with a relative decreases the quality-adjusted child care price for white American families by 67 percent. In addition, grandparent-provided child care is usually trustworthy and considered the "next best thing" (compared to mother's care) (Falk and Falk 2002; Wheelock and Jones 2002).

Since intergenerational support for working women is not a new phenomenon, it is useful to begin with the literature of intergenerational support in different countries and cultures and then look at how immigration has transnationalized it into the U.S. labor market.

The evidence on this topic from Europe is abundant and often focuses on regional differences. Many European studies are comparative analyses using panel data to control for unobserved family factors (Aassve, Arpino, and Goisis 2012; Albertini, Kohli, and Vogel 2007; García-Morán and Kuehn 2013; Hank and Buber 2008). In addition to confirming that

Xiaochu Hu is project specialist for economic evaluation at the University of the District of Columbia.

© 2018 Russell Sage Foundation. Hu, Xiaochu. 2018. "Filling the Niche: The Role of the Parents of Immigrants in the United States." *RSF: The Russell Sage Foundation Journal of the Social Sciences* 4(1): 96–114. DOI: 10.7758/RSF.2018.4.1.06. Direct correspondence to: Xiaochu Hu at hxch.peking@gmail.com, University of the District of Columbia, Building 44, Room 119, 4200 Connecticut Avenue NW, Washington, D.C. 20008.

grandparent-provided child care affects female labor force participation, they all agree that grandparenting practices vary among the countries under study. Family ties in southern Europe are known to be stronger than in the rest of Europe (Albuquerque and Passos 2010). Marco Albertini, Martin Kohli, and Claudia Vogel (2007) note that family ties in southern European countries are different from family ties in Continental or Nordic countries. In southern Europe, multigenerational families are more common and more resource exchange takes place between the generations. Studying ten European countries, Karsten Hank and Isabella Buber (2008) discover, using the Survey of Health, Ageing, and Retirement in Europe (SHARE), that the pattern may be more complex than a dichotomy of "strong versus weak" or "Scandinavian versus Mediterranean." They find three distinctive regional groups in terms of grandparent caring: Danish, Dutch, French, and Swedish grandparents are the most likely to provide care but the least likely to provide regular care; grandparents in the Mediterranean countries are less likely to provide care, but the most likely to provide regular care; and Austrian, German, and Swiss grandparents are in the middle. The SHARE data also reveal that European grandparents vary with respect to whether they feel obligated to provide care to their young grandchildren: in the Netherlands and Denmark, fewer than 60 percent of grandparents agree that it is their duty to provide weekly care, but 95 percent of Greek grandparents see caring for their grandchildren as their duty.

Naohiro Ogawa and John F. Ermisch (1996) document the child-caring role of coresiding grandparents in Japan, an established industrialized country that suffers from low female labor force participation. Margaret Maurer-Fazio and her colleagues (2009) examine the topic in the context of rural-to-urban migration in China, using Chinese census data from 1982 to 2000. They conclude that coresidency with parents or in-laws increases the labor force participation rate of nonmigrant urban women by 4.6 percentage points. Maurer-Fazio and her colleagues hypothesize that because housing constraints have not been a major issue for most urban Chinese families since around 2000, elderly parents who coreside with their children are more likely to be frail and therefore add to the burden of the working female in the family. Thus, their finding of a positive impact of the presence of parents and in-laws on labor market outcomes is unexpected. Because in broader Asian culture women are expected to do the housework, I would expect to find a more significant supporting role for working mothers being filled by grandmothers—particularly the maternal grandmother, since she typically does the housework that is considered the mother's responsibility.

Although the impact of intergenerational support on female labor force participation has been well studied, research has not examined such intergenerational support in the light of immigration. Care-providing parents of immigrants play a unique role in the receiving economy. My research unifies the intergenerational support practices of different countries and cultures in the U.S. labor market context. It also contributes to the immigration literature by providing possible explanations for the labor force participation rates of foreign-born females and the relationship between those rates and the level of intergenerational support they receive.

Destination countries and home countries may differ not only in their grandparenting practices but also in the impacts of those practices. First, the international immigration process, both permanent and temporary, is characterized by strong positive selection: the most willing and able grandparents come to the United States to offer care. Hence, I expect to find a larger positive effect of grandparental support on the immigrant mothers' labor force participation compared to the non-immigrant coresiding mothers. Second, foreign-born grandparents who follow their children to the United States—that is, who are not first-generation or primary immigrants—are less independent financially and psychologically and more likely than their American counterparts and their counterparts in the home country to coreside with their children. Third, the help-receiving immigrants may have less competition for this parental support from siblings, owing to geographic separation from them. Finally, foreign-born grandparents' age at migration, language restrictions, citizenship status, and low mobility (from an inability to drive) make them less likely than native grandparents to be in the paid labor force and, therefore, more likely to contribute to child care and other housework.

Since the 1990s, the age composition of immigrants to the United States has changed: the share of seniors (ages sixty-five and older) has increased from 9 to 12 percent. Senior immigrants also have a growing representation in legal permanent resident (LPR) admissions, in part because, as Jeanne Batalova (2012) points out, previous immigrants took advantage of U.S. immigration policy's family preference and sponsored their parents to come to this country.

In examining the extent to which intergenerational support exists in U.S. immigrant families, such support should not only be put in the context of the immigrants' ethnic groups in the home country but also analyzed in comparison with the host country. Part of that context in the United States is its cultural emphasis on independence and the nuclear family. In addition, the geographical distance between the host and home countries may severely limit grandparents' ability to provide child care and household assistance (Fields, O'Connell, and Downs 2011). Eva García-Morán and Zoë Kuehn (2013) exclude the foreign-born from the samples in their study using German data because both "availability of child care by relatives" and "residence relative to parents" may be determined by very different factors. Studies of intergenerational support using U.S. data are sparse. Josefine Posadas and Marian Vidal-Fernandez (2013) quantify that grandparents' provision of child care increases female labor force participation rate by 15 percent.

In my research, I compare the education levels of immigrant mothers who receive intergenerational help. Recent literature diverges in its assessment of which level of education brings a bigger motherhood penalty for women. Yanka Byker's study (2016) shows that new mothers at the very high end of the education scale (master's degree or higher) and those at the low-middle and low end (non-college-educated) experience steeper drops in labor force participation than those in the middle (bachelor's degree). Paula England and her colleagues (2016) find that high-skilled, high-paid women experience the largest motherhood penalty, and Olena Nizalova, Tamara Sliusarenko, and Solomiya Shpak (2016), using data from Ukraine, find that low-educated women suffer the largest motherhood penalty. In looking at family networks and low-skilled immigration, Patricia Cortés and José Tessada (2011) find that low-skilled immigration increases paid labor market work hours for women at the top quartile of the pay scale because the economic return for highly educated females is larger in that market. However, evidence for the opposite impact can also be found: in her work using U.K. Time Use Survey data, Anne Grey (2005) concludes that there is a significant difference between mothers' labor force participation with and without grandparental help, and that this difference is especially large for non-college-educated mothers.

IDENTIFYING THE NICHE

Susan Eckstein and Giovanni Peri (this issue) define an immigrant niche as "occupations in which a high percentage of workers are foreign-born." If providing nonpaid, contingent child care is an "occupation," then immigrants' parents definitely occupy a niche: a higher percentage of foreign-born than native-born grandparents coreside with and provide care to their grandchildren. Compared to other labor market niches discussed in this issue, the niche occupied by immigrants' care-providing parents is "flatter": these grandparents are a relatively homogenous group, they are older, and their expected "work" time is short. Once the children are no longer dependents, and as these immigrants' parents become older, they may receive care themselves and become consumers of welfare if they stay in the country.

The support of their own parents may free immigrants who are parents (most likely the mothers) from child care and household chores and allow them to be engaged in the paid labor force or to pursue the type of work that best matches their skills. This effect is similar to the complementarity effect observed between new low-skilled immigrants, on the one hand, and high-skilled natives and existing immigrants, on the other (Borjas 1999; Peri and Sparber 2009, 2011). The complementarity effect within families is even more direct and efficient because the inflow of foreign-born grandparents is totally demand-driven—foreign-born parents are always tied to an existing immigrant family, and there is a perfectly matched position for them. Research has documented that the presence of grandparents in immigrant households has a positive impact on the children's language development and assimilation (Tran 2010), as well as on the maintenance of family and ethnic ties (Waters et al. 2011). In the extreme case where a new mother trusts only her own mother to look after the baby (Falk and Falk 2002), the market cannot provide alternative care and this niche will go unfilled if the grandmother is absent. Even if grandparents' work could be replaced with day care services, one could argue that, given the shortage of day care services in most U.S. cities, the inflow of caregiving grandparents, rather than taking jobs from American day care workers, probably adds new day care "workers" to the market.

In discussing grandparent care preferences in their comparative study of European countries, Arnstein Aassve and his colleagues (2012) develop a typology of families in terms of the mother's labor force participation and the grandmother's care preferences: (1) modern families with highly motivated working women, weak family ties, and working grandmothers; (2) traditional families with a negative preference for working mothers, strong family ties, and a preference for family child care; and (3) mixed families with highly motivated working mothers mismatched with the available grandmothers. In U.S. immigrant families, the first family type (modern) may not be observed as often, since those grandmothers who prefer working or other retired activities other than caring for grandchildren are less likely to end up in the United States. Families with coresiding grandparents are likely to be either the second type (traditional) or the third (mixed), and the most important factor distinguishing these two types of families may be the mother's education level.

This typological analysis points to two competing mechanisms that my research tests empirically: (1) in traditional immigrant families, the presence of a grandparent will not increase the mother's labor force participation; and (2) in mixed immigrant families, although mothers and grandparents come from the same country and culture and may have similar preferences, being primary immigrants and more likely to be risk-seeking makes it more likely that these immigrant mothers are the modern type of mother, and therefore that intergenerational support will increase their labor force participation.

To explore regional differences, figure 1 illustrates the correlation of grandparent-provided care (proxied by a grandparent's presence in the same household) with the labor force participation of immigrant mothers by region. If we consider the U.S. average as the original and divide the panel into four quadrants, we have three groups of regions with different preferences for the working and caretaking roles of mothers and grandparents. The upper-right quadrant, where both the percentage of households with a coresiding grandparent (GPinhh) and immigrant mothers' labor force participation rate (FLPR) are higher than the U.S. average, encompasses those regions represented by the traditional type of grandparents and modern mothers (mixed families). East and Southeast Asia and Africa fall into this category. Regions in the lower-right quadrant have larger percentages of coresiding grandparents in the household and lower female labor force participation rates (traditional families). Central and South America, Southwest Asia, Southern Europe, and the Middle East fall into this category. In the lower-left quadrant—with rates lower than the U.S. average of coresiding grandparents and female labor force participation rates—we find the modern type of grandparents mixed with traditional mothers (Central and Eastern Europe, Western Europe, Northern Europe, and North America, not including Mexico). No regions are located in the upper-left quadrant. Note that this division applies only to immigrants in the United States from those regions, not to the actual populations of those regions.

Figure 1. Correlation of Labor Force Participation of Immigrant Mothers Ages Sixteen and Older with the Percentage of Households with a Coresiding Grandparent, by Region of Birth, 2014

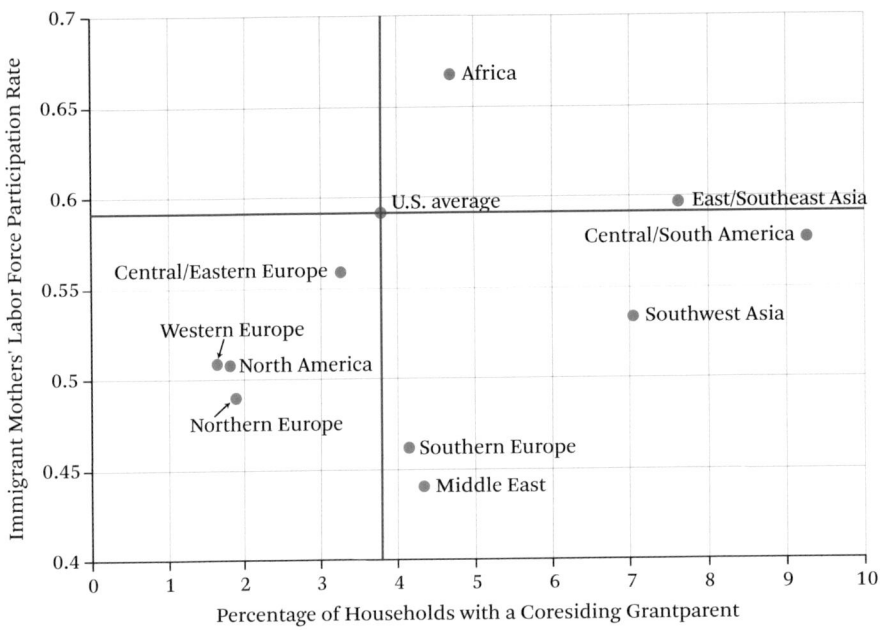

Source: Author's calculation using 2006–2015 Current Population Survey (CPS) all-month data. For region of birth, see 2014 American Community Survey (ACS) five-year data.

DATA AND METHODS

To examine the relationship between grandparents' presence and female immigrants' labor force participation, the empirical analysis uses CPS data sets obtained through the Integrated Public Use Microdata Series (IPUMS). Managed by the Bureau of Labor Statistics (BLS), the CPS follows one family for four months and then, eight months later, follows up with the family for another four months. Thus, each family is interviewed for a total of eight months during a span of sixteen months. Taking advantage of the CPS's longitudinal design, I construct a panel of linked households across interview periods using the unique household and person identifications produced by Julia Drew, Sarah Flood, and John Warren (2014) for IPUMS CPS data.

My research examines the effects of the non-first-generation foreign-born grandparents' co-residence on the labor force participation of primary (first-generation) female immigrants by focusing on foreign-born female household heads and spouses, who are more likely to be primary immigrants.

The key explanatory variable, GPinhh (grandparent in the same household), is created by using information on household relations. (I recode relations into generational marks, then identify multigenerational families as GPinhh.) A grandparent's presence in any given family can vary from period to period, as can the dependent variable, female labor force participation. Because CPS data do not contain information about whether a coresiding grandparent provides care for the children in the household, I make the plausible assumption that coresiding grandparents are providing such care and also helping with household chores to some extent. This assumption is supported by the positive selection inherent in the international migration process: the most willing and able grandparents are most likely to migrate. Although the presence of non-coresiding grandparents who live nearby and provide occasional or regular care has been documented to have a positive impact, the CPS does not provide this information, and therefore it is not possible for me to examine the impacts of non-coresiding grandparents.[1] As discussed earlier, foreign-born grandparents who are nonprimary immigrants are more likely to live with their children; unfortunately, those who reside elsewhere are not included in this research.

Panel Regression

The first empirical approach I take is a panel regression using CPS data. For convenience, I use a linear probability model (LPM) for panel data with fixed effects for a binary dependent variable (labor force participation of immigrant mothers).

$$P_{i,t} = \alpha_0 + \alpha_1 GPinhh_{i,t} + X_{i,t} + \gamma_i + \gamma_t + u_{i,t}. \quad (1)$$

Since our key independent variable is also binary (having a parent in the same household), using an LPM is more reasonable than an ordinary least squares (OLS) model, and the "fitted probabilities are simply the average y_i within each cell defined by the different values of x and no need to worry about probabilities less than zero or greater than one" (Wooldridge 2002, 454–57).

Let i denote an individual woman who is age eighteen or older, foreign-born, the mother of preschool-age children (under age six), and either a household head or the spouse of a household head, and let t denote the combination of year and month (the variable "mish"). $Y_{i,t}$ indicates the labor force participation outcome of women i at time t; $GPinhh_{i,t}$ indicates whether a grandparent is in the same household of women i at time t; $X_{i,t}$ presents a vector of time-varying characteristics that include age, age squared, years of education, citizenship status (only for foeign-born: noncitizen or naturalized citizen), marriage status (dummy), birth region, and family income. Individual and time fixed effects are included in order to control the individual-invariant characteristics, such as location and personal preferences, as well as the time-invariant factors, such as the overall labor market environment.

I group birth countries into nine regions according to geographic adjacency as well as differences in European grandparenting practices, as suggested by the literature (Hank and Buber 2008): North America (excluding the United States), Central and South America, Northern Europe, Western Europe, Southern Europe, Central and Eastern Europe plus the Russian Empire, East and South Asia, India and Southwest Asia, the Middle East, and Africa.

Construction of the Panel Data and the Instrumental Variable

To better establish the causal relationship between a coresiding grandparent and a mother in the labor force, the previously used instrumental variable (IV) was the maternal grandmother being alive (Aassve, Arpino, and Goisis 2012; Posadas and Vidal-Fernandez 2013). Since this information is not provided by the CPS, I choose to use the source country's retirement age as IV. I argue that earlier retirement directly increases the availability of grandparents and that retired grandparents are more likely to travel to the United States to coreside with their adult immigrant children and care for their grandchildren. At the same time, the retirement age in the parents' source country is not likely to affect the labor force participation (dependent variable) of female household heads or spouses in the United States. I use retirement age data on sixty-seven countries, ranging from age fifty (China) to age sixty-seven (Iceland, Norway, and Greece), with some countries setting the retirement age in increments of 0.3 years (four months) and 0.4 years (three months).

In many cases, the grandmother came to the United States alone or, if she traveled with her husband, stayed for a longer period than her husband. Both child care experience and retirement age are factors in explaining why grandmothers more often provide child care, and for longer periods, than grandfathers. Because grandmothers outnumber grandfathers

---

1. On the positive impacts of non-co-residing grandparents, see two studies that use SHARE data: Hank and Buber 2008 and García-Morán and Kuehn 2013.

Table 1. The Impact of a Coresiding Grandparent on the Female Labor Force Participation Rate: Panel Regression Descriptive Statistics

	Native Mothers		Foreign-Born Mothers	
	Mean	Standard Deviation	Mean	Standard Deviation
In labor force	0.678	0.467	0.479	0.500
Ln(hrs)	3.414	0.598	3.486	0.486
Parent	0.030	0.172	0.058	0.234
Age	31.875	6.876	32.648	6.637
Education year	14.051	2.459	12.364	3.946
Married	0.779	0.415	0.874	0.332
Naturalized	—	—	0.280	0.449
High education (HE) dummy	0.382	0.486	0.309	0.462
Medium education (ME) dummy	0.321	0.467	0.161	0.367
Low education (LE) dummy	0.296	0.457	0.530	0.499
Observations	514,946		123,598	

Source: Author's compilation based on 2006–2014 CPS monthly data (Flood et al. 2015).
Notes: Sample contains females who were age eighteen or older, mothers of at least one child under the age of six, and household heads or spouses of household heads. The hours worked sample is constructed using "in labor force" samples only (with therefore fewer observations). The table shows unweighted means and standard deviations.

and are more likely to provide care when they coreside with children, when the retirement age for a source country differs for males and females—for example, in China women retire at age fifty-five while men retire at sixty—I choose to use the female retirement age.

Technically, testing the effect of having a grandparent in the household on labor force participation requires a binary panel data model with endogeneity. To keep the methods simple, I choose to implement panel regression with fixed effects using two-stage least squares (2SLS) with instruments for both binary outcomes (labor force participation) and continuous outcomes (hours worked last week).

Table 1 presents the descriptive statistics of the dependent and independent variables of the panel regressions. The variable "in labor force" for foreign-born mothers (47.9 percent) is substantially lower than that for natives (67.8 percent), with the standard deviation around 0.5 (50 percent) for both. The logged hours worked last week for those in the labor force are relatively equal (3.41 and 3.49). Foreign-born mothers are almost twice as likely to have a parent present in the same household as native mothers (5.4 percent versus 2.9 percent). Foreign-born mothers are also more likely than natives to be married (87.4 percent versus 77.9 percent). With an average of 14.0 years of education, native mothers are better-educated overall compared to foreign-born mothers (12.4 years), but the standard deviation for foreign-born mothers is larger, reflecting a more widespread distribution. High education (HE) and medium education (ME) dummies are defined as "college degree and above" and "some college education but no degree." A third education category, low education (LE)—defined as "high school diploma and less than high school education"—is omitted by the regression owing to collinearity. Indeed, a much larger portion of foreign-born mothers belong to the low-education group (53 percent) compared to natives (29.6 percent).

The Difference-in-Differences Method: Following Women Before and After They Give Birth

Another empirical approach I use is a difference-in-differences model to identify the effect of a grandparent on new (immigrant) mothers. Handling "having a child" and "having a coresiding parent" as two independent treatments, this approach improves on the panel regression, where only mothers are examined, by allowing me to examine both women with children and those without children. Specifically, using 2006–2015 CPS data, I identify the month (interview period) in which a woman gave birth and mark all months after that as postpartum months. The other treatment—whether or not a parent resides in the same home—is the same variable as in the panel regression. The two treatments are independent, which means that they may or may not happen during the same period. Because the CPS follows individuals only over a span of sixteen months, this model focuses only on women with a child under two years old. (Assuming that a woman gives birth in the second period during which she and her family are interviewed by the CPS, the baby will be fifteen months old in the last period in which they are interviewed.) Most of the new births happen during the eight months when families are not interviewed. In other words, the period in which I see a change in the number of children is not likely to be the month in which the new baby was born. Hence, paid maternity leave is less of a concern for disrupting regression results. It would be ideal to know the exact months when women gave birth, but this information is not provided in the CPS.

The difference-in-differences model is constructed as a panel linear probability regression:

$$Y_{i,t} = \alpha_0 + \alpha_1 GPinhh_{i,t} + \alpha_2 Child_{i,t} + \alpha_3 GPinhh *Child_{i,t} + X_{i,t} + u_{i,t}. \quad (2)$$

$Y_{i,t}$ indicates the labor force participation outcome—whether a woman is in the labor force (dummy variable) and hours worked per week at all jobs—of women i at time t. (Notice that this is different from $Y_{i,t}$ in a panel regression.) $GPinhh_{i,t}$ indicates whether a parent lives in the same household as a woman i at time t; $Child_{i,t}$ indicates whether a woman i is in a postpartum month at time t; $GPinhh*Child_{i,t}$ is the interaction term of having a coresiding parent and having given birth; $X_{i,t}$ presents a vector of

Table 2. The Impact of a Coresiding Grandparent on the Labor Force Participation Rate of Foreign-Born Mothers: Difference-in-Differences Regression Descriptive Statistics

	Mean	Standard Deviation
In labor force	0.632	0.482
Post-childbirth	0.077	0.270
Grandparent in the household	0.059	0.236

Source: Author's compilation based on 2006–2014 CPS monthly data (Flood et al. 2015).
Notes: Sample contains 148,981 observations of eighteen- to forty-five-year-old female household heads or spouses of household heads. Only individuals appearing eight times are included.

time-varying characteristics that include age, years of education, naturalized citizen (dummy), and marriage status (dummy). The coefficient, α_3, is the difference-in-differences estimator.

Table 2 presents the descriptive statistics of the dependent and independent variables of the difference-in-differences regressions. The sample contains eighteen- to forty-five-year-old foreign-born females who are household heads or spouses of household heads. For a better before-and-after comparison, only individuals appearing eight times are included. A total of 18,705 women are included in the regression, and about 14.7 percent of them gave birth during the period followed in the data.

EMPIRICAL RESULTS

Regression Results

Table 3 presents the results for equation 1 (panel LPM regression with fixed effects) using CPS all-month data from 2006 to 2015. Except for column 4, all other models' standard errors are clustered. Column 1 shows results for the labor force participation of native-born mothers who have at least one preschool-age child and are household heads or spouses of household heads. The key explanatory variable, "parent present in the same household," has a significantly negative effect on labor force participation: with everything else controlled, having a coresiding parent in the household is estimated to reduce the probability of participating in the labor force by about 4 percent (0.042). This may reflect the American culture and also the negative selection of elderly coresiding grandparents: women may opt out of the labor force because they are more likely to care for coresiding parents than to get help from them. In addition, being married and having one additional preschooler are estimated to reduce the probability of participating in the labor force by 11 and 8 percent, respectively.

Column 2 shows results for the labor force participation of foreign-born mothers of at least one preschool-age child who are household heads or household heads' spouses. Everything else controlled, having a coresiding parent significantly increases the probability of participating in the labor force for a foreign-born female with a preschooler by about 7 percent (0.074). This result is highly significant. The magnitude of this effect of intergenerational support on female labor force participation falls in between what Posadas and Vidal-Fernandez (2013) find (15 percent) using Southern European data and what Maurer-Fazio and her colleagues (2009) find (4.6 percent) using Chinese data. This result is plausible considering that the U.S. immigration population includes so many nationalities and cultural norms. Later in my analysis, regional interactions will shed light on this issue. Unlike Posadas and Vidal-Fernandez, who can clearly identify care-providing grandparents in their study, I have to proxy coresiding with care-providing, and this may discount the effect to some extent. That I find a larger effect than what Maurer-Fazio and her colleagues find may be due to the strong positive selection that international migration offers: compared to coresiding grandparents in native households, grandparents who are willing and able to travel internationally are more likely to provide care and to enable women to join the paid labor force.

In addition, column 2 shows that being a naturalized citizen (compared to being a noncitizen or legal permanent resident) increases the probability of participating in the labor force by 15 percent. For immigrant mothers, being married and having one additional preschooler are estimated to reduce the probability of participating in the labor force by 22 and 8 percent, respectively. This model also controls for the immigrant's birth region; the results show that mothers from India, Southwest Asia, and the Middle East are less likely to be in the labor force, while those from Southern Europe and Africa are more likely to be in the labor force.

Column 3 uses the same variables as column 2, but here the key explanatory variable is instrumented. The coefficient of "parent" on the second stage becomes implausibly large, denoting a weak instrument. The fitness of the model is also poor. Table 4 shows the first-stage estimates of this 2SLS. The F-statistic of the first-stage estimates is 37.7, well above the threshold of IV qualification (10.0). "Parent" is statistically significant, but the coefficient is tiny (−0.002). Retirement age is a weak IV, possibly because variation (which is not large) occurs only by country, not by year. Also, working grandparents' eligibility in many countries to take family leave to visit and take care of their U.S.-based grandchildren may also weaken the effectiveness of using retirement age as an IV in this analysis.

Columns 4 and 5 of table 3 combine the regional dummy and each region's interaction terms with "parent" to reveal the regional difference in grandparental support and its impact on mothers' labor force participation in the United States without clustered standard errors (column 4) and with clustered standard errors (column 5). In the model without clustered standard errors, the regional interaction terms of "India and Southwest Asia" and "East and Southeast Asia" have significantly positive effects. Considering that preschoolers' mothers from these two regions have a lower probability of participating in the labor force, having a parent in the household is estimated to increase the probability of the mother being in the labor force for families from these two regions. In other words, for immigrant women from these two regions, grandparental support has a fairly large positive effect on their labor force participation. However, with the standard errors clustered, all regional interactions' significant effects disappear (column 5).

Table 3. Female Immigrants' Labor Force Participation Response, by Parents' Presence

Y = In Labor Force (1,0)	(1) Native-Born	(2) Foreign-Born	(3) Foreign-Born with Instrumental Variable	(4) Foreign-Born, Region, and Parent Interaction (Without Clustered Standard Error)	(5) Foreign-Born, Region, and Parent Interaction	(6) Foreign-Born, Education, and Parent Interaction
Parent present in the same household	−0.042*** (−0.003)	0.074*** (0.004)	4.728*** (0.790)	0.064*** (0.024)	0.563 (68.204)	0.062*** (0.006)
Years of mother's education	0.079*** (0.001)	0.060*** (0.001)	0.103*** (0.007)	0.061*** (0.001)	0.061*** (0.001)	
Age	0.009*** (0.000)	0.020*** (0.001)	0.038*** (0.004)	0.020*** (0.001)	0.020*** (0.001)	0.020*** (0.001)
Age squared	−0.000*** (0.000)	−0.000*** (0.000)	−0.000*** (0.000)	−0.000*** (0.000)	−0.000*** (0.000)	−0.000*** (0.000)
Married	−0.111*** (0.001)	−0.224*** (0.0025)	0.038 (0.030)	−0.225*** (0.003)	−0.225*** (0.003)	−0.220*** (0.003)
Number of children under age six	−0.076*** (0.001)	−0.079*** (0.002)	−0.064*** (−6.060)	−0.079*** (0.002)	−0.079*** (0.002)	−0.078*** (0.002)
Naturalized citizen		0.153*** (0.003)	−0.003 (0.006)	0.153*** (0.003)	0.153*** (0.002)	0.158*** (0.003)
North America (not including the United States and Mexico)		0.037* (0.020)	n.o.	omitted	0.181*** (0.018)	0.023** (0.020)
Latin America		0.006 (0.018)	−0.168*** (0.026)	−0.029*** (0.009)	0.015*** (0.016)	−0.029 (0.019)
Northern Europe		0.027 (0.019)	−0.020 (0.020)	−0.005 (0.013)	0.176*** (0.020)	0.015 (0.019)
Western Europe		omitted	−0.016 (0.020)	−0.037** (0.018)	0.144*** (0.024)	omitted
Southern Europe		0.059*** (0.022)	−0.084 (0.042)	0.031* (0.016)	0.215*** (0.019)	0.037*** (0.022)
Central Europe		−0.017 (0.018)	−0.185*** (0.029)	−0.052*** (0.010)	0.128*** (0.017)	−0.030 (0.018)
East and Southeast Asia		0.027 (0.019)	−0.333*** (0.056)	−0.014 (0.010)	0.167*** (0.016)	0.009 (0.019)
India and Southwest Asia		−0.141*** (0.018)	−0.396*** (0.043)	−0.181*** (0.010)	−0.002 (0.016)	−0.148*** (0.019)
Middle East		−0.153*** (−7.490)	n.o.	−0.182*** 0(.020)	omitted	−0.168*** (0.023)
Africa		0.050*** (0.019)	−0.298*** (0.046)	0.014 (0.010)	0.193*** (0.017)	0.025** (0.019)
N America_parent interaction					−0.115 (0.099)	−0.605 (68.835)
Latin_parent interaction					−0.013 (0.024)	−0.512 (120.345)

(continued)

Table 3. (*cont.*)

Y = In Labor Force (1,0)	(1) Native-Born	(2) Foreign-Born	(3) Foreign-Born with Instrumental Variable	(4) Foreign-Born, Region, and Parent Interaction (Without Clustered Standard Error)	(5) Foreign-Born, Region, and Parent Interaction	(6) Foreign-Born, Education, and Parent Interaction
N Europe_parent interaction				−0.327***	−0.829	
				(0.068)	(130.285)	
W Europe_parent interaction				−0.663**	−1.159	
				(0.333)	(141.142)	
S Europe_parent interaction				−0.213***	−0.711	
				(0.062)	(136.196)	
Central Europe_parent interaction				−0.028	−0.525	
				(0.033)	(113.526)	
East/Southeast Asia _ parent interaction				0.058**	−0.441	
				(0.026)	(50.908)	
India/SW Asia_ parent interaction				0.087***	−0.410	
				(0.027)	(73.661)	
Middle East_ parent interaction				−0.351***	−0.851	
				(0.118)	(61.069)	
Africa_parent interaction					−0.499	
					(59.400)	
High-edu (dummy)						0.144***
						(0.003)
Middle-edu (dummy)						0.104***
						(0.003)
HE_parent interaction						0.024**
						(0.010)
ME_parent interaction						0.011
						(0.010)
Constant	0.482***	0.204	0.304***	0.235***	0.062***	0.132***
	(0.003)	(0.026)	(0.026)	(0.018)	(0.023)	(0.026)
Group number	120	120	120	120	120	120
Observations	752,120	178,206	115,328	178,206	178,206	178,206
Within R-squared	0.056	0.114	0.020	0.114	0.114	0.108
Between R-squared	0.06	0.006	0.200	0.006	0.006	0.010
Overall R-squared	0.056	0.113	0.020	0.113	0.113	0.107

Source: Author's compilation based on 2006–2014 CPS monthly data (Flood et al. 2015).
Notes: Sample includes foreign-born females who were mothers of at least one child under age six. Robust standard errors are reported in brackets. n.o. = no observation.
*p < .10; **p < .05; ***p < .01

Table 4. First-Stage Estimates of the Relationship Between the Probability of a Parent's Presence and Retirement Age in a Fixed-Effects Model

	Dependent Variable: Parent Present in the Same Household
Retirement age coefficient	−0.002***
(t-statistic)	(0.000)
F-statistics for IV	37.700
Between R-squared	0.137
N (group number)	115,328 (120)

Source: Author's compilation based on 2006–2014 CPS monthly data (Flood et al. 2015).
Notes: Other independent variables include education, age, age squared, marital status, region dummies, and citizenship.
***$p < .01$

Finally, the regression on column 6 of table 3 includes college-educated (HE) and medium-educated (ME) dummies and allows interactions between these education indicators and a parent's presence in the same household in order to examine whether parental support helps highly educated immigrant women more than their less-educated counterparts. The interaction term of college-educated and parent's presence being highly significant indicates that the effects of grandparental support on labor force participation for college-educated immigrant mothers are larger than the effects on their less-educated counterparts. Everything else controlled, a college-educated immigrant mother living with a parent has a 16.8 percent higher probability of being in the labor force than an immigrant mother with a high school education or less who lives with a parent.[2] This is also evidence that the labor force niche of immigrants' parents has an economic rationale: it is more economically beneficial for a grandparent to provide child care and enable the higher-educated mother to work because highly educated women are paid more in the labor market. The interaction of being medium-educated with having a parent present in the household is not statistically significant; thus, the benefit from having a grandparent present is significant only when the mother is college-educated. This finding echoes the research by Cortés and Tessada (2011), who find that low-skilled immigration increases work hours for highly paid and high-skilled women.

To test the robustness I ran the same sets of fixed-effects panel OLS regressions on logged hours worked last week. The results (signs, significance levels, and relative magnitudes of the key explanatory variable) are similar. (Results are not shown here but are available upon request.)

Difference-in-Differences Regression Results

Table 5 shows the unweighted relations of the two treatments—having a newborn and having a coresiding parent. Foreign-born females from eighteen to forty-five years old who gave birth during the sixteen-month interview period are included. The labor force participation rate of the group with no parent present in the same household drops about five percentage points postpartum, compared to almost no change for the group with a parent present.

Table 5. Labor Force Participation Rate of Foreign-Born Women Ages Eighteen to Forty-Five Before and After Giving Birth, by Parent Presence in the Same Household

	No Parent in the Household	Parent in the Household	Total Observations
Before new birth	58.21%	65.31%	10,451
After new birth	53.51%	65.08%	11,449
Total observations	20,301	1,599	21,900

Source: Author's compilation based on 2006–2014 CPS monthly data (Flood et al. 2015).
Notes: Unweighted. Only women who were interviewed for eight completed periods, had given birth during the interview period, and were household heads or spouses of household heads are included.

2. College (highly educated) dummy's coefficient (0.144) plus interaction term's coefficient (0.024).

Table 6. Female Immigrants' Labor Force Participation: Difference-in-Differences Regression Results

Y = In Labor Force (1,0)	(1) Foreign-Born		(2) Native-Born	
Observations	148,981		771,627	
R-squared	0.0971		0.0396	
Post-childbirth	−0.067	(−14.330)***	−0.063	(−35.600)***
Coresiding parent	0.051	(9.390)***	−0.047	(−15.700)***
Child-parent interaction	0.033	(2.040)**	0.024	(2.880)
Years of education	−0.0200	(61.660)***	−0.0300	(155.910)***
Age	0.009	(40.770)***	0.002	(32.240)***
Marital status	−0.216	(−69.510)***	−0.083	(−79.170)***
Naturalized	0.129	(50.450)***	—	
Constant	0.206	(24.080)***	0.335	(90.600)***

Source: Author's compilation based on 2006–2014 CPS monthly data (Flood et al. 2015).
Note: Sample contains eighteen- to forty-five-year-old females who were household heads or spouses of household heads.
*p < .10; **p < .05; ***p < .01

Table 6 presents the results of the difference-in-differences method implemented by a regression with interaction terms of the two treatments. Column 1 shows that the difference-in-differences estimator is statistically significant at the 5 percent level. The coefficients of the first three explanatory variables show that for a foreign-born woman who does not have a coresiding parent, the probability of being in the labor force declines 6.7 percent after she has a child, compared to a decline of 3.4 percent for those who have a coresiding parent. In other words, having a coresiding parent significantly alleviates the decline in labor force participation of new immigrant mothers.

Column 2 presents the results of the same model run on the native-born counterparts of these foreign-born mothers. Both having a newborn and having a coresiding parent decrease the probability of being in the labor force for a native mother. The difference-in-differences estimator is positive (meaning having a coresiding parent may alleviate the postpartum labor force participation decline), but it is not statistically significant.

When I run the same regressions using logged hours worked as the dependent variable, the difference-in-differences estimator is not statistically significant. The effect on hours worked may not be as significant as on labor force participation because, with the CPS data following women for only a relatively short period (sixteen months), there might not be much difference in work hours for women who have already shortened their work hours prior to giving birth. On the other hand, pregnant women who intend to stop working are likely to stay in their job (although cutting down their hours) until the baby's arrival and then choose not return to work. Therefore, using CPS data and this research design, labor force participation is a better outcome to examine rather than hours worked.

NON-IMMIGRANT PARENTS AND THE CASE OF CHINA

More recently arrived parents of immigrants are more likely to be on non-immigrant visas (usually the B-2 type), and they are not well represented in CPS or census data. As discussed earlier, the non-immigrant parents of immigrants can obtain LPR status and eventually become naturalized citizens through family sponsorship from their immigrant children. Not much attention has been paid, however, to the recent rise in the number of older temporary visitors. We can better understand the current magnitude and the future trend of this caregiving population by examining the non-immigration visa data.

Figure 2 shows the recent fifteen-year trends in B-2 admissions for those age fifty and older

Figure 2. B-2 Admissions for Tourists and Visitors Age Fifty and Older from Selected Countries (Not Including Mexico), 2000–2014

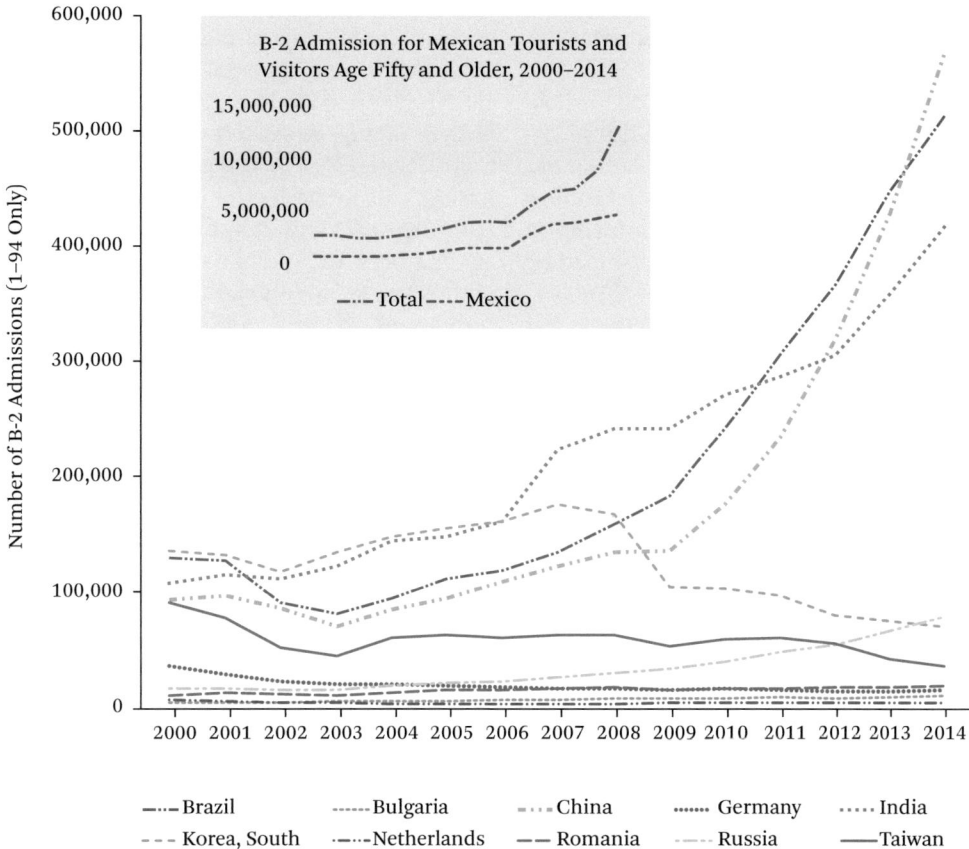

Source: U.S. Department of Homeland Security, "Nonimmigrant Admissions (1-94 Only) by Selected Class of Admission (B2 Only), Selected Category of Age (Fifty and Above), Regional and Selected County of Citizenship: Fiscal Year 2000 to 2014." Washington: U.S. Department of Homeland Security.

Notes: Beginning in 2010, the number of I-94 non-immigrant admissions has greatly exceeded the totals reported in previous years owing to a more complete count of land admissions, and the number of I-94 non-immigrant admissions in 2013 and 2014 greatly exceeded the totals reported in previous years because Canadian air and sea admissions were counted more completely.

from selected countries. B-2 visas are issued for tourists and for those visiting friends and family in the United States temporarily. Given that we do not have detailed information about the purpose of these visits, we have to assume that some of these visitors are care-providing grandparents. Numbers for these grandparents are mixed in with those for tourists and temporary visitors in this age group. While the care-providing visitors typically stay longer than others (usually up to six months, the maximum length of stay allowed by this visa), we have no specific information about their length of stay that would give us a better estimate of their numbers.

In figure 2, data for Mexico, which has experienced the most drastic increase in B-2 admissions,[3] has been graphed separately so as

---

3. This might in part be due by a change in counting methods by the Department of Homeland Security (DHS). Until 2005, typically only the initial land admission of an I-94 non-immigrant was recorded by the DHS. That

not to dwarf the changes in B-2 admissions from the other countries. China, Brazil, and India are the other three countries that have recently sent a soaring number of older B-2 visitors to the United States—a trend that echoes the observation earlier in this article that the cultures and practices of Latin America and East and Southeast Asian countries are among the most noteworthy in providing grandparental support. The dramatic increases in older B-2 visitors may also be explained by the rise of the middle class in these countries, as well as the existing immigrant population from these countries in the United States. It is also interesting to compare China with Taiwan and South Korea, two other countries that have similar Confucian cultures and that emphasize intergenerational support. The economies and immigration inflows to the United States of these two countries took off prior to the more recent period of Chinese economic development and increasing immigration inflows, their fertility rates have been low, and their "grandparent" inflow has been stable. (We even see a decline in the number of older B-2 visitors from South Korea.) Examining the older B-2 visitor trends helps us understand how the caregiving grandparents' niche is perpetuated by family ties to earlier immigrants as well as by the economic development of the major immigrant-sending countries.

I examine China not only because of its grandparental culture but also because, in the current Chinese economic and political context, more parents of current Chinese immigrants are expected to arrive. Chinese elderly are highly involved with their grandchildren. Studies have found that this tradition is maintained in Chinese immigrant families in the United States and that grandparents in Chinese immigrant families do more than take care of children and help with household chores: they also educate children about Chinese language and culture (Xie and Xia 2011), provide role models, and maintain the family's historical continuity (Falk and Falk 2002, 134–36).

Many Chinese immigrants who arrived in the last couple of decades were at the prime age for getting an education or taking a high-skill job. Immigrants in this wave were mostly born after the implementation of China's one-child policy and are likely to be the only child in their family; as such, they are accustomed to their parents' care. As these highly educated immigrants settle in the United States and have their own children, their parents follow as caregivers. In light of the financial success of the Chinese middle class, it is likely that the number of migrating Chinese grandparents will continue to increase in the near future.

To supplement the quantitative analysis of non-immigrant, care-providing Chinese grandparents, I conducted semistructured interviews with fifteen Chinese immigrant families that include grandparents who are on B-2 visas. Although the limited sample does not permit generalization, this qualitative part of the research allows me to describe the dynamics of this special population in greater detail.

Yang came to the United States for an advanced degree in 2004 and currently holds a full-time job on the East Coast. Both Yang and her highly educated husband, also born in China, are the only children in their families. Even when Yang was in school, her mother would come to the United States for a couple of months to provide care and cook for her during critical exam times. When Yang had her first daughter, their family had the typical "4-2-1" family structure of Chinese households after the implementation of the one-child policy (which stayed in place for over a generation): four grandparents, two parents, and one child. Recently Yang and her husband had a second daughter. Ever since Yang's older child was born, her parents (mostly her mother) and her in-laws have been taking turns staying with the family, each for around six months, and this pattern has continued with the addition to the family. Besides taking care of the kids, her parents and her in-laws also cook and help around the house when they have a chance. Yang's

---

year, the DHS began an effort to record all land admissions. For more information, see Department of Homeland Security, "The Impact of Counting Changes on Nonimmigrant Admissions: An Update," 2012, available at: https://www.dhs.gov/sites/default/files/publications/Impact%20of%20Counting%20Changes%20on%20NI%20Admissions%20August%202012.pdf (accessed June 2, 2017).

older daughter, now three, speaks mostly Chinese so far, since Chinese is the only language spoken at home. Yang considers herself very lucky to have both sets of parents providing care: "It saves us so much money. If not for their help, I don't think it would make sense for me to go to work while sending both kids to day care. I told them they do not need to take care of the elder one after she turns two, and was thinking about sending her to day care. But they insist on keeping her at home for longer." Yang and her husband are legal permanent residents and in the process of being naturalized. They plan to sponsor their parents for LPR status as soon as they become eligible.

Wang and her two-year-old son followed her husband, who took a faculty position at a Midwestern U.S. university in 2011. Wang has been working on a PhD degree at the same university. Their son was born in Singapore in 2009, when Wang's husband held a postdoc position there, and Wang's mother went to Singapore to take care of her and the baby. Later, they moved back to a city not far from Wang's hometown in China, and her mother often visited them there to help out. Since they moved to the United States, her mother has visited three times, each visit lasting three to six months. Wang's daughter was born in 2015. Because her mother was experiencing health issues at that time, her in-laws came from China to stay with them right before the baby arrived to provide care. During that period, her father-in-law's own father in China became sick and he had to return. Her mother-in-law stayed for the whole six months allowed by her B-2 visa. Wang has a younger brother who has stayed in Canada after going there for his master's degree. He and his wife are expecting a child, and Wang's mother plans to help them when the new grandchild arrives. She will stay for only two weeks, however, since her daughter-in-law's parents will also be there and plan to be the primary caregivers.

In Wang's case (and her brother's), we see the strong preference for the maternal grandmother as the first choice of caregiver. The first month after childbirth, known as yuezi (meaning "month"), is crucial for both mother and baby in Chinese culture and practice. Because new mothers are expected to lie down whenever possible, they need help taking care of the baby as well as themselves. Traditionally, most women married into the husband's family and the paternal grandmother was the main caregiver during the yuezi period. Now that more and more young couples live apart from their parents, however, the first choice for this role is the maternal grandparents—especially the maternal grandmother, because she knows best the new mother's eating and living preferences.

Zhang came to the United States for an advanced degree in 2009. Her husband is a third-generation Chinese immigrant born and raised in a Latin American country. They recently moved from the South to the West Coast while Zhang was pregnant, and her husband took a job there. After their baby arrived, Zhang's parents came to stay with them to take care of the baby, and when the baby was three months, Zhang happily went back to work in a new job. Without her parents' support, according to Zhang, it would have been a lot more difficult for her to return to the labor force. "I know that they will do a good job, a better job than I perhaps," said Zhang. She also mentioned that her in-laws, who are second-generation Chinese immigrants living in Latin America, are not likely to offer such child care, partly because they are still working in their country, but also because, being more Westernized, they are not used to the idea of offering to care for grandchildren, as Zhang's parents are. Zhang has applied for an extended stay for her parents of another six months so that they can remain until her baby is close to a year old and more ready for day care.

In the absence of grandparents willing and able to provide care, my interviewees' backup plans included care by the mother herself, care by the other set of grandparents, day care, and nanny service. No one mentioned "satellite babies" as an option: in an earlier prevalent practice, Chinese immigrants sent infants back to China to be raised by members of their extended families (Bohr and Tse 2009; Skeldon 1997; Waters 2001).

All child-caring grandparents I interviewed had close social network ties in China. Some had other grandchildren who also needed care, and some were caregivers for their own parents in China. Their double caregiving role and close social ties back in China required that they travel frequently. At the same time, their limited free time while providing care, cultural differences, language barriers, and the low walkability of American cities made Chinese grandparents more socially dependent during their time in the United States than they were back in China.

The one-child policy may have reduced the competition for attention from other grandchildren, but when the only child lives overseas, the China-based parents face a difficult choice about where to settle long-term. I gleaned from my interviews that the main consideration in determining the long-term plan is whether the immigrant is the only child. If they have other children in China, the parents tend to say that they will eventually go back to China. Those with an only child who lives in the United States, especially widowed parents, seem to be indecisive and concerned about the future. Huang, the only child of her family, came to the United States for her PhD, is now married to a U.S. citizen, and has a two-year-old son. She told me: "I grew increasingly worried about my mother after my father passed away four years ago. I feel obliged to call her every day to make sure she is doing well when she is in China. My mother is happier here to see us every day, but I can tell she still misses her sisters and friends at home. In another ten years, her friends and sisters may all leave our hometown and stay near their own children in other cities. It's almost definite that she will need to stay with us in the future, although she says she is undecided."

Other concerns about staying in the United States include the language barrier, lifestyle differences, lack of health insurance, and social dependency. Song, a sixty-two-year-old caregiving grandmother in the United States, told me that once when she had to be hospitalized, the doctor gave a long explanation and instructions to her through her daughter, but her daughter translated it into only a few sentences in Chinese. "I feel very frustrated, not being able to understand anything," Song said. Liang, a caregiving grandfather I interviewed, said, "Even in China nowadays, young people do not want to live with their elderlies because it is not convenient that way. We do not want to live with them [his children] either. We are freer by ourselves. Not to mention in the United States we do many things differently." Although most of the China-based grandparents I interviewed were middle-class, they spoke no English or very limited English. Most of them could not afford housing in a major U.S. city and also found it socially hard to maintain a household by themselves in the United States. In China, they might have been leading a happy retired life, just without their beloved grandchildren. The advantages of staying in the United States mentioned by these grandparents included being close to children and grandchildren, the nice weather and environment, better economic and educational opportunities for children and grandchildren, and readily available Chinese produce.

CONCLUSIONS AND DISCUSSION

Overall, I find that immigrants' parents fill an important yet often overlooked niche in the U.S. labor market—providing care for their grandchildren and freeing up female immigrants to participate in the paid labor market. Although grandparental support is not a new phenomenon and has been analyzed in the literatures of many regions, it has not been examined and documented in the context of immigration before; nor has it received much attention from immigration researchers and policymakers. Care-providing parents of immigrants work for free, and their economic contribution is largely hidden. Foreign-born, care-providing grandparents are unpaid contingent workers in the U.S. labor market who fill a niche that otherwise might not be filled (in the case of stay-at-home mothers).

My empirical analysis using panel regression finds that having a coresiding grandparent increases the labor force participation probability of immigrant new mothers by about 7.4 percent and that the effects differ by birth region or country and educational level. Further, my difference-in-differences analysis shows that coresiding parents significantly alleviate the labor force participation decline of new immigrant mothers.

A case study of China-based care-providing parents illustrates that the role of immigrants' parents goes beyond lifting female immigrants into the paid labor market. Over the long term, their presence and caregiving may improve the health of their immigrant children and grandchildren as well as the grandchildren's school performance. The time and help that immigrants' parents devote to the third generation also seem to increase their own mental health.

Because of limited data availability, this study assumes that coresiding grandparents provide care, since the CPS does not provide this information. Therefore, I have examined the impact of coresiding grandparents only, not of those who live nearby and provide care. Also, the short longitudinal coverage of the CPS confines the difference-in-differences analysis to children between ages zero and fifteen months. This is reasonable for examining the impact of grandparents visiting and providing temporary care, but it is not ideal for looking at those who are permanent legal residents—that is, the parents of children who have become naturalized citizens. As for the dependent variable, I use women's labor force participation as a measurement of the impact of intergenerational support, on the assumption that coresiding grandparents provide child care to an extent that affects the mother's decision to be employed in paid work. Though providing child care might not necessarily lift mothers to the paid labor force, help from coresiding grandparents could influence a number of other factors. Future research should examine other labor market outcomes, such as the family wage gap, gender inequality, and related health outcomes such as women's fertility rate and postpartum health.

Finally, both the availability of immigrants' parents and their future in this country are largely shaped by U.S. immigration policy. Many primary immigrants who are in their child-bearing years (the time when they need help the most) are work-visa holders, LPRs, or working on becoming naturalized, which is a lengthy process. The caregiving parents of this population arrive on B-2 visas and are restricted by the six-months-per-year rule (and three months for those from Visa Waiver Program [VWP] member countries, who are traveling without a visa). These parents' path toward naturalization is determined by U.S. naturalization policy, which differs by country of birth and sponsor's citizenship status. In addition to immigration status, foreign-born grandparents providing child care face many other challenges that call for policy responses, including health insurance coverage, language barriers, and adaptation to U.S. life. Even those grandparents who have become LPRs face the tough choice as they grow older and overseas travel becomes increasingly inconvenient between living with their children and grandchildren in the United States, with all the language and cultural barriers, and remaining in their home country and not being able to see their extended family in the United States—perhaps their only remaining family.

REFERENCES

Aassve, Arnstein, Bruno Arpino, and Alice Goisis. 2012. "Grandparenting and Mothers' Labor Force Participation: A Comparative Analysis Using the Generations and Gender Survey." *Demographic Research* 27(3): 53–84.

Albertini, Marco, Martin Kohli, and Claudia Vogel. 2007. "Intergenerational Transfer of Time and Money in European Patterns–Different Regimes?" *Journal of European Social Policy* 17(4): 319–34.

Albuquerque, Paula, and Jose Passos. 2010. "Grandparents and Women's Participation in the Labor Market." Working paper. Lisbon: Technical University of Lisbon.

Batalova, Jeanne. 2012. "Senior Immigrants in the United States." Washington, D.C.: Migration Policy Institute.

Bohr, Yvonne, and Connie Tse. 2009. "Satellite Babies in Transnational Families: A Study of Parents' Decision to Separate from Their Infants." *Infant Mental Health Journal* 30(3): 256–86.

Borjas, George. 1999. "Economic Analysis of Immigration." In *Handbook of Labor Economics*, vol. 3, edited by Orley C. Ashenfelter and David Card. Amsterdam: Elsevier.

Byker, Yanya. 2016. "The Opt-Out Continuation: Education, Work, and Motherhood from 1984 to 2012.: *RSF: The Russell Sage Foundation Journal of the Social Sciences* 2(4): 34–70.

Cortés, Patricia, and José Tessada. 2011. "Low-Skilled Immigration and the Labor Supply of Highly Skilled Women." *American Economic Journal: Applied Economics* 3(3, July): 88–123.

Drew, Julia A. Rivera, Sarah Flood, and John Robert

Warren. 2014. "Making Full Use of the Longitudinal Design of the Current Population Survey: Methods for Linking Records Across 16 Months." *Journal of Economic and Social Measurement* 39(3): 121–44. DOI: 10.3233/JEM-140388.

Eckstein, Susan, and Giovanni Peri. 2018. "Immigrant Niches and Immigrant Networks in the U.S. Labor Market." *RSF: The Russell Sage Foundation Journal of the Social Sciences* 4(1): 1–17. DOI: 10.7758/RSF.2018.4.1.01.

England, Paula, Jonathan Bearak, Michelle J. Budig, and Melissa J. Hodges. 2016. "Do Highly Paid, Highly Skilled Women Experience the Largest Motherhood Penalty?" *American Sociology Review* 81(6): 1161–89.

Falk, Ursula Adler, and Gerhard Falk. 2002. *Grandparents: A New Look at the Supporting Generation*. Amherst, N.Y.: Prometheus Books.

Fields, Jason, Martin O'Connell, and Barbara Downs. 2011. "Grandparents in the United States, 2001." Washington: U.S. Department of Commerce, U.S. Census Bureau, Economic Statistics Division.

Flood, Sarah, Miriam King, Steven Ruggles, and J. Robert Warren. 2015. *Integrated Public Use Microdata Series: Version 4.0* (machine-readable database). Minneapolis: University of Minnesota.

García-Morán, Eva, and Zoë Kuehn. 2013. "With Strings Attached: Grandparent-Provided Child Care and Female Labor Market Outcomes." SOEP Papers on Multidisciplinary Panel Data Research 610-2013. Berlin: German Socio-Economic Panel Study at DIW Berlin.

Grey, Anne. 2005. "The Changing Availability of Grandparents as Carers and Its Implications for Childcare Policy in the U.K." *Journal of Social Policy* 34(4): 557–77.

Hank, Karsten, and Isabella Buber. 2008. "Grandparents Caring for Their Grandchildren: Findings from the 2004 Survey of Health, Ageing, and Retirement in Europe." *Journal of Family Issues* 30(1): 53–73.

Heckman, James J. 1974. "Effects of Child-Care Programs on Women's Work Efforts." *Journal of Political Economy* 82(2, pt. 2, March–April): S136–63.

Maurer-Fazio, Margaret, Rachel Connelly, Chen Lan, and Lixin Tang. 2009. "Childcare, Eldercare, and Labor Force Participation of Married Women in Urban China: 1982–2000." IZA Discussion Paper 4204. Bonn: Institute for the Study of Labor (June).

Nizalova, Y. Olena, Tamara Sliusarenko, and Solomiya Shpak. 2016. "The Motherhood Penalty in Times of Transition." *Journal of Comparative Economics* 44(1): 56–75.

Ogawa, Naohiro, and John F. Ermisch. 1996. "Family Structure, Home Time Demands, and the Employment Patterns of Japanese Married Women." *Journal of Labor Economics* 14(4): 677–702.

Peri, Giovanni, and Chad Sparber. 2009. "Task Specialization, Immigration, and Wages." *American Economic Journal: Applied Economics* 1(2): 135–69.

———. 2011. "Highly Educated Immigrants and Native Occupational Choice." *Industrial Relations: A Journal of Economy and Society* 50(3): 385–411.

Posadas, Josefine, and Marian Vidal-Fernandez. 2013. "Grandparents' Childcare and Female Labor Force Participation." *IZA Journal of Labor Policy* 2: 14.

Skeldon, Ronald. 1997. "Migrants on a Global Stage: The Chinese." In *Pacific Rim Development: Integration and Globalization in the Asia-Pacific Economy*, edited by Peter J. Rimmer. Crows Nest, Au.: Allen and Unwin.

Tran, Van C. 2010. "English Gain vs. Spanish Loss? Language Assimilation Among Second-Generation Latinos in Young Adulthood." *Social Forces* 98(September): 257–84.

Waters, Johanna L. 2001. "The Flexible Family? Recent Immigration and 'Astronaut' Households in Vancouver, British Columbia." Vancouver: Vancouver Centre of Excellence, Research on Immigration and Integration in the Metropolis.

Waters, Mary C., Patrick Carr, Maria Keflas, and Jennifer Holdaway, eds. 2011. *Coming of Age in America: The Transition to Adulthood in the Twenty-First Century*. Berkeley: University of California Press.

Wheelock, Jane, and Katharine Jones. 2002. "Grandparents Are the Next Best Thing: Informal Childcare for Working Parents in Urban Britain." *Journal of Social Policy* 31(3): 441–63.

Wooldridge, Jeffery. 2002. *Econometric Analysis of Cross-section and Panel Data*. Cambridge, Mass.: MIT Press.

Xie, Xiaolin, and Xia Yan. 2011. "Grandparenting in Chinese Immigrant Families." *Marriage and Family Review* 47(6): 383–96.

Bridging the Service Divide: Dual Labor Niches and Embedded Opportunities in Restaurant Work

ELI R. WILSON

Restaurants and other interactive service workplaces in the United States serve as labor niches for two very different kinds of workers doing different tasks. Immigrant Latinos primarily work "back-of-the-house" jobs doing manual tasks, while class-privileged whites work "front-of-the-house" jobs performing customer-facing tasks. How do these social and structural cleavages between dual labor niches affect the workplace dynamic? Drawing on ethnographic research in upscale Los Angeles restaurants, I describe the closed boundaries between these distinct labor niches and the valuable bridging between them performed by certain workers who are able to ease social tensions and buffer the service labor process. I discuss the implications of these findings for the study of contemporary immigrant labor niches and the nature of the opportunities within them and between them.

Keywords: immigrant niches, second generation, restaurants, labor markets, Latinos

In many global U.S. cities, a growing number of restaurants, hotels, and other "interactive" service workplaces serve as employment niches for two distinct types of individuals doing two distinct and unequal types of labor. On the one hand, unskilled Latino immigrants work the majority of the "back-of-the-house" jobs, with tasks like cleaning, stocking, and cooking. On the other hand, class-privileged whites fill "front-of-the-house" jobs whose primary tasks involve customer service. Although often stationed just feet apart in the workplace, these two different worker cohorts have little in common: most would not only be unable to perform the other's job but could not even communicate in the same language.

How does the presence of *dual* employment niches affect the labor dynamic within contemporary interactive service workplaces? How are these niches maintained, and with what consequences for workers? Traditional scholarship on labor relations focuses primarily on the tension between workers and management (Burawoy 1979) or, more recently, between workers and customers (see Leidner 1993; Lopez 2010). Yet these perspectives, with a few notable exceptions (for example, Kanter 1977), tend to neglect or downplay *intra*-worker relations in the

---

Eli R. Wilson received his PhD from the University of California–Los Angeles and is visiting scholar at UCLA's Institute for Research on Labor and Employment.

© 2018 Russell Sage Foundation. Wilson, Eli R. 2018. "Bridging the Service Divide: Dual Labor Niches and Embedded Opportunities in Restaurant Work." *RSF: The Russell Sage Foundation Journal of the Social Sciences* 4(1): 115–27. DOI: 10.7758/RSF.2018.4.1.07. I would like to thank Rubén Hernández-León, Roger Waldinger, Neil Gong, three anonymous reviewers, and this issue's journal editors, Susan Eckstein and Giovanni Peri, for their comments on previous drafts of this article. Any remaining errors are my own. Direct correspondence to: Eli R. Wilson at eli.revelle.wilson@gmail.com, 264 Haines Hall, 375 Portola Plaza, Los Angeles, CA 90095.

workplace. Similarly, existing literature on immigrant and ethnic labor niches provides us with valuable insight into the high concentration of particular immigrant groups in certain lines of work (Filipinas in nursing, Vietnamese women in nail salons, Mexican men in agriculture, and so on), but the analytical toolkits that scholars usually deploy are geared toward capturing either descriptive employment trends of immigrant groups or the process of niche formation itself (Eckstein and Peri, this issue; Waldinger and Lichter 2003). This leaves us with an incomplete understanding of the worlds of work within which immigrant niches are embedded. As a consequence, we remain unclear on how immigrant niches in particular industries today are affecting the labor process, shop-floor social relations between members and nonmembers (who themselves may be members of other niches), and the nature of opportunity in these workplaces.

Restaurants in immigrant gateway cities like Los Angeles provide excellent settings in which to examine contemporary labor niches up close. The food and beverage industry has grown into one of the largest sectors of the U.S. economy, generating billions of dollars in annual revenue and employing 14.4 million Americans nationwide.[1] With 276,000 food and drink establishments in the city alone, Los Angeles is the nation's largest regional restaurant industry (Restaurants Opportunities Center of Los Angeles 2011). It also employs an extremely diverse group of workers: nearly two-thirds of all Los Angeles restaurant workers are Hispanic, and over half (55.2 percent) are foreign-born, mostly from Mexico, Central America, and Asia (ROC-LA 2011). Many of these non-white immigrant workers are concentrated in low-wage, manual-labor positions such as cooking, dishwashing, and bussing tables. By contrast, white men and women are concentrated in customer-facing restaurant jobs such as serving, bartending, and management (Restaurants Opportunities Centers United 2014). In effect, the strong patterning found in Los Angeles restaurants by race, class, and gender reflects two distinct labor niches in these workplaces: a white front of the house and an immigrant Latino back of the house.

This study draws on over two years of ethnographic fieldwork within upscale, full-service Los Angeles restaurants in which I examined how the two unequal labor niches in restaurant work are maintained and kept closed against one another. On this divided shop floor, I show that some workers, as a function of their particular skills and attributes, are able to function as crucial agents helping to bridge social and structural inequalities between workers and facilitate the flow of food service. I close by discussing how this research advances the study of contemporary immigrant labor niches, particularly those located in expanding interactive service industries.

METHODS AND FIELD SITES

The research discussed in this article is part of a larger project examining labor, immigration, and inequality in the Los Angeles restaurant industry. I derive the data from participant observation within two upscale Los Angeles restaurants in which I was employed as a waiter ("server"). My fieldwork within the first restaurant described here lasted fourteen months between 2012 and 2013, and my fieldwork within the second restaurant lasted five months, from the fall of 2015 to the spring of 2016. At each field site, as I worked two to five shifts per week (totaling twelve to thirty-five hours), I recorded observations on a wide variety of work-related events such as hiring interviews, employee training sessions, daily service on "the floor," and post-shift parties. I compiled notes immediately following fieldwork each day, storing them on dated, password-protected files on a personal computer. All of the individuals I interacted with regularly, including management, were made aware of my research intention.

Participant observation is a unique methodological tool for understanding shop-floor dynamics since it allows the researcher to examine the unfolding of micro-relationships in

---

1. National Restaurant Association, "News and Research: Facts at a Glance," November 18, 2016, available at: http://www.restaurant.org/News-Research/Research/Facts-at-a-Glance (accessed November 20, 2016).

a particular context. My initial approach to this fieldwork followed the tenets of grounded theory (Glaser and Strauss 1967), according to which a researcher enters the field without formal hypotheses or theoretical assumptions and allows the ensuing analysis to emerge inductively. After initial data collection, I began to focus on refining my working theories by actively seeking out "deviant cases" in the field (see Timmermans and Tavory 2012). Following this logic, I decided to enter a second field site with slightly different characteristics so as to expand, contrast, and cross-check my overall body of data.[2] Additionally, I supplemented my data with a series of in-depth, nonrandom interviews with workers from both restaurants. Each interview lasted between thirty and ninety minutes on average and centered on three broad discussion topics: personal work history, workplace social relations, and long-term goals and career aspirations.

Field Site 1: Match Restaurant
Match (pseudonym) is a popular, casual-upscale restaurant located in an affluent area of west Los Angeles near the posh neighborhoods of Santa Monica, Venice, and Brentwood. As an exclusive site for upper-middle-class consumption, Match has a primary clientele of white young professionals, in their twenties and thirties, who are local residents, nearby office workers, and foreign tourists. Dining at Match is expensive, though not unusually so for the area. For example, lunch averages $25 per person, and dinner is $40 before tip, tax, and alcohol.

As of 2013, Match had roughly half a dozen managers and eighty workers split evenly between the front and back of the house. The demographic breakdown of these employees closely resembled patterns found in many other higher-end U.S. restaurants: servers, bartenders, hosts, and baristas were primarily young, white, and college-educated, whereas cooks, dishwashers, bussers, and food runners were almost exclusively first- or second-generation Latino men of working-class backgrounds.

Field Site 2: Terroir Restaurant
Terroir is an upscale restaurant on the west side of Los Angeles. Formally opened in the fall of 2015 after several years as a "pop-up" (temporary) restaurant, Terroir offers chef-driven, pan-Asian cuisine. The average cost of a meal per person is $30 at lunch and $50 to $80 at dinner, excluding tax, alcohol, and tip. In contrast to Match's yuppie clientele, Terroir's regulars tend to be middle-aged and monied; most are either white or Asian American.

Terroir is a modest-sized operation compared to Match; it has a smaller seating capacity (80 compared to 120), and a full staff of three managers and forty employees. Like Match, Terroir has mostly white front-of-the-house workers in lead positions, while the kitchen and support workers are primarily Latino immigrant men. At both restaurants, the compensation structure for employees is roughly in line with industry standards nationwide: front-of-the-house workers rely heavily on tips to supplement their minimum-wage earnings, whereas kitchen-based employees do not earn tips but instead make slightly higher hourly wages (approximately $9 to $15). At Match, servers and bartenders get to keep what they make after "tipping out" their support staff (host, busser, runner, and so on). By slight contrast, tips are "pooled" at Terroir: tips are combined at the end of the night and distributed based on a fixed percentage to all customer-facing workers. (Back-of-the-house workers are excluded.) The effect is that tip-based earnings are more volatile at Match than at Terroir, where a slow night can mean no tips for the staff.

INSIDE RESTAURANT WORK
Like other interactive service workplaces (Sherman 2007), restaurant work requires coordinating, producing, and distributing a service that is to be consumed on-site and under time con-

---

2. I do not treat my two field sites as formally comparative cases. Rather, I appraise them as having a family resemblance—both are upscale, full-service Los Angeles restaurants—but with variations in their social and organizational characteristics.

straints (Whyte 1948). This demands a close coordination between different employees: a server must relay specific customer orders to the kitchen (and drink orders to the bar), where the correct dishes (and drinks) are assembled. The dish is handed off to a food runner who must successfully relay it to the correct table. At the conclusion of the meal, a busser clears the table, and the host is notified that the table may be reseated.

This sequence of service tasks is divided into "front-of-the-house" and "back-of-the-house" labor. Each has its own logic, norms, and internal job ladders. Those in lead front-of-the-house positions, such as servers, cashiers, and bartenders, are primarily responsible for guest relations and must ensure that diners leave satisfied ("the customer is always right"). Particularly in higher-end establishments, this labor requires that front-of-the-house workers monitor their emotional and physical displays, which scholars refer to as "emotional" or "aesthetic" labor (Hochschild 1983; Warhurst and Nickson 2009). Food runners, barbacks, bussers, and hosts interact less frequently with guests and are commonly referred to as the "support" staff at the front of the house. Functionally, however, their role is no less important to the overall operation. Support staff often must provide assistance to multiple groups of actors in the workplace, such as customers, managers, cooks, and servers. For example, a host greets guests at the door but also must stay in frequent contact with servers and managers in order to know when new tables are ready to be seated. Similarly, a food runner communicates—often using thick industry slang—with kitchen workers to help shuttle food out to the dining room. Once there, he or she must formally introduce each dish to diners.

Back-of-the-house workers prep, stock, clean, and assemble food items in the restaurant, often behind the scenes. They labor on goods and materials instead of with people. Back-of-the-house labor thus demands different capabilities and skills from front-of-the-house labor: physical strength, dexterity (for example, knife skills), and stamina (an ability to endure, for instance, ten- to twelve-hour shifts), not to mention hot, loud, and often dangerous job conditions. Playing out largely outside customers' view, the norms of the back-of-the-house shop-floor culture often contrast with the hospitality focus of the front of the house to include cursing, shouting, sexual jokes, and even physical violence (see Bourdain 2000; Fine 1996; Whyte 1948). With the exception of management, many back-of-the-house workers acquire their skills informally and on the job (Hagan, Hernández-León, and Demonsant 2015), relying on informal training systems to first learn the work by shadowing incumbent workers (Bailey and Waldinger 1991; Fine 1996) and then later demonstrating the proficiency necessary for kitchen-based promotions (see Lowe, Hagan, and Iskander 2010).

Relations between front- and back-of-the-house restaurant workers periodically swell into conflict. The sociologist William F. Whyte (1948) noted more than half a century ago that waitresses and male cooks in restaurants were frequently at odds. Cooks, attempting to achieve an efficient work rhythm in the kitchen, would view any special requests (or errors) coming from the front of the house as a nuisance at best, a disruption meriting retaliation at worst. Waitresses, focused on maximizing their tips from customers, were primarily interested in bending rules to please diners—regardless of the headaches this created for the kitchen.

In the United States, the divides between front- and back-of-the-house workers are accentuated by the earnings inequality between the two kinds of labor. Cooks, dishwashers, and other pantry workers earn low hourly wages and average scarcely more than minimum wage. With limited job benefits, little employment security, and usually no advancement opportunities, most back-of-the-house restaurant work is seen as dead-end labor—as quintessentially "bad" jobs in the service industry (Kalleberg 2011). In California, front-of-the-house workers earn a minimum wage of $9 an hour plus tips (as of 2015). Tip earnings, however, can be quite substantial at many full-service restaurants, particularly in fine-dining establishments where check averages are higher. For example, a recent multi-city study found that restaurant servers averaged roughly $22 an hour in gross earnings—and sometimes much more (Haley-Lock and Ewert 2011).[3] Food runners, bussers, and those in other support positions earn slightly less. In most restaurants, they are each apportioned a smaller share of tips each night ("tipped out"); recent ethnographic accounts suggest that food runners and bussers typically earn around half the tips that servers and bartenders make (see Gomberg-Muñoz 2011).

MAINTAINING UNEQUAL LABOR NICHES

Today front-of-the-house restaurant workers often do not share the same social characteristics as those scrubbing pots and sweating over a hot grill behind kitchen doors. Particularly in diverse metropolitan centers such as Los Angeles, New York, and Chicago, high-earning serving and bartending jobs function as an employment niche for middle-class white men and women, while back-of-the-house jobs serve as employment niches for Latinos, especially the foreign-born (Gomberg-Muñoz 2011; Jayaraman 2014; ROC-LA 2011; Sherman 2007; Waldinger and Lichter 2003).[4]

A series of overlapping processes channel different restaurant workers into one of the two employment niches. Hiring biases are a powerful way in which management niches employment from the outset. For example, research shows that hiring managers often favor Latino immigrants for the more labor-intensive, low-paying back-of-the-house jobs. As the anthropologist Ruth Gomberg-Muñoz (2011) observes, restaurant managers often see immigrant Latino men as a source of reliable hard workers who are relatively complacent about low wages and difficult working conditions. Such racialized and stereotyped hiring preferences for these positions are found throughout the industry. In many immigrant-heavy areas of the country, cooking, bussing, and janitorial restaurant jobs are now paradigmatic of the "brown-collar" work (Cantazarite 2000) into which Latino immigrants are channeled (Barret 2006).

Discriminatory hiring also reinforces the class-privileged white labor niche in the front of the house. Research shows that employers consistently prefer applicants who they believe possess "soft skills" and other personality-based attributes, such as a "friendly demeanor" (Moss and Tilly 2001). As the sociologist Mary Gatta and her colleagues Heather Boushey and Eileen Appelbaum (2009) have noted, managers' reliance in their hiring decisions on an assemblage of looks, personality, and poise is often a smoke screen for a preference for hiring white, middle-class young adults (Warhurst and Nickson 2009; Williams and Connell 2010). Managers may also share sociocultural traits with those whom they offer the more desirable jobs, reinforcing networks of inequality in the workplace (Rivera 2012). Similarly, the non-white immigrants who do manage to obtain lead front-of-the-house jobs often are more European in appearance and have urbane, middle-class mannerisms (Zukin 1995, 154–73).

The boundaries between the two employment niches of restaurant work are further reinforced through social networks. As the sociologist Mark Granovetter (1974/1995) famously noted, workers often help those in their social circles connect to jobs by alerting them when jobs become available and vouching for their character and skills when talking with employers. These social ties are specific and highly directional: they help connect certain people to similar jobs already held by others in their social network (Granovetter 1985).

Because individuals within a network tend to have similar social traits—a principle known as homophily—social networks contribute to the uniformity of labor niches. This contribution has been well documented among immigrant laborers, who often lean heavily on network ties to gain employment in niche worksites (Hagan 1998; Hondagneu-Sotelo 2001; Massey, Durand, and Malone 2002; Waldinger and Lichter 2003). In this way, back-of-the-house restaurant jobs (as well as some sup-

---

3. This earnings figure may be low, since tip earnings are notoriously underreported. However, yearly earnings figures are often lower for many front-of-the-house workers because they do not work forty-hour weeks (and do not accrue vacation time when they take time off).

4. Many fast-food (or "quick-serve") establishments, particularly in poorer urban areas, are staffed by minorities, immigrants, and those with little education—regardless of position (see Ehrenreich 2001; Newman 1999).

port jobs) can become "colonized" by networks of male, immigrant Mexicans and Central Americans (Massey, Durand, and Malone 2002; Waldinger and Lichter 2003). Network dynamics pattern front-of-the-house jobs in similar ways, but within very different social circles. In step with managerial preferences for hiring the right "look" for customer-facing positions, white middle-class servers and bartenders are often able to "hook up" their friends with similar jobs. Employers may even reach out to workers who appear to exemplify the right traits for the job to see if they have any friends who want to "join the team" (Besen-Cassino 2014; Warhurst and Nickson 2007).

Thus, for the well-connected individuals who fit the right profile for the right restaurant positions, social networks lubricate their entrance into different labor niches in the workplace. These same forces also foreclose access to, or movement *between,* the two niches. Thick social networks threaded with race, class, and other social characteristics severely curtail the prospect of workers within different labor niches switching from back-of-the-house to front-of-the-house jobs, or vice versa. This goes beyond a mere mismatch of skill. Plainly, few employees fit into both social worlds of work. Being embedded in one labor niche (immigrant Latinos working in the back of the house) necessarily means not being a part of the other niche (middle-class whites working in the front of the house). The processes that encourage in-group membership in certain labor niches also close the niches off from one another.

BETWEEN NICHES: TENSION, DISTANCE, AND CONFLICT

At Match and Terroir, the social inequalities between white, middle-class workers and immigrant Latino workers are accentuated by their structural differences as front- and back-of-the-house employees, respectively. The tensions that often ripple along these fault lines manifest in a variety of ways. Most commonly, front- and back-of-the-house workers simply ignore each other at work, as I noted while working at Match:

I take my lunch meal to the break area beyond the kitchen. It is prime break time—right before the lunch rush—and there are two tables already taken. Around one [sit] three white servers who alternate between furious texting on their cell phones and chatting loudly with one another. [Around] the other [sit] four immigrant Mexican cooks, three of [whom] are hastily shoving food into their mouths. The fourth is fast asleep. I hear Charlie, one of the servers seated at the first table, call out my name: "Eli, so glad you could make it to the party!"[5] He speaks loudly and directly over the heads of the cooks, including his sleeping coworker. "Crystal [a server] and I were just talking about where to head for a beer after work!" (October 7, 2012).

Charlie's actions here suggested that he registered only his young, white tablemates as colleagues and social peers. Similarly, often no one in the front of the house was aware when the Mexican immigrant dishwashers, prep cooks, and line cooks at Match clocked in and out. Even floor managers, for example, usually did not notice when the Mexican cook Xeno left for the day and José took over his job working on the kitchen line.

The social distance between those in each labor niche was also clearly illustrated by who knew whose name in the workplace: many white servers did not know the names of their coworkers preparing the food, nor did the Latino cooks know who was serving it. José, a first-generation line cook at Match in his early forties, would occasionally flag me down to ask who "the one with glasses" was (Jerry) or to relay a message to "the blond girl" (Pamela) about the chicken sandwich ticket she had just entered into the point of sale (POS) system. Servers were just as oblivious toward their back-of-the-house coworkers. "There are so many of them," complained Pip, a white waitress in her midtwenties who had worked at Match for two years. "Besides, all I care about is that the food comes out quickly with no errors, you know?"

The smaller scale of operations at Terroir eased the estrangement between front- and

---

5. I have changed names to protect the privacy of those cited in this study.

back-of-the-house workers, but did not necessarily eliminate it. With about half as many workers compared to Match during even the busiest shifts, Terroir presented more intimate opportunities for them to interact across the front- and back-of-the-house labor divide. Bobby, a white server in his late thirties, quickly became well liked among the Mexican dishwashers for the deft sexual jokes he would direct at them when he dropped off dirty plates ("did I hear you say you wanted my culo, Papi? Absolutely, I'll give it to you. Can you wait until after work or should we head into the walk-in [fridge] right now?"). Few other white front-of-the-house workers went to such lengths to establish rapport with their Latino back-of-the-house coworkers. For example, after I witnessed Reggie, a white waiter in his early twenties, chatting with the head chef and two Mexican line cooks stationed in the kitchen, Reggie leaned over to me and whispered, "Hey, Eli, is our new line cook's name Ana?"

Tips also brightened the boundaries between the two labor niches. Despite the different tip distribution structures at Match and Terroir (individualized tips versus pooled tips), tips always flowed primarily to the white server staff, trickled down to the Latino support staff, and stopped short of the kitchen—an unequal reward for a busy day of labor at the restaurant that prompted tense interactions. I made the following field note at the end of a hectic Sunday brunch at Match:

> I was happy that all my tables went smoothly today. They also tipped well, averaging over 20 percent of each bill. Before leaving, I ducked into the kitchen to crack a joke with Xeno and Juan [cooks] and thank them for doing a good job on the line today: I had received no customer [complaints] and lots of compliments on the food. Xeno, looking weary after nine-plus hours of hard cooking, approached me and said, "[It] was really busy today, yeah? You guys must have made a lot of money in tips. Like, what, two hundred dollars maybe?"
>
> "Yeah, we did [okay]," I say, thrown by the line of inquiry. We both stare off towards the dining room. "But not two hundred . . ." I protested.
>
> "How much you made then?" he interrupted, staring at me and looking tired.
>
> "Uhhh, we don't make *that* much money here . . ." I stammered while Xeno turned and walked away without a word. (February 5, 2013)

As several Mexican cooks also suggested to me, they perceived their white coworkers in the front of the house as lazy gringos who did not work very hard for the money they earned. It is worth noting, however, that few complained to management or otherwise attempted to address the issue.

Managerial practices also affect the boundaries between labor niches. Though managers at both Match and Terroir preached collectivist sentiments such as "we are all one family" and "let's take care of each other out there," actual workplace practices suggested the opposite was true. For example, staff meetings for the whole staff were rarely held at Match; instead, meetings were announced as being for "servers and bartenders only," or as "mandatory for all kitchen personnel." At Terroir, during pre-opening training, the general manager, a white man in his forties named Jim, painstakingly welcomed new front-of-the-house staff to "the team." He spent the beginning hour of each day leading group icebreakers, encouraging us to be goofy and to share something unusual about ourselves. By striking contrast, I was never formally introduced to any of the cooks or dishwashers at the restaurant.

Other policies actually *inhibited* interaction between employees in the front and back of the house. For instance, Match servers were not allowed to communicate directly with line cooks during service, as I learned when I tried to correct an order:

> A guest flags me down to say she forgot to mention to put the cream sauce on the side instead of directly on top of her [omelet]. I hurry back to the kitchen to convey the message to the cooks. I go directly to Juan, who I know is manning the egg station today. I begin to explain the instruction to him when [executive] chef Eric screams over to me, "Hey! Don't talk directly to him, you give *me* the instruction, then *I'll* relay the message!"

Humiliated, I repeat the special instructions to him while all the cooks look on. (October 5, 2012)

Match management argued that forcing servers to follow a formal chain of command and to not communicate directly with line cooks had a practical purpose: the person responsible for directing the flow of kitchen production expected to know what was happening in the kitchen at all times. Yet, in practice, following this protocol was sometimes had operationally clunky and socially alienating results. Servers and cooks separated by only a few feet were forced to speak to a third party—the chef—to convey even the simplest of information ("sauce on the side for the omelet on twenty-one!").

Cleavages between niched restaurant workers can also threaten the flow of the food service. White servers who were unable (or unwilling) to appreciate the occupational stresses that Latino kitchen workers regularly faced would inadvertently create more problems for them, and in turn create more problems for themselves as well. As I found out from Xeno only after months of working with him, servers at Match frequently ordered dishes during the heart of the lunch or dinner rush that had been out of stock ("eighty-sixed") for hours, or that required the most labor-intensive preparation. The resulting bottlenecks in kitchen production then caused delays in getting food to the tables. Oblivious to the kitchen issues they had created, servers, dealing with frustrated diners, saw only the cooks' collective ineptitude. A comment during one such delay from Jerry, a white, twenty-six-year-old waiter, is a case in point: "Jeez, it's like all of them [the Latino cooks] went out partying last night and are hungover this morning!"

Personal beefs on the shop floor can also spill over into food service problems. For example, a white Terroir waitress named Dorothy, who could not understand Spanish, complained that Carlos and Jorge, two Guatemalan prep cooks, were "talking shit" about her in Spanish. When management proved reluctant to get involved, Dorothy took matters into her own hands. She announced loudly that she refused to enter the area where Carlos and Jorge were working, which happened to be next to the dishwashing station. Her refusal left her front-of-the-house coworkers scrambling—and none too pleased about it—to help buss her tables and bring dirty dishes to the dish pit. This added duty in turn decreased the time they could spend attending to the needs of guests. Similarly, Antonio, a second-generation Mexican American food runner, told me that he was going to "slack off" with his job duties since he was frustrated about the paltry tips he was receiving. He made it clear that his diminished efforts would not be noticeable enough that management would call him out, but servers would nevertheless have to work harder to run food, clear plates, and reset tables in their sections (thus affecting their tips).

BRIDGING THE SERVICE DIVIDE

If the social and structural cleavages between the two labor niches can disrupt the food service process, the same forces also give value to skills, people, and technologies that can alleviate these disruptions. Electronic POS systems, for example, are an automated means by which restaurants like Match and Terroir can enable different restaurant workers to communicate customer orders using standardized language and procedures. POS systems reduce a restaurant's dependence on the traditional face-to-face communications between servers and kitchen workers—through verbal orders, handwritten ticket stubs, and so on.[6] No less importantly, technological restaurant systems also allow immigrant workers with poor English abilities to function adequately in the kitchen by learning how to interpret a few basic commands.

Yet the growing use of sophisticated POS systems and other smart restaurant technology has had the unintended consequence of rein-

---

6. Other restaurant technologies that have become commonplace have had similar deskilling effects in different areas of the labor process. The software Open Table, for instance, generates an electronic system for online guest reservations, and Hot Schedules is an online employee scheduling hub that centralizes (and digitizes) time-off requests and shift swaps for managerial approval.

forcing the *social* boundaries between immigrant Latino kitchen workers and white dining room workers. Although such technology further reduces the need for interpersonal dialogue between the two sets of coworkers, it cannot entirely eliminate it; restaurant guests frequently and inevitably voice questions, suggest menu revisions, and make special requests that servers need to convey directly to the kitchen. Here lies the distinct advantage of having on staff individuals with the skills to bridge social divides between the white niche and the Latino niche.

A number of Los Angeles restaurants advertise employment opportunities for workers who are bilingual in English and Spanish. Consider the following hiring ads posted to the Craigslist Los Angeles "Food and Beverage" job forum in April 2016:

HIRING NOW Bilingual Spanish/Eng Cashiers & Cooks

COME WORK AT A HAPPY, FUN & FAST PACE ENVIRONMENT

Hiring Cashiers & Cooks with Great growth opportunity.

Job Requirements:

- Must be at least 18 years of age
- Able to work varied shifts including holidays & weekends
- Excellent customer service skills
- Positive attitude
- Attention to detail and quality
- *Bilingual in English & Spanish Preferred*
- May lift materials and/or product up to 50 pounds or more. (italics added)

Kitchen Manager for Popular Restaurant!

Long-standing restaurant group with concepts based on the westside and greater LA area with multiple locations is seeking a Kitchen Manager!

Please have previous experience with managing a high-volume kitchens, maintaining consistency in menu execution, carrying out health and safety standards. Having full knowledge of administrative responsibilities is expected, as well as having an understanding of financials (food/labor costs, P&Ls).

Must also have great communication skills as this person will be supervising, training, coaching, and motivating staff by giving constructive feedback. Looking for a true and honest leader in the kitchen! *Must be fluent in English and Spanish.* (italics added)

As both of these ads attest, being bilingual in Spanish and English has become an increasingly essential skill for restaurant work in Los Angeles. To be sure, some of this skill demand stems from growing ethnic consumer bases in the immigrant neighborhoods of East and South Los Angeles. Yet L.A. restaurants, I argue, also seek bilingual workers to buffer internal employee relations. This is evident in the fact that the positions in these Craigslist ads do *not* require customer engagement (cooks, kitchen manager) and may in fact be located in predominantly white, English-speaking neighborhoods of the city ("westside").

At both Terroir and Match, bilingual workers function as crucial social bridges, facilitating communication between the white and Latino labor niches. They fill what social network scholars refer to as a "structural hole"—a lack of ties between two or more social groups within a given network (Burt 2005). At Terroir, the chef-owner's self-proclaimed right-hand man for the past ten years has been a Mexican immigrant named Jon. Forty-one years old and originally from Veracruz, Mexico, Jon speaks English and Spanish fluently, though his English remains heavily accented. By most measures, Jon would make for an excellent kitchen hire in any restaurant: he is exceptionally hardworking, skilled in a variety of culinary techniques, and intensely loyal to the chef. That said, arguably Jon's greatest value to Terroir—which he demonstrates daily—is his ability to manage Spanish-speaking back-of-the-house workers and coordinate their work with the front of the house. He swiftly translates communication back and forth between cooks, servers, managers, and even the head chef, who does not speak Spanish. Jon conducts hiring interviews for new line cooks and dishwashers, sets kitchen schedules, and mediates the occasional dispute between kitchen employees, all in Spanish. As a result, when Jon is around the restaurant—which is almost always, given his salaried sous chef position—the head chef seldom has to say a word to any of the Spanish-speaking Mexican and Central American back-of-the-house workers whom he employs. After years of working with Jon at his side, he simply trusts Jon to get the job done.

Jon's ability to fill structural holes in the workplace has undoubtedly played a part in helping him achieve his status as a salaried sous chef in an upscale restaurant like Terroir. He and other bilingual Spanish-English kitchen workers possess the skills necessary to orchestrate food service across the two socially distinct labor niches. However, as central as Jon is to Terroir's operation, his pride in his Veracruzano-born heritage makes him less relatable to his white and middle-class coworkers in the front of the house. Jon speaks lovingly of salsa dancing in Latin clubs on his days off and is outspoken in his belief that beer "should be ice-cold and light, like Modelo, not that bitter India Pale Ale shit that Americans want to drink these days!" Out of touch with the cultural milieu of his front-of-the-house coworkers (as well as of many of the restaurant's patrons), Jon remains socially embedded within the immigrant Latino niche. Like other immigrant Latino workers at Terroir, I never once witnessed Jon being invited to go out after work for a drink with his front-of-the-house colleagues.

Jon and other bilingual immigrants may lubricate work-based relations between the two niches of restaurant employment, but they do little to close the social and cultural cleavages between the niches. This is where second-generation Latino restaurant workers like Pedro have an edge. Pedro is a thirty-two-year-old Mexican American born in South-Central Los Angeles to Guadalajaran parents. Despite holding only a high school degree, Pedro has rapidly risen through Match's kitchen ranks in the sixteen months since he began working there. Having grown up speaking both Spanish and English, Pedro was first hired as a dishwasher at minimum wage ($9 at the time). Six months later, he was promoted to prep cook. He continued climbing the kitchen ladder until he was—in his words—"at the top of the heap": he became the lead line cook at Match, working just under the sous chef, with responsibility for the primary grill and pizza-baking stations. He now makes $15 an hour.

Like Jon, Pedro says that he benefited from his ability to translate between English and Spanish, both of which he speaks natively and without an accent. When I met him in late 2012, while he was still a prep cook, it was clear that Pedro was already the point person in Match's kitchen for front- and back-of-the-house workers alike. Pedro would hustle around the kitchen furiously chopping vegetables while talking just as fast in two languages. Unlike Jon, Pedro's bi-*cultural* fluency deepened his rapport with front-of-the-house workers and managers beyond his ability merely to deliver translation services. During meal breaks at Match, Pedro liked to joke around with young, white servers like Charlie and Amy. To Charlie, he would exclaim, "What's up, doggie! How was that bar you hit up last Friday? Meet any niiiiiccee chicas?" With Amy, Pedro would chat excitedly about developments in their mutual favorite TV show, *The Walking Dead*. Back on the kitchen line during busy meal rushes, Pedro would hum popular Mexican hits playing on the radio alongside the immigrant cooks. Mid-song, he could code-switch back to American youth slang when a white server stopped by to ask him a question or momentarily hang out. Before I left Match in the summer of 2013, Pedro had received yet another promotion—this time to kitchen manager and regional trainer of Match's newly opened second location near Hollywood. Having been with Match less than two years, Pedro had skills that had enabled him to make a remarkably fast ascent up the back-of-the-house hierarchy.

Pedro's central position within multiple employee networks at Match made him an indispensable figure in a workplace spliced into divergent occupational communities. Other second-generation Latino workers were also able to carve out similarly advantageous positions for themselves. Twenty-year-old Victor, a second-generation Mexican American, began at Match as a busser—the lowest position in the dining room hierarchy. Within six months, management promoted Victor to food runner, a position that allowed Victor to leverage his bilingual skills from outside the kitchen. As a food runner, Victor conversed with kitchen workers in Spanish about the dishes he received, then turned around and described the food to English-speaking diners. Within a year, Victor had his eye on what he viewed as "the next step" for him: becoming a "flex" employee at the restaurant, working part-time as a cook and part-time as a waiter. He was convinced that he could do it. Victor told me one day, gesturing toward a group of white servers, "It's pretty simple what they do. I mean, I can do that *for sure:* just bullshit with customers, get them what they want, then make a bunch of tips." He envisioned a kitchen role as also coming easily for him: he had always helped his mother cook for the family and had past work experience assembling sandwiches at a local Subway.

When I left Match in 2013, it remained to be seen whether Victor would be given the unprecedented opportunity to work in both front- and back-of-the-house capacities—straddling the divided labor niches. Management had seemed favorable to the idea. In Victor, personal ambition was coupled with an attractive mixture of social and cultural competencies that the restaurant could have used. Able to schmooze with Match's white customers in English while double-checking the accuracy of the food coming out of the kitchen in Spanish, Victor, like Pedro, bridged the service divide in the workplace.

CONCLUSION

The growth of the service economy alongside continued migration from Latin America is reshaping not only local labor markets but also shop-floor dynamics in the workplaces in which immigrants are concentrated. Drawing from ethnographic data on full-service Los Angeles restaurants, my research examined a workplace characterized by dual labor niches: immigrant Latinos employed in back-of-the-house capacities and middle-class whites employed in front-of-the-house capacities. I have shown that the social (race, class, gender, immigration status) and structural asymmetries of these labor niches, reinforced by employer hiring preferences and unequal social networks, effectively close them off to each other. As a result, the bright boundary between the class-privileged white niche and the immigrant Latino niche can produce everyday shop-floor tensions, food service snafus, and lingering inequalities in the workplace.

I argue that dual-niched workplaces hold situational opportunities for those able to bridge the divide. Bilingual English-Spanish workers at both restaurants studied here put their linguistic skills to use by brokering communication between an English-speaking front of the house (and management) and a Spanish-speaking back of the house. They smoothed the food service process while simultaneously acting as a social bridge on the shop floor between otherwise profoundly divided employees.

Individuals with dual social and cultural competencies may be of even greater utility in such workplaces. Because many of the bilingual, second-generation workers in this study not only linguistically code-switched when interacting with different worker cohorts (see Hernández-León and Lakhani 2013; Morando 2013) but also deployed appropriate sociocultural scripts as needed, they could serve affluent white guests in line with managerial expectations and socialize with both white coworkers and immigrant Latino coworkers. For many second-generation Latino workers, this ability to partially transcend the boundary between the two labor niches proved valuable, helping them secure promotions, raises, and greater job responsibilities at the restaurants (see also Wilson 2017). As other recent scholarship also indicates, individuals' ability to showcase their "cross-cultural" capital is likely to be valuable in increasingly diverse institutional settings (Agius Vallejo 2012; Da Cruz, this issue; Lee 1998).

In sum, this research contributes to our understanding of contemporary immigrant labor markets in two primary ways. First, it showcases the complicated interaction of race, class, and immigration on "global" shop floors. As the case of restaurants illustrates, a given immigrant labor niche may be only one slice of a firm's larger social organization in which other types of individuals are concentrated in different aspects of the work (see, for example, Peri and Sparber 2009). Drawing attention to the broader organizational contexts within which immigrant labor niches are embedded is crucial to understanding the worlds of work—their labor relations, opportunity structures, inequalities, and shop-floor experiences—that immigrants and their offspring are encountering today. Second, this study provides a valuable supplement to macro-level data suggesting the intergenerational "stagnation" of Latinos on the lower rungs of the U.S. labor market (Portes and Rumbaut 2006; Telles and Ortiz 2008; Waldinger, Lim, and Cort 2007). Although the Latino workers in this study remain in the marginalized service sector—few stood to make giant leaps in socioeconomic mobility—other workers, as this study demonstrates, are encountering nuanced mobility pathways at the intersection of personal skills and competencies with the social organization of work. Against a backdrop of the larger structural barriers facing Latino immigrants and their offspring, it remains to be seen how far these intangible and contextualized "skills" can take workers as they continue building work careers.

REFERENCES

Agius Vallejo, Jody. 2012. "Socially Mobile Mexican Americans and the Minority Culture of Mobility." *American Behavioral Scientist* 20(10): 1–16.

Bailey, Thomas, and Roger Waldinger. 1991. "Primary, Secondary, and Enclave Labor Markets: A Training Systems Approach." *American Sociological Review* 56(4): 432–45.

Barret, Rusty. 2006. "Language Ideology and Racial Inequality: Competing Functions of Spanish in an Anglo-Owned Mexican Restaurant." *Language in Society* 35(2): 163–204.

Besen-Cassino, Yasemin. 2014. *Consuming Work: Youth Labor in America*. Philadelphia: Temple University Press.

Bourdain, Anthony. 2000. *Kitchen Confidential: Adventures in the Culinary Underbelly*. New York: HarperCollins.

Burawoy, Michael. 1979. *Manufacturing Consent: Changes in the Labor Process Under Monopoly Capitalism*. Chicago: University of Chicago Press.

Burt, Ronald S. 2005. *Brokerage and Closure: An Introduction to Social Capital*. Oxford: Oxford University Press.

Cantazarite, Lisa. 2000. "Brown-Collar Jobs: Occupational Segregation and Earnings of Recent-Immigrant Latinos." *Sociological Perspectives* 43(1): 45–75.

Da Cruz, Michaël. 2016. "Offshore Migrant Workers: Return Migrants in Mexico's English-Speaking Call Centers." *RSF: The Russell Sage Foundation Journal of the Social Sciences* 4(1): 39–57. DOI: 10.7758/RSF.2018.4.1.03.

Eckstein, Susan, and Giovanni Peri. 2018. "Immigrant Niches and Immigrant Networks in the U.S. Labor Market." *RSF: The Russell Sage Foundation Journal of the Social Sciences* 4(1): 1–17. DOI: 10.7758/RSF.2018.4.1.01.

Ehrenreich, Barbara. 2001. *Nickel and Dimed: On (Not) Getting By in America*. New York: Henry Holt & Co.

Fine, Gary A. 1996. *Kitchens: The Culture of Restaurant Work*. Berkeley: University of California Press.

Gatta, Mary, Heather Boushey, and Eileen Appelbaum. 2009. "High-Touch and Here-to-Stay." *Sociology* 43(5): 968–89.

Glaser, Barney G., and Anselm L. Strauss. 1967. *The Discovery of Grounded Theory*. New York: Aldine.

Gomberg-Muñoz, Ruth. 2011. *Labor and Legality: An Ethnography of a Mexican Immigrant Network*. New York: Oxford University Press.

Granovetter, Mark. 1985. "Economic Action and Social Structure: The Problem of Embeddedness." *American Journal of Sociology* 91(3): 481–510.

———. 1995. *Getting a Job: A Study of Contacts and Careers*. 2nd ed. Chicago: University of Chicago Press. (Originally published in 1974.)

Hagan, Jacqueline Maria. 1998. "Social Networks, Gender, and Immigrant Incorporation: Resources and Constraint." *American Sociological Review* 63(1): 55–67.

Hagan, Jacqueline, Rubén Hernández-León, and Jean-Luc Demonsant. 2015. *Skills of the Unskilled: Work and Mobility Among Mexican Migrants*. Berkeley: University of California Press.

Haley-Lock, Anna, and Stephanie Ewert. 2011. "Waiting for the Minimum: U.S. State Wage Laws, Firm Strategy, and Chain-Restaurant Job Quality." *Journal of Industrial Relations* 53(1): 31–48.

Hernández-León, Rubén, and Sarah Morando Lakhani. 2013. "Gender, Bilingualism, and the Early Occupational Careers of Second-

Generation Mexicans in the South." *Social Forces* 92(1): 59–80.

Hochschild Arlie. 1983. *The Managed Heart: Commercialization of Human Feeling.* Berkeley: University of California Press.

Hondagneu-Sotelo, Pierette. 2001. *Doméstica: Immigrant Workers Cleaning and Caring in the Shadows of Affluence.* Berkeley: University of California Press.

Jayaraman, Saru. 2014. *Behind the Kitchen Door.* Ithaca, N.Y.: Cornell University Press.

Kalleberg, Arne. 2011. *Good Jobs, Bad Jobs: The Rise of Polarized and Precarious Employment Systems in the United States, 1970s–2000s.* New York: Russell Sage Foundation.

Kanter, Rosabeth Moss. 1977. *Men and Women of the Corporation.* New York: Basic Books.

Lee, Jennifer. 1998. "Cultural Brokers: Race-Based Hiring in Inner-City Neighborhoods." *American Behavioral Scientist* 41(7): 927–37.

Leidner, Robin. 1993. *Fast Food, Fast Talk: Service Work and the Routinization of Everyday Life.* Berkeley: University of California Press.

Lopez, Steven. 2010. "Workers, Managers, and Customers: Triangles of Power in Work Communities." *Work and Occupations* 37(3): 251–71.

Lowe, Nicolai, Jacqueline Hagan, and Natasha Iskander. 2010. "Revealing Talent: Informal Skills Intermediation as an Emergent Pathway to Immigrant Labor Market Incorporation." *Environment and Planning A* 42(1): 205–22.

Massey, Doug, Jorge Durand, and Nolan Malone. 2002. *Beyond Smoke and Mirrors: Mexican Immigration in an Era of Economic Integration.* New York: Russell Sage Foundation.

Morando, Sarah J. 2013. "Paths to Mobility: The Mexican Second Generation at Work in a New Destination." *Sociological Quarterly* 54(3): 367–98.

Moss, Philip, and Chris Tilly. 2001. *Stories Employers Tell: Race, Skill, and Hiring in America.* New York: Russell Sage Foundation.

Newman, Katherine. 1999. *No Shame in My Game: The Working Poor in the Inner City.* New York: Russell Sage Foundation.

Peri, Giovanni, and Chad Sparber. 2009. "Task Specialization, Immigration, and Wages." *American Economic Journal: Applied Economics* 1(3): 135–69.

Portes, Alejandro, and Ruben Rumbaut. 2006. *Immigrant America: A Portrait.* 3rd ed. Berkeley: University of California Press.

Restaurant Opportunities Centers United (ROC). 2014. "The Great Service Divide: Occupational Segregation and Inequality in the U.S. Restaurant Industry." New York: Restaurant Opportunities Centers United (October 22).

Restaurant Opportunities Center of Los Angeles (ROC-LA). 2011. *Beyond the Kitchen Door.* New York: Restaurant Opportunities Centers United (February 14).

Rivera, Laura. 2012. "Hiring as Cultural Matching: The Case of Elite Professional Service Firms." *American Sociological Review* 77(6): 999–1022.

Sherman, Rachel. 2007. *Class Acts; Service and Inequality in Luxury Hotels.* Berkeley: University of California Press.

Telles, Edward, and Vilma Ortiz. 2008. *Generations of Exclusion: Mexican-Americans, Assimilation, and Race.* New York: Russell Sage Foundation.

Timmermans, Stefan, and Iddo Tavory. 2012. "Theory Construction in Qualitative Research: From Grounded Theory to Abductive Analysis." *Sociological Theory* 30(3): 167–86.

Waldinger, Roger, and Michael Lichter. 2003. *How the Other Half Works: Immigration and the Social Organization of Labor.* Berkeley: University of California Press.

Waldinger, Roger, Nelson Lim, and David Cort. 2007. "Bad Jobs, Good Jobs, No Jobs? The Employment Experience of the Mexican American Second Generation." *Journal of Ethnic and Migration Studies* 33(1): 1–35.

Warhurst, Chris, and Dennis Nickson. 2007. "Employee Experience of Aesthetic Labour in Retail and Hospitality." *Work Employment Society* 21(1): 103–20.

———. 2009. "'Who's Got the Look?' Emotional, Aesthetic, and Sexualized Labour in Interactive Services." *Gender, Work, and Organization* 16(3): 385–404.

Whyte, William F. 1948. *Human Relations in the Restaurant Industry.* New York: McGraw-Hill.

Williams, Christine L., and Catherine Connell. 2010. "'Looking Good and Sounding Right': Aesthetic Labor and Social Inequality in the Retail Industry." *Work and Occupations* 37(3): 349–77.

Wilson, Eli R. 2017. "Stuck Behind Kitchen Doors? Assessing the Work Prospects of Latter-Generation Latino Workers in a Los Angeles Restaurant." Unpublished paper. University of California, Los Angeles.

Zukin, Sharon. 1995. *The Culture of Cities.* Oxford: Blackwell.

PART III

New Immigrants in Growing Sectors: High- and Low-Skilled Labor Market Niches

Israeli Infotech Migrants in Silicon Valley

STEVEN J. GOLD

Prior to the 1980s, Israel's national ideology discouraged emigration and entrepreneurship among its citizens. Yet, by the late 1990s, Israeli emigrants were one of the leading immigrant nationalities in Silicon Valley. Drawing on interviews, fieldwork, a literature review, and perusal of social media, I explore the origins of Israeli involvement in high-tech activities and the extensive linkages between Israeli emigrants and the Israeli high-tech industry. I also summarize the patterns of communal cooperation that permit emigrant families to maintain an Israel-oriented way of life in suburban communities south of San Francisco, and I compare these patterns with those of Indians, a nationality engaged in the same pursuit. I conclude by considering the impact of infotech involvement on Israeli immigrants and on the U.S. economy.

Keywords: immigrant entrepreneurs, transnationalism, ethnic communities, Silicon Valley

Israeli immigrants have among the highest rates of entrepreneurship of all national-origin groups in the United States, and they sustain similar patterns in other places where they have settled in Europe, South Africa, Australia, and Asia. Their rate of self-employment in 2000, according to that year's U.S. census, was 33.4 percent. Areas of economic specialization include garments, jewelry, construction and real estate, entertainment, restaurants, grocery stores, media, moving companies, and multiple professions (Y. Cohen 2009; Gold 2002).

Among their various realms of economic specialization, information technology has received the most interest because of its global economic importance as well as the particular conditions associated with its emergence. Indeed, Israelis and migrants from other countries who work as entrepreneurs, professionals, and financiers in high-tech and are engaged in other cutting-edge economic activities have been the focus of a growing body of attention. Regarded as the world's most powerful engines of economic growth and innovation, they are associated with the establishment of Silicon Valley and similar locations in other regions and national settings (Kotkin 1992; Rebhun and Lev Ari 2010; Saxenian 2006; Senor and Singer 2009). According to a report produced for the U.S. Small Business Administration, high-tech migrants have been found "to account for a disproportionate share of job creation and economic growth" in recent years (Hart, Acs, and Tracy 2009, 5).

Steven J. Gold is professor of sociology at Michigan State University.

© 2018 Russell Sage Foundation. Gold, Steven J. 2018. "Israeli Infotech Migrants in Silicon Valley." *RSF: The Russell Sage Foundation Journal of the Social Sciences* 4(1): 130–48. DOI: 10.7758/RSF.2018.4.1.08. Direct correspondence to: Steven J. Gold at gold@msu.edu, Department of Sociology, Berkey Hall, Room 316, 509 East Circle Drive, Michigan State University, East Lansing, MI 48824-1111.

The economic desirability of these entrepreneurs has now been recognized by business experts, academics, government officials, journalists, and policymakers who had previously paid little attention to immigrant entrepreneurship (Hart, Acs, and Tracy 2009; Hohn 2012; Light 2010). Multiple nations now compete to attract these immigrants with ever more generous incentives, and high-tech immigrants have become associated with economically advanced host societies like the United States. At the same time, their countries of origin are well aware of their value. Seeking to benefit from their development magic, the homelands of these entrepreneurs have reformed long-standing policies regarding citizenship, offshore investment, government financing, money transfer, and taxation. As a consequence, environments that formerly favored protectionism now encourage global engagement through "tax incentives, government grants and funding of R&D, training grants, incubators for start-ups and support for venture capital" (Saxenian 2006, 104; Cohen 2010; Ray 2013).

In addition to reworking their financial and business-related policies, high-tech migrants' countries of origin have also revisited national understandings of patriotism, identity, occupation, military service, and place of residence. In many cases, perspectives on family, gender, culture, and religious practices have been transformed to encourage and endorse emigrants' involvement in the global economy (Frenkel 2008). Drawing on opportunities and resources associated with multiple locations, acquired from assorted nation-states, networks, and organizations, and motivated by an array of loyalties, affinities, and relationships, Israeli immigrants' extensive involvement in information technology is a product of such a transnational process.

Because "infotech" entrepreneurs enjoy unprecedented levels of income, state-granted permission to work and travel, and access to elite institutions, some observers argue that this group represents a fundamentally new category in the realm of migration. These migrants are distinct not only from laborers but also from other skilled migrants such as merchants and professionals (Saxenian 2006; Senor and Singer 2009). Such is the contention of Israel Drori, Benson Honig, and Mike Wright (2009, 1003–4), who identify infotech migrants as "transnational entrepreneurs (TEs)" and assert that they "are not simply passive adherents to institutional constraints, but actively mold them to suit their own unique initiatives.... TEs modify and create environments including new and existing institutions, as well as structures, inclusive of rules and procedures, that go on to define new and emergent 'rules of the game.'"

Drori and his colleagues point out that immigrant entrepreneurs are "frequently obligated to rely on their group's ethnic resources and social capital," of the type associated with enclaves or ethnic economies, for their economic viability, and their experience is codified with the language of marginality, as suggested in concepts like "Pariah people," "middleman minorities," "marginal men," and "disadvantage" theory (Drori, Honig, and Wright 2009, 1004; Portes 2010; Light and Gold 2000). On the contrary, transnational infotech entrepreneurs are able to obtain services, investment funds, and business contacts from mainstream sources. They are welcomed to the host societies' corridors of power—places to which, until quite recently, persons of their nationality, religion, or race had little access (Wishingrad 2015).

Given that "the debate on whether ethnic niches are harmful or beneficial for earnings continues to interest immigration scholars," infotech migrants' productivity and status can be seen as challenging widely accepted assumptions in the study of international migration (Lee 2013, 748; Portes 2010; Sanders and Nee 1996; Waldinger and Bozorgmehr 1996; Xie and Gough 2011). Accordingly, their achievements and the contexts that produce them are topics worthy of scholarly research.

This article explores the experience of immigrants from Israel who are employed in the United States in infotech and related high-level occupations—such as academics, engineers, managers, and venture capitalists—in order to gain insight into the ways in which highly skilled immigrants are involved in entrepreneurship. To consider the place of occupation versus nationality in the development of the high-tech niche, I include a cursory comparison of Israeli emigrants' patterns of involvement in infotech to those of Indians, the migrant nationality most heavily represented in this endeavor both in Silicon Valley and nationally (Wadhwa, Saxenian, and Siciliano 2012). Finally, I consider the implications of involvement in the infotech industry, both for immigrants themselves and for American society.

METHODS

This multi-sited ethnography focuses on interviews with twenty-one Israelis employed in infotech and related high-level occupations such as academics, engineers, and venture capitalists. Interviews were conducted between 1991 and 2016 in California and among returnees (including former California residents) in Israel by the author and two Israeli women research assistants. Additional interviews and fieldwork data were provided by an Israeli journalist living with her family in Silicon Valley. Contacts were established through snowball referrals and via the networks of the author and research assistants. Four respondents were interviewed on multiple occasions.

Background information was obtained from additional interviews and fieldwork with about one hundred Israeli emigrants (forty-four women and fifty-three men, including both the wife and husband of nine couples) between 1991 and 2014. Locations included California and, for returned emigrants, several places in Israel. Further, interviews were conducted with persons with special knowledge of Israeli emigrant communities, including community activists, journalists, and employees of Jewish community agencies. Interviews were open-ended, but based on an interview guide. Most were audio-recorded, translated into English (if conducted in Hebrew), and transcribed. All names of respondents in this report are pseudonyms (Gold 2002; Gold and Hart 2013). Finally, additional data were collected through a review of the academic and journalistic literature, an examination of surveys and official statistics, and a perusal of websites regularly used by members of the Israeli high-tech community.

FROM CONDEMNATION TO ENCOURAGEMENT OF EMIGRANT ENTREPRENEURSHIP

Israel's status as a recently formed nation engaged in protracted conflict with many of its neighbors and populated by Jews from throughout the world suggests some of the reasons why members of its population have been well represented among high-tech immigrants. Israelis' propensity for emigration is explained by the population's relatively short tenure in Israel. As of 2007, almost 30 percent of Israelis were foreign-born, and 90 percent had resided there for three generations or less (Jewish Virtual Library 2014; Senor and Singer 2009). Thus, many Israelis possess abilities, expectations, language skills, cultural knowledge, citizenship, and contacts associated with the places where their families once lived. Israelis facing the difficulties associated with their careers, the Israeli cost of living, and the country's social or political alienation, security, and other concerns may find a solution in emigration (Gold and Hart 2013).

Israeli emigrants' inclination toward entrepreneurship can be traced to Jews' long history of self-employment as well as the presence of extensive Jewish and Israeli ethnic economies in the major points of settlement (Gold 2002; Kotkin 1992).[1] Their significant representation in technical occupations is associated with the importance of defense to the country's survival. Finally, the sheer number of Israelis with high-tech training can be attributed to the country's institutions of higher education and the arrival of almost 1 million immigrants from the former Soviet Union during the 1990s; many thousands of these Soviet immigrants had been trained as scientists, engineers, and technical specialists (Gold 2015).

Estimates of the number of Israeli emigrants in the United States have been subject to controversy and exaggeration by journalists and Israeli government sources (Gold 2002). The U.S. Census Bureau's 2011–2013 American

---

1. See O'Keefe and Quincy, this issue, for a description of Jewish immigrants' entrepreneurship in a very different time and context.

Community Survey (ACS) estimates that there were 139,980 Israel-born persons in the United States during that period (U.S. Census Bureau 2013). Drawing on U.S. and Israeli census data, Uzi Rebhun and Lilach Lev Ari (2010, 15) assert that the total population of Israelis in the United States—including those born in Israel, those born in other countries, and their U.S.-born children and American spouses—is 250,000. The actual number involved in infotech occupations is impossible to determine (as is their residency status in the United States—citizen, student visa, tourist, and so on), but journalistic sources and community activists claim that between 50,000 and 200,000 reside in the greater San Francisco Bay Area (Orpaz 2014).

The Israeli population is well endowed with contacts, skills, and aspirations conducive to migration, but the country's national narrative emphasizes settlement. Israel came into being to provide a homeland for the world's Jews following the Holocaust. Zionism (Israel's state-building ideology) called for the ingathering of the exiles and reviled departure. From its formation in 1948 until the 1980s, the country identified emigration as a personal failing and a threat to its military, economic, and demographic survival (Cohen 2010; Goldscheider 1996). For a brief time emigration was even illegal, and afterward it remained heavily stigmatized. Until recently—and to a lesser extent still—emigrants were depicted in political discourse, social science research, journalism, and popular culture as disillusioned, lonely, impoverished, subject to family breakdown and loss of Jewish identity, and alienated from coreligionists in points of settlement (Sabar 1999; Shokeid 1988; Sobel 1986, 55). In a famous 1970s statement, Prime Minister Yitzhak Rabin called Israeli emigrants "moral lepers," "the fallen among the weaklings," and "the droppings of insects" (Ritterband and Zerubavel 1986, 113).

In addition to discouraging emigration, some forms of Israeli ideology prior to the 1990s denigrated entrepreneurship—a common means of survival that had been practiced by Jews in the Diaspora for millennia. Early Zionism posited that Israel was the location where Jews could finally extricate themselves from the debased livelihood of doing business in other people's countries. Instead, living on their own land, Israelis would become "new Jews" and make the desert bloom, often through ennobling agriculture (Almog 2000). Hence, whether in Israel or beyond, a Jewish business owner was regarded as a relic of the Diaspora—a self-serving tax evader incapable of living as a proud and self-confident Jew (Freedman and Korazim 1986, 144).

By the 1990s, however, the country's increased involvement in the global economy—in large part through activities and links established by Israeli emigrants in global centers of innovation and commerce—altered Israeli views about going abroad and engaging in infotech entrepreneurship. Such activities undergirded the country's transformation from a business-averse collectivist society with triple-digit inflation whose largest export was citrus to what is now celebrated as the "Start-up Nation," with high rates of entrepreneurial innovation, ties to the world's leading companies, extensive access to venture capital, and sustained economic growth (Senor and Singer 2009).

In addition to enjoying greater tolerance for travel abroad, infotech migrants have also benefited from the Israeli public's unique view of their occupation. Unlike the reviled Diaspora entrepreneur, Israeli infotech migrants are seen in a positive light and viewed as pursuing an endeavor that is "more than a tool for individual success or making profit. Rather, it contributes to the national project and Israel's political, economic and security needs." Such an endeavor is collectively oriented and associated with "transforming the world through the mastery of scientific knowledge" (Zilber 2006, 289). Although a garment manufacturer in Los Angeles and a software engineer in Palo Alto are both Israeli exiles running a business in California, Israelis would tend to see them as occupying different moral universes and would condemn the former while celebrating the latter.

In sum, Israel's migration-driven involvement in high-tech activities has transformed popular understandings of both emigration and entrepreneurship, reducing the disparagement of these activities and legitimizing their benefits. These new understandings have allowed today's emigrants to be more confident and outspoken about their presence abroad than was the case for emigrants prior to the late 1990s.

ISRAELI EMIGRATION AND THE ORIGINS OF ISRAELI IMMIGRANTS' INVOLVEMENT IN HIGH-TECHNOLOGY OCCUPATIONS

Israelis began migrating to the United States soon after the country's formation in 1948, and the development of Israeli communities in the United States had begun to receive academic and communal attention by the early 1980s (Ritterband and Zerubavel 1986). Members of those communities were diverse in ethnicity, religiosity, and class background, but the population generally included young families with children (Y. Cohen 2009). Many earned a living through self-employment or as professionals. Israeli émigrés lived and worked within established Jewish neighborhoods in major cities, such as New York and Los Angeles (Gold 2002; Rebhun and Lev Ari 2010). Unlike most other Jewish immigrants, Israelis have often expressed ambivalence about living in the United States and raising their children as Diaspora Jews.

Israeli emigrants in high-tech occupations are in many ways similar to the broader Israeli-American population. However, their desirable job skills and American degrees make it easier for them to acquire legal resident status, earn more money, and be much less dependent on Israeli and Jewish ethnic enclaves in the United States for finding employment and a coethnic community. Finally, the largest concentration of infotech Israelis is found in ethnically diverse communities south of San Francisco rather than in the Jewish neighborhoods of West Los Angeles, Greater New York City, and Miami (Gold 2016).

In this environment, infotech Israelis maintain a communal orientation that underlies their creation of an ethnic economy and ethnic community. Ivan Light and I (Light and Gold 2000, 4) have defined an ethnic economy as "coethnic self-employed and employers, and their coethnic employees," and we discuss the conditions under which the development of symbiotic solidarity and trust between a group and its entrepreneurs facilitates the social and economic advancement of both. The literature on immigrant entrepreneurship documents the importance of shared resources to the business success of a wide range of populations—from Hausa cattle dealers in post-independence Nigeria to Korean greengrocers in contemporary New York City (Cohen 1969; Min 2008).

As a highly entrepreneurial group, Israeli emigrants display these patterns wherever they settle. However, Israel is a highly diverse and recently settled country whose subgroups vary in nationality, religiosity, educational level, and ideological outlook, as well as in a variety of other ways. When Israelis emigrate, they therefore tend to interact and build communities with the conationals whose backgrounds, occupations, and identities they share—Yemenis with Yemenis, Kibbutznicks with Kibbutznicks, Ultra-Orthodox Hassidim with Ultra-Orthodox Hassidim, and so on (Gold 2002; Rebhun and Lev Ari 2010).

Israeli infotech emigrants make up such a subgroup in the United States: their social ties are based on their shared military and educational experiences, their similar occupations, and their common residential location south of San Francisco. Lacking close ties with Americans, American Jews, and Israeli immigrants from backgrounds unlike their own, they collaborate in both their work lives and their social lives, as documented in ethnography and journalism. "They don't strive to become American. They see themselves as Israelis who live in the U.S." (Handwerker 2014; Saxenian 2006). Not surprisingly, then, their strongest collective commitments in the United States are to the other infotech Israelis with whom they work, socialize, and engage in activities that maintain their favorite aspects of Israeli life while living in the United States.

THE ORIGINS OF THE INFOTECH NICHE

Israeli emigrants' extensive involvement in information technology and other high-tech ventures can be traced to the 1970s, when the Jewish state languished through a period of geopolitical conflict and inflation. Seeking opportunities, young Israelis increasingly went abroad in search of advanced training and education. In her study of Silicon Valley, AnnaLee Saxenian (2006, 105) notes that between 1978 and 2000, more than 14,000 Israeli professional and technical workers emigrated to the United States. Upon completion of their degrees, a fraction stayed on to work. With training in engineering, science, and technology, many found jobs in leading U.S. electronics and computer firms, first in the Route 128 area near Boston and later near San Francisco.

Although Israeli emigrants in high-tech come from diverse backgrounds, many are affiliated with the male Sabra (native-born Israeli) elite. Brought together in selective high schools, youth programs, military units, and universities, they received advanced training in science and math while mastering leadership skills as military officers. For example, a significant number of veterans of Unit 8200, a division of the Israel Defense Forces (IDF) devoted to cybersecurity, have gone on to take leadership roles in international high-tech industries (Swed and Butler 2015; Tendler 2015).

Israeli military and technical organizations provide an environment of shared training and service that catalyzes the lifelong, cooperative relationships that underlie Israel's innovative and collaborative high-tech culture (Senor and Singer 2009). In contrast, Israelis who do not share this background of combined high-tech military training and service—including recent immigrants, persons of lower-status origins, those from religious families, and women (who, though eligible for these programs, are underrepresented in them)—have less access to these networks and the resources and opportunities they provide and are less involved in high-tech professions (Swed and Butler 2015).

Sharing common backgrounds, infotech émigrés retained close yet informal connections as they built lives and careers in the United States. Along the way, they acquired contacts among American Jews, sometimes through the Israeli Economic Consulate in San Francisco. Israeli emigrants were also actively involved with U.S. investors, and their mastery of American ways of doing business facilitated cross-fertilization between the United States and Israel. Saxenian (2006, 109) quotes an infotech CEO who was also a retired IDF officer about the formation of this nexus: "One quarter of my university graduating class went to the United States and then stayed on to work in high-tech in Silicon Valley. They all started coming back to be entrepreneurs . . . they knew how to hire U.S. marketers and business developers."

Israeli infotech workers' degrees from American universities enable them to find excellent jobs in leading American corporations. When some of those who wanted to return home accepted employers' offer of the option of creating Israeli branches of American firms, the result was the expansion of leading American firms into the Middle East. "Intel and National Semiconductor set up integrated circuit design centers in Israel in the 1970s," notes Saxenian (2006, 106), "in order to retain highly valued [Israeli] engineers." IBM, Motorola, DEC, and Microsoft followed suit. Most of these plants flourished, and today the largest offshore research facilities of several U.S. electronics firms are located in Israel.

At present, a tremendous amount of social capital is shared among high-tech Israelis at home and abroad, as well as among Israelis and their friends and colleagues in diverse businesses in the United States and elsewhere. Sharing social capital serves as a vehicle for a variety of groups, nationalities, and industries to collaborate and to exchange know-how, investments, and innovative ways of doing business (Saxenian 2006).

Israeli emigrants' initial successes in the high-tech and computer industries impressed Israeli politicians, business leaders, and policymakers and seemed to suggest a viable solution to Israel's economic challenges. Given the nation's exceptional number of highly skilled workers, the idea of employing them in the burgeoning computer industry seemed practical. However, Israel lacked the investment capital and management skill needed to bankroll and supervise the requisite level of industrial expansion. Toward this end, and as the country was evolving rightward politically from socialism to neoliberalism, Israel changed many of its economic regulations in such a way as to encourage the generation of investment capital—for instance, by removing restrictions on offshore investors and by allowing Israeli companies to compete in global markets (Goldberg 2012, 28).

The Israeli labor force was technologically proficient but lacking in knowledge of finance and management; however, because venture capitalists commonly provide their clients with mentoring and management training as well as funds, workers were able to acquire these skills from their investor colleagues as they developed technology companies (Davone 2007). A major step in this process was the Yozma program, created by the Israeli government during the early 1990s to generate venture capital for Israeli start-ups (Avnimelech 2009). By 2009, the program had generated over $3 billion worth of investment and support for Israeli companies. Not only was the program successful in providing start-up funding for Israeli firms, but it also helped offshore investors and international corporations overcome their fear of investing in Israeli companies (Senor and Singer 2009, 168–70).

Indeed, as of 2008, Israel had more high-tech ventures per capita than any other nation. It led the world in civilian research-and-development spending per citizen and ranked second behind the United States in the number of companies listed on the high-tech NASDAQ stock exchange. With a 2008 population of less than 8 million, Israel attracted as much venture capital as France and Germany combined (with a total population of 140 million) (Brooks 2010; Senor and Singer 2009, 33).

The simultaneous and transnational development of infotech industries in Israel and by Israeli emigrants in Silicon Valley provided benefits to the growth and expansion of both. Emigrants in California helped Israel develop contacts with U.S. and international firms, facilitated the opening of branches of American companies in Israel, fostered access to large sources of venture capital, and generated contracts for Israel-based facilities. Emigrants shared with colleagues back home their familiarity with the social, business, and communication styles of American managers, investors, and firms. Finally, emigrants' participation in the dynamic, diverse, and creative "melting pot of ideas" environment of Silicon Valley allowed them to interact with a global network of partners (Orpaz 2014). In turn, research-and-development tasks requested by offshore colleagues were performed in Israel, which also provided additional workers.

Saxenian (2006, 105) argues that Israeli migrants' immersion in and familiarity with "technology centers in the U.S." propelled the country's phenomenal growth in high-tech. In contrast, she points out, larger, more affluent, and "more advanced industrialized nations that boasted well-developed technical education and research capabilities, such as Germany and France, failed to develop the entrepreneurial and technological dynamism that characterizes Israel today."

From the 1990s to the present, Israeli immigrants and firms that bridge Silicon Valley and Israel have played important roles as innovators and leaders in infotech. Companies that they started have been purchased or financed by major American and international infotech companies. Saxenian (2006, 110) cites the acquisition of Mirabilis's ICQ software by AOL in 1998 for over $400 million as the turning point. Created by a group of Israelis living in San Jose, the company gave its software to users for free, thus establishing "viral marketing."

Eric Benhamou, a Sephardic Jew born in Algeria and educated at the Ecole Nationale Supérieure d'Arts et Métiers in Paris and at Stanford University, was another early success story. From 1990 to 2010, he was CEO or chairman of 3Com. The company, which was ranked as high as 294 on the Fortune 500 list, was sold to Hewlett-Packard for $2.7 billion in cash in 2009. Benhamou remains active in venture capital, start-ups, philanthropy, and business education, serves on the boards of several Silicon Valley firms, and speaks passionately about Israelis' "natural talent for entrepreneurship" (Scheck 2009; Shelah 2006).[2]

With continued growth, Israelis became not only sellers but also buyers of U.S. infotech firms. In 2003, Israel's largest high-tech company, Ness Technologies, purchased APAR Infotech, an information services firm with corporate headquarters in Pittsburgh, Penn-

---

2. See the Benhamou Global Ventures (BGV) website at: benhamouglobalventures.com.

sylvania, for $360 million (Hermoni and Dar 2003).

COETHNIC COOPERATION IN BUSINESS ACTIVITIES

In addition to profiting from offshore ties, the Israeli infotech community in Silicon Valley benefits from high levels of in-group cooperation. Members jointly engage in business, social, and philanthropic activities. A variety of volunteer and for-profit organizations and business accelerators provide recent arrivals with socialization, networks, and lessons in doing business with Americans (Efrati 2012). Initially informal, Israeli emigrants' associations have now become more visible, better organized, and more likely to be affiliated with the Israeli consulate (Orpaz 2014). These centers of collaboration are supplemented by newspapers, websites, and forms of social media useful for getting oriented in the Bay Area. Finally, community members often shop and socialize in a variety of Israeli-style shops and restaurants. Bucks of Woodside is well known as the restaurant where countless Silicon Valley projects were brainstormed over coffee and eggs, but Oren's Hummus, created by Oren Dobronsky—who had developed and sold four high-tech start-ups before entering the restaurant business—is a popular equivalent for Israeli immigrants (Pine 2012; Pollock 2014).

A unique aspect of the Israeli infotech subculture appears to be its high level of cooperation, as discussed in news stories and documented in our own interviews. That cooperation offers a rather striking contrast to the patterns generally observed among entrepreneurial ethnic groups—including Israelis engaged in other occupations (Gold 1994, 2002; Granovetter 1995). Ethnic businesses often operate within highly competitive, even parasitical, environments in which owners conceal practices and contacts from firms run by country men and women who often have skills, contacts, and business resources remarkably like their own (Gold 2002). For example, my research found that Israeli emigrant restaurateurs, garment manufacturers, and building contractors avoided collaborating with coethnics in order to protect their access to consumers and profit margins (Gold 1994, 2002).

In contrast, the infotech sector appears to reward openness and collaboration (Freedman 2008). Informants attributed this to conational loyalty, common emotional styles, shared language (Hebrew), ease in evaluating and communicating with coworkers and subcontractors, and acceptance of flexible work-family arrangements (Bluestein 2012; Gold 2002; Orpaz 2014). Although they occasionally referred to the presence of other nationalities, Israeli infotech migrants in Silicon Valley were most concerned with conationals and seldom described Indians or Chinese as competitors or rivals (Banerjee 2007). In a 2016 interview, a journalist who had lived with her family among infotech Israelis in Silicon Valley for almost a decade explained its increasingly cooperative culture:

> As a person who has been working in Israeli high-tech all my life, I can tell you that firgun [a Hebrew term meaning "unselfish delight in the success of others" (Kordova 2014)] wasn't the norm fifteen or twenty years ago, but has become the norm. There are tech meetups, open source, community activities, and they drive people to think well and help. Also, the innovation process requires many feedback loops. Connections are worth money, and cooperation too. People pride themselves in the "karma" they get by helping. If you help, it means you are someone. Also, let's say I am a good high-tech Israel exec in The Valley—it is in my interest to behave well, even towards competitors, since I may start-up a future company with them, get valuable connections through them, etc.

Finally, the structure of the infotech industry often requires cooperation because teams of workers with complementary skill sets are most likely to be funded by venture capitalists—as suggested in a leading entrepreneur's presentation at an event organized by the Silicon Valley–based Israeli Executives and Founders Forum (IEFF) on "The Art of Building Billion Dollar Start-ups." The speaker advised his audience that "the ideal start-up size is 2-3 people; a hacker, a designer and a hustler. A one-person start-up can't easily address those three roles" (Soffer 2015).

BUSINESS SUCCESS AND COMMUNAL SATISFACTION

Much of the research on immigrant-driven infotech entrepreneurship has focused on production techniques, capital acquisition, willingness to take risks, and other business-related concerns. By contrast, social science research about immigration, ethnic entrepreneurship, and transnationalism emphasizes that the maintenance of relations between distant groups and locations relies on social, ethnic, national, and familial connections. These personal and affective ties and relationships underlie efficiency, good communication, innovation, trust, and successful collaboration (Kanter 1977; Nonini and Ong 1997; Saxenian 2006).

In other words, migrants' sentiments and decisions with regard to broader aspects of their collective life are not just peripheral to "the real story" of making money, but instead vital to the ability of transnational entrepreneurs to engage in economic activities. Moreover, it is important to remember that decisions about economic activities are not just made by the largely male groups of entrepreneurs but also depend on the appraisals of their spouses, children, extended families, networks, and communities (Aneesh 2003; Gold 2013; Kobayashi and Preston 2007; Ray 2013). It follows, then, that skilled immigrant entrepreneurs' identities and social engagements are worthy topics of consideration within a study of transnational entrepreneurship.

Indeed, research exploring diverse populations of high-level migrants has consistently emphasized the importance of non-economic factors in shaping transnational behavior (Salaff, Wong, and Greve 2010). In her research on Indian entrepreneurs traveling between their homeland and the United States, Manashi Ray (2013, 95) has found that "the family played a significant role both as the end goal and the means to achieve global migration and return . . . migrants' new ways of imagining migration and return and future work were guided as much by their own personal life-stage transition issues, nostalgia for the Indian way of life and feelings of nationalism as by the possibility of taking advantage of business opportunities."

Israelis involved in Silicon Valley's infotech industries are often economically successful and enjoy the area's high standard of living and good educational opportunities for their children. Like Yael, many value the tolerant and multicultural environment of the Bay Area over the culture of Israel:

> Well, I have been out of Israel for eight years, and I do feel an enormous difference. On the intellectual side, I always had a critique of how Israel treats Arab citizens, etc. But only after being here [in the United States] and seeing what ethnic equality looks like—it puts Israel in a very unfavorable light.
>
> [During a visit,] we were just floored by some of the racist comments that very good friends made that we were not aware of when we [previously] lived in Israel because either we made them [ourselves] or we were deaf.

Nevertheless, many Israeli emigrants claim that they don't feel fully comfortable in the United States and remain committed to Israel (Gold 2002; Sabar 1999). They often attribute this to cultural, linguistic, political, and national differences between Israel and Western points of settlement. (Remember that Israel's international involvement in infotech can be traced to the desire of Israelis working in the United States to return home.) An article in a Bay Area Jewish newspaper describes these differences:

> They're drawn here by the promise of affluence, lower tax rates and an entrepreneur-friendly culture. While some become U.S. citizens, they retain strong ties to the Jewish State—both personally and professionally. "It's very easy to take the Israelis out of Israel, but almost impossible to take Israel out of the Israelis," said [Shuly] Galili [executive director of the California Israel Chamber of Commerce (CICC)], who counts more than 200 members [in her organization]. (Brandt 2000)

Many emigrants claim that they would prefer to reside in Israel eventually, with their relatives and amid the country's familiar culture, language, and system of national identity. In fact, many Israelis do return home. Despite their relatively comfortable positions in Diaspora communities and lengthy stays, many highly educated Israeli families do not consider their settlement to be permanent. In the words of an Israeli woman who, with her infotech worker husband and three children, spent eight years in Palo Alto:

> Israelis have a lot of problems about staying here. They say, "We will stay here for the time being." I went to school here [in the United States] growing up, and now my child is going to school here too. I have a lot of good feelings about [U.S. schools] compared to the Israeli school system. But we want to go back now. I have come to the conclusion that I can't bear this permanent sojourn anymore. Hopefully, we will be back in less than a year.

Religious, national, and linguistic identities are especially pertinent in shaping infotech emigrants' impression of the United States. Some high-tech Israeli emigrants appreciate U.S. forms of Judaism (Gold 2002), but most of them, coming from a secular and nationalistic background, resenting the influence of the Orthodox community in Israeli life, and unfamiliar with the Reform and Conservative denominations with which most North American Jews affiliate, disdain the idea of maintaining their Jewish identity, and especially their children's Jewish identity, through participation in American Jewish activities (Gold 2002; Shokeid 1988).

Accordingly, Israeli infotech workers with children were more likely to want to return home. Many had been raised as members of the elite of Israeli society, and many of them were very concerned about their children being deprived of a childhood similar to their own. Further, because Israeli culture emphasizes the centrality of a series of shared experiences to socialization and national identity, a child growing up abroad will be excluded from these forms of engagement, which are essential for both social membership and occupational success. Deborah and Havah, two Israeli parents, described their distance from American Jews:

> Deborah: Most of them [American Jews] go by the Reformed stream, and I tend to actually like it because it's more modern and it doesn't conflict with family life as much as the other streams of Judaism do. But I think that from a Jewish life perspective, it's really a lot like Christianity. There isn't that much difference.

> Havah: There is a big inability to relate to American Jews.... If I meet an East Coast kind of typical Jew, I don't know what I should do. I feel that there is a minority mentality there that I can't decipher. It is very embarrassing for me. He is trying to communicate in a way that is fathomable to another American Jew, and I can't figure it out.

GENDER AND ADAPTATION

Because of the class, gender, and ethnic characteristics of the Israelis who are most active in high-tech occupations (most are educated male military veterans), the resources and benefits of migration are unequally distributed among the population. In nearly every study of high-tech Israelis in the United States, we find that, even when migration was a "family decision" and the family as a whole has enjoyed economic benefits as a result of migration, the decision to migrate was generally made by the men, who were seeking expanded educational and occupational opportunities in the United States (Lev Ari 2008). Once in the United States, men often enjoy the benefits of such expanded opportunities and feel more comfortable in the country. Women and dependent children, however, have more negative views of migration and of life abroad. Men often wish to stay on, but women frequently exert pressure to return to Israel to participate in familiar social activities, interact with family members, and raise children according to Israeli and Jewish values.

Consequently, in the view of many Israeli infotech emigrant families, the high-paying jobs available to male Israeli workers do not fully compensate for the unfamiliar environment in which their children must be raised. In the words of a Silicon Valley resident: "Nobody knows if Israelis [in Silicon Valley] can perpetuate their culture. The only ones that have are the ones that have sent their kids back for military service."

In this way, infotech immigrants' cooperation with each other, enduring ties to Israel, their country of origin, and selective consumption of Jewish communal services stem from their collective discomfort living in the United States. While they rely on coethnic networks to get into business, Israeli emigrants also depend on another set of collective activities to retain an Israeli outlook for themselves and their families in the United States.

RETAINING ISRAEL-NESS IN AMERICA

Israelis and their family members involved in the infotech industry patronize and sometimes run shops, restaurants, grocery stores and boutiques that satisfy their consumer and social needs. Other enterprises provide child care, recreation, Hebrew-speaking doctors and dentists, catering, and real estate and relocation services. Various political organizations, including the recently created Israeli American Council, provide a venue for Israeli Americans to express their views on the U.S. political system in order to expand their political influence (Gold 2016).

Reflecting Israel's desire to retain the interest and loyalty of infotech emigrants and encourage their eventual return, its government provides a package of cultural and economic services (N. Cohen 2009), including summer-in-Israel programs that allow Israeli-American youth to maintain language skills and an Israeli identity in the United States. The homeland also offers the Lone Soldiers Program, which enables Americans and others around the world to serve in the Israel Defense Forces. Finally, the Israeli government provides immigrants with a wide range of services and subsidies—assistance with job finding, renting an apartment, obtaining access to health care, and orienting children to Israeli life—if they seek to return. Such benefits are less generous than those available to olim (newly arrived Diaspora Jews), but they are nonetheless worth thousands of dollars.[3]

Emigrants' own activities and the services delivered by the Israeli government allow them to avoid involvement with American Judaism. At the same time, local Jewish organizations extend a variety of services to their cousins from the Middle East. Despite Israelis' feeling of distance from American Jews and the synagogues and community centers that they have created, many families are willing to participate in these activities because they fear that, without some form of institutional Jewish engagement, their children will lose their identity as Israelis and Jews (Gold 2002; Pine 2012).

Prior to the 1980s, in keeping with Israeli policies intended to discourage emigration, the American Jewish establishment withheld outreach or assistance to Israeli newcomers. Once Israel reversed its stance on the issue, however, local American Jews began to provide a number of services to emigrants. Such efforts can be understood as reflecting the host group's desire to assist coreligionists in need. At the same time, welcoming Israelis allows American Jews to replenish their own community, which has been subject to depletion by age, assimilation, and intermarriage. Toward these ends, American Jewish agencies, synagogues, and organizations have established Israeli-oriented chapters of philanthropic organizations, employed Hebrew-speaking staff members for communal services, created Israeli-style Hebrew school classes, child care centers, folk dancing, and sing-along events, and scheduled celebrations of Israeli holidays.

Despite their consumption of these services, many Israeli families are still uncomfortable in the United States and eventually decide to return home. (Visas also mandate their departure.) In fact, the incidence of return among infotech Israelis is so high that respondents spontaneously told me that they dreaded the summer months—many of their closest conational friends would be leaving then (Gold 2002). As Orly explained during an interview conducted in the summer of 2006:

> I am very tired of the Israeli community here because it is so transient. A lot of good friends have gone back. There was a huge episode of that this year—150 families at least went back. My son's day care was decimated because everybody left. The day cares in Palo

---

3. For more information, see the Ministry of Aliyah and Integration website at: http://www.moia.gov.il/English/Pages/default.aspx (accessed November 16, 2016).

Alto don't want Israeli kids because they have everybody leave at some point. And I like the people that go back better than the people who stay. In many respects, I think it is right to go back, although it's a more complex life in Israel.

Other members of the Israeli emigrant population besides those involved in infotech express a desire to return (Gold 2002; Lev Ari 2008; Shokeid 1988). Moreover, rates of return are associated with economic and security conditions. Larger numbers of emigrants tend to return during times of relative peace and economic growth in Israel (as well as during U.S. recessions). Upticks in violence in Israel restrain remigration (Y. Cohen 2009).

Because of their valuable skills, infotech and other high-level professionals can be confident of finding a good job upon return. Drawing on work-based connections and their access to resources through government-run anti-brain-drain programs, infotech professionals are able to set up employment prior to remigration and are well represented among remigrants.[4]

In reflecting on their multiple migrations, some returned émigrés suggested that rather than solving their economic, affiliational, and family predicaments, the ever-present possibility of geographic mobility became a problem in itself. A woman in the midst of a difficult readjustment to Israel described migration as a Pandora's Box that she regretted opening. "I think we would have been happier," she opined, "if we had not traveled to the U.S. that first time."

Several factors tend to discourage high-tech migrants' permanent settlement: the availability of jobs abroad, the relatively easy process of migration and return, and personal and family-based ambivalence about various points of residence. In fact, these factors work to sustain transnational careers. Although regular travel may be frustrating for infotech emigrants and their families, and difficult for their countries of origin and settlement, their continuous travel across borders may also contribute to the industry's ongoing transformation as it creates new markets, delivers new sources of capital and labor, and introduces new systems of production.

A BRIEF COMPARISON OF ISRAELI AND INDIAN INFOTECH MIGRANTS IN SILICON VALLEY

Israelis are not the only migrant group known for their high-tech entrepreneurship; a sizable body of research demonstrates that Chinese, Taiwanese, and Indians helped to establish Silicon Valley and continue to play leading roles in its continuity (Saxenian 2006). Among these migrant groups, Indians are by far the most dominant population in both Silicon Valley and throughout the United States (Saxenian 2006; Wadhwa, Saxenian, and Siciliano 2012). A brief comparison of Israelis and Indians can reveal the importance of ethnic versus industry-based factors in determining these two migrant populations' involvement in infotech.

According to Vivek Wadhwa, AnnaLee Saxenian, and David Siciliano (2012, 2), who analyzed a random sample of 1,882 out of the 107,819 engineering and technology companies formed in the United States between 2006 and 2012, 24.3 percent of these companies had at least one immigrant founder. India was the number-one source of immigrants starting engineering and technology companies in the United States during this period, accounting for 33.2 percent of the total. Israel was the sixth-largest source, contributing founders of 3.5 percent of all immigrant-created engineering and technology companies during the period (ibid., 3). Looking at Silicon Valley alone between 2006 and 2012, Indians accounted for 32 percent of the immigrant-founded companies, while Israelis created about 2.5 percent (ibid., 26).

Perhaps the greatest difference between these two nations is in their population. Israel has approximately 8 million citizens. In contrast, India is the second-largest country in the world with 1.252 billion citizens. With over 3 million residents in the United States, there are approximately twelve times as many Indians here as Israelis, who number 250,000 (Cen-

---

4. See the Israel Brain Gain Program website at: http://www.israel-braingain.org.il/article.aspx?id=7120 (accessed November 18, 2016).

tral Intelligence Agency 2013). Despite Israel's smaller population, Israeli Americans have close and enduring relations with the sizable, educated, and influential American Jewish population of some 6 million.

Their differences in size notwithstanding, the two countries have a number of features in common. Both became independent in the late 1940s, share a legacy of British colonialism, and are noted for their extensive and entrepreneurial diasporas (Dossani and Kenney 2002). Immigrants from both countries are better educated than both the average American and the average member of their country of origin (Cohen 1996).

Given Indian immigrants' high educational levels and sizable numbers, high-tech is only one of several professional niches they occupy in the United States; they are also employed as engineers, health care professionals, managers and administrators, and supervisors and proprietors of sales jobs (Eckstein and Peri, this issue). In contrast, infotech is the only well-known realm of Israeli professional specialization in Silicon Valley and the United States.

Israeli emigrants had an earlier start in Silicon Valley than Indian immigrants; their involvement dates back to the early 1990s. Moreover, Israeli infotech emigrants are more likely to have U.S. degrees, and more of them have attained permanent resident status than workers from India. As of 2012, Indians held the largest share of the 262,569 H-1B skilled worker visas in the United States with 168,367, or 64 percent. Israelis were not listed among the top twenty H-1B nationalities and held fewer than 1,000 such visas (Arora and Gambardella 2004; U.S. Department of Homeland Security 2013). These figures reflect the different modes of entry into the United States taken by Indian and Israeli infotech migrants. Israelis find it easier to stay on.

Both Israel and India rely on ties between immigrants in Silicon Valley and home-country institutions to foster infotech growth at home and abroad. Owing to Israel's higher level of national development, more advanced infrastructure, and cutting-edge research and development facilities, Israeli transnationals can link up with profitable high-tech firms back home that specialize in, for instance, research and development as well as hardware design and manufacturing.[5] In contrast, India-based firms are best known for providing low-cost software. In their report on the globalization of the software industry, Ashish Arora and Alfonso Gambardella (2004, 12) assert that, "at the risk of some exaggeration, one can say that multinational firms came to Israel to do R&D [and] to India for inexpensive skilled workers."

Despite their later start in Silicon Valley, Indians had increased their involvement by 2012 in a wide variety of industrial activities, yielding expanded access to venture capital and a growing number of start-ups (Chadha 2015; Dahad 2015). A 2015 article in the Indian newspaper *Firstpost* noted that Sundar Pichai and Satya Nadella were the CEOs of Google and Microsoft, respectively, Vinod Khosla was cofounder of Sun Microsystems, Amit Singhal was a senior vice president of Google, Shantanu Narayen was president and CEO of Adobe, and Padmasree Warrior was chief technical officer of Cisco. Their many MBA degrees and their high levels of English fluency (compared to other migrant nationalities) have made Indians especially well represented among the ranks of managers of U.S. infotech firms (Dossani 2002, 26).

Fieldwork and journalism conducted in Israeli and Indian infotech communities reveal that ethnic networks are of vital importance to both populations in providing referrals, advice, access to funds, and sources of mentoring (Eischen 2011). Israelis and Indians alike pragmatically reach out to conationals in the United States and their country of origin for work-related information and connections. Members of both communities also mention being motivated by national loyalty and pride to support the advancement of their coethnics and their homelands in high-tech.

I have already reviewed Israeli emigrants' tendency to cling to their home-country identity and social practices even as they pursue careers in the United States. In a like manner, Indians are said to "look to their [country] of birth as [a place] to return to, subject to the

---

5. Israel's literacy level is close to 98 percent, while India's is about 75 percent (Central Intelligence Agency 2013).

right conditions such as professional opportunities" (Dossani 2002, 26). The leading infotech scholar Vivek Wadhwa explains the theory and practice underlying Indian immigrants' networks:

> One reason . . . Indian entrepreneurs have a very strong support network here in the U.S. [is that] thirty years ago, when Indians began building momentum in Silicon Valley, that first generation of successful startup founders worked hard to help those who followed. They built organizations and created a U.S. ecosystem of successful Indian entrepreneurs—and, crucially, angel funders—to accelerate the success of newcomers.
>
> They decided to forget which part of India they were born in and just to focus on the cause. When the first generation of Indians in Silicon Valley succeeded in shattering the glass ceiling, they decided to help others follow their path. They realized that they had all surmounted the same obstacles. And that they could reduce the barriers to entry for others behind them by sharing their experiences and opening some doors. (Chadha 2015)

In sum, the patterns of involvement of Israeli and Indian infotech immigrant communities in Silicon Valley and with conationals back home reveal surprising similarities. This is striking given the two countries' vastly different sizes and disparate histories, cultures, and levels of development. These common patterns can be traced to not only the structure of the infotech industry but also the two migrant communities' shared interactions and experiences of studying and working together.

In fact, fieldwork, journalism, and academic research reveal a significant amount of intergroup collaboration among Israeli and Indian infotech entrepreneurs in Silicon Valley (Kapur and McHale 2005; Mohan 2013; Sheth 2007). Acting as host during Indian president Pranab Mukherjee's visit to the Knesset (the Israeli Parliament), Israeli prime minister Benjamin Netanyahu indicated his awareness of India's and Israel's accomplishments in global infotech as he joked, "Hindi and Hebrew are the main languages of the Silicon Valley, [although] you sometimes also hear English" (*Times of India* 2015).

The importance of nationality in fostering cooperation and accessing home-country resources allows groups like Indians, Chinese, and Israelis to limit other nationalities' access to the infotech niche, thus imposing social closure. At the same time, however, the nationally diverse "melting pot of ideas" milieu of Silicon Valley encourages collaboration among varied populations who exchange complementary skills and assets in a mutually beneficial manner (Orpaz 2014; Saxenian 2006).

Social science research often attributes migrants' social patterns to essentialized cultural characteristics. This brief comparison of Israeli and Indian infotech entrepreneurs in Silicon Valley suggests that structural and industry-related factors should also be considered as important explanations for the strikingly similar social practices of apparently dissimilar groups engaged in the pursuit of common ends.

COMMUNITY-BASED IMPACTS OF ISRAELI EMIGRANTS' CONCENTRATION IN INFOTECH

Israeli migrants' infotech involvement has had considerable impacts on both migrants themselves and on American society.

Through their extensive involvement in high-tech, Israeli immigrants enhanced their access to income and self-determination. They are now much freer to travel, to live where they wish, and to pursue more lucrative and prestigious careers than would have been possible had they followed other pursuits. Further, through their immersion in transnational spaces like Silicon Valley, they can enjoy the affluence and what many describe as the "quiet life" outside of Israel while simultaneously interacting with fellow Israelis. They find satisfaction in visiting the homeland regularly, contributing to its development through their careers, providing philanthropic support, and lobbying host-country governments on Israel's behalf.

At the same time, a considerable fraction of Israeli emigrants involved in high-tech entrepreneurship remain ambivalent about being outside of the home country. Israeli women find it difficult to raise children in U.S. suburbs and often feel isolated from family, friends, and home-country institutions that permit married women in Israel to maintain a more satisfying work-family mix than is available in the United States (Gold 2002; Lev Ari 2008). The children of Israeli immigrants feel compelled to make momentous decisions about their future place of residence while still teenagers, since prospects for full participation in Israeli society are hindered for those who do not serve in the Israel Defense Forces.

Israeli migrants involved in infotech have also had a significant impact on the United States. Since the start of the Great Recession in 2008, economists, policymakers, business leaders, and journalists have expressed concern about the country's reduced ability to attract and compete for high-tech entrepreneurs on a global scale. This finding is emphasized in a recent report by Wadhwa, Saxenian, and Siciliano (2012), who determined that the number of Silicon Valley start-ups created by immigrants was substantially reduced between 2005 and 2012. In 2005, 52.4 percent of new enterprises included at least one key founder who was an immigrant. By 2012, that proportion had dropped to 43.9 percent. Even more ominous, the study concluded that "immigrant founded companies' dynamic period of expansion has come to an end" (Wadhwa, Saxenian, and Siciliano 2012, 2). Viewing as a major threat the international competition for migrant entrepreneurs coming from countries that offer more attractive subsidies or better economic conditions than the United States, U.S. politicians, CEOs, and business experts have endorsed policies and incentives to ensure the continued supply and retention of this valuable form of human capital (Bluestein 2012; Hart, Acs, and Tracy 2009). Exemplifying this perspective, the CEO of the U.S. Chamber of Commerce, Thomas J. Donohue, asserted in 2012, "We should allow the world's most creative entrepreneurs to stay in our country. They are going to contribute and succeed somewhere—why shouldn't it be in the United States?" (Hohn 2012). Such sentiments underlie the implementation of immigrant investor visas.[6]

Israel continues to be a reliable source of skilled workers. To ensure their availability, leading Silicon Valley institutions have collaborated with Israeli immigrant organizations. For example, in October 2014, the first California Israel International Business Summit was held at Microsoft's Mountain View campus. The event drew 25 companies and 400 attendees (Cherney 2014). Similarly, in 2015, the Stanford University Graduate School of Business (GSB) held its third annual Israeli Entrepreneurship Fair, with the target constituency being Silicon Valley firms with at least one Israeli founder. Sponsored by the GSB's career center and the university's Jewish student association, the event sought to identify employment opportunities for recent graduates while pursuing goals shared by Israel and the GSB (Wishingrad 2015).

From the U.S. perspective, Israeli émigrés' enduring interest in the U.S. economy is gratifying. While the number of high-tech workers from Taiwan, once a major source country, has recently flat-lined, Israelis and emigrants from other countries continue to enter the United States at a good clip. Policymakers hope that these migrants will continue to supplement America's high-tech labor needs over the long term.

CONCLUSION

Israeli infotech migration began when individuals sought opportunities abroad during a period when Israel discouraged both emigration and entrepreneurship. Relying on social and human capital they had already acquired in Israel, they achieved economic success in a manner that both drew on and contributed to the growth of the infotech industry in Israel and the United States. In response, Israel transformed its economic and labor market policies in order to enhance high-tech immigrants' participation in the global economy.

Despite the increased legitimacy of such endeavors, we see that migrants' choices are not simply economically based. Rather, Israeli em-

---

6. See U.S. Department of State, Bureau of Consular Affairs, "Immigrant Investor Visas," available at: travel.state.gov/content/visas/en/immigrate/Immigrant-Investor-Visas.html.

igrants evaluate the quality of life where they settle in the host country in light of numerous factors, including opportunities for retaining religious, cultural, and national identities. California offers many benefits, but Israeli emigrants remain nostalgic for home and find the Bay Area to be a less than ideal location for socializing Israeli children. In response, immigrants, the Israeli government, and American Jewish organizations provide services to make the environment more acceptable to these emigrants.

Our cursory comparison of Israelis with Indians—the largest group of immigrant entrepreneurs both nationally and in Silicon Valley—reveals marked similarities in their means for succeeding in California while also facilitating home-country development. Both groups stress in-group collaboration, national loyalty, and a desire to overcome exclusion.

In conclusion, transnational strategies can provide infotech migrants with significant options and resources both at home and abroad, but only if they endure unfamiliar and sometimes uncomfortable environments that test their identities and create difficulties for their families. Migrants often deal with such challenges by reinforcing their ties with conationals and their country of origin. In this, we see that collective, familial, and identificational issues still shape patterns of work and travel in the contemporary global economy and thus deserve continuing attention in studies of global migration.

Dealing with expanded options for work and travel may make life more complex for migrant families and more challenging for their countries of origin and settlement. At the same time, however, regular travel among infotech migrants may contribute to the ongoing exchange of ideas and the maintenance of networks that generate innovation.

REFERENCES

Almog, Oz. 2000. *The Sabra: The Creation of the New Jew.* Berkeley: University of California Press.

Aneesh, A. 2003. "Between Fantasy and Despair: The Transnational Condition and High-Tech Immigration." In *Immigrant Life in the U.S.: Multidisciplinary Perspectives,* edited by Donna Gabaccia and Colin W. Leach. London: Routledge.

Arora, Ashish, and Alfonso Gambardella. 2004. "The Globalization of the Software Industry: Perspectives and Opportunities for Developed and Developing Countries." Working Paper 10538. Cambridge, Mass.: National Bureau of Economic Research.

Avnimelech, Gil. 2009. "VC Policy: Yozma Program 15-Years Perspective." Paper presented at the 2009 summer conference of the Copenhagen Business School. Frederiksberg, Denmark (June 17–19).

Banerjee, Neela. 2007. "In Jews, Indian-Americans See a Role Model in Activism." *New York Times,* October 2.

Bluestein, Adam. 2012. "The Most Entrepreneurial Group in America Wasn't Born in America." *Inc.,* October 15.

Brandt, Joshua. 2000. "Israeli Entrepreneurs, Alumni of Technion Institute Deepen Ties to Booming Silicon Valley." *Jewish News Weekly of Northern California,* September 1.

Brooks, David. 2010. "The Tel Aviv Cluster." *New York Times,* January 12.

Central Intelligence Agency (CIA). 2013. *The World Factbook.* Available at: https://www.cia.gov/library/publications/the-world-factbook/index.html (accessed June 17, 2016).

Chadha, Sunainaa, 2015. "More Than Just Pichai and Nadella: Indians Now the Biggest Power Players in Silicon Valley." *Firstpost,* August 12.

Cherney, Max. 2014. "Israeli Firms Seek Partners at Silicon Valley Summit." *Jewish News Weekly of Northern California,* November 6.

Cohen, Abner. 1969. *Custom and Politics in Urban Africa: A Study of Hausa Migrants in Yoruba Towns.* Berkeley: University of California Press.

Cohen, Nir. 2009. "Come Home, Be Professional: Ethno-nationalism and Economic Rationalism in Israel's Return Migration Strategy." *Immigrants and Minorities* 27(1): 1, 1–28.

———. 2010. "From Legalism to Symbolism: Anti-Mobility and National Identity in Israel, 1948–1958." *Journal of Historical Geography* 36: 19–28.

Cohen, Yinon. 1996. "Economic Assimilation in the United States of Arab and Jewish Immigrants from Israel and the Territories." *Israel Studies* 1(2): 75–97.

———. 2009. "Migration Patterns to and from Israel." *Contemporary Jewry* 29(2): 115–25.

Dahad, Nitin. 2015. "Indian Tech Innovation: Hardware Still Poor Second to Software." *The Next Silicon Valley,* February 11.

Davone, Richard. 2007. "Diasporas and Development." Washington, D.C.: World Bank. Available at: http://documents.worldbank.org/curated/en/2007/01/7527868/diasporas-development (accessed March 24, 2016).

Dossani, Rafiq. 2002. "Chinese and Indian Engineers and Their Networks in Silicon Valley." Stanford, Calif.: Stanford University, Asia/Pacific Research Center (March).

Dossani, Rafiq, and Martin Kenney. 2002. "Creating an Environment for Venture Capital in India." *World Development* 30(2): 227–53.

Drori, Israel, Benson Honig, and Mike Wright. 2009. "Transnational Entrepreneurship: An Emergent Field of Study." *Entrepreneurship Theory and Practice* 33(5, September): 1001–22.

Eckstein, Susan, and Giovanni Peri. 2018. "Immigrant Niches and Immigrant Networks in the U.S. Labor Market." *RSF: The Russell Sage Foundation Journal of the Social Sciences* 4(1): 1–17. DOI: 10.7758/RSF.2018.4.1.01.

Efrati, Amir. 2012. "Israelis Tap in to Silicon Valley." *Wall Street Journal,* February 16.

Eischen, Kyle. 2011. "Immigrants' Globalization of the Indian Economy." Unpublished paper. University of California, Santa Cruz.

Freedman, Marcia, and Joseph Korazim. 1986. "Israelis in the New York Area Labor Market." *Contemporary Jewry* 7(1): 141–53.

Freedman, Matthew L. 2008. "Job Hopping, Earnings Dynamics, and Industrial Agglomeration in the Software Publishing Industry." *Journal of Urban Economics* 64(3): 590–600.

Frenkel, Michal. 2008. "Reprogramming Femininity? The Construction of Gender Identities in the Israeli Hi-Tech Industry Between Global and Local Gender Orders." *Gender, Work, and Organizations* 15(4): 352–74.

Gold, Steven J. 1994. "Patterns of Economic Cooperation Among Israeli Immigrants in Los Angeles." *International Migration Review* 28(105): 114–35.

———. 2002. *The Israeli Diaspora.* London and Seattle: Routledge and University of Washington Press.

———. 2013. "Enhanced Agency for Recent Jewish Migrants to the U.S." *Contemporary Jewry* 33(1–2, April–July): 145–67.

———. 2015. "Adaptation and Return Among Israeli Enclave and Infotech Entrepreneurs." In *Immigration and Work,* edited by Jody Agius Vallejo. Bingley, U.K.: Emerald.

———. 2016. "Patterns of Adaptation Among Contemporary Jewish Immigrants to the U.S." In *American Jewish Yearbook 2015,* vol. 115, edited by Arnold Dashefsky and Ira M. Sheskin. DOI 10.1007/978-3-319-24505-8_1.

Gold, Steven, and Rona Hart. 2013. "Transnational Ties During a Time of Crisis: Israeli Emigration, 2000 to 2004." *International Migration* 51(3): 1–34.

Goldberg, Uri. 2012. *What's Next for the Startup Nation? A Blueprint for Sustainable Innovation.* Bloomington, Ind.: Author House.

Goldscheider, Calvin. 1996. *Israel's Changing Society: Population, Ethnicity, and Development.* Boulder, Colo.: Westview Press.

Granovetter, Mark. 1995. "The Economic Sociology of Firms and Entrepreneurship." In *The Economic Sociology of Immigration: Essays on Networks, Ethnicity, and Entrepreneurship,* edited by Alejandro Portes. New York: Russell Sage Foundation.

Handwerker, Haim. 2014. "Proud to Be Israeli in the U.S." *Haaretz,* October 19.

Hart, David M., Zoltan J. Acs, and Spencer L. Tracy Jr. 2009. "High-Tech Immigrant Entrepreneurship in the United States." Washington, D.C.: Small Business Administration, Office of Advocacy (July).

Hermoni, Oded, and Zuri Dar. 2003. "Ness Technologies Acquires APAR Infotech." *Haaretz,* May 13.

Hohn, Marcia Drew. 2012. "Immigrant Entrepreneurs: Creating Jobs and Strengthening the Economy." Washington, D.C.: U.S. Chamber of Commerce, Labor Immigration and Employee Benefits Division (January).

Jewish Virtual Library. 2014. "Latest Population Statistics for Israel (Updated January 2014)." Available at: http://www.jewishvirtuallibrary.org/latest-population-statistics-for-israel (accessed February 21, 2015).

Kanter, Rosabeth M. 1977. *Men and Women of the Corporation.* New York: Basic Books.

Kapur, Devish, and John McHale. 2005. "Sojourns and Software: Internationally Mobile Human Capital and High-Tech Industry Development in India, Ireland, and Israel." In *From Underdogs to Tigers: The Rise and Growth of the Software Industry in Some Emerging Economies,* edited by Ashish Arora and Alfonso Gambardella. Oxford: Oxford University Press.

Kobayashi, Audrey, and Valerie Preston. 2007. "Transnationalism Through the Life Course: Hong Kong Immigrants in Canada." *Asia Pacific Viewpoint* 48(2, August): 151–67.

Kordova, Shoshona. 2014. "Word of the Day: Firgun: The Art of Tooting Someone Else's Horn." *Haaretz*, August 25.

Kotkin, Joel. 1992. *Tribes: How Race, Religion, and Identity Determine Success in the New Global Economy.* New York: Random House.

Lee, Jennifer C. 2013. "Employment and Earnings in High-Tech Ethnic Niches." *Social Forces* 91(2): 747–84.

Lev Ari, Lilach. 2008. *The American Dream—For Men Only? Gender, Immigration, and the Assimilation of Israelis in the United States.* El Paso, Tex.: LFB Scholarly Publishers.

Light, Ivan. 2010. "Transnational Entrepreneurs in an English-Speaking World." *Die Erde* 141(1–2): 1–16.

Light, Ivan, and Steven J. Gold. 2000. *Ethnic Economies.* San Diego: Academic Press.

Min, Pyong Gap. 2008. *Ethnic Solidarity for Economic Survival: Korean Greengrocers in New York City.* New York: Russell Sage Foundation.

Mohan, Mukund. 2013. "The Indian Startup Ecosystem Should Look at Israel as a Role Model." Best Engaging Communities (blog), March 24, available at: https://bestengagingcommunities.com/2013/03/24/the-indian-startup-ecosystem-should-look-at-israel-as-a-role-model/ (accessed June 21, 2016).

Nonini, Donald, and Aihwa Ong. 1997. "Introduction: Chinese Transnationalism as an Alternative Modernity." In *Ungrounded Empires: The Cultural Politics of Modern Chinese Transnationalism,* edited by Aihwa Ong and Donald Nonini. New York: Routledge.

O'Keefe, Siobhan, and Sarah Quincy. 2018. "Old Immigrants, New Niches: Russian Jewish Agricultural Colonies and Native Workers in Southern New Jersey, 1880–1910." *RSF: The Russell Sage Foundation Journal of the Social Sciences* 4(1): 20–38. DOI: 10.7758/RSF.2018.4.1.02.

Orpaz, Inbal. 2014. "Israeli Mafia Thrives in Silicon Valley but Can't Escape High Cost of Living." *Haaretz*, January 29.

Pine, Dan. 2012. "Little Herzliya: Israeli Ex-pats Reshape South Bay Jewish Life." *Jewish News Weekly of Northern California,* April 20.

Pollock, Miriam. 2014. "The Sabras of Silicon Valley." *The Tower* (Stanford University) 19(October).

Portes, Alejandro. 2010. *Economic Sociology: A Systematic Inquiry.* Princeton, N.J.: Princeton University Press.

Ray, Manashi. 2013. "The Global Circulation of Skill and Capital—Pathways of Return Migration of Indian Entrepreneurs from the United States to India." In *Diaspora Engagement and Development in South Asia,* edited by Tan Tai Yong and Md Mizanur Rahman. Houndmills, Basingstoke, U.K.: Palgrave Macmillan.

Rebhun, Uzi, and Lilach Lev Ari. 2010. *American Israelis: Migration, Transnationalism, and Diasporic Identity.* Boston: Brill.

Ritterband, Paul, and Yael Zerubavel. 1986. "Introduction: Special Supplemental Section: Conference Reports on Israelis Abroad." *Contemporary Jewry* 7(1): 111.

Sabar, Naama. 1999. *Kibbutzniks in the Diaspora.* Albany: State University of New York Press.

Salaff, Janet, Siu-lun Wong, and Arent Greve. 2010. *Hong Kong Movers and Stayers: Narratives of Family Migration.* Chicago: University of Illinois Press.

Sanders, Jimy M., and Victor Nee. 1996. "Immigrant Self-employment: The Family as Social Capital and the Value of Human Capital." *American Sociological Review* 61(2): 231–49.

Saxenian, AnnaLee. 2006. *The New Argonauts: Regional Advantage in a Global Economy.* Cambridge, Mass.: Harvard University Press.

Scheck, Justin. 2009. "H-P to Acquire 3Com for $2.7 Billion." *Wall Street Journal,* November 11.

Senor, Dan, and Saul Singer. 2009. *Start-Up Nation: The Story of Israel's Economic Miracle.* New York: Twelve.

Shelah, Shmulik. 2006. "Eric Benhamou Has Apparently Discovered the Gene Responsible for Technological Entrepreneurship in Israel." Israel Valley, April 30, available at: http://israelvalley.com/articles/1427-eric-benhamou-has-apparently-discovered-the-gene-responsible-for-technological-entrepreneurship-in-israel (accessed June 21, 2016).

Sheth, Niraj. 2007. "Thread: Indian and Israeli Communities Work Together in Silicon Valley." *East Bay Times,* August 20.

Shokeid, Moshe. 1988. *Children of Circumstances: Israeli Emigrants in New York.* Ithaca, N.Y.: Cornell University Press.

Sobel, Zvi. 1986. *Migrants from the Promised Land.* New Brunswick, N.J.: Transaction.

Soffer, Stuart. 2015. "Meanwhile in Silicon Valley: IEFF as Central Exchange in Israeli Silicon Valley Start-up Ecosystem." *Jerusalem Post,* March 2.

Swed, Ori, and John Sibley Butler. 2015. "Military Capital in the Israeli Hi-Tech Industry." *Armed Forces and Society* 41(1): 123–41.

Tendler, Idan. 2015. "From the Israeli Army Unit 8200 to Silicon Valley." TechCrunch, March 20. Available at: https://techcrunch.com/2015/03/20/from-the-8200-to-silicon-valley/ (accessed June 21, 2016).

Times of India. 2015. "'Hindi, Hebrew Main Languages of Silicon Valley.'" *Times of India,* October 14.

U.S. Census Bureau. 2013. *2011–2013 American Community Survey Three-Year Estimates.* Washington: U.S. Government Printing Office.

U.S. Department of Homeland Security (DHS). 2013. "Characteristics of H-1B Specialty Occupation Workers, Fiscal Year 2012." Annual Report to Congress, October 1, 2011, to September 30, 2012. Washington: DHS.

Wadhwa, Vivek, AnnaLee Saxenian, and F. David Siciliano. 2012. "Then and Now: America's New Immigrant Entrepreneurs, Part VII." Kansas City, Mo.: Kauffman: The Foundation of Entrepreneurship (October).

Waldinger, Roger, and Mehdi Bozorgmehr, eds. 1996. *Ethnic Los Angeles.* New York: Russell Sage Foundation.

Wishingrad, Sarah. 2015. "GSB [Graduate School of Business] Hosts Israeli Entrepreneurship Fair." *Stanford Daily,* April 8.

Xie, Yu, and Margaret Gough. 2011. "Ethnic Enclaves and the Earnings of Immigrants." *Demography* 48(4, November): 1293–1315.

Zilber, Tammar B. 2006. "The Work of the Symbolic in Institutional Processes: Translations of Rational Myths in Israeli High-Tech." *Academy of Management Journal* 49(2, April): 281–303.

Caring and Carrying the Cost: Bicultural Latina Nurses' Challenges and Strategies for Working with Coethnic Patients

MING-CHENG M. LO AND EMERALD T. NGUYEN

In an emergent type of labor market niche, bicultural immigrants serve as cultural brokers between clients and workers and among different groups of workers whose communications are hindered by cultural and language barriers. We focus on the bicultural Latino nurses who are recruited as cultural brokers to facilitate "culturally competent care" in a predominantly white institution that serves an increasingly diverse patient population, with Hispanics being the majority-minority group. Through a qualitative study based on twenty-six in-depth interviews in Northern California, we find that these nurses adopt "code hybridization" strategies to manage their roles as cultural brokers. We discuss the larger institutional contexts that shape the successes and impacts of these strategies, as well as the theoretical implications for assimilation theories.

Keywords: nurses, Latino immigrants, cultural brokers, health care, immigrant assimilation

Scholars have richly depicted the span of immigrant labor market niches in the United States from one end of the spectrum to the other—from the most labor-intensive sectors to the very high-skilled sectors (for a comprehensive review, see Eckstein and Peri, this issue). Building upon and advancing these insights, this article, along with some new studies (for example, Da Cruz, this issue; Wilson, this issue), identifies and explores an emergent type of niche that is filled by bicultural immigrants (including second and later generations) who serve as cultural brokers between clients and workers and among workers whose communications are hindered by cultural and language barriers. These immigrant workers' unique skill set supposedly lies in their bilingualism and their alleged familiarity with both cultures.

This study focuses on bicultural Latino nurses, including licensed practical nurses (LPNs), registered nurses (RNs), and nurse-practitioners (NPs). As one of the most rapidly expanding sectors of the economy, health care

---

Ming-Cheng M. Lo is professor of sociology at the University of California–Davis. **Emerald T. Nguyen** earned a PhD in sociology from the University of California–Davis and was a 2016–2017 American Sociological Association Congressional Fellow.

© 2018 Russell Sage Foundation. Lo, Ming-Cheng M., and Emerald T. Nguyen. 2018. "Caring and Carrying the Cost: Bicultural Latina Nurses' Challenges and Strategies for Working with Coethnic Patients." *RSF: The Russell Sage Foundation Journal of the Social Sciences* 4(1): 149–71. DOI: 10.7758/RSF.2018.4.1.09. We would like to acknowledge the financial support we received from the University of California–Davis Center for Poverty Research. An earlier version of this article was presented at the 2016 American Sociological Association annual meetings. We are grateful for the comments from the discussant and other participants on our panel. Direct correspondence to: Ming-Cheng M. Lo at mmlo@ucdavis.edu, Department of Sociology, University of California, 1 Shields Avenue, Davis, CA 95616; and Emerald T. Nguyen at etnguyen@ucdavis.edu.

has long been known to rely on immigrant workers to address its labor force shortages—for example, foreign-trained nurses from the Philippines (Ortiga, this issue) and Indian doctors who fill the jobs that native doctors avoid (Eckstein and Peri, this issue). The hiring of bicultural Latino nurses, however, is a response to a different demand. Instead of being asked to fill the overall RN shortage or to take undesirable jobs shunned by native workers, these nurses are being recruited as cultural brokers to facilitate "culturally competent care" in a predominantly white institution that serves an increasingly diverse patient population, with Hispanics having become the majority-minority group (Bosch, Doshier, and Gess-Newsome 2012; Institute of Medicine 2001; Thacker 2005). Put differently, we can view bicultural Spanish-speaking nursing as a niche formed by the long-term flows over the last few decades of Mexican and Central American immigrants who have flocked to the United States for low-income, labor-intensive jobs and who have become clients for health care services.

The need for bicultural Latino nurses has been extensively documented (for a literature review, see Bosch, Doshier, and Gess-Newsome 2012), and so has the shortage of these health care professionals. Citing the U.S. Census Bureau, the National Association of Hispanic Nurses (NAHN) reports that the Hispanic population reached 53 million in 2012, representing a 50 percent increase since 2000. The NAHN also reports that 41 percent of adult Hispanics did not speak English proficiently, yet Hispanics made up only 4.8 percent of RNs and 7.5 percent of LPNs (U.S. Census Bureau 2007). Indeed, the underrepresentation of minority health care professionals was recognized as an important health care concern in *Healthy People 2010,* a U.S. Department of Health and Human Services (2000) report that set the goal of awarding 12 percent of nursing degrees to underrepresented racial and ethnic groups by 2010. Current efforts to address the shortage of bicultural Latino nurses include: Spanish-English bilingual nursing programs at community and four-year colleges; state-funded scholarships for Hispanic nursing students; Spanish-competency training programs (sponsored by NAHN); and certification by the National Board of Certification for Medical Interpreters (CMI), among other initiatives. In short, the rise of the bicultural Latino nursing niche is a response to the rapid increase in the Hispanic immigrant patient population, and it is now recognized by policymakers, health care professionals, and educators as an important yet underaddressed area of expertise in health care.

Situated against this background, our research focuses on the question: How do bicultural Latino nurses address the tensions and challenges of "cultural brokerage"?[1] Although we join other scholars in highlighting the shortage of bicultural nurses and underscoring the importance of their recruitment, our purpose here is to problematize the assumption that knowing both cultures is tantamount to being able to successfully engage in cultural brokerage. More specifically, we situate bicultural Latino nurses in a workplace context—a white, mainstream institution—in which they are expected to adhere to professional norms and organizational regulations while simultaneously addressing their coethnic patients' cultural understandings, practices, and other life-context concerns, with the former expectation routinely regarded by most colleagues as more important than the latter. How do they work in this context as cultural brokers? How do these immigrant health care professionals, straddling both worlds, manage to develop a coherent workplace identity, if any at all? How does the larger organizational environment shape their strategies and challenges?

Drawing on twenty-six in-depth interviews in Northern California, our research addresses

---

1. Originally developed by the anthropologists Eric Wolf and Clifford Geertz, the notion of "cultural brokerage" has generally been defined as bridging, linking, or mediating between groups or persons from different cultures. Scholars have applied this notion to the context of clinical interactions, especially for studying the roles of nurses and medical interpreters. Informed by Lo's earlier work on patient culture, we further specify cultural brokerage as the mutual inclusion of seemingly incongruent sets of schemas or cultural orientations (Lo 2010).

these questions in a qualitative study. As detailed in the findings section, we find that nurses' practice of cultural brokerage is hardly uniform and instead involves diverse strategies of what we term "code hybridization"—namely, blending different parts of two cultures to avoid (or to confront) certain social tensions and power hierarchies.

THEORETICAL FRAMEWORK AND CONTRIBUTIONS

To address our questions about bicultural Latino nurses' cultural brokerage strategies and workplace identities, we borrow theoretical insights from two bodies of sociological literature: studies of ethnic concordance and cultural competency, and research on immigrant and minority middle-class identities. The former helps us conceptualize the tensions of cultural brokerage; the latter offers a frame for discussing cultural brokers' strategies. More broadly, our research has important theoretical implications for assimilation theories in that it highlights the function of bicultural immigrants' "biculturality"—rather than assimilation or ethnic retention—as a special job skill in today's American labor market.

Does Ethnic Concordance Promote Cultural Competency?

In almost all sociological literature, it is assumed that assimilated Latino immigrants (including second and later generations) are the natural candidates for bridging the two cultures. This assumption resonates with the larger policy discourse on "ethnic concordance" within health care—the matching of the ethnicity of patients and health care workers. In these policy discussions, increasing the ethnic concordance between patients and health care workers is promoted as a measure to deliver "culturally competent health care" and thereby improve the quality of clinical interactions for minority patients in the United States (Brown et al. 2007; Cooper et al. 2003; Institute of Medicine 2001). Proponents of ethnic concordance argue that coethnics are likely to share similar cultural beliefs and social experiences and thus will develop mutual respect and trust (Cooper et al. 2003; LaVeist and Nuru-Jeter 2002), communicate better, and achieve greater partnership in the patient's health care (Meghani et al. 2009).

This assumption is challenged by an ambiguous empirical picture. On the one hand, research does document that some patients report a preference for an ethnically concordant provider (Garcia et al. 2003) or that they evaluate concordant health care encounters as more satisfying and communicative (Cooper et al. 2003; LaVeist and Nuru-Jeter 2002; LaVeist, Nuru-Jeter, and Jones 2003). Some studies show that patients receive better care and are more likely to use care services when in an ethnically concordant relationship with their provider (King et al. 2004; Modi, Whetstone, and Cummings 2007).

However, just as many studies report the opposite finding. Several studies find that concordance is not correlated with patients' ratings of care, clinical experiences, or health outcomes (Clark, Sleath, and Rubin 2004; McKinlay et al. 2002; Saha, Arbelaez, and Cooper 2003; Stevens, Shi, and Cooper 2003). Janice Blanchard, Shakti Nayar, and Nicole Lurie (2007) report that, for Latinos, concordance has negative effects—patients are more likely to rate clinical encounters with coethnic providers as disrespectful. Other studies show that the effects of ethnic concordance vary widely across racial groups (Blanchard, Nayar, and Lurie 2007; Garcia et al. 2003). Even within the same ethnic group, ethnic concordance assumes different levels of significance in the varying life contexts of patients (Bender 2007; Garcia et al. 2003; Malat and Hamilton 2006).

More fundamentally, many sociologists challenge the core premise of ethnic concordance policies for its simplistic view of patient culture. Concordance policies rest on the assumption that coethnics share crucial values and cultural practices, and that this common set of values and practices, in turn, facilitates clinical interactions. Explicitly or implicitly, this assumption has been questioned by countless studies, which reveal that patient culture is shaped not only by ethnicity but also by gender, class, educational background, immigration status, and other social forces manifested in the patient's life context (for a comprehensive review, see Lo and Stacey 2008). Rather than equating patients' culture with their ethnicity, these studies suggest that patients' culture should be understood more broadly and flexibly as the patients' sense-making schema shaped by diverse social forces (ibid.). Patients resort to such schemas or frameworks for understanding clinical procedures and interactions and situating their medical decisions amid competing priorities in their lives.

Viewing culture as intersectional, these researchers argue that the key to accommodating patient "culture" in the clinic lies not in matching the ethnicity of patients and health care workers, but in prompting health care workers to allow and help patients to situate their health and health care in relevant life contexts. In an influential framework for these discussions, a patient's life context is conceptualized as the patient's "lifeworld," which can be briefly defined as the patient's contextually grounded experiences of events and problems in everyday life whose significance depends on the patient's biographical situation and position (for reviews of the literature on patient lifeworld, see Barry et al. 2001; Lo and Bahar 2013). It is argued that the quality of care is compromised when, in clinical interactions, the "voice of medicine" (which is dominated by doctors' biomedical framework and oriented toward the goal of patient compliance) overpowers or marginalizes the "voice of lifeworld" (which is inclusive of patients' preferences and experiences and oriented toward doctor-patient consensus through negotiation) (Barry et al. 2001; Greenhalgh, Robb, and Scambler 2006; Leanza, Boivin, and Rosenberg 2010; Mishler 1984; Porter 1998; Stevenson and Scambler 2005). Health care professionals, in general, are reported to be inclined to disengage from the patient's lifeworld, but they are found to be particularly likely to do so with minority or immigrant patients, whose lifeworlds are socially and culturally more marginalized (Lo 2010; Lo and Bahar 2013).

As Sarah Willen and Elizabeth Carpenter-Song (2013) put it, scholars and practitioners have now reached the point where it will be fruitful to move beyond rearticulating these well-published critiques of ethnic concordance and cultural competency policies. To the extent that "patient culture" still functions as a placeholder for talking about many dimensions of social experiences in the clinic (in other words, the patient lifeworld), it should not be treated merely as a conceptual category to be criticized and retheorized (Good et al. 2011). Instead, analyzing the ways in which health care workers discuss and address "patient culture"—however imperfectly or simplistically they may define it—provides us with an important window to understanding the on-the-ground challenges and creativity of health care workers who have begun to wrestle with these messy lifeworld issues. For example, immigrant health care professionals are still commonly expected to perform the role of cultural brokers at hospitals and clinics, despite the aforementioned research challenging the very rationale of this expectation. Yet we have little understanding of how these health care workers manage being assigned the task of bridging the norms of the clinic and the lifeworlds of coethnic patients. Documenting and theorizing their challenges and coping strategies will help us better understand the complexity of cultural brokerage in health care.

The Identities of Immigrant Professionals: Code-Switching or Code-Hybridizing?

We take up this task by focusing on the experiences of Latina nurses who regularly care for Latino patients. We incorporate insights from the literature on immigrant and minority middle-class identities to help frame the patterns emerging from our interview data. More specifically, this literature sensitizes us to the interclass boundaries (with coethnics) and interethnic tensions (with white colleagues) that middle-class minorities and immigrant professionals are challenged to negotiate. Our interviewees reported similar (but not identical) patterns of boundary-crossing in their experiences. Meanwhile, studies on Latino and other middle-class minorities generally identify "code-switching" as their main coping strategy—for example, signaling white middle-class cultural cues at work and in public and engaging in ethnic cultural practices when visiting coethnics (Agius Vallejo 2012; Agius Vallejo and Lee 2009, Neckerman, Carter, and Lee 1999). Furthermore, some of these middle-class minorities may establish ethnic professional organizations that enable them to collectively process the stress of straddling two social worlds and reflect on the meanings of their identities as middle-class blacks, Latino teachers, and the like. Similar to what Nancy Fraser (1995) describes as counterhegemonic publics, these ethnic professional associations provide a "training ground" for upwardly mobile minorities to experiment with ways of hybridizing multiple cultural codes. But in coethnic clinical interactions, multiple sets of tension are compressed into the singular social space of the clinic, accentuating both ethnic and professional identities in a mainstream institution, which in turn renders unusable the common coping strategies of code-switching and counterhegemonic publics. Indeed, our interviewees were expected to provide "culturally sensitive" care to coethnic patients and *simultaneously* adhere to clinical regulations and norms and conduct themselves professionally in front of patients, doctors, and other hospital staff. We investigate how these Latina nurses developed new coping strategies—which we term "code hybridization"—in this context.

How Does "Biculturality" Function as a Job Skill for Immigrants?

Our case study of bicultural Latina nurses has broad theoretical implications beyond the discussions of cultural brokers in health care settings and their workplace identity strategies. For immigration scholars in general, the workplace experiences of our Latina nurses, who were both first- and later-generation immigrants, broaden the framework of the segmented assimilation theory (Portes and Zhou 1993). Extending segmented assimilation theory's argument that immigrants' "biculturality" can function as an advantage for school-age youths, our study is among the first to show how biculturality can also function as a job skill for immigrant adults. Meanwhile, we caution that cultural blending as a job skill can be put to use most effectively—benefiting not only bicultural immigrant professionals themselves but mainstream American society—only when appropriate institutional support is in place. Furthermore, we qualify segmented assimilation theory's assumption that, for immigrant youths straddling two cultures, cultural blending occurs more or less automatically. Indeed, our findings will concretely illustrate how immigrant and American cultures are blended on the ground.

The segmented assimilation theory has been extremely influential in demonstrating the benefits of biculturalism for immigrant youths. Scholars observe that bicultural immigrant youths learn English and participate in American cultural activities at school, while embracing their parents' languages and cultural practices at home. The sharing of languages and cultures in the home space, in turn, allows parents to offer guidance and support, protecting these youths from the oppositional cultures in inner cities. Statistically, the second-generation immigrants who follow this path—termed "selective acculturation" in this literature—appear to perform better in school and garner better economic prospects than those who opt for either complete assimilation or oppositional ethnic pride (Kasinitz et al. 2008; Portes and Rumbaut 2001). However, as Mary Waters and her associates (2010) have argued, these insights about immigrants' bicultural advantage rest almost exclusively on the empirical evidence about school-age children. To date, little is known about whether, and how, bicultural second-generation immigrants translate their bicultural advantage from educational settings to the job market. Our study is one of the first to illustrate how immigrant professionals (including, in our case, first-, second-, and later-generation immigrants) can enjoy a special market niche thanks to their cultural blending skills.

Furthermore, while cultural hybridization lies at the core of the selective acculturation model, the concrete processes of hybridization tend to be assumed rather than analyzed in this literature. To be sure, scholars have documented the mechanisms that can encourage the preservation of home cultures for immigrant youths—such as ethnic networks or civic organizations in their ethnic enclave. But little is said about how these youths actually *blend* their ethnic culture with American ways, or how they resolve the tensions that arise from such cultural blending. Being immersed in two cultures is often assumed as tantamount to naturally knowing how to mix them. Substantiating as well as qualifying such assumptions, our findings illustrate *how* Latina nurses can deploy ethnic identities at work, and integrate them with their professional identity, when they have access to particular resources and cultural flexibility in their workplace settings. In the absence of such institutional support, as our findings indicate, their ethnic identities can pose challenges to bicultural nurses' professional status or identities. We elaborate these theoretical insights in the conclusion.

METHOD AND DATA

Design and Setting

We use in-depth interviews and grounded theory methodology to understand bicultural Latina nurses' experiences with Latino patients in health care contexts in Northern California. Northern California is one of the most diverse regions in the United States, with a long history of receiving immigrants from Asia and Latin America. While nationwide Hispanic Americans are the largest minority group (16 percent according to the 2010 census), California is the state with the largest Hispanic population. In Northern California, almost one-quarter of the residents are Hispanic.

The Hispanic residents of Northern California generally mirror their national counterparts in terms of education and poverty levels. As shown in appendix figure A1, compared to the national average, Hispanics are both more likely to have less than a high school education and less likely to be college-educated. Compared with other racial groups, Hispanics lag behind Asians, non-Hispanic whites, and African Americans. The trends in Northern California are similar.

Nationally, Hispanics (along with African Americans) are also more likely to live in poverty (see appendix figure A2). Similar patterns are found in Northern California. Appendix figure A2 shows the average proportion of individuals from each group who are Medicaid-eligible—that is, those whose individual incomes are 133 percent of the federal poverty level or less. In Northern California, almost 30 percent of Hispanics are Medicaid-eligible, compared to fewer than 20 percent of non-Hispanic whites and Asians.

To meet the health care demands of the large and socioeconomically disadvantaged Hispanic group, many policy prescriptions center on increasing the numbers of Hispanic health care professionals as cultural brokers, as discussed earlier. But as also noted, there has been a significant lag in the actual implementation of these policies (Sánchez et al. 2015). This national trend is largely mirrored in Northern California. In 2012–2013, Hispanics made up 6 percent of the physician workforce nationwide, and a little over 4 percent in Northern California. Hispanics are also underrepresented among registered nurses (4.7 percent nationwide, 6.4 percent in Northern California) and nurse-practitioners (4.1 percent nationwide, 11.1 percent in Northern California) (see appendix figure A3). In focusing here on Latina nurses, we set aside the experiences of Latino physicians for future research, given that the two groups differ greatly in professional status, workplace identity, and relationships with patients.

Recruitment

Most, if not all, ethnic concordance policies assume that immigrants (including second and later generations) are the natural candidates to fill the bicultural nursing niche. But as we discussed earlier, an intersectional understanding of culture has led most sociologists to debunk the overly simplistic equating of ethnicity with culture. Empirically, bicultural nurses familiar with Latino cultures are mostly, *but not exclusively,* Latino immigrants (both foreign-born and later-generation). Acknowledging this observation, our study includes a small number of white Spanish-bilingual nurses; their experiences accentuate the unique identity challenges faced by our main group of interviewees, bicultural Latina nurses.

Those meeting our criteria for recruitment were Spanish-bilingual nurses who had worked with Latino patients in a health care setting for at least six months. After receiving ethics approval from the institutional review board at the University of California–Davis, we recruited nurses by posting information about the project in medical facilities and on social media sites relevant to Latino nursing groups. Snow-

Table 1. Demographic Characteristics of Spanish Bilingual Nurses in the Sample

Race	
Hispanic	80.8%
White	15.4
Biracial (Hispanic-white)	3.8
Ethnicity	
Colombian	3.8
Costa Rican	3.8
El Salvadoran	15.4
Guatemalan	11.5
Mexican	34.6
Nicaraguan	3.8
Peruvian	3.8
Multiethnic Latino	3.8
White	15.4
Biracial	3.8
Immigrant generation	
First generation	7.7
1.5 generation	34.6
Second generation	42.3
Third or later generation	15.4
Workplace	
Community clinic	23.1
Hospital	38.5
Public health	30.8
Other	7.7

Source: Authors' calculations of Bicultural Nurses' Study data.

ball sampling was also utilized to recruit nurses.

The Sample

Table 1 offers a summary of the demographic characteristics of the nurses in our sample: twenty-two Hispanics and four fluently bilingual, non-Hispanic whites. In a female-dominated profession, male nurses (n = 1) were less available than female nurses (n = 25) to be interviewed. About 60 percent of our interviewees were U.S.-born (second- and third-generation immigrants); 40 percent were foreign-born. They worked in community clinics, hospitals, and county public health services, where they provided primary, acute, and specialty care.

Data Sources

Data were collected between July 2012 and October 2013 through in-person, in-depth, audio-recorded interviews with each nurse. The interviews were conducted in English by the authors or research assistant and lasted roughly one to two hours. We provided a summary of the research project and obtained written informed consent at the start of each interview. A flexible interview schedule guided participants through a conversation on three broad topics. The first set of questions pertained to the interviewee's educational and professional trajectory and previous and current workplace settings. The second set of questions asked the nurses to discuss their interactions with Latino patients and reflect upon what they viewed as the key challenges, rewards, and professional goals in serving co-ethnic patients. We encouraged them to describe these experiences and reflections in their workplace contexts, including organizational resources, regulations, cultural norms, and interactions with other patients, fellow nurses, providers, or other hospital personnel. Finally, we invited them to reflect on their ethnic identity and describe their relationship to their ethnic community. Throughout the interview, nurses were encouraged to offer specific examples.

Data Analysis

Interviews were transcribed by trained research assistants and analyzed with a grounded theory approach. We first read interview transcripts in their entirety to gain a holistic understanding of the nurses' experiences. Using themes that emerged from these readings, we generated broad codes. We then refined and reapplied critical codes to the data, which allowed us to inductively identify analytical patterns. Also, we observed relationships between these analytical patterns, both within and across interviews. This coding process was inductive and recursive, totaling three rounds of double-coding by both authors. In each round, each author coded all transcripts independently, and any discrepancies between coders were resolved through discussions and clarifications of the meanings of specific codes. To preserve confidentiality, we used pseudonyms to refer to all people and places in the nurses' accounts.

FINDINGS

Expected to provide "culturally sensitive" care to coethnic patients while simultaneously operating within clinical regulations and professional norms, the Latina nurses in our study engaged in practices that we describe as code hybridization. Most of them embraced the key professional norms, such as the scientific superiority of biomedicine, the rationality or at least necessity of institutional procedures, and the value of professional universalism—that is, the principle that all patients were to be cared for equally well regardless of racial or ethnic bonds, social status, and other nonprofessional identity markers. At the same time, many (though not all) of them endorsed a countercurrent within the medical institution: an emphasis on the importance of patient lifeworld—namely patients' experiences of everyday events and problems whose meanings are shaped by the patient's larger life context (Barry et al. 2001). Latina nurses found their voices in the counterhegemonic professional ideal of lifeworld communications, through which they articulated how their shared ethnic heritage improved and enriched their clinical interactions with coethnic patients. Furthermore, some nurses developed a vision of what we term "relational communities within the clinic," which featured shared emotional bonds and vulnerable moments between caregivers and care-receivers. For these nurses, relational communities with coethnic patients were not merely instrumental in providing better biomedical care; they were valuable in themselves for empowering both nurses and their coethnic patients in a white-dominant institution. More broadly, they viewed relational communities as a means to restoring culture and humanity to the practice of health care. In mixing biomedical norms with ethnic bonds and cultural perspectives, Latina nurses resorted to, and at times broadened, counterhegemonic professional discourses in U.S. health care institutions.

However, significant and often unresolved tensions accompanied nurses' practices of cultural blending. Many found that professional universalism and relational communities were difficult principles to reconcile; the institutional norms of efficiency often pushed against the space for lifeworld communications, and the desire to form ethnic bonds and the quest for professional status were at times in competition. These tensions could impose costs and present challenges to the nurses' careers.

How, and how well, our interviewees managed these tensions and challenges differed according to their specific mode of code hybridization. At the same time, code hybridization patterns suggest different emergent workplace identities among Latina nurses. Specifically, our findings suggest four patterns of code hybridization and workplace identity among Latina nurses.

The Cross-Functional Professionals

Working within the biomedical framework, these nurses expressly incorporated concerns from their patients' lifeworlds; doing so, they emphasized, facilitated biomedical approaches rather than interfered with them. Their medical and ethnic representations blended together to facilitate professional interactions that were culturally meaningful to patients. We describe these nurses, who engaged in the most robust form of code hybridization, as "cross-functional professionals." However, nurses only become cross-functional professionals if they enjoy strong institutional support—for example, adequate resources, autonomy over their work schedule, and a workplace culture supporting their unconventional practices. Not surprisingly, only a few Latina nurses in our study derived their workplace identity from being able to work cross-functionally.

Cross-functional professionals articulated a nuanced and in-depth understanding of how coethnic patients' lifeworlds were imminently relevant to their health care and could not be bracketed. They illustrated this perspective with countless examples of clinical communications and medical goals being thwarted by doctors' misunderstandings about Latino patients' styles of interaction, their cultural capital deficits shaped by ethnicity, class, immigration status, and so on, and the material constraints they experienced from the competing priorities in their everyday lives. Alba, a fifty-seven-year-old Mexican American pediatric nurse-practitioner, described herself as the institution's "acculturation coordinator"; she consulted with patients who had been "yelled at by their doctors" for repeatedly disobeying their doctor's recommendations of lifestyle changes to control their diabetes, hypertension, or other chronic diseases. She explained to her patients that the doctors "are worried about you. But they don't have time to explain everything." In contrast, she did take the time to situate clinical conversations about diet changes in the context of a patient's everyday food choices:

> I understand that when they go to make food choices in the supermarket, because they don't speak the language, because they don't read or write, sometimes either in English or Spanish, they look at pictures to make . . . a healthy choice. So we have to talk a lot about when you see a picture of an apple on a juice can, that doesn't mean it's healthy. But they think it does. . . . We also talk about . . . McDonald's, the fast-food burgers, because they talk to me about affording to feed their family on the Dollar McDonald whatever. And I have to tell them that the whole reason it's affordable is because it's high-fat. Fat is affordable and fat's hurting you. . . . So I have to talk to them a lot about marketing and advertisement, of how it works here in the United States, and the kind of ingredients they use in the United States, because it's different from what they use in Mexico. And I know that because I lived in both countries.

Similarly, Suzanna, a twenty-nine-year-old public health nurse, engaged in a contextualized discussion about following a medical regimen with her coethnic patient who got into a "yelling match" with the provider:

> This provider had been with this family for several months. And since the beginning I think she could only see the patient as neglectful. . . . And I feel like a lot of interactions, the providers don't give the education or the tools or the knowledge to succeed, and work to meet the clients with where they're at. They expect perfection from the beginning. But these are people with very low education, language barriers, and cultural barriers. So, with this client, they got into a yelling match. And at some point I had to jump in and kind of ask some more questions. So I said, "Why didn't you give them [the client's children] medication on time?" She [the client] said, "Oh, it's summer. We're out and about. And seven o'clock is really early. And it's light out. So I forget what time it is, and when we realized what time it is when we get home, I think it's already too late." [Then I ask], "Well, what time do you get home?" [The client replies], "Well, I get home about 7:45 to 10:30." And so then, the doctor says, "Well, you can take the medication at 7:45, or you know, as late as 8:30, nine o'clock." So that gave the parent a little more information to be able to administer the medication correctly. So after that, she didn't miss a day of the medication because she knew she had wiggle [room].

These nurses' perspective resonates with the sociological research on lifeworld communications in the clinic (Barry et al. 2001; Greenhalgh, Robb, and Scambler 2006; Leanza, Boivin, and Rosenberg 2010; Mishler 1984; Porter 1998; Stevenson and Scambler 2005) in illustrating that the quality of care is often compromised when the "voice of lifeworld" (which is inclusive of patients' experiences and oriented toward doctor-patient consensus) becomes distorted by the "voice of medicine" (which is dominated by doctors' biomedical framework and is oriented toward the goal of patient compliance).

In addition to being able to engage in in-depth communications, cross-functional professionals address the lifeworld constraints faced by Latino patients, who are mostly low-income, by connecting them with resources both inside and outside the system. As illustrated in Reyna's account, lifeworld communication is not only about being respectful of patients' styles or perspectives but also, and equally importantly, about finding the resources they need to address their lifeworld constraints:

A lot of them come to the city from towns ... where they can't get the treatment they need.... So they bring family from these faraway places, and our policy is that only one person can stay, and I know they don't have the resources to go stay at a hotel. And that's really hard for me, and I tend not to tell them, "Only one person can stay." I usually try to accommodate at least two in the room, and the other ones, I'll say, "Okay, you can go to the waiting room, I'll bring you blankets, I'll bring you sheets."... Because I know they don't have the resources, and their family member just got out of surgery at like six or seven o'clock at night, and then they [would] have to drive two and a half hours [if they were to go home].... The next day I communicate with the oncoming nurse, "They need social work, they need a case manager." Social work means to give them food vouchers, talk to the family and see what they might be able to afford. There's a church really close to us, and they have little dorms. So they work with them, on trying to get them a place to stay. Or I'll tell them, "I'm going to be the nurse for the next three nights. Your loved one is going to be in my hands, they're going to be fine. You can go home and get some rest and come back."

While these nurses offered an intersectional view of their coethnic patients' lifeworlds, they nonetheless emphasized that sharing a cultural background with coethnic patients gave them a unique set of cultural resources to use in addressing these patients' (intersectional) lifeworld concerns. Alba believed that her understanding of how the Mexican food market and health care system differ from their counterparts in the United States facilitated her cultural brokerage work for her Latino patients. Suzanna's Mexican background, she felt, helped inform the types of questions and concerns she addressed with her coethnic patients. These nurses did acknowledge their differences from their coethnic patients, but they used what they believed to be their shared culture as a basis for bridging these differences. Suzanna, for instance, recognized that, though she and her coethnic patients shared the Spanish language, she needed to go out of her way to learn some specific cultural colloquialisms:

> I think all Spanish-speaking people understand that there's some general type of Spanish, but then there are colloquial types of words that we use. And so I know that, when I say a certain word but you are Salvadoran and you have a different word for that, we know that there's a difference and we reconcile it pretty easily.

Maria, a fifty-two-year-old El Salvadoran nurse who worked at a women's health clinic, felt that her language abilities allowed her to provide better care and have a warm relationship with her Spanish-speaking patients, but she had to speak more simply with these patients, as well as tune in to a different cultural style of interaction:

> You can talk right, but [my coethnic patients] can't, [because of] the low education. We need to go to their level and explain the stuff more slowly and more carefully. And for them, they feel more confident when somebody speak the language.... It's [also] cultural; [Hispanic] people are afraid to [ask questions]. Because [providers] explain something, but [the patients] don't know clearly what they say but they are afraid to ask questions. *I am more sensitive in that point.*

Further, even though they had secured remarkably higher education and socioeconomic statuses than most of their coethnic patients, the cross-functional nurses said that their Latino patients often reminded them of their own immigrant parents and relatives. Accordingly, they expressed an emotional closeness with these patients as well as a strong motivation to help and care for them. Reyna, a Mexican American nurse who worked in surgical oncology, empathized with her coethnic patients and wanted to help empower them. This desire stemmed in part, she said, to having witnessed her own mother's struggles in the U.S. health care system:

> One of the greatest things about nursing [is] that I can get to know my patients and help

them heal and get better, and educate them. . . . "This is your body, this is your life. Don't hesitate to ask questions, 'cuz no question is dumb." You know, and a lot of people can come in that way, and *I know my mom did too,* and she was educated, and she had a daughter who was working in the health field, but she still felt she couldn't ask questions.

As illustrated by these examples, lifeworld-sensitive care requires not only an in-depth understanding of lifeworld issues and a willingness to help but also time, material resources, and the professional autonomy to flexibly adjust work schedules and adapt regulations to accommodate patients' needs. Indeed, stories featuring a cross-functional professional identity were told only by interviewees who described having significant institutional autonomy and access to relevant resources. Alba explicitly portrayed her cultural brokerage work as not only approved but greatly appreciated by her colleagues, and it was clear that institutional support gave her flexibility and latitude over her schedule and pace at work. Suzanna worked with providers who did not tell her to simply do what the doctors had ordered, but allowed her to jump in and intervene. Reyna had the institutional autonomy to bend the rules and let extra family members stay in patients' rooms, and case workers at her institution worked with her to help patient families gain access to food vouchers. These nurses also mentioned gift cards, financial support for motels, and transportation assistance (for example, sending a community volunteer driver to pick up a patient) as concrete measures taken at their institution to help patients obtain the treatment they needed.

In short, the cross-functional professionals can be described as "code hybridizing" in that they expand professional boundaries to accommodate ethnic bonds, an approach that is accepted at their institutions as an effective way to provide high-quality and lifeworld-sensitive care. Such an organizational environment seems to prevail, however, in only a few small pockets within U.S. health care. Among the Latina nurses in our study, the cross-functional professionals were unique in being able to achieve a coherent workplace identity that validated both their professional and ethnic identities.

The Reformers Within

The nurses who were "reformers within" had similar goals for addressing patient lifeworlds as their "cross-functional" counterparts, but had fewer resources, less institutional autonomy, and sometimes deeper conflicts between their workplace duties and visions of lifeworld-sensitive care. Lacking adequate institutional support, yet unwilling to compromise their professional visions, these nurses felt that they were going it alone with their efforts. These "reformers within" were nurses who articulated deeper criticisms of the dominant norms in their institution than other interviewees, as well as more progressive counterhegemonic visions of care. They also incurred greater professional costs.

The reformers nurses often challenge workplace norms directly—for example, by confronting doctors who are rude or culturally insensitive, giving patients permission to modify doctors' orders, making room for alternative medicine, and honoring the "wisdom" in the community—and go out of their way to help patients navigate the system and cobble together resources. Gabrielle, a triage nurse, said, "I sometimes push a little bit further with the doctor, and then I'll just call the patient directly." Yolanda, a fifty-two-year-old public health nurse whose parents were migrant farmworkers from Mexico, described similar interactions: "I remember turning my back to [a doctor] and apologizing for the doctor and saying, 'We can do it his [the doctor's] way. Or we can do it the way that you will find more comfortable or that you know you can accomplish. The goal is to make it successful for your son.'" Commenting on helping her low-income Latino patients in general, Yolanda said that "you have to go begging sometimes" in order to find resources for these patients. Both Gabrielle's and Yolanda's examples illustrate the lengths to which reformers will go to advocate on behalf of their patients, even sometimes risking their professional standing by disagreeing with physicians or taking it upon themselves to "go begging."

Often feeling alienated in their work environment, the reformers develop a counterhegemonic vision of a "relational community in the clinic" in which health care workers build rich relationships with patients that go beyond the goal of professional rapport. In these relationships, reformer nurses position themselves as both givers of care and recipients of warmth and love. These relationships allow immigrant nurses and patients alike to be, as one nurse put it, "empowering each other in the care." Isabella, a twenty-eight-year-old Guatemalan intensive care unit nurse, described caring for and cleaning a patient. She emphasized the vulnerability and trust involved in the act:

> People trust you and invite you into their little worlds [to clean their bottoms], and I actually appreciate that a human being is willing to let another human being take care of them. I think it's actually one of the most beautiful parts of our job, even though it's kind of the most demeaning part—*seen* as demeaning by other people. . . . But a lot of us, I think, fight to be the advocate for the patient. We do care.

These nurses' experiences are illustrative of Arthur Frank's (1996) "wounded healer," who, in the process of giving care, expressing compassion, and developing companionship, recovers her own humanity. Their accounts of these day-to-day interactions also place Frank's vision in concrete institutional settings. The reformer nurses reported having little institutional support; consequently, they individually bore the costs of "doing the right thing," from putting in extra work and dealing with time management difficulties to suffering the disapproval of colleagues and physical and emotional burnout. Dolores was a twenty-eight-year-old Mexican American nurse working in primary care who had previously worked in a public health clinic. She would go out of her way to assist her patients, even taking one to her appointment at Planned Parenthood on her own time. Maintaining the same sense of mission at her current position, but with less institutional support, Dolores felt as if she was doing two separate jobs: empowering culturally marginalized patients while meeting the demands of her daily routine:

> You're providing medical care, getting vital signs, giving the injection, but then you're also trying to—if you care a lot—you're trying to give the patient space to express their culture, and then having to interpret that to the provider who maybe doesn't care, maybe has their own stereotypes. . . . I haven't burnt out yet, but a lot of nurses get burnt out eventually.

Furthermore, deviating from the norm of professional detachment, nurses in the relational community allow themselves to be emotionally vulnerable to patients' deaths, losses, and judgments. Isabella described this emotional vulnerability:

> I think one of the hardest things working with transplant patients is, they're my favorite patients, but I remember when I lost my first transplant patient. . . . Her name was [also] Isabella, and she was my same age, and she had gotten a heart transplant and then four months later, she died. . . . So I think that hits you when you start establishing relationships and you're young, 'cause I was twenty-three at the time. And you see, you know, these are people, but they're also—they're ticking time bombs in a sense, their days are limited.

She elaborated:

> I'm glad that I was there. I tend to always be there when my favorite patients die, and I don't know why that ends up happening. You know, I admit them and I'm there and help them pass on. But, I like being there. Because I don't feel like I would trust anybody else to do it as good as I could do it, and be there, and the family needs me. . . . We've built this relationship, and it's just appropriate that I'm there, so I feel closure in that sense, or satisfaction in knowing that this is the best way it could be.

This is an eloquent description of how a nurse and her "favorite" patients (and their families) grant each other support with their presence during such final moments. For Isabella, the emotional bond had grown beyond what was prescribed by her professional role—she would not "trust anybody else to do it" and she needed to be there when a patient died to "feel closure."

By the same token, and notwithstanding the ideal of professional universalism, these nurses admit that they feel greater emotional affinity with coethnic patients than any other patient group. Isabella's "relational community" with coethnic patients developed easily because they reminded her of "my loud, obnoxious Hispanic mother" and because "we Hispanics are loud, cynical people." She contrasted these relationships with her interactions with Chinese patients, whom she experienced as culturally distanced from her and therefore challenging to bond with. Such explicit celebration of ethnic solidarity in the clinic, however, can invite colleagues' questioning or disapproval. Dolores's supervisors sometimes reprimanded her for not being "a team player" with the other health care workers when she advocated for her coethnic patients, and her coworkers often asked her: "Why is race such a big deal for you?"

If the cross-functional nurses engage patient lifeworlds to ensure that they provide quality care, the reformer nurses enter the relational community as a goal in itself—to secure a space for themselves and for their coethnic patients to express their culture and humanity within an otherwise sterile and bureaucratized social world. Reformer nurses make their workplace identity coherent largely by prioritizing ethnic relationships over institutional norms—but with certain costs to their careers.

The Medical Missionaries

In contrast to the reformers, some Latina nurses fully endorse the dominant cultural and bureaucratic norms of the clinic. They embrace ethnic bonds with coethnic patients only as a means to helping them assimilate into the world of modern medicine. We describe these nurses as "medical missionaries."

Medical missionaries have a fairly black-and-white perception of biomedicine and institutional regulations, which they consider utterly superior and non-negotiable. Patient cultures and other lifeworld perspectives, in their view, are merely "excuses" for noncompliance or obstacles to assimilation. Xena, a nurse who worked in a mobile clinic, said that she did not "try to sugarcoat" what the patient said when she reported to her supervisors, nor did she offer anything "out of the scope of what we do" to patients. Beatrice put the responsibility on her patients to learn and adopt norms of clinical communication. Rather than empathizing with her coethnic patients, who tended to be fearful about offending authority figures with questions, disagreements, or explanations for their "noncompliance," Beatrice faulted them for being "deceitful." She elaborated:

> [Hispanic patients] don't want to tell you the whole story. Because they might feel embarrassed for something that they did, or didn't do. . . . I think they have more tendency to hide information. . . . I tell them, "If you want us to help you, the only way we're going to help you is if you give me all the info."

Sometimes medical missionaries get exasperated with coethnic patients whose views of medicine might appear far-fetched and misguided. Zola explained that her patients from Mexico believed that, in coming to the United States, with its advanced medical practices and technology, they would automatically be cured. She was impatient with these inaccurate perceptions: "Sir, you are paraplegic; you're not going to get any better. Do you know who Superman [actor Christopher Reeve] is? He had all the money in the world, and he didn't get better. If you're paraplegic, you're paraplegic."

Despite their hard-liner attitudes, most medical missionaries explicitly convey a sense of communal affinity with Latino patients. Like their cross-functional counterparts, they are often reminded of their immigrant parents and relatives by their coethnic patients and thus feel particularly obligated to help this patient group. Their "help," however, comes primarily in the form of top-down education rather than cultural flexibility toward interactional styles and other lifeworld practices. Julia, a specialty nurse, saw Latino patients' barriers in terms of their deviation from the cultural norms of the clinic—for example, not educating themselves, not asking enough questions, and being too accepting of authority—and saw medical education as the solution. At the same time, she recognized these issues in her own family and felt sympathetic: "[Even] in my own family . . . what the providers say is what it is, and there's no questioning of what the provider's asking for."

Like the reformers, medical missionaries are able to resolve most tensions between their professional and ethnic identities, but they do so differently. Instead of prioritizing ethnic relationships, medical missionaries resort to institutional norms and procedures to define patient deservingness (asking, for example, "are they willing to be assimilated?") and the scope of what even a caring professional can do ("my hands are tied"). Beatrice stated that "all I can do is to give them the information, and then it's their choice." Xena noted that a nurse following professional norms may seem distant and cold to patients, but she was not apologetic about creating that impression. She defended and abided by those professional norms.

In short, the medical missionaries' workplace identity is primarily informed by professional cultures and institutional norms, and their ethnic identity gives them only an enthusiasm for assimilating coethnics into the world of modern medicine.

The Conflicted Coethnics
It is noteworthy that the workplace identity of almost half of our Latina interviewees was that of what we term the "conflicted coethnic." These nurses found it important to engage in coethnic patients' lifeworlds, yet in doing so, they reported, they encountered many institutional barriers. For instance, they were sensitive to Latino patients' styles of interaction (for example, storytelling, being overly deferential), but they needed direct information to work with; they wanted to provide meaningful support to coethnic patients and take more time to help with their cultural capital deficit, but they faced pressure from supervisors and hospital management to adhere to a fast-paced work schedule; and they wanted to bond with and offer extra care for coethnic patients, but they felt uncomfortable with the implication of favoritism.

Whereas the cross-functional professionals can resort to institutional autonomy and resources to deal with similar tensions, and the reformers and medical missionaries can do so by prioritizing, respectively, ethnic bonds and professional norms, the conflicted coethnics cannot articulate a consistent framework for integrating their ethnic and professional identities. Instead, they seem to invoke one set of norms or the other on an ad hoc basis.

Specifically, if conflicted coethnic nurses find a needy coethnic patient "deserving," they tend to expand the professional boundaries of care by redefining their relationship with the patient in pseudo-familial terms. They may feel critical of the coethnic patient's behaviors, but these behaviors also remind them of their own family and relatives. They therefore display extra patience in taking care of these coethnic—if admittedly challenging—patients and derive more emotional reward from doing so. Francesca described how she managed her coethnic patients' extensive "storytelling": "You ask the question and they come up with a long answer. If they're going and going and going, I just go, 'Okay. So does that mean yes or does that mean no?' [*laughs*]." But she also repeatedly said that she "worries about my Hispanic patients more," because "I know they will forget [to take their medicine]. Because my relatives in Mexico are like that." She regularly called these patients back to check on them and said that they reminded her of her own immigrant parents. Likewise, Nancy illustrated how conflicted coethnic nurses try to manage the communication styles of their less-assimilated coethnic patients, while reminding themselves to be more patient and accommodating:

> But this way of communicating through storytelling gets in the way of me doing my [job], me being more efficient with my time. I can see how I could get exasperated and just be like, "Okay, can you get to the point? Can you just answer my question?" At the same time, I feel like, I know that we [Hispanic people] communicate with stories. And I know that I get more information when they

tell me stories. So, I hope that I'm not one of those people that get exasperated and cuts them off.

Laura described the way the familial nature of her patient relationships could complicate the line between her professional duties and her coethnic loyalties: "I felt like I'm taking care of my uncle. So that part was, yeah, and I was super-aware of it. . . . My boundaries were not really as sharp as they could have been."

At the same time, these nurses are anxious about letting such boundary expansion go too far; they worry about the situation becoming unfair, about letting these patients take advantage of the system, about the extra work for themselves simply becoming unmanageable. When a patient gives cues that trigger these worries, a "needy" coethnic patient becomes a "greedy" one. Nurses, in these situations, highlight their professional boundaries to fend off the "greedy" patient's "excessive" demands. Laura wanted to do more for her Latino patients, but also noted that their demands sometimes needed to be curbed:

> Sometimes they want more. . . . But you cannot give more because there's no more. We wish there was more to give, but. . . . As much as I want to, I can't today. . . . I remember one family, I moved everything for them. Like food-wise, I was ordering double portions so that they could eat, but then that was not enough. They wanted this specific soda, and these specific things. And I was like, "I gave you my hand and now you're taking my elbow, my shoulder, you're jumping all the way up." . . . Or also the sense of time, [they think] we have much more. The sense of time for Latinos, it's like a chewing gum.

Ursula was a Peruvian public health nurse whose workplace, the county's tuberculosis center, had several resources to help address patients' many financial constraints. Given the infectious nature of tuberculosis, Ursula persuaded her clients to be compliant using a variety of resources available to her, such as gift cards and travel vouchers. Her account illustrates especially well the dilemma of nurses who are committed to advocating for Latino patients yet feel obligated to draw the boundary between need and greed:

> I have to advocate more for the Spanish-speaking patients. . . . Like, I have to try to read what is in their minds because sometimes they are shy or they are embarrassed or they don't feel comfortable. . . . And of course there is the other extreme. The [Hispanic] people who want to take advantage of, "Oh, I'm in a private hospital. I want a double tray." Or the ones that ask for everything. "Give me soap." That's the other extreme. They are the ones who want to take advantage of the system, and we see that here also.
>
> There are situations where we have to pay for a motel because no one wants the patient. It happened a few months ago with one of my patients. Nobody wants the patient back home because the patient was infectious, so they can't [go home]. They had to pay for a motel, but only for a number of days. After that, the patient, if he or she is not infectious anymore, the patient has to find a place to go. But this person demanded, "No, you must find me a place to live or you have to find me a job." Oh, it's ridiculous! That's the other extreme.
>
> With those, we have to set limits. "I'll give you two gift cards and that's it." Or, "I'll give you three gift cards a week until you find a job. Once you find a job, I'll bring it down to one or two." And then they get mad. "No, why are you giving me less gift cards? I still need them." "Because you have a job. Because there are other people who don't have a job. They need more gift cards."

As richly illustrated here, Ursula had to know when to draw the line and limit the amount of resources she doled out to her Latino patients, whom she otherwise felt committed to advocating for. The task of defining need versus greed on a case-by-case basis is a source of tension for these nurses' workplace identity.

Furthermore, conflicted coethnics find their own biases and power struggles embedded in ethnic communities and cultures. Their sympathy for, and cultural affinity with, coethnics' values and cultural practices notwithstanding, these nurses also think that professional distance sometimes protects patients from nurses' moral judgments about certain behaviors and can also serve as a defense for nurses against coethnic patients' internalized racism. (By the same token, professionalism protects Latina nurses from the ethnic biases of white patients and colleagues.) Further challenging a romanticized version of ethnic bonds in the clinic was the observation of some nurses that they felt excluded by other ethnic "relational communities" in the clinic. For example, several interviewees described feeling uncomfortable and unwelcome in their own work space when their Filipino coworkers became "cliquey" by speaking in Tagalog during work hours or otherwise blending professional and communal space.

Straddling their professional world and their ethnic community, and constantly on guard against one infringing on the other, conflicted coethnic nurses experience high workplace stress. Lacking a coherent workplace identity, they become very anxious when challenged by different groups to demonstrate where their singular loyalties lie: "Are you a team player with the rest of the doctors and nurses?" Or, "Are you too close with your people, and therefore a less competent nurse?" Or, "You are one of us; you are not really a medical professional."

The Sympathetic Outsiders: Spanish-Speaking White Nurses

Despite the policy focus on using minority health care workers as cultural brokers for coethnic patients, nurses who speak Spanish and self-identify as cultural brokers are not exclusively from Latino communities. Our study also includes four white Spanish-speaking nurses whose experiences accentuate the identity dilemma of the Latina nurses. In general, we find that the white Spanish-speaking nurses cared about their Latino patients' lifeworld constraints and were committed to helping these patients bridge the gap between their lifeworld and the clinic. However, their racialized outsider status provided them with a buffer between these challenges and their professional identity. They often described unresolved cultural tensions as part of "their culture," for instance, rather than as part of a shared experience.

The white Spanish-speaking nurses in our study seemed devoted to addressing Latino patients' lifeworld constraints, but they also described themselves as "bridge-builders" who understood aspects of Latino communities without being members of them. In their "bridging" efforts, they focused on the gap between "cultures of poverty" and biomedical priorities, deemphasizing the importance of ethnicity beyond language. They were critical of mainstream health care for making it difficult for all low-socioeconomic-status patients, not just Latino patients, to access quality care.

Instead of talking about ethnic solidarity or community empowerment, these white nurses characterized their relationships with Latino patients in terms of "rich cultural exchanges." (One nurse even talked about being more in touch with her emotional side in Spanish than in English.) Their self-positioning as sympathetic outsiders vis-à-vis Latino communities allowed them to avoid confronting certain tensions between patient lifeworlds and the clinic—for example, they saw the practice of bringing large families to the ICU as "their culture," which "I don't understand but respect." In contrast, Latina nurses facing similar tensions tended to feel pressured to state a position on what to do about "our culture." Unlike the Latina nurses, Spanish-speaking white nurses never talked about having to fend off overdemanding Latino patients. When asked about such patients, they said that their Latino patients "never complain" and "never ask for anything." Some of them observed that Latino nurses were pressured to distance themselves from unassimilated coethnic immigrants and that, being white, they faced no such pressure.

Although not the focus of this study, Spanish-speaking white nurses' experiences highlight the identity challenges faced by Latina nurses. Regardless of their ethnicity, all nurses in this study described tensions, many of them unresolved, between patient lifeworlds and the norms and regulations of the clinic. When self-positioning as outside helpers reaching out to the Latino community, the white Spanish-speaking nurses could look at the unresolved tensions as too deeply embedded in "the community" to come within their professional reach. Such experiences exemplify the very stance that is *un*available to the Latina nurses. Identified as insiders in both their ethnic and professional communities, Latina nurses' workplace identities largely hinge on addressing the very tensions that "sympathetic outsiders" opt to bracket.

CONCLUSION

This study has examined how bicultural Latina nurses bridge patient cultures and clinical norms in performing their roles as cultural brokers for coethnic patients. Our findings indicate that these health care professionals cannot succeed in bridging the clinic and coethnic patients' lifeworlds without larger institutional transformations in place—for example, greater access to resources, more flexible institutional regulations, and an organizational culture committed to diversifying biomedical norms, as illustrated in the experiences of the "cross-functional professionals." Most of the Latina nurses in our study, lacking such structural support, had only several options: they were forced to internalize the cost (the "reformers within"); they became socialized into a narrow view of patient culture (the "medical missionaries"); or, as happened with more than half of them, they were left to struggle with institutional tensions as personal workplace problems (the "conflicted coethnics"). Overall, these Latina nurses' practices of code hybridization were often costly to their career (through, for example, difficulty with time management, disapproval from colleagues, doing extra work on their own time), but these practices often enriched the institutional culture of their workplace (for example, by creating richer understandings of patient lifeworlds and providing more room for relational bonds between patients and caregivers).

Our findings are likely to raise the question of *why* a bicultural nurse engages in a particular practice of code hybridization as opposed to another. This question lies beyond the scope of this article. Future research with a large and representative sample is needed to address whether and how immigrant generation, types of clinics, or other variables explain bicultural nurses' choice of code hybridization strategy.

Here, it remains only to elaborate on the policy and theoretical implications of our research.

For policymakers, our study confirms that meaningful cultural brokerage in health care should focus on helping patients understand and situate health care procedures and decisions in their life contexts, and that such efforts on the part of health care providers require significant amounts of time, material resources, and a respectful and flexible institutional culture. Using immigrant professionals as cultural brokers will be a successful policy only if it also focuses on implementing relevant institutional changes. It is worthwhile to reemphasize our earlier clarification that "patient culture" is not simply patient ethnicity, but instead should be understood as a set of meaning-making schemas, shaped by intersecting social structures such as class, ethnicity, and immigration status. The Hispanic patient population discussed by our interviewees was by and large low-income and undocumented; these patients spoke little English and were more familiar with Latin American than North American cultures. Their sense-making schema for having to miss work to keep a medical appointment, for example, was not simply informed by being Hispanic, or poor, or non-English-speaking; it was precisely how these factors intersected in their lives that shaped their decision-making process. A Latina nurse may not automatically understand or sympathize with these patients' sense-making schemas, especially when working under pressure to adhere to mainstream professional norms. By the same token, a white doctor who speaks Spanish might learn to incorporate such lifeworld "cultures" into clinical communications (this possibility being, of course, beyond what our data can address). But more importantly, since current policy proposals continue to focus on ethnic concordance as a shortcut to addressing linguistic and cultural barriers in the clinic, it makes sense to improve upon existing policies rather than start from scratch. A sensible policy recommendation, we argue, is to give Latina nurses who are expected to work as cultural brokers the necessary institutional support, both cultural and material, to do so.

For scholars of immigrant labor market niches, our article offers a qualitative discussion of the emergent niche of cultural brokers who facilitate the interactions between an increasingly diverse patient population and a white-dominant health care system. Our study highlights the social and cultural tensions faced by these cultural brokers, their familiarities with both languages and cultures notwithstanding. Our observations resonate with existing studies. For example, Ming-Cheng Lo and Roxana Bahar (2013) have found that Hispanic patients experience complex and tension-ridden relationships with coethnic nurses. Virginia Elderkin-Thompson, Roxane Cohen Silver, and Howard Waitzkin (2001) suggest that Latino nurses' social and professional standing might mitigate their willingness to advocate for coethnic patients or explain medical conflicts to their professional superiors. Advancing this line of conversation, ours is among the first studies to show that nurses can and do proactively address these tensions, with varying degrees of success, as illustrated in the patterns of code hybridizing reported here.

Furthermore, our findings have broader theoretical implications beyond the discussions of cultural competency policies and niche labor markets. The workplace experiences of our Latina nurses broaden the framework of segmented assimilation theory (Portes and Zhou 1993). As an extremely influential theory in recent debates about immigrant incorporation, segmented assimilation theory raises alarm about the danger of downward assimilation for the second generation of racialized minority groups, especially when immigrant parents and their American-born children adapt at different speeds (termed "dissonant acculturation" in this literature). In the context of this worrisome trend, it is particularly noteworthy that some minority immigrant children are observed to be protected against the danger of downward assimilation. Scholars argue that this happens when they adopt behaviors from the American mainstream that help them fit in, while retaining immigrant languages and cultural values, which work as a conduit for them to receive parental guidance and support (Portes and Zhou 1993). Described as "selective acculturation," this cultural blending has been shown to allow these immigrant children to reach parity with native-born whites and even surpass them in educational attainment and occupational status (Jiménez and Horowitz 2013; Kasinitz et al. 2008; Lee and Zhou 2015).

Our findings advance the segmented assimilation theory's argument in a number of ways. First, while this literature focuses mainly on school-age youths, our study is among the first to show how "biculturality" can function as a job skill for immigrant and later-generation adults. Mirroring the pattern of selective acculturation, our Latina nurses largely sought to make mainstream American institutional practices "work" for an immigrant population through the support of shared language and communal ties. But in this context, the elderly in the community were on the receiving end, not the giving end, of guidance and emotional support. The role of the cultural broker in health care—which is one of the fastest-growing industries in the United States—may be indicative of a growing market niche for bicultural professionals who can provide a bridge between predominantly white mainstream institutions and their increasingly diverse clienteles. Immigrants and their offspring are certainly not the only ones capable of becoming bicultural, but their experience of straddling both cultural worlds may predispose them to developing cultural blending skills.

Second, and relatedly, our findings illustrate how such cultural blending actually occurs on the ground. In the segmented assimilation literature, it is often assumed that children of immigrants, by virtue of being exposed to two cultures, naturally know how to blend them and resolve the tensions therein. To the extent that existing research has described concrete patterns of cultural blending, it has done so by and large in terms of "code-switching"—for example, adopting mainstream cultural styles at school or at work and switching back to ethnic cultural practices at home and in ethnic communities. Our study moves the discussion on the issue forward by challenging researchers to recognize that the boundaries between immigrants' social worlds are not always so clear-cut. With social boundaries becoming increasingly blurred, the practices of code hybridization are as important as they have been understudied.

Insights borrowed from the literature on black and Latino middle-class identities support the observation that cultural blending does not happen easily or automatically. As reviewed earlier, these studies suggest that middle-class minorities and immigrants engage in "code-switching" as a main strategy in straddling two cultural worlds. Sometimes middle-class immigrants establish ethnic professional organizations in order to have small cultural spaces where they can experiment with hybridizing both cultures. That the major mechanisms for embracing bicultural identity are code-switching and creating small cultural laboratories suggests that cultural blending *is not really happening in mainstream institutions*. It follows, then, that we have little understanding of how bicultural immigrants blend both cultures in mainstream institutions—in the rare cases where they do.

Our study offers an example of the diverse forms taken by code hybridization, with divergent impacts on individuals and institutions. The most robust practices of code hybridization not only empower both immigrant professionals and their clients but also engender critical reflections of institutional norms. But placed in an unsupportive workplace, code hybridization practices can become professionally costly for immigrant professionals. Other practices are lopsided, primarily reinforcing dominant institutional norms through a minority language. Being based on a case study, these findings are not meant to be generalized to other institutional contexts, but they do debunk the assumption that cultural blending happens automatically among bicultural immigrants and highlight the need for future research to focus on the patterns, potential, and limitations of various practices of cultural hybridization.

We must emphasize that, even as "biculturality"—achieved through selective acculturation, code hybridization, or other patterns yet to be uncovered—is proven to be an advantage rather than a barrier on the path to integration, integration is still fraught with challenges wrought by American mainstream institutions themselves. These institutions recognize the need to hire bicultural immigrants and their offspring as cultural brokers, but they rarely provide these individuals with the tools to achieve success alongside their non-immigrant coworkers. We have demonstrated, for instance, how the burden of the double duty—to achieve parity with white colleagues *while also* addressing their coethnic patients' needs—is put on Latina nurses themselves. We have also shown that occasionally institutions do provide such support, and that Latina nurses' bicultural skills can be best utilized when they do. Institutional contexts matter a great deal.

These findings suggest a cautionary note against the optimism that bicultural immigrants will automatically become agents of social change to usher in the new era of multiculturalism in mainstream America (Alba and Nee 2003). By the same token, these observations underscore that cultural brokerage, in its scope and importance, goes beyond how well immigrant professionals manage their workplace identities or help coethnic clients. Future research is called for to better understand how and why different forms of code hybridization take place and contribute to diversifying larger institutional cultures.

APPENDIX

Figure A1. Educational Attainment of Americans, by Race, 2012

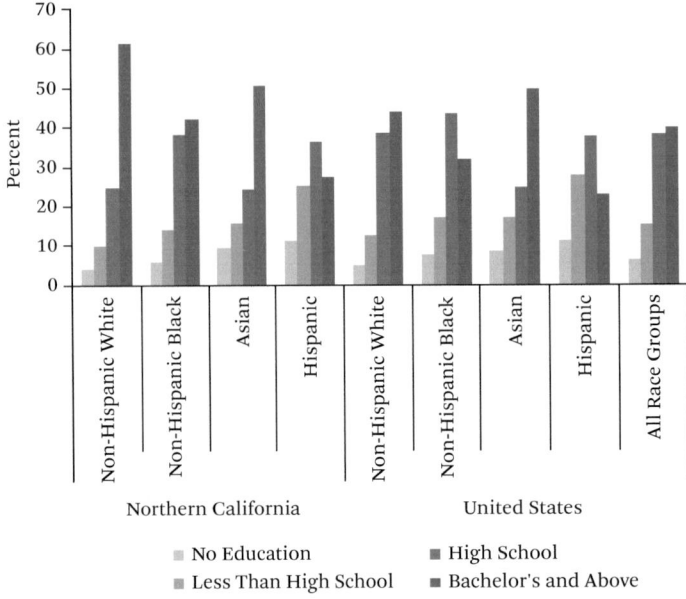

Source: Authors' calculations based on the 2012–2013 American Community Survey (ACS).

Figure A2. Medicaid Eligibility of Americans, by Race, 2012

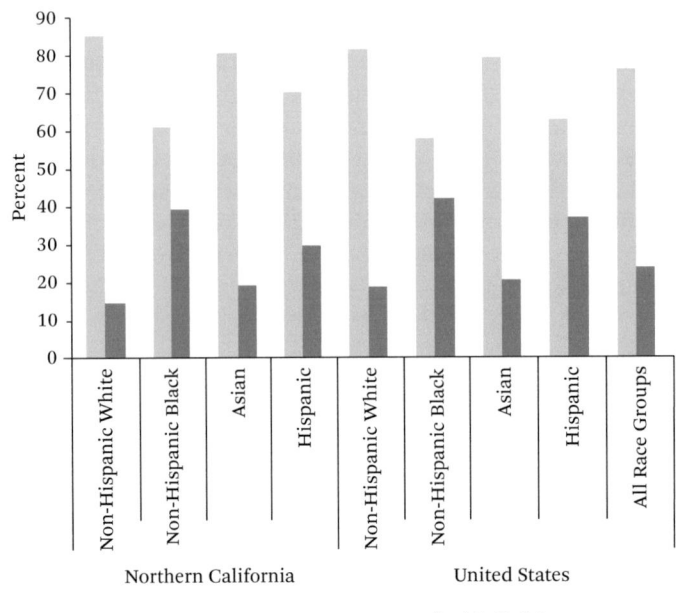

Source: Authors' calculations based on the 2012–2013 ACS.
Note: Medicaid eligibility is based on income up to 133 percent of the federal poverty line.

Figure A3. Americans in Medical Occupations, by Race, 2012

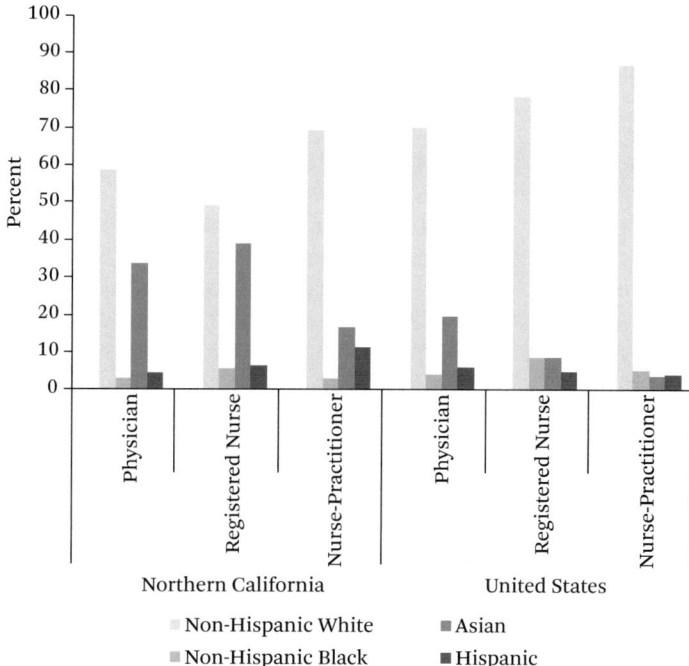

Source: Authors' calculations based on the 2012–2013 ACS.

REFERENCES

Agius Vallejo, Jody. 2012. "Socially Mobile Mexican Americans and the Minority Culture of Mobility." *American Behavioral Scientist* 56(5): 666–84. DOI:10.1177/0002764211433807.

Agius Vallejo, Jody, and Jennifer Lee. 2009. "Brown Picket Fences: The Immigrant Narrative and 'Giving Back' Among the Mexican-Origin Middle Class." *Ethnicities* 9(1): 5–31. DOI:10.1177/1468796808099902.

Alba, Richard, and Victor Nee. 2003. *Remaking the American Mainstream: Assimilation and Contemporary Immigration.* Cambridge, Mass.: Harvard University Press.

Barry, Christine A., Fiona A. Stevenson, Nicky Britten, Nick Barber, and Colin P. Bradley. 2001. "Giving Voice to the Lifeworld. More Humane, More Effective Medical Care? A Qualitative Study of Doctor-Patient Communication in General Practice." *Social Science and Medicine* 53(4): 487–505. DOI:10.1016/S0277-9536(00)00351-8.

Bender, Daniel J. 2007. "Patient Preference for a Racially or Gender-Concordant Student Dentist." *Journal of Dental Education* 71(6): 726–45.

Blanchard, Janice, Shakti Nayar, and Nicole Lurie. 2007. "Patient-Provider and Patient-Staff Racial Concordance and Perceptions of Mistreatment in the Health Care Setting." *Journal of General Internal Medicine* 22(8): 1184–89. DOI:10.1007/s11606-007-0210-8.

Bosch, Paul C., Sally A. Doshier, and Julie Gess-Newsome. 2012. "Bilingual Nurse Education Program: Applicant Characteristics That Predict Success." *Nursing Education Perspectives* 33(2): 90–95.

Brown, Tony N., Koji Ueno, Carrie L. Smith, Noel S. Austin, and Leonard Bickman. 2007. "Communication Patterns in Medical Encounters for the Treatment of Child Psychosocial Problems: Does Pediatrician-Parent Concordance Matter?" *Health Communication* 21(3): 247–56. DOI:10.1080/10410230701307717.

Clark, Trina, Betsy Sleath, and Richard H. Rubin. 2004. "Influence of Ethnicity and Language Concordance on Physician-Patient Agreement About Recommended Changes in Patient Health Behavior." *Patient Education and Counseling* 53(1): 87–93. DOI:10.1016/S0738-3991(03)00109-5.

Cooper, Lisa A., Debra L. Roter, Rachel L. Johnson, Daniel E. Ford, Donald M. Steinwachs, and Neil

R. Powe. 2003. "Patient-Centered Communication, Ratings of Care, and Concordance of Patient and Physician Race." *Annals of Internal Medicine* 139(11): 907–15. DOI:10.7326/0003-4819-139-11-200312020-00009.

Da Cruz, Michaël. 2018. "Offshore Migrant Workers: Return Migrants in Mexico's English-Speaking Call Centers." *RSF: The Russell Sage Foundation Journal of the Social Sciences* 4(1): 39–57. DOI: 10.7758/RSF.2018.4.1.03.

Eckstein, Susan, and Giovanni Peri. 2018. "Immigrant Niches and Immigrant Networks in the U.S. Labor Market." *RSF: The Russell Sage Foundation Journal of the Social Sciences* 4(1): 1–17. DOI: 10.7758/RSF.2018.4.1.01.

Elderkin-Thompson, Virginia, Roxane Cohen Silver, and Howard Waitzkin. 2001. "When Nurses Double as Interpreters: A Study of Spanish-Speaking Patients in a U.S. Primary Care Setting." *Social Science and Medicine* 52(9): 1343–58. DOI:10.1016/S0277-9536(00)00234-3.

Frank, Arthur W. 1996. *The Wounded Storyteller: Body, Illness, and Ethics*. Chicago: University of Chicago Press.

Fraser, Nancy. 1995. "Politics, Culture, and the Public Sphere: Toward a Postmodern Conception." In *Social Postmodernism: Beyond Identity Politics*, edited by Linda Nicholson and Steven Seidman. New York: Cambridge University Press.

Garcia, Jorge A., Debora A. Paterniti, Patrick S. Romano, and Richard L. Kravitz. 2003. "Patient Preferences for Physician Characteristics in University-Based Primary Care Clinics." *Ethnicity and Disease* 13(2): 259–67.

Good, Mary-Jo DelVecchio, Sarah S. Willen, Seth Donal Hannah, Ken Vickery, and Lawrence Taeseng Park. 2011. *Shattering Culture: American Medicine Responds to Cultural Diversity*. New York: Russell Sage Foundation.

Greenhalgh, Trisha, Nadia Robb, and Graham Scambler. 2006. "Communicative and Strategic Action in Interpreted Consultations in Primary Health Care: A Habermasian Perspective." *Social Science and Medicine* 63(5): 1170–87. DOI:10.1016/j.socscimed.2006.03.033.

Institute of Medicine. 2001. *Crossing the Quality Chasm: A New Health System for the Twenty-First Century*. Washington, D.C.: National Academies Press.

Jiménez, Tomás R., and Adam L. Horowitz. 2013. "When White Is Just Alright: How Immigrants Redefine Achievement and Reconfigure the Ethnoracial Hierarchy." *American Sociological Review* 78(5): 849–71. DOI:10.1177/0003122413497012.

Kasinitz, Philip, John H. Mollenkopf, Mary C. Waters, and Jennifer Holdaway. 2008. *Inheriting the City: The Children of Immigrants Come of Age*. New York: Russell Sage Foundation.

King, William D., Mitchell D. Wong, Martin F. Shapiro, Bruce E. Landon, and William E. Cunningham. 2004. "Does Racial Concordance Between HIV-Positive Patients and Their Physicians Affect the Time to Receipt of Protease Inhibitors?" *Journal of General Internal Medicine* 19(11): 1146–53.

LaVeist, Thomas A., and Amani Nuru-Jeter. 2002. "Is Doctor-Patient Race Concordance Associated with Greater Satisfaction with Care?" *Journal of Health and Social Behavior* 43(3): 296–306. DOI:10.2307/3090205.

LaVeist, Thomas A., Amani Nuru-Jeter, and Kiesha E. Jones. 2003. "The Association of Doctor-Patient Race Concordance with Health Services Utilization." *Journal of Public Health Policy* 24(3): 312–23. DOI:10.2307/3343378.

Leanza, Yvan, Isabelle Boivin, and Ellen Rosenberg. 2010. "Interruptions and Resistance: A Comparison of Medical Consultations with Family and Trained Interpreters." *Social Science and Medicine* 70(12): 1888–95. DOI:10.1016/j.socscimed.2010.02.036.

Lee, Jennifer, and Min Zhou. 2015. *The Asian American Achievement Paradox*. New York: Russell Sage Foundation.

Lo, Ming-Cheng Miriam. 2010. "Cultural Brokerage: Creating Linkages Between Voices of Lifeworld and Medicine in Cross-Cultural Clinical Settings." *Health* 14(5): 484–504. DOI:10.1177/1363459309360795.

Lo, Ming-Cheng Miriam, and Roxana Bahar. 2013. "Resisting the Colonization of the Lifeworld? Immigrant Patients' Experiences with Co-ethnic Healthcare Workers." *Social Science and Medicine* 87(June): 68–76. DOI:10.1016/j.socscimed.2013.03.022.

Lo, Ming-Cheng Miriam, and Clare L. Stacey. 2008. "Beyond Cultural Competency: Bourdieu, Patients and Clinical Encounters." *Sociology of Health and Illness* 30(5): 741–55. DOI:10.1111/j.1467-9566.2008.01091.x.

Malat, Jennifer, and Mary Ann Hamilton. 2006.

"Preference for Same-Race Health Care Providers and Perceptions of Interpersonal Discrimination in Health Care." *Journal of Health and Social Behavior* 47(2): 173–87. DOI:10.1177/002214650604700206.

McKinlay, John B., Ting Lin, Karen Freund, and Mark Moskowitz. 2002. "The Unexpected Influence of Physician Attributes on Clinical Decisions: Results of an Experiment." *Journal of Health and Social Behavior* 43(1): 92–106.

Meghani, Salimah H., Jacqueline M. Brooks, Trina Gipson-Jones, Roberta Waite, Lisa Whitfield-Harris, and Janet A. Deatrick. 2009. "Patient–Provider Race-Concordance: Does It Matter in Improving Minority Patients' Health Outcomes?" *Ethnicity and Health* 14(1): 107–30. DOI:10.1080/13557850802227031.

Mishler, Elliot George. 1984. *The Discourse of Medicine: Dialectics of Medical Interviews.* New York: Ablex Publishing Corporation.

Modi, Seema C., Lauren M. Whetstone, and Doyle M. Cummings. 2007. "Influence of Patient and Physician Characteristics on Percutaneous Endoscopic Gastrostomy Tube Decision-Making." *Journal of Palliative Medicine* 10(2): 359–66. DOI:10.1089/jpm.2006.0145.

Neckerman, Kathryn M., Prudence Carter, and Jennifer Lee. 1999. "Segmented Assimilation and Minority Cultures of Mobility." *Ethnic and Racial Studies* 22(6): 945–65. DOI:10.1080/014198799329198.

Ortiga, Yasmin Y. 2018. "Learning to Fill the Labor Niche: Filipino Nursing Graduates and the Risk of the Migration Trap." *RSF: The Russell Sage Foundation Journal of the Social Sciences* 4(1): 172–87. DOI: 10.7758/RSF.2018.4.1.10.

Porter, Sam. 1998. *Social Theory and Nursing Practice.* New York: Macmillan.

Portes, Alejandro, and Rubén G. Rumbaut. 2001. *Legacies: The Story of the Immigrant Second Generation.* Berkeley: University of California Press.

Portes, Alejandro, and Min Zhou. 1993. "The New Second Generation: Segmented Assimilation and Its Variants." *Annals of the American Academy of Political and Social Science* 530(1): 74–96. DOI:10.1177/000271629353000106.

Saha, Somnath, Jose J. Arbelaez, and Lisa A. Cooper. 2003. "Patient-Physician Relationships and Racial Disparities in the Quality of Health Care." *American Journal of Public Health* 93(10): 1713–19. DOI:10.2105/AJPH.93.10.1713.

Sánchez, Gloria, Theresa Nevarez, Werner Schink, and David E. Hayes-Bautista. 2015. "Latino Physicians in the United States, 1980–2010: A Thirty-Year Overview from the Censuses." *Academic Medicine* 90(7). DOI: 10.1097/ACM.0000000000000619.

Stevens, Gregory D., Leiyu Shi, and Lisa A. Cooper. 2003. "Patient-Provider Racial and Ethnic Concordance and Parent Reports of the Primary Care Experiences of Children." *Annals of Family Medicine* 1(2): 105–12. DOI:10.1370/afm.27.

Stevenson, Fiona, and Graham Scambler. 2005. "The Relationship Between Medicine and the Public: The Challenge of Concordance." *Health* 9(1): 5–21. DOI:10.1177/1363459305048091.

Thacker, Karen. 2005. "Academic-Community Partnerships: Opening the Doors to a Nursing Career." *Journal of Transcultural Nursing* 16(1): 57–63.

U.S. Census Bureau. 2007. *The American Community—Hispanics: 2004.* Washington: U.S. Government Printing Office.

U.S. Census Bureau, American Community Survey, 2012–2013. American Community Survey 1-Year Estimates; generated by Emerald T. Nguyen; using Integrated Public Use Microdata Series Version 6.0, available at: https://usa.ipums.org/usa/index.shtml (accessed September 1, 2015).

U.S. Department of Health and Human Services (DHHS). 2000. *Healthy People 2010.* Washington: U.S. Government Printing Office.

Waters, Mary C., Van C. Tran, Philip Kasinitz, and John H. Mollenkopf. 2010. "Segmented Assimilation Revisited: Types of Acculturation and Socioeconomic Mobility in Young Adulthood." *Ethnic and Racial Studies* 33(7): 1168–93. DOI:10.1080/01419871003624076.

Willen, Sarah S., and Elizabeth Carpenter-Song. 2013. "Cultural Competence in Action: 'Lifting the Hood' on Four Case Studies in Medical Education." *Culture, Medicine, and Psychiatry* 37(2): 241–52. DOI:10.1007/s11013-013-9319-x.

Wilson, Eli R. 2018. "Bridging the Service Divide: Dual Labor Niches and Embedded Opportunities in Restaurant Work." *RSF: The Russell Sage Foundation Journal of the Social Sciences* 4(1): 115–27. DOI: 10.7758/RSF.2018.4.1.07.

Learning to Fill the Labor Niche: Filipino Nursing Graduates and the Risk of the Migration Trap

YASMIN Y. ORTIGA

Overseas recruitment has become a common strategy in filling nurse shortages within U.S. health institutions, sparking the proliferation of nursing programs in the Philippines. Export-oriented education exacerbates a mismatch, however, between available jobs (in both the Philippines and the United States) and the number of nursing graduates, thus increasing joblessness and underemployment among Filipino youth. Pursing higher education as a means to migrate also puts Filipino students at risk of getting caught in a migration trap, where prospective migrants obtain credentials for overseas work yet cannot leave when labor demands or immigration policies change. Such problems highlight the complicated impact of immigrant labor niches in places like the United States on developing nations, beyond the brain drain narratives that dominate academic and policy discussions.

Keywords: nursing, migration, labor niche, higher education, the Philippines

As policymakers highlight the growing health care demands of the aging populations of developed nations, foreign nurse recruitment has become the fastest and most common strategy to fill local manpower needs (Brush and Berger 2002; Rother and Lavizzo-Mourey 2009). With scholars estimating a shortage in the United States as severe as 1 million registered nurses by 2020, the United States has emerged among receiving countries as the most active recruiter (Buchan 2006; Keuhn 2007). This demand has created an immigrant labor niche within the American health care system: foreign nurses now fill positions in large urban hospitals as well as in a growing number of rural hospitals and nursing homes (Brush 2008). To date, the largest group of foreign-born nurses comes from the Philippines, a country whose colonial ties with the United States have facilitated nurse migration for more than a century (Brush 2010; Choy 2003).

Scholars have raised concerns about the impact of such migration flows on nurse migrants' countries of origin, given that the U.S. health care system, which employs the largest professional nurse workforce of any country in the world, exerts "a strong pull on global nurse resources" (Aiken 2007, 1300). Policy discussions also warn of the disastrous implications of "brain drain"—the exodus of trained nurses from poorer nations, which need them the most (Brush 2010; Lorenzo et al. 2007). Yet

Yasmin Y. Ortiga is a lecturer at the College of Alice and Peter Tan, National University of Singapore.

© 2018 Russell Sage Foundation. Ortiga, Yasmin Y. 2018. "Learning to Fill the Labor Niche: Filipino Nursing Graduates and the Risk of the Migration Trap." *RSF: The Russell Sage Foundation Journal of the Social Sciences* 4(1): 172–87. DOI: 10.7758/RSF.2018.4.1.10. Direct correspondence to: Yasmin Y. Ortiga at yasmin.ortiga@nus .edu.sg, College of Alice and Peter Tan, University Town, National University of Singapore, 8 College Avenue East, #B1-50, Singapore 138615.

these problems, while important, do not completely capture how U.S. nursing shortages affect migrant nurses' home countries.

The brain drain narrative depicts emigration as a pressing issue in many developing nations, but it fails to recognize that a growing number of migrant-sending countries now regard emigration as an economic strategy and train workers specifically for overseas markets in order to maximize future monetary remittances (Cabanda 2015; Rodriguez 2010). Studies have shown that U.S. hospitals' aggressive recruitment of foreign nurses has sparked the proliferation and expansion of nursing programs in the Philippines; the country's mostly private colleges and universities are now eager to offer aspiring migrants the chance to take advantage of overseas opportunities (Masselink and Lee 2010; Ortiga 2014). The promise of immigrant success in the United States has also encouraged Filipino families to invest in higher education as a means to migration and created a widespread demand for nursing degrees (Asis and Batistella 2013; Ortiga 2017). International policymakers have largely praised such efforts as an effective "supply response" to global demands and a valid alternative to previous government efforts to prevent nurses from leaving the country (Tan 2009, 8).

This article challenges such celebratory notions of export-oriented education by discussing how attempts to educate aspiring migrants to fill overseas labor demands actually exacerbates the problems of deskilling, youth unemployment, and a growing mismatch between postsecondary education and available jobs within the local labor market. Drawing on two years of ethnographic research within Philippine nursing schools, I argue that as Filipino aspiring migrants educate themselves to fill the U.S. nursing labor niche, they also risk getting caught in two types of traps. The first is the *migration trap* (Jimenez-David 2008): aspiring migrants obtain specific credentials in the hope of working overseas, yet are unable to leave when labor demands or immigration requirements change. In the context of the most recent U.S. nursing shortage, a backlog of immigrant visa applications in the mid-2000s severely curtailed the outflow of Filipino nurses to the United States (Acacio 2011), and the financial crisis in 2008 reduced migrant nurse hires around the world (International Centre on Nurse Migration 2012). Lacking public funds, Philippine hospitals could not offer permanent positions to the staggering number of nursing graduates within the country, leaving many unemployed and unable to obtain the work experience needed for jobs in alternative destinations like Japan and Singapore. Filipino nursing graduates caught in this situation then find themselves in an *opportunity trap* (Brown 2003): the never-ending need to collect credentials in order to secure a positional advantage in the job market.

The struggles of Filipino nursing graduates caught in these two traps show that however much the continuous need for foreign nurses benefits migrants and the U.S. hospitals in need of their labor, the impact of such immigrant niches on migrant-sending countries is far more complicated. Even as researchers predict a global demand for nurse labor, aspiring migrants grapple with the loss of time and money in an effort to remain "employable" for jobs they have yet to obtain. Rather than brain *drain,* I argue, the U.S. migrant nurse labor niche is more likely to lead to a problem of brain *waste* as qualified nursing graduates find themselves in industries and jobs that have little need for their skills.

THE U.S. NURSING LABOR NICHE
For the past fifty years, a cyclical demand for registered nurses (RNs) within the American health care system has led to inflows of foreign-educated nurses into the United States (Glaessel-Brown 1998; Goodin 2003). Such inflows have come in fits and starts, largely defined by massive structural changes within U.S. health care institutions and policy responses seeking to address the impact of these shifts on American health professionals.

Nurse shortages in the 1980s were attributed to hospital expansions and changes in the Medicare payment system that increased nurse-to-patient ratios. Foreign nurses played a significant role in filling this need until the recession of the early 1990s, when hospitals offered higher salaries to entice more Americans to enter the nursing profession (Glaessel-Brown 1998; Gordon 2005). The recruitment of foreign nurses increased again toward the turn of the century as American nurses became disillusioned with the emergence of managed care—a set of structural changes designed to make hospitals operate in line with a corporate model of efficiency and financial viability (Aiken 2007). Already faced with heavier workloads and more administrative duties, American nurses also encountered higher risks of retrenchment, given the entry of more "unlicensed assistive personnel," such as nurse's aides and licensed practical nurses (LPNs), who took on some of nurses' work (such as changing beds and turning patients). Hospital administrators justified this change as a way to decrease the number of nurses needed on the hospital floor, yet they still expected nurses to take on the extra work of monitoring nurse's aides (Gordon 2005). When these conditions led to another exodus of nurses from U.S. hospitals, the most recent wave of recruitment for nurse labor overseas began. According to researchers, one of the largest inflows of foreign nurses occurred during this particular period: more than 50,000 migrant nurses entered the United States from 2000 to 2006 (Acacio 2011).

Nursing salaries increased again in the mid-2000s, sparking local interest in nursing programs and encouraging former nurses to return to the workforce (Rother and Lavizzo-Mourey 2009). At the same time, the financial crisis of 2008 led to the scaling back of migrant nurse recruitment in most destination countries, like the United States, the United Kingdom, and Canada (Buchan, O'May, and Dussault 2013; International Centre on Nurse Migration 2012). Some scholars argue that these changes signaled a temporary reprieve from the nursing shortage (Buerhaus, Auerbach, and Staige 2009), while others warn that the U.S. nursing labor deficit is far from over and that foreign recruitment will eventually resume and intensify in the next decade (Cortés and Pan 2014; Kingma 2008).

In seeking to understand the pervasive nursing shortages in the United States, scholars have pointed to the inability of U.S. nursing programs to train a sufficient pool of registered nurses for local hospitals. The majority of U.S.-educated nurses possess a three-year associate degree obtained from a community college, while roughly one-third hold a four-year baccalaureate degree from a college or university. In recent years, nursing schools have offered an eighteen-month "accelerated program" for applicants who already have a bachelor's degree (Ellenbecker 2010). Despite these different pathways to a nursing credential, U.S. colleges and universities continue to admit only limited numbers of students owing to the lack of qualified nursing faculty (Aiken, Cheung, and Olds 2009; Gordon 2005; Rich and Nugent 2010). Nurses who hold an associate degree are less likely to pursue graduate studies and take on a faculty position, and more likely to take longer when they do. Thus, recruiting foreign nurses continues to be the quickest way to address nursing needs (Buchan 2006; Rother and Lavizzo-Mourey 2009).

Establishing the Labor Niche

Nurse migrants have moved across U.S. borders in a variety of ways, taking advantage of education and training opportunities in the United States or, in the case of the Philippines, previous colonial ties (Brush 2010; Choy 2003; George 2005). What differentiates post-1965 nurse migration is the emergence of brokers: private agencies that facilitate the entry of foreign nurses into local hospitals (Acacio 2011; Aiken 2007; Kingma 2006). Agency representatives take on the work of advertising open positions in source countries like the Philippines and navigating the bureaucratic process of preparing foreign nurses' paperwork for emigration (Guevarra 2010; Kingma 2008; International Council of Nurses 2006).

Contemporary nurse migration has also seen the emergence of different immigration policies to hasten the entry of nurses into the United States. Unlike other recruiting countries like Japan, the United States did not establish bilateral ties with source countries to facilitate the entry of nurses. However, U.S. officials introduced visa categories that would ease the entry of foreign-educated nurses (Kingma 2007). In the 1980s, U.S. lawmakers established the H-1A visa, a specific category to admit foreign-educated nurses. Subsequently, the Immigration Nursing Relief Act of 1989 enabled foreign nurses with H-1A visas to apply for permanent residence after three years as a registered nurse. This act was allowed to lapse in 1995, when the nursing shortage was perceived as having ended (Glaessel-Brown 1998). During the most recent shortage, foreign nurses entered the United States through the EB-3 visa program; this permanent immigrant visa is reserved for applicants who work in preferred occupations or professions. The United States granted more than 50,000 EB-3 visas to health professionals and their families from 1999 to 2007 (Acacio 2011). The issuance of such visas slowed after the recession in 2008, thereby stemming the flow of migrant nurses into the United States.

Despite foreign nurses receiving special considerations in U.S. immigration policy, American requirements for the entry of migrant nurses are the most stringent among receiving countries. Applicants must pass an English proficiency test, a review of credentials, and the National Council Licensure Examination for Registered Nurses (NCLEX-RN). In fact, foreign nurses were more likely than their local counterparts to possess a bachelor's degree and to have more work experience (Polsky et al. 2007). Patricia Cortés and Jessica Pan (2015) argue that there is a strong positive selection among Filipino migrant nurses in particular, given that those who make it through this process are likely to come from more highly educated families and possess more social capital. As of 2010, 8 percent of the U.S. nursing labor force was made up of foreign nurses (Cortés and Pan 2015). Filipino nurses are the largest group of foreign-born nurses in the United States, with other groups originating from the Caribbean and Latin America.

The next section illustrates how institutions within foreign nurses' countries of origin have also sought to take advantage of nurse shortages in the United States, eventually exploiting the nursing labor niche as a lucrative source of profit. Focusing on the Philippines, I discuss the role of private colleges and universities and its impact on aspiring migrants and their families.

EDUCATING FOR EXPORT: THE PHILIPPINE MODEL

As one of the largest migrant-sending countries in the world, the Philippines has been well known for its response to overseas labor demands, with state-run institutions playing a key role in certifying migrants' exit papers and qualifications, ensuring their safety, and brokering their labor to potential employers (Goss and Lindquist 1995; Rodriguez 2008, 2010).[1] In the case of nursing, the Philippine state promoted Filipino nurses as an ideal source of labor to address global nursing shortages, and government-regulated agencies marketed Filipino women's inherent ability to do care work (Guevarra 2010).[2] These efforts have resulted in a steady increase over the years in the number of professional nurses deployed overseas, and Filipino nurses now work in a wide range of countries, including the United States (see figure 1).

Although given less attention in the migration literature, the growth of commercial industries catering to Filipino nurse migration came with the expansion of nursing programs within Philippine colleges and universities—all eager to produce the nursing graduates their U.S. counterparts were unable to provide. Corporations and family-owned businesses op-

---

1. As political instability and economic problems pushed more Filipinos to seek overseas employment, migration industries grew within the country, offering placement services for individual workers hoping to find better opportunities abroad (Asis 2006; Rodriguez 2010). In the 1970s, then-president Ferdinand Marcos chose to institutionalize the migration process: "labor export" was turned into an economic strategy for national development. This period saw a general policy shift toward "managing" migration outflows instead of trying to prevent people from leaving the country (Acacio 2008, 104). Government bodies made concentrated efforts to direct the movement of people through "official channels," thus "allowing for greater transparency in labor transfers, employment conditions, migrant earnings, and foreign exchange remittances" (Acacio 2008, 104).

2. Although Filipino aspiring migrants saw the United States as their ideal destination, Philippine nursing schools took on the task of educating their students for a "global" market—for instance, by introducing language electives for countries like Japan and Germany and offering courses on "transcultural nursing." Elsewhere (Ortiga 2014) I have written about the pressures this puts on Filipino nurse educators.

Figure 1. Filipino Professional Nurses Deployed Overseas, 2000–2015

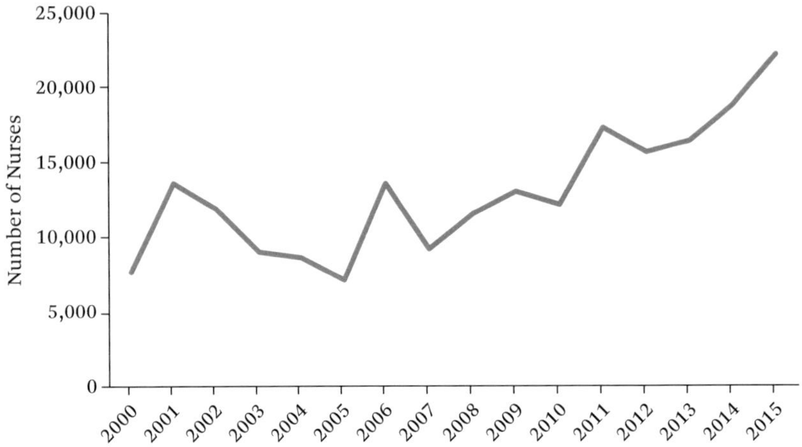

Source: Author's calculations based on Philippine Overseas Employment Agency 2015.

erated the majority of these schools and relied completely on student tuition for profit. Although Philippine media reports highlighted the dubious operations of "fly-by-night" nursing schools (Bagaoisan and Ching 2009; Uy 2008), most private colleges and universities actually complied with standards set by the Philippine Commission on Higher Education (CHED) and were state-recognized institutions.[3]

Research studies on migration and development have tended to highlight the negative impact of out-migration on educational attainment within sending communities. Although overseas remittances allow migrant households to pay for tuition and school supplies, such benefits are supposedly outweighed by the costs of absent parents and increasing household responsibilities (Creighton, Park, and Teruel 2009; McKenzie and Rapoport 2011; Nobles 2011). In contrast, the Philippines has emerged as a rare "success" story: the prevalence of migration actually leads to better school attendance and increased college enrollment (Yang 2008). The surges of demand and decline in enrollment in Philippine nursing schools have been in line with the cyclical nature of nursing shortages in the United States (Choy 2003). The most recent wave of foreign nurse recruitment to the United States sparked the largest demand for nursing degrees, which peaked at 450,000 new nursing students in 2005 (Ortiga 2014).

Although the Philippine state brokers Filipino nurse labor to many destination countries, the United States remains the students' ideal destination—a preference strongly informed by the country's history as a former American colony, but also reinforced by the promise of higher wages and the best possibility of permanent settlement, as compared to other receiving nations like Japan and Saudi Arabia (Buchan 2006). Thus, Filipino families invest in nursing education with the hope that their children will eventually be able to work in the United States and send remittances home.

Until the mid-2000s, Philippine state officials celebrated the expansion of nursing education as an opportunity for both aspiring migrants and the Philippines as a whole. On the one hand, nursing shortages in the United States encouraged aspiring migrants to work toward obtaining higher education, which

---

3. After the Philippines achieved independence in 1946, the war-torn government barely had the capacity to run its universities, much less establish new institutions. Budgetary constraints continue to this day, and the bulk of the state's education budget is still allotted for basic education. To date, 88.1 percent of the country's 1,934 higher education institutions are privately owned (Philippine Commission on Higher Education 2016).

both policymakers and migration scholars associate with immigrants' likelihood of success. Studies have shown that the better social networks and resources of highly educated migrants make it easier for them to be economically incorporated into their host society (Csedo 2008; Menjivar 2010; Portes, Fernandez-Kelly, and Haller 2005).

On a broader scale, the rise of Philippine nursing schools reflects an increasingly popular strategy of educating migrants for "export": migrant-sending countries create "surpluses of certain categories of the highly skilled" on the assumption that these individuals will find lucrative positions overseas and eventually contribute to the development of their home communities (De Haas 2005, 1272; Ortiga 2017). Individuals with higher skill levels also incur lower migration costs, thus decreasing the risk of being exploited or abused (Martin 2012). As such, Philippine state officials have tended to regard skilled professionals like nurses as "ideal migrants" because they are less likely to need protections from the state (see Rodriguez and Schwenken 2013).

Such positive interpretations of the Philippines nursing education boom have faced opposition from nursing activists and academics, who question what the outflow of Filipino nurses has meant for local institutions and health care delivery. Researchers have cautioned government agencies on the problematic implications of brain drain: the loss of valuable labor in Philippine hospitals (Buchan, Kingma, and Lorenzo 2005; Lorenzo et al. 2007). The policy analyst Nicola Yeates (2009, 2010) warns that while nursing schools could produce new graduates to replace those who leave, nurse migration to the United States still leaves Philippine hospitals with a lack of experienced nurses with more professional expertise.

However, the growth of the foreign nurse labor niche in the United States has also led to problematic outcomes not easily captured in the brain drain narrative. Given the Philippines' largely private higher education system, aspiring migrants pay the cost themselves of enhancing their overseas employability, leaving the Philippine state free to benefit from their future remittances without having to invest in their education. Aspiring migrants also absorb the risk involved in obtaining necessary qualifications for future jobs in the context of an unstable market. Although these uncertainties affect undergraduates all over the world, they are magnified in the Philippine context, where both students and schools aim to fill nursing labor needs beyond national borders. When the most recent nursing "boom" that propelled an outflow of Filipino nurses to the United States ground to a halt during the 2008 financial crisis, stemming the recruitment of foreign nurses, visa processing for Filipino immigrants went into "retrogression"—the term used by embassy officials when the number of visa applicants exceeds the number of visas available (Acacio 2011). Here I discuss the implications of such events for the everyday lives of Filipino nurse graduates and their plans for the future.

METHODS

This article stems from a larger project analyzing the ways in which Philippine universities attempt to educate graduates for "export" to the global market by adjusting school policies and curricula to meet the anticipated needs of foreign employers. From 2011 to 2014, I conducted fieldwork in Manila, where I interviewed educators and students from programs associated with overseas jobs, such as nursing programs and hotel and restaurant management (HRM) programs. My findings are based on a total of 104 interviews with nursing students, instructors, and graduates. This sample includes fifty-three nurse educators and twenty-one nursing students who were working and studying at private nursing schools at the time I conducted my fieldwork. I also interviewed thirty individuals who graduated from nursing programs between 2005 and 2011 but were unable to find work overseas.

It is important to note that in nursing the boundaries between instructors, students, and graduates are often blurred. At the height of the nursing boom, fresh graduates were immediately hired as instructors, often within six months, and even if they had limited hospital experience. I found that many of the "nursing graduates" who had left the profession were actually former clinical instructors who had moonlighted in nursing schools at one point in their careers. These interviewees shifted between different perspectives, speaking sometimes as a former nursing student or instructor, and sometimes as a former nurse who was no longer practicing the profession.

I recruited participants by circulating an invitation letter through school associations and asking participants to refer me to other faculty, students, and recent nursing graduates. At the time I conducted my interviews, some graduates had entered government programs that deploy unemployed nursing graduates to rural communities; many others had left the profession and were working as call center agents or sales representatives. Interviewees were relatively privileged, given that only one-third of Filipino high school graduates are able to pursue higher education (Asis and Batistella 2013). Nursing is also one of the most expensive degrees in the Philippines. Nevertheless, I would not consider my respondents part of Manila's wealthy elite. Most upper-class students attended universities that were far more expensive than the nursing schools I visited. At the same time, many of my interviewees had overseas relatives who sponsored their school fees, without which they would not have been able to afford to go.

I asked interviewees why they decided to pursue nursing as a profession, how they experienced the decline in demand for nursing degrees, and what happened when they looked for work after graduation. This article is limited in that I did not interview nursing graduates who had succeeded in finding work in the United States.

LEARNING TO FILL THE LABOR NICHE

Despite the growing emphasis on academic credentials, the global economy has seen a decline in permanent employment and increasing instability within workplaces (Brown, Lauder, and Ashton 2011; Kalleberg 2009; Smith 2010). As a result, students today spend more on schooling but are less likely to get the jobs they want (Brown and Hesketh 2004; Tomlinson 2008). Yet the promise of higher education and future immigrant success remains a convincing reason for many Filipino students to pursue a four-year degree in nursing. A quick glance at Philippine migration statistics shows that an aspiring migrant could easily leave the country as a domestic helper or construction worker, with little need for academic training or credentials. Still, my interviewees wanted to obtain jobs with better wages, higher social status, and protections against employer abuse—privileges that many of their migrant relatives had not been able to enjoy. College education thus served as an expensive "investment" in a better future and a better migration experience. Joey, a 2011 graduate, explained that the idea of becoming a nurse came from his mother, who was working as a domestic helper in Italy:

> Mama was jealous of her friends whose children were able to get good jobs in Italy because they were nurses.... So the reason I took nursing was so we could swap, I will be the one to work there and she can finally come home. It's hard now because [*pause*] she's not legally allowed to be there.

Joey was lucky to get a scholarship that covered most of his tuition at a private university. However, his mother still struggled to remit enough money for miscellaneous fees, field trips, uniforms, and the countless supplies that nursing students had to bring with them during clinical rotations. "For every visit to the [hospital], you had to buy surgical gloves, cotton, medicine... if your nursing kit was not complete, the instructors would take points off your grade," Joey said. "After one semester, I could tell Mama was starting to regret choosing this major, but she worked hard to make sure I graduated."

Other interviewees did not have a parent who funded their education but relied instead on "sponsors" or relatives working overseas. Most of these sponsors perceived higher education as a means to pass on to a younger member of the family the responsibility of supporting the family. Some sponsors worked in blue-collar positions, like Joey's mother, but many were also professionals within the health field. These migrants chose a young family member to finance through college with the hope that they would eventually be able to go overseas as well. Nestor, who graduated in 2014, said that he owed his college degree to his dad's sister, a nurse working in the United States.

> My tita [aunt] has a lot of influence in our family. She's really successful in the U.S., and she was able to help everyone in our family. I'm the eldest grandson, so everyone [in the family] said that I should take nursing like her. Then I can be the one to help my family when I graduate.... But if you ask me, I wouldn't take nursing. I wanted to take architecture or business management. Those fields are more of my forte. But I don't really have a choice. I can't just pick a major because I like it. I have to think of my family too.

Pursuing a higher education degree as a step toward emigration is not a misguided plan. One needs academic credentials to obtain professional work, and in many migrant-receiving countries, higher degrees are an increasingly important factor in deciding which immigrants are granted entry (Kofman 2007). This rationale has justified the promotion of export-oriented strategies among local universities and the push in migrant-sending states like the Philippines for academic programs that train students for labor niches overseas (Ortiga 2017). Yet, as mentioned earlier, the pursuit of higher education as a means to finding overseas work exacerbates the risk for college-educated graduates in the Philippines of getting caught in one or both of two types of traps that can lead to underemployment and brain waste.

The Migration Trap

The opportunity offered by the U.S. nursing labor niche to Filipino nurses is often fleeting and unstable. Open positions are filled very quickly, and U.S. officials change immigration policies depending on nationality quotas and domestic conditions. Thus, Filipino students who invest in certain degrees in the hope of migrating often discover that they are unable to leave the country because they have graduated at the end of an overseas job trend. This is the problem of the migration trap.

Rina Jimenez-David (2008) describes the migration trap as a problem for those who have already obtained their degree, but aspiring migrants among my interviewees shared that they felt "trapped" even before they graduated. As students, many of them were well aware that overseas opportunities for Filipino nurses were dwindling; subsequently, many were left stuck in the Philippines and struggling to find work. Gina, a nurse who graduated in 2006, said that even while the number of students enrolled in her college was still high, she started to hear stories about previous cohorts who could not find work:

> I could tell something was wrong [in senior year] when I would see some of our graduates around town. I would ask them what they've been doing, and they'd say, "Wala!" [Nothing!], or, "Nasa bahay lang, tambay!" [Just hanging out at home!] Or sometimes I would see them in the hospital, working as volunteers ... with no salaries! That's when I started to wonder what would happen to me.

Despite these signs, many nursing students did not want to "waste" the money they had already spent on books and nursing courses by shifting to another program. Daisy, who graduated in 2014, said that after she graduated from high school, "my parents told me that nursing is a very expensive major so they really asked me if I could handle the load. They said, 'Once you start, no more shifting to another major!'" Similarly, Patrick, Daisy's classmate, shared that college was a "luxury" for his family. As such, paying extra money for more classes would have been out of the question. He explained, "My mother told me that college is a one-shot deal. If I flunk a class or drop a class, they will pull me out. I think it's because the money for my tuition is not from them, it's from my aunt in Canada. So yeah, just one shot." Although Patrick and Daisy knew that the opportunities for migrant nurses had waned, financial and time constraints prevented them from pursuing other courses of study. Because Philippine college curricula require students to take major subjects as early as the first semester, it is harder for students to shift majors without worrying about delaying their graduation.

Caught in the migration trap, nursing graduates said that they became depressed with their situation: still being required to continue with the difficult clinical rotations and board exam reviews amid such career uncertainty. Few students wanted to practice as nurses in the Philippines given the low wages and deplorable working conditions in local hospitals (Guevarra 2010; Lorenzo et al. 2007). The nursing profession attains high social status in the Philippines only when associated with possible emigration. Otherwise, nursing is seen as a thankless, undesirable job. "It's disappointing and degrading," said Jay, who graduated in 2012. "Before, people would look at you and say 'Wow, nursing student!' They look up to you. Now, after the decline, it's like, 'Ah, laos na course mo, maghanap ka nalang ng iba.' [Your major is obsolete, find something else to study.] But I was in my third year already, so what else can I do but finish?"

Looking back at their educational experience, nursing graduates shared that timing was the trickiest part of choosing the right college major. Parents and relatives had little idea of whether the demand for nurses in the United States would last until their children completed a four-year degree. Mira, who took nursing as a "second course," shared that she always had "bad luck" in choosing college majors. She first pursued microbiology as a pre-med major in 1998, but realized as she approached her senior year that her parents could not afford to send her to medical school. Not wanting to go into research or teaching, she took a job at one of the many call centers in Manila. In 2003, her parents suggested that she take up nursing, and an aunt who lived in the United States volunteered to pay her tuition. Mira recalled that there had been about two thousand students in her cohort, about one hundred of whom were also pursuing nursing as a second degree. "I thought I had chosen a good time to go back to school. We were so many," she admitted. Yet by the time Mira graduated and passed her board exams in 2008, the number of nurses leaving for the United States had started to decline, and the sheer number of nursing graduates had overwhelmed Philippine hospitals. Feeling trapped with another degree that "doesn't lead anywhere," Mira returned to call center work.

For other interviewees, the problem of bad timing was made worse by employer demands for international certification, appropriate work experience, and language tests (Kingma 2006). Lorna, who obtained her nursing degree in 2004, claimed that she had completed all her requirements for immigration by 2006, right when U.S. hospitals started to stem the hiring of foreign nurses.

My sister-in-law passed all her requirements in 2005, and they processed all her papers in less than a year. I thought I would still make it, but it was too late. Maybe because of the financial crisis in the U.S., they became stricter with visa applications. The agency tells me there's still a demand. The government just doesn't want to bring in more people. . . . Now, I just think that if a new opportunity comes again, at least I'll be the first in line.

Lorna comforted herself with the idea that her investments in certification would open up the possibility of migration in the future. Yet she was unsure as to when the "next time" would be, and she admitted that some of her exam results would become invalid in five years. She would then face the risky decision of whether to invest even more money in her migration plans, given the unpredictable timing of nurse recruitment in destination countries.

These Philippine aspiring migrants were not stereotypical Third World immigrants, desperate to leave under any circumstances, but rather sought particular conditions for emigration. Even though caught in the migration trap, they did not necessarily have no means of leaving the country. Rather, they were unable to leave in the manner they had envisioned and in which they had invested. At the time of my interviews, government agencies still reported a need for nurses in places like Yemen, Jordan, and Saudi Arabia. However, few of my interviewees would consider working in the Middle East, mainly because of what they had heard about Arab employers. Tanya, a 2014 nursing graduate, said that employers in the Middle East were "violent" and "abuse women." Although she knew little about Middle Eastern countries, she said that she had seen enough on TV to decide that she did not want to work in the region. Similarly, Mara, a 2011 nursing graduate, said that her parents wanted her to work only in the United States and that "they would worry too much if I went anywhere else."

These views reveal that nursing graduates' decision to emigrate is often more nuanced than simply a quest to earn higher wages. Philippine nursing students pursued higher education in the hope of gaining access to the United States even with no assurance that their college degree would automatically lead to a job in an American hospital. Studies of college students in other countries echo this trend: students spend exorbitant amounts on higher degrees with no clear notion of the difficulties they will face after graduation (Arum and Roksa 2011; Brooks and Everett 2009). In the Philippines, however, this problem is made worse by an export-oriented education system that directs students toward the promise of opportunities beyond national borders.

The Opportunity Trap

Nursing graduates caught in the migration trap face two choices: find other ways to practice nursing, or leave the profession altogether. Yet, whichever decision they make, nursing graduates often find themselves caught in another difficult situation: struggling to accumulate more and more credentials to improve their chances in a poor job market. The sociologist Phillip Brown (2003) calls this the problem of the opportunity trap: individuals continuously pursuing training and education to obtain tough-entry jobs, despite little evidence that more qualifications will lead to better opportunities. As more people engage in this strategy, the harder it becomes for anyone to get ahead. Yet few can forgo this race for credentials given the risk of completely losing out in the end.

In the Philippines, the massive number of nursing students has worsened the effects of the opportunity trap. As the number of jobs in the United States began to drop, graduates scrambled to differentiate themselves from the thousands of others with the same academic qualifications. Many of my interviewees remained hopeful that the U.S. market would open up for the recruitment of migrant nurses in the future and worked fervently to "build up" their résumés with extra training and certification. With only limited open positions, however, Philippine hospitals were unable to absorb the thousands of nurses flooding the market. Mirielle Kingma (2007), a consultant for the International Council of Nurses, notes that this problem is common in countries that experience high rates of nurse migration, not because of a lack of need, but because local hospitals lack funds and support for staff. Desperate for work experience, many of my interviewees resorted to paying for their own professional development, thereby adding to the thousands of pesos their families had already invested in their education.[4]

One expensive option was pursuing a master's degree in nursing. For many of my interviewees, "going back to school" seemed like a better way to spend their time, given the lack of hospital jobs for nurses in the current market. Yet these nurses had only a vague idea of whether such a credential would actually lead to higher returns in the United States. Rey, a nurse who graduated in 2007, was one of the lucky few who found full-time work, at a children's hospital in Manila. He attended graduate classes during his free time and eventually obtained a master's degree in nursing. Rey admitted that he was not really sure what opportunities a master's degree would bring, but he had enrolled in the program because his colleagues were doing the same thing:

> A lot of people believe that a [master's] will help you get to the U.S., but that's not true. I took it because I would hear all the other

---

4. Interviewees did not mention their parents borrowing money or going into debt for their education, although it would not be surprising if this was the case for many of them. Rather, interviewees talked about their parents using hard-earned savings or relying on remittances from a relative working overseas.

nurses talking about wanting to take a master's. There would be all this talk about how their master's will be credited abroad or how it will make sure you get a higher rank when you go abroad. Now I find it funny because they wanted the degree, but they don't really know what it involves.

Research does indicate a need for more nurses with postgraduate degrees, mainly to take on faculty positions in understaffed nursing schools in the United States. Yet, with foreign recruitment mainly channeling migrant nurses into hospitals and nursing homes (Keuhn 2007), it is unclear whether a master's degree from the Philippines would be an advantage to them. Nurses like Rey are most probably overqualified for the positions they are likely to obtain in the United States.

For nursing graduates who find pursuing a master's degree too costly and time-consuming, enrolling in short-term "training sessions" can be a more viable alternative. Offered by both public and private hospitals, these sessions provide nursing graduates with "certified" skills in specialized areas of the hospital. Amy, who graduated in 2008, shared that since she passed the board exams, her mother had spent 26,000 pesos (about U.S.$523) on two training sessions: a three-week seminar on inserting intravenous tubes, and a six-week session on being a dialysis nurse. Amy confided that she was ashamed to ask her mother for more money, given that her parents had already financed her college education. However, her mother had insisted that she go for the training rather than give up and work at a call center. Sheila, who graduated in 2007, paid for two training seminars; focused on occupational health and safety, they catered to would-be company nurses. Like Amy, Sheila paid for her extra training with the help of a cousin in the United States, who also funded her nursing education. She believed that the extra investment increased her ability to perform certain hospital tasks, thereby enhancing her employability. Both Amy and Sheila rationalized their decision to undergo further training by arguing that training certificates would be useful when applying for work overseas.

Although such training certificates do provide nurses like Amy and Sheila with some advantage over their peers, they represent a costly investment that is fully absorbed by individuals and their families. The head nurse of a local private hospital confided that such training sessions used to be offered as free professional development seminars for hospital staff. With the large number of unemployed nursing graduates in need of "exposure," hospital administrators opened these sessions to the public, thus garnering a very lucrative source of extra income.

Although paying for what was once offered for free may have seemed unfair, many nursing graduates felt that enrolling in these training sessions was still better than volunteering at local hospitals. With nurses outnumbering the available positions in Philippine hospitals, many resorted to providing their labor for free, just to get the work experience required by many foreign employers. At one point, local hospitals even started charging nursing graduates for the "experience" of working in the hospital. One interviewee shared that administrators in her university charged their own graduates 6,000 pesos for only three months of "exposure" in the campus hospital. The fees were higher for work in specialized areas such as kidney dialysis. Eventually, news of nurses paying to work led to a public uproar, prompting Philippine politicians to ban hospitals from collecting these fees. However, hospitals—both public and private—could still accept nurse "volunteers," thus continuing to benefit from their free labor.

Sadly, these volunteer experiences do not always pay off. Aside from paying for training sessions, Sheila also volunteered in two medical institutions: a public community hospital and a larger private hospital in her home province. Both hospitals gave her a certificate designating her a "Volunteer Nurse," but unfortunately, recruitment agencies refused to accept it. "They said that the hospitals [overseas]," she complained, "will not accept a nurse who only had experience as a volunteer. My COE [certificate of experience] said I was a 'Volunteer Nurse,' not a 'Staff Nurse,' but we did the same work as the hospital's nurses! Of course the staff nurses did most of the difficult procedures, but in most wards, there were only two staff nurses. Everyone else working were volunteers!"

In response to this problem, Philippine state agencies implemented short-term programs that employed nurses in health centers and provincial hospitals in the country's rural areas. Interviewees saw this program as a temporary way to pay the bills, but not as a training ground to enhance their chances of migration. Patrick, who finished a one-year stint with this program, did not find the experience useful in his migration plans because he had been limited to routine procedures like administering vaccines and taking vital signs. In fact, his nursing job was so "easy" that he worked part-time at his aunt's convenience store and transcribed interviews for a researcher at a local university. Many of his classmates avoided these government programs, despite the lack of nursing jobs elsewhere. "No one really wants to work in [rural communities]," Patrick said. "Your work there is not credited if you want to go abroad, so it's pretty useless." The only "break" Patrick caught came when the head nurse at the government hospital where he was volunteering secretly gave him a certificate of experience as a staff nurse. "Actually, what she did was illegal, because we were volunteers, not full-time staff. Naawa lang talaga siya sa amin [She just felt so sorry for us]." With his COE, Patrick applied for a nursing job on a cruise ship. He had given up on making it to the United States.

Given the resources needed to remain in the nursing field, more than half of my interviewees opted to leave the profession altogether. Facing pressures to contribute to the household income, many of them could no longer afford to spend more money for training, work experience, or certification. Unfortunately, the decision to leave nursing did not always lead to freedom from the opportunity trap. Jimenez-David (2008) argues that many nursing graduates are also likely to receive the "short end of the employment stick," partly because potential employers fail to recognize their qualifications and skills. As a result, nursing graduates seeking new professional careers must still pursue credentials in order to gain entry into other fields. A few parents allowed their children to go back to college and major in other areas like education or business management. Most opted for cheaper alternatives such as technical vocational (tech-voc) certificates awarded by the Philippine Department of Labor and Employment. Although a tech-voc certificate was considered a "demotion" from a college degree, nursing graduates rationalized that many tech-voc courses were related to health and lent some professionalism to their résumé. Arnel, a 2007 nursing graduate, became a certified "spa therapist" after obtaining a tech-voc certificate in massage therapy. He initially paid for a tech-voc certificate in caregiving, thinking that he could still go to Canada to work as a live-in caregiver. However, available openings for caregivers had declined by the time he finished the course, so he was now focused on teaching massage therapy to other nursing graduates like himself. He admitted that, despite his successful change in career, his job carried a certain stigma among family and friends. "Someone once told me, 'Nag-nursing ka pa eh ngayon masehista ka lang.' [All that work to be a nurse and now you just give massages for a living.] I just keep quiet and then post pictures of myself on Facebook, lecturing my class on massage therapy."

While nursing graduates like Arnel were determined to remain within the health field, others entered other industries where employers were not choosy about academic degrees, mostly in the field of business process outsourcing (BPO). In the Philippines, call center agencies actively recruit new graduates to answer customer queries, transcribe meeting notes, and process company databases. These jobs offer much higher pay than nursing positions in Philippine hospitals, yet interviewees perceived call center work as requiring few skills—especially the kind they worked hard to develop in their professional education.

Other nursing graduates settled for either domestic work or low-skilled service work, both locally and overseas; such jobs were readily available and did not require too much paperwork. Darlene, a 2007 graduate, found work as a cashier at a factory canteen after working as a salesgirl and a grocery store attendant. She had spent the first few years after graduation as a volunteer nurse in a public hospital, but because she had to care for her elderly father, she decided that she could no longer afford to work for free. Now, almost a decade after she passed the nursing board exams, she was considering applying for domestic work positions in Singapore. Unlike Darlene, Kim, a 2009 graduate, had spent little time looking for nursing jobs or investing in further training. Her parents had used most of their savings on her nursing degree, and she was expected to help pay for her younger siblings' education after graduation. After a few months of unsuccessfully trying to find work as a nurse, she took on a housekeeping job at a hotel in New Zealand. Despite her current situation, Kim said that she would like to return to nursing as a profession. Yet her family's financial needs made it hard for her to spend more time and money keeping herself employable for the next time nurse recruitment resumed.

CONCLUSION

In seeking to enhance their chances of migration through education, nursing graduates face the risk of getting caught in the migration trap and the opportunity trap—continuously upgrading their skills and credentials in the hope of getting jobs that do not exist. These problems do not affect only migrant-sending countries. As noted by the sociologist Vicki Smith (2010, 280), today's global economy has made it the responsibility of individuals to prove their employability—that is, the "professional and personal capacity to maximize one's employment potential." Even nonmigrant graduates in wealthy nations encounter problems of underemployment and joblessness; many are unable to practice in the field for which they have been educated and end up working in jobs that do not require a college degree (Asis and Batistella 2013; Brown, Lauder, and Ashton 2011). In the Philippines, however, the promise of higher education has been incorporated into a state-led system of labor export that encourages students to become educated in fields that will fill overseas labor gaps. As such, growing labor niches in desirable destination countries like the United States, as we have seen with nursing, can create massive change within Philippine higher education institutions, as schools take advantage of the thousands of aspiring migrants seeking to enhance their overseas employability.

These export-oriented education strategies complicate typical narratives about the impact of U.S. nursing labor shortages on source countries. On the one hand, the influx of Filipino nurses into the United States motivates young Filipinos to pursue four-year degrees in nursing, thus increasing the number of students seeking higher education in the country. As an immigrant labor niche, nursing is very dynamic in that it offers opportunities for professional growth and vertical mobility not offered by other occupations (Eckstein and Peri, this issue). The cyclical nature of the U.S. nursing labor shortage then provides long-term opportunities for aspiring migrants looking to invest in nursing education. Although changing visa requirements and domestic work conditions have temporarily stopped the influx of foreign nurses, U.S. nursing schools are still unable to produce enough graduates for American health care institutions. Thus, overseas recruitment of nurses is likely to continue in the future.

On the other hand, export-oriented education can exacerbate a mismatch between available jobs (both locally and overseas) and the actual number of graduates produced by colleges and universities. Philippine private schools bear no responsibility for placing their students in appropriate jobs after graduation, and Philippine government agencies do little to address the needs of nursing graduates who are unable to find work when overseas opportunities decline. Studies have highlighted the ways in which migration costs usually disadvantage workers, especially those from lower socioeconomic backgrounds, yet most of these studies have focused on recruitment costs paid to private placement agencies (see Martin 2012). This article elucidates the enormous cost and effort incurred by Filipino students seeking higher education in order to remain employable for their future U.S. employers, sometimes with little idea of how long such labor demand will last.

In the end, few of my interviewees had the luxury of waiting for the long-term benefits of their higher education, and as such, their experiences indicated a looming problem of brain *waste* rather than brain *drain*. Given the dismal work conditions for nurses in the Philippines and the lack of funding for hospital staff, having more nursing graduates does not necessarily translate into more nurses working in Philippine hospitals. Instead, thousands of qualified nurses find themselves back in school, working in call centers, or leaving the country as domestic and service workers. What is wasted is not just the money spent on college tuition, but the time and effort invested in becoming a professional nurse, with expert knowledge and health care delivery skills. Meanwhile, Philippine government agencies, such as the Commission on Higher Education, lament the continued dearth of qualified college graduates in fields that would benefit local industries, such as marine biology, mathematics, dentistry, and social work (Gamil 2011; Pazzibugan 2013).

Despite the problems faced by nursing graduates, Philippine state agencies are unlikely to prevent private nursing schools from expanding their programs when the recruitment of foreign nurses to work in the United States resumes. At the same time, the Philippines faces increasing competition in the migrant nurse labor market as other countries, like China, India, and Vietnam, adopt similar strategies to facilitate the out-migration of their citizens (Brush and Sochalski 2007). This continuous push toward export-oriented education strategies amid rising uncertainty forewarns us about future problems—problems not fully captured in the prevailing brain drain narratives—as new immigrant niches continue to emerge within large destination countries like the United States.

REFERENCES

Acacio, Kristel. 2008. "Managing Labor Migration: Philippine State Policy and International Migration Flows, 1969–2000." *Asia and Pacific Migration Journal* 17(2): 103–18.

———. 2011. "Getting Nurses Here: Migration Industry and the Business of Connecting Philippine-Educated Nurses with United States Employers." PhD diss., University of California, Berkeley.

Aiken, Linda H. 2007. "U.S. Nurse Labor Dynamics Are Key to Global Nurse Sufficiency." *Health Services Research* 42(3): 1299–1322.

Aiken, Linda H., Robyn B. Cheung, and Danielle M. Olds. 2009. "Education Policy Initiatives to Address the Nurse Shortage in the United States." *Health Affairs* 28(4): w646–w56.

Arum, Richard, and Josipa Roksa. 2011. *Academically Adrift: Limited Learning on College Campuses*. Chicago: University of Chicago Press.

Asis, Maruja M. B. 2006. "The Philippines' Culture of Migration." Washington, D.C.: Migration Policy Institute (January 1). Available at: http://www.migrationpolicy.org/article/philippines-culture-migration/ (accessed June 29, 2016).

Asis, Maruja M. B., and Graziano Batistella. 2013. *The Filipino Youth and the Employment Migration Nexus*. Philippines: UNICEF Philippines.

Bagaoisan, Andrew Jonathan, and Mark Angelo Ching. 2009. "Defying CHED Rules, Substandard Nursing Schools Churn Out Graduates." *GMANewsOnline*, June 16. Available at: http://www.gmanetwork.com/news/story/165082/news/specialreports/defying-ched-rules-substandard-nursing-schools-churn-out-graduates (accessed June 29, 2016).

Brooks, Rachel, and Glyn Everett. 2009. "Post-graduation Reflection on the Value of a Degree." *British Educational Research Journal* 35(3): 333–49.

Brown, Phillip. 2003. "The Opportunity Trap: Education and Employment in the Global Economy." *European Educational Research Journal* 2(1): 141–79.

Brown, Phillip, and Anthony Hesketh. 2004. *The Mismanagement of Talent: Employability and Jobs in the Knowledge Economy*. New York: Oxford University Press.

Brown, Phillip, Hugh Lauder, and David Ashton. 2011. *The Global Auction: The Broken Promises of Education, Jobs, and Incomes*. Oxford: Oxford University Press.

Brush, Barbara L. 2008. "Global Nurse Migration Today." *Journal of Nursing Scholarship* 40(1): 20–25.

———. 2010. "The Potent Lever of Toil: Nursing Development and Exportation in the Postcolonial Philippines." *American Journal of Public Health* 100(9): 1572–83.

Brush, Barbara L., and Anne M. Berger. 2002. "Sending for Nurses: Foreign Nurse Migration, 1965–2002." *Nursing and Health Policy Review* 1(2): 103–15.

Brush, Barbara L., and Julie Sochalski. 2007. "International Nurse Migration: Lessons from the Philippines." *Policy, Politics, and Nursing Practice* 8(1): 37–46.

Buchan, James. 2006. "The Impact of Global Nursing Migration on Health Services Delivery." *Policy, Politics, and Nursing Practice* 7(3): 16S–25S.

Buchan, James, Mireille Kingma, and F. Marilyn Lorenzo. 2005. "International Migration of Nurses: Trends and Policy Implications." Geneva, Switzerland: International Council of Nurses, Global Nursing Review Initiative.

Buchan, James, Fiona O'May, and Gilles Dussault. 2013. "Nursing Workforce Policy and the Economic Crisis: A Global Overview." *Journal of Nursing Scholarship* 45(3): 298–307.

Buerhaus, Peter I., David I. Auerbach, and Douglas O. Staige. 2009. "The Recent Surge in Nurse Employment: Causes and Implications." *Health Affairs* 28(4): w657–w68.

Cabanda, Exequiel. 2015. "Identifying the Role of the Sending State in the Emigration of Health Professionals: A Review of the Empirical Literature." *Migration and Development* (December 28). DOI: 10.1080/21632324.2015.1123838.

Choy, Catherine Ceniza. 2003. *Empire of Care: Nursing and Migration in Filipino American History*. Durham, N.C.: Duke University Press.

Cortés, Patricia, and Jessica Pan. 2014. "Foreign Nurse Importation to the United States and the Supply of Native Registered Nurses." *Journal of Health Economics* 37(C): C164–C80.

———. 2015. "The Relative Quality of Foreign Nurses in the United States." *Journal of Human Resources* 50(4): 1009–50.

Creighton, Mathew, Hyunjoon Park, and Graciela Teruel. 2009. "The Role of Migration and Single Motherhood in Upper Secondary Education in Mexico." *Journal of Marriage and Family* 71(5): 1325–39.

Csedo, Krisztina. 2008. "Negotiating Skills in the Global City: Hungarian and Romanian Professionals and Graduates in London." *Journal of Ethnic and Migration Studies* 34(5): 803–23.

De Haas, Hein. 2005. "International Migration, Remittances, and Development: Myths and Facts." *Third World Quarterly* 26(8): 1269–84.

Eckstein, Susan, and Giovanni Peri. 2018. "Immigrant Niches and Immigrant Networks in the U.S. Labor Market." *RSF: The Russell Sage Foundation Journal of the Social Sciences* 4(1): 1–17. DOI: 10.7758/RSF.2018.4.1.01.

Ellenbecker, Carol H. 2010. "Preparing the Nursing Workforce of the Future." *Policy, Politics, and Nursing Practice* 11(2): 115–25.

Gamil, Jaymee T. 2011. "PRC Lists in Demand College Courses." *Philippine Daily Inquirer*, November 18.

George, Sheba Mariam. 2005. *When Women Come First: Gender and Class in Transnational Migration*. Berkeley: University of California Press.

Glaessel-Brown, Eleanor E. 1998. "Use of Immigration Policy to Manage Nursing Shortages." *Journal of Nursing Scholarship* 30(4): 323–27.

Goodin, Heather J. 2003. "The Nursing Shortage in the United States of America: An Integrative Review of the Literature." *Journal of Advanced Nursing* 43(4): 335–50.

Gordon, Suzanne. 2005. *Nursing Against the Odds: How Health Care Cost Cutting, Media Stereotypes, and Medical Hubris Undermine Nurses and Patient Care*. Ithaca, N.Y.: Cornell University Press.

Goss, Jon, and Bruce Lindquist. 1995. "Conceptualizing International Labor Migration: A Structuration Perspective." *International Migration Review* 29(2): 317–51.

Guevarra, Anna Romina. 2010. *Marketing Dreams, Manufacturing Heroes: The Transnational Labor Brokering of Filipino Workers*. Piscataway, N.J.: Rutgers University Press.

International Centre on Nurse Migration (ICNM). 2012. "The Impact of the Financial Crisis on Nurses and Nursing: A Comparative Overview of 34 European Countries." *ICNM News*. Geneva, Switzerland: International Council of Nurses.

International Council of Nurses (ICN). 2006. *The Global Nursing Shortage: Priority Areas for Intervention*. Geneva, Switzerland: ICN.

Jimenez-David, Rina. 2008. "The Migration Trap," *Philippine Daily Inquirer*, June 17.

Kalleberg, Arne 2009. "Precarious Work, Insecure Workers: Employment Relations in Transition." *American Sociological Review* 74(1): 1–22.

Keuhn, Bridget M. 2007. "No End in Sight to Nursing Shortage." *Journal of the American Medical Association* 298(14): 1623–25.

Kingma, Mireille. 2006. "Nurse Migration: Mini-Business, Big Business." *Harvard Health Policy Review* 7(1): 102–12.

———. 2007. "Nurses on the Move: A Global Overview." *Health Services Research* 42(3): 1281–1300.

———. 2008. "Nurse Migration and the Global Health Care Economy." *Policy, Politics, and Nursing Practice* 9(4): 328–33.

Kofman, Eleonore. 2007. "The Knowledge Economy,

Gender, and Stratified Migrations." *Studies in Social Justice* 1(2): 122–35.

Lorenzo, Fely Marilyn E., Jaime Galvez-Tan, Kriselle Icamina, and Lara Javier. 2007. "Nurse Migration from a Source Country Perspective: Philippine Country Case Study." *Health Services Research* 42(3): 1406–18.

Martin, Philip. 2012. "Reducing Migration Costs and Maximizing Human Development." In *Global Perspectives on Migration and Development: GFMD Puerto Vallarta and Beyond*, edited by Irene Omelaniuk. New York: Springer.

Masselink, Leah E., and Shoou-Yih Daniel Lee. 2010. "Nurses, Inc.: Expansion and Commercialization of Nursing Education in the Philippines." *Social Science and Medicine* 71(1): 166–72.

McKenzie, David, and Hillel Rapoport. 2011. "Can Migration Reduce Educational Attainment? Evidence from Mexico." *Journal of Popular Economics* 24(4): 1331–58.

Menjivar, Cecilia. 2010. "Immigrants, Immigration, and Sociology: Reflecting on the State of the Discipline." *Sociological Inquiry* 80(1): 3–27.

Nobles, Jenna. 2011. "Parenting from Abroad: Migration, Nonresident Father Involvement, and Children's Education in Mexico." *Journal of Marriage and Family* 73(4): 729–46.

Ortiga, Yasmin Y. 2014. "Professional Problems: The Burden of Producing the 'Global' Filipino Nurse." *Social Science and Medicine* 115: 64–71.

———. 2017. "The Flexible University: Neoliberal Education and the Global Production of Migrant Labor." *British Journal of Sociology of Education* 38(4): 485–99. DOI: 10.1080/01425692.2015.1113857.

Pazzibugan, Dona Z. 2013. "CHED Identifies 'Priority Courses' to Fill Needs of Workforce.'" *Philippine Daily Inquirer*, August 7.

Philippine Commission on Higher Education (CHED). 2016. "Higher Education in Numbers." Last modified June 1, 2016. Available at: http://ched.gov.ph/central/page/higher-education-data-infographics-2016 (accessed May 23, 2017).

Philippine Overseas Employment Agency (POEA). 2015. "OFW Statistics." Available at: http://www.poea.gov.ph/ofwstat/ofwstat.html (accessed May 24, 2017).

Polsky, Daniel, Sara J. Ross, Barbara L. Brush, and Julie Sochalski. 2007. "Trends in Characteristics and Country of Origin Among Foreign-Trained Nurses in the United States, 1990 and 2000." *American Journal of Public Health* 97(5): 895–900.

Portes, Alejandro, Patricia Fernandez-Kelly, and William J. Haller. 2005. "Segmented Assimilation on the Ground: The New Second Generation in Early Adulthood." *Ethnic and Racial Studies* 28(6): 1000–40.

Rich, Karen L., and Katherine E. Nugent. 2010. "A United States Perspective on the Challenges in Nursing Education." *Nurse Education Today* 30(3): 228–32.

Rodriguez, Robyn M. 2008. "The Labor Brokerage State and the Globalization of Filipina Care Workers." *Signs* 33(4): 794–800.

———. 2010. *Migrants for Export: How the Philippine State Brokers Labor to the World*. Minneapolis: University of Minnesota Press.

Rodriguez, Robyn M., and Helen Schwenken. 2013. "Becoming a Migrant at Home: Subjectivation Processes in Migrant-Sending Countries Prior to Departure." *Population, Space, and Place* 19(4): 375–88.

Rother, John, and Risa Lavizzo-Mourey. 2009. "Addressing the Nursing Workforce: A Critical Element for Health Reform." *Health Affairs* 28(4): w620–24.

Smith, Vicki. 2010. "Review Article: Enhancing Employability: Human, Cultural, and Social Capital in an Era of Turbulent Unpredictability." *Human Relations* 63(2): 279–303.

Tan, Edita. 2009. *Supply Response of Filipino Workers to World Demand*. Philippines: International Organization of Migration.

Tomlinson, Michael. 2008. "'The Degree Is Not Enough': Students' Perceptions of the Role of Higher Education Credentials for Graduate Work and Employability." *British Journal of Sociology of Education* 29(1): 49–61.

Uy, Jocelyn. 2008. "CHED Fails to Shut Down Low-Performing Nursing Schools—COA." *Philippine Daily Inquirer*, June 12.

Yang, Dean. 2008. "International Migration, Remittances, and Household Investment: Evidence from Philippine Migrants' Exchange Rate Shocks." *Economic Journal* 118(528): 591–630.

Yeates, Nicola. 2009. "Production for Export: The Role of the State in the Development and Operation of Global Care Chains." *Population, Space, and Place* 15(2): 175–87.

———. 2010. "The Globalization of Nurse Migration: Policy Issues and Responses." *International Labour Review* 149(4): 423–42.